World War I: A Compact Chronology

1914

June 28: Assassination of Archduke Franz Ferdinand and wife Sophie in Sarajevo, Bosnia (Austria-Hungary), provokes war.

July 28: Austria-Hungary declares war on Serbia, which it accuses of provoking the assassination.

July 28–August 6: A tangle of European alliances aligns Germany with Austria-Hungary against Russia, France, and Great Britain. Italy remains temporarily neutral.

July 29–December 9: Austria-Hungary invades Serbia but is repeatedly repulsed.

August: Executing its "Schlieffen Plan," Germany invades Belgium and France (in the battles of the Frontiers, Lorraine, Ardennes, Sambre, Le Cateau, and Guise), coming within 30 miles of Paris.

August 17–19: Russia invades East Prussia.

August 23–September 2: Austria-Hungary invades Russian Poland (Galicia).

August 26–31: Russia suffers a massive defeat at the Battle of Tannenberg.

September 5–10: The Germans suddenly turn at the Marne, and the French counterattack in the First Battle of the Marne. The German advance is arrested, and the Western Front hardens into a static line of trenches.

September 9–14: Russia suffers another total defeat at the First Battle of the Masurian Lakes.

September 15–November 24: In the "race to the sea," the opposing armies on the Western Front attempt to outflank one another in a push toward the English Channel coast (in the battles of the Aisne, Verdun, and St.-Mihiel; the First Battle of Ypres; and the First Battle of Champagne).

September 17–28: The Austro-German offensive occurs in western Poland.

October 29: Turkey enters the war on the side of the Central Powers.

1915

January 1–March 30: Allies stage an offensive in Artois and Champagne; the results are costly and indecisive.

January 19–20: German zeppelins bomb English cities.

February 4: Germans initiate U-boat attacks on Allied and neutral merchantmen.

February 7–21: The Russians are badly mauled at the Winter Battle (the Second Battle of the Masurian Lakes).

February–April: The Austro-Hungarian offensive in Russian Poland (Galicia) collapses, and the Russians counterattack.

February–August: An Allied amphibious assault on the Dardanelles and Gallipoli ends with the Turkish siege of the Allied invaders—the worst disaster in modern British military history.

April–May: Armenians under Turkish control rebel after suffering massacre by the Turks on suspicion of aiding the Russians.

April–June: The Germans focus on the Eastern Front, breaking through Gorlice-Tarnow and forcing the Russians out of much of Poland.

April 22–May 25: The Germans unleash poison gas at the Second Battle of Ypres.

May 7: U-boat sinks the British liner *Lusitania* with a loss of American lives; this creates a U.S.–German diplomatic crisis.

May 23: Abrogating agreements with the Central Powers, Italy declares war on Austria-Hungary.

June 23–December 2: The Italians launch futile and costly offensives against Austro-Hungarians in the First through Fourth Battles of the Isonzo.

September 25–November 6: The Allies launch a second Artois and Champagne offensive, suffering huge losses.

October–November: Austro-German-Bulgarian forces invade Serbia, driving the Serbian army out of its own country; survivors are evacuated by French and Italian ships to Corfu.

December 17: Sir Douglas Haig replaces Field Marshal Sir John French as British overall commander.

1916

February 21–December 18: At great cost to both sides, the French repel German offensives against the Verdun fortresses and then counterattack successfully.

March 11–November 14: The fruitless and costly Italian offensives are continued in the Fifth through Ninth Battles of the Isonzo.

April: British forces in Mesopotamia begin a long advance on Baghdad (see **March 11, 1917**).

May 31–June 1: The Battle of Jutland, the biggest naval battle in history, is a tactical victory for the Germans but a strategic victory for the British.

June–August: Turks led by Enver Pasha are defeated by the Russians in the Caucasus.

June 4–September 20: The Russian Brusilov Offensive in Carpathia nearly knocks Austria-Hungary out of the war.

June 5: With the support of the British (led by T.E. Lawrence, "Lawrence of Arabia"), Hussein, grand sherif of Mecca, and his son Faisal lead an Arab revolt against the Turks in the Hejaz.

August–December: Romania enters the war on the side of the Allies and is quickly overrun by German forces.

June 24–November 13: Franco-British forces stage an offensive at the First Battle of the Somme, making small gains at great cost. The British employ tanks for the first time.

alpha
books

World War I: A Compact Chronology   (continued)

1917

January 31: Germany proclaims unrestricted submarine warfare.

February 3: The United States severs diplomatic relations with Germany.

February 23–April 5: German troops begin withdrawal to strong positions on the Hindenburg Line.

March 1: The Zimmermann Telegram, a German proposal of an alliance with Mexico against the United States, is published.

March 11: Baghdad falls to British General Sir Frederick Maude.

March 12: The Russian Revolution overthrows Czar Nicholas II.

April 6: The United States declares war on Germany.

April 9–20: The Nivelle Offensive (the Second Battle of the Aisne, the Third Battle of Champagne) ends in a massively costly French failure.

April 29–May 20: Mutiny breaks out throughout the French army.

May 12–October 24: The Tenth through Twelfth Battles of the Isonzo are fought. The Twelfth is also called the Battle of Caporetto and nearly destroys the thoroughly demoralized, mutinous Italian army.

June–July: Douglas Haig leads a British offensive in Flanders, including the monumentally costly Third Battle of Ypres (Passchendaele) and the Battle of Cambrai.

June 27: Greece enters the war on the Allied side.

September 1: German General Oscar von Hutier stages the Riga Offensive, taking the northernmost end of the Russian front.

November 7: The Bolshevik Revolution installs Lenin's communist government in Russia.

December 9: Jerusalem falls to British forces under General Edmund Allenby.

December 15: The Bolsheviks conclude a "separate peace" with Germany by the Armistice of Brest-Litovsk; Russia withdraws from the war.

1918

January–September: T.E. Lawrence ("Lawrence of Arabia") leads Arab guerrillas in a successful campaign against Turkish positions in Arabia and Palestine.

January 8: President Woodrow Wilson lays down his "Fourteen Points" as the "only possible program" for peace.

March 21–July 19: German Generalissimo Erich Ludendorff mounts five major offensives against the Allies. Costly to the Allies as well as the Germans, the offensives ultimately fail.

April 12: Haig issues his do-or-die "backs to the wall" order during Ludendorff's Second (Lys) Offensive.

May 28: American troops are victorious in their first major action, the Battle of Cantigny.

May 30–June 17: American troops prevail at the Battles of Château-Thierry and Belleau Woods.

June 15: Under General Armando Diaz, the Italians prevail against Austro-Hungarian forces at the Battle of the Piave.

July 15–17: Allied generalissimo Ferdinand Foch takes the offensive in the Second Battle of the Marne.

July 18–August 5: Franco-American forces push back the Marne salient during the Aisne-Marne Offensive.

August 8–September 4: British General Haig directs the successful Amiens Offensive, forcing all German units back to the Hindenburg Line. Ludendorff calls August 8 the "Black Day" of the German army.

September 12–16: American troops clear out the St.-Mihiel salient; during the battle, U.S. Colonel William "Billy" Mitchell leads the greatest air assault of the war.

September 15–29: The Battle of the Vardar pits Serb, Czech, Italian, French, and British forces under General Franchet d'Esperey against Bulgarian forces, culminating in the Bulgarian Armistice of September 29.

September 18–October 30: Allenby, with Lawrence and Faisal, drives the Turks to their own border. The Battle of Megiddo (September 19–21) is the most brilliant British victory of the war. Turkey concludes an armistice on October 30.

September 26–November 11: Foch masterminds the Meuse-Argonne Offensive, the final Franco-American offensive of the war.

September 27–October 17: Haig's forces storm the Hindenburg Line, breaking through at several points.

September 28–October 14: Belgian troops attack at Ypres.

October 6: In a message to President Wilson, Prince Max of Baden, Germany's new chancellor, requests an armistice.

October 17–November 11: The British advance to the Sambre and Schledt rivers, taking many German prisoners.

October 27: Erich Ludendorff resigns.

October 29–November 10: Revolution breaks out in Germany (beginning with the mutiny of the High Seas Fleet). Forced to abdicate (November 9), Kaiser Wilhelm II flees to Holland (November 10).

November 3: Trieste falls to an Allied naval expedition; Austria-Hungary concludes an armistice.

November 7–11: German negotiators led by Matthias Erzenberger meet in Ferdinand Foch's railway carriage headquarters at Compiègne to hammer out an armistice.

November 11: Armistice Day; fighting stops at 11 A.M.

November 23: The brilliant German guerrilla general Paul von Lettow-Vorbeck surrenders his undefeated army in East Africa; it is the last German force to lay down its arms.

December: The Allies occupy the Rhineland.

1919

May 7–June 28: The Treaty of Versailles is drafted and signed.

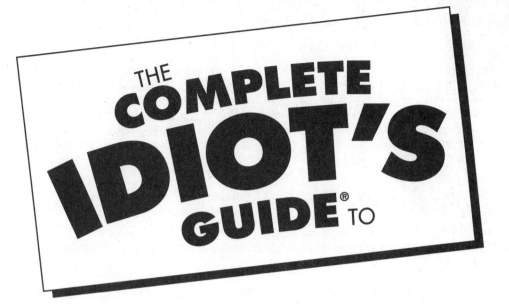

THE **COMPLETE IDIOT'S GUIDE**® TO

World War I

by Alan Axelrod

alpha books

Macmillan USA, Inc.
201 West 103rd Street
Indianapolis, IN 46290

A Pearson Education Company

For Anita and Ian, victorious always

Copyright © 2000 by Alan Axelrod

THE COMPLETE IDIOT'S GUIDE TO and Design are registered trademarks of Macmillan USA, Inc.

International Standard Book Number: 0-02-863902-2
Library of Congress Catalog Card Number: Available from the Library of Congress.

02   01   00   8   7   6   5   4   3   2   1

Interpretation of the printing code: The rightmost number of the first series of numbers is the year of the book's printing; the rightmost number of the second series of numbers is the number of the book's printing. For example, a printing code of 00-1 shows that the first printing occurred in 2000.

Printed in the United States of America

Publisher
Marie Butler-Knight

Product Manager
Phil Kitchel

Managing Editor
Cari Luna

Acquisitions Editor
Randy Ladenheim-Gil

Development Editor
Michael Thomas

Production Editor
Billy Fields

Copy Editor
Krista Hansing

Illustrator
Jody P. Schaeffer

Cover Designers
Mike Freeland
Kevin Spear

Book Designers
Scott Cook and Amy Adams of DesignLab

Indexer
Amy Lawrence

Layout/Proofreading
Angela Calvert
John Etchison

Contents at a Glance

Contents

Appendixes

Foreword

The Great War came as no surprise. Planned for in excruciating detail, its major players knew exactly how the scenario would play out, based on lessons from their earlier wars, the Austro-Prussian War in 1866 and the Franco-Prussian War of 1870–71. The Germans had their Schlieffen Plan, conceived in the 1890s, and the French had their Plan XVII, developed even earlier. Despite different objectives, both plans shared a strategic emphasis on attack in overwhelming force. Neither side expected a long war, given their timetables for lightning moves. All that held them back was the starting gun.

Alan Axelrod reveals in fascinating detail the background and progress of this great war, which failed to turn out as any initial combatant planned. A complex phenomenon that eventually embroiled some thirty-six nations, it requires his great skills of narrative and timing to take a reader successfully through its major campaigns and political skulduggery. Early on, Axelrod wonders why so few Americans really know in any detail this important war, which truly changed the course of human history—in contrast to the huge and knowledgeable following for the much earlier American Civil War. Perhaps a key to this puzzle lies in whatever has drawn some 20,000 Americans into regularly reenacting Civil War battles. No one could possibly be enticed into reliving the unspeakable horrors of trench warfare. Axelrod goes on to identify the palpable differences between the two wars when he characterizes World War I as "a conflict marked by stalemate and slaughter rather than movement and conquest."

For the Germans the Schlieffen Plan worked as long as there was forward momentum. When progress was halted by the French at the Marne, the combatants finally discovered what differences advances in ordnance had forced on their tactics. Suddenly it was clear that fortune no longer favored the bold; the better part of valor was a good defensive position. Within months, both sides had dug in, creating trench networks straddling no man's land from the Belgian coast to the borders of Switzerland. As 1915 began, four million soldiers occupied pestilential trenches along the front, and nothing would change their relative positions for nearly four years. A poet accurately characterized the Western Front this way:

> Five hundred miles of Germans
> Five hundred miles of French
> And English, Scotch and Irish men
> All fighting for a trench.
> And when the trench is taken
> And many thousands slain,
> The losers, with more slaughter,
> Retake the trench again.

What made the difference in ground warfare was the machine gun—and rifled, breech-loading field artillery.

More than half a century earlier, at the Battle of Gettysburg, about 15,000 men advanced in formation across open fields to charge an enemy position a mile away. Established upon a ridge and behind a low stone wall, the Union forces held their fire until the Confederates were well within range, a restraint Rebels laid to a two-hour barrage that prepared their way. What they didn't know was that their guns had progressively overshot the target as each blast pounded a cannon's tailpiece deeper into the soft earth. And because black powder created such billows of smoke, the gunners could rarely observe where their shots were falling.

When General Pickett's men neared their objective, the center of the Union line, they advanced into point-blank fire; even so, a handful of Southerners did reach the stone wall—at least temporarily. That as many as 5,000 Confederates actually returned unhurt to their lines was something of a miracle, owed mostly to the inaccuracy of the day's weapons and to firing time lost in reloading by muzzle.

There were many comparable infantry charges in World War I, but the outcome was quite different: Hardly anyone who charged over the top survived the defenders' savage fire. With developments in smokeless powder and in high-velocity ammunition, the machine gun of 1914 could fire 600 rounds per minute at ranges that exceeded 1,000 yards. Two or three machine guns would have made quick work of a Pickett's Charge. Robert E. Lee, who ordered the charge, would not make such a mistake again, but the generals of World War I did— again and again.

Axelrod further differentiates the two wars by pointing out that in World War I getting killed became a rather more impersonal event—"rarely was there any individual opponent to outwit, outrun, or outthink." Breech-loading had shortened the interval between firings, and field guns now had recoil systems that took up the counterforce of propulsion without jolting the gun carriage, which saved time readjusting the aim. And rifled barrels and high-velocity shells had pushed possible targets far beyond human sighting—some seventy miles for Germany's Paris guns. Death just dropped out of the sky—with no warning.

But some things had begun to change before the United States entered the fighting in late spring 1918. With Russia out of the war that winter, Germany took advantage of armies withdrawn from the Eastern Front to direct all efforts toward finally crushing the British and the French forces—before Americans arrived in threatening numbers. A series of five major German offensives against the Western Front brought both sides out of the trenches and into the open, which was just fine with General John J. Pershing, commander of the American Expeditionary Force, who had long resisted feeding his men as they arrived into the deadly trenches to die under foreign commanders. In 110 days of heavy combat, fighting at last under the American flag and now two million strong, the AEF played a decisive role in causing the defeat of the German Empire. Now let Alan Axelrod tell you in greater detail how it all unfolded.

—Walton Rawls

Walton Rawls is the author of *Wake Up, America!: World War I and the American Poster.* His other books include *Great Civil War Heroes and Their Battles,* a Book-of-the-Month Club alternate selection, and *Disney Dons Dogtags: The Best of Disney Military Insignia from World War II.* He was a contributor to the *Oxford Companion to American Military History.*

Introduction

In a century defined by cataclysms, the only event more cataclysmic than World War I was the war that it spawned, World War II. Without an understanding of the first world war, we cannot fully comprehend the second. More important, without knowledge of World War I, the entire century becomes something of a mystery. The frenetic despair of the 1920s, the economic disaster of the 1930s, the great dichotomies of communism versus capitalism and of totalitarianism versus democracy, the simultaneous desire for and fear of a one-world mentality, the progress of science and technology, the emergence of much that characterizes popular culture—all these have roots in the "Great War." This is the event that launched, forged, and battered our times into shape.

Yet probably never have so many known so little about an event so momentous.

For most Americans, World War I has loomed in what seems a remote past—more remote, somehow, than the nineteenth-century past of the Civil War, which even the most casual history buff embraces. What accounts for this remoteness and lack of understanding?

Born of grand, sweeping strategies, World War I was nevertheless a conflict marked by stalemate and slaughter rather than movement and conquest. Animated by nationalist fervor, world-embracing idealism, and self-sacrificing patriotism, it was nevertheless characterized far more deeply by misery than by heroism. World War II was ultimately far bloodier, but not more dismal. World War I seems to defy and resist understanding. As one battered French soldier put it, "Humanity must be mad."

Moreover, because the United States entered the war at a late stage, much of the conflict seems even farther away, a struggle among foreigners. Yet the American experience of the war instantly transformed the United States into a great world power, a position that it has held consistently since 1917–1918. For Americans—and for others—World War I is an end and a beginning. It is the sharp, violent—unspeakably violent—end of the Old World, and it is the equally violent beginning of the New World. The war ushered in a host of new technologies, new moralities, new visions of society, new political philosophies, new political realities, new art and music, and maybe even new emotions.

World War I is more present—far less remote—than we may think. Today's headlines produced by the volatile politics of the Middle East and of Balkan Europe grow directly from the war and its immediate aftermath. Much of the structure of modern Europe is a product of the Treaty of Versailles. The sense so many Americans have that their country is obligated and destined to champion democracy throughout the world is a sense that was born during the Great War.

World War I is well worth understanding, and this book is intended to help.

Part 1, "The Lamps Go Out," begins with a comprehensive overview of the war, including its origins, course, and outcome. It includes chapters on the European background of the war, the network of alliances that made war all but inevitable, and the resources and plans of each of the belligerent nations. The last chapter of this part tells how a political assassination in an obscure Balkan capital triggered the greatest conflict the world had known up to that time.

Part 2, "Home Before the Leaves Fall," details the opening days, weeks, and months of the war, emphasizing the great German offensive that, in the space of a month, roared through Belgium and France to within 30 miles of Paris. The extraordinary Allied counterattack at the First Battle of the Marne is narrated, and the start of trench warfare is explained. This part also explores the early disasters of the Eastern Front, including the calamitous Battle of Tannenberg. It concludes with the entry of Turkey into the war and the early action at sea.

Part 3, "We Are the Dead," focuses on the war's second and third years, a time of stalemate unrelieved by battles as bloody as they were fruitless. Included are the British catastrophe at Gallipoli, the entry of Italy into the war on the side of the Allies, and the heroic and monumentally costly defense of Verdun.

Part 4, "Troubled Seas and Fiery Skies," is devoted to the sea war between the British Grand Fleet and the German High Seas Fleet, which culminated in the biggest naval battle the world has ever seen, at Jutland. World War I also took to the skies in an entirely new kind of warfare, aerial combat, including dogfights between "winged knights" and bombing and ground attack missions.

Part 5, "Doughboys," narrates U.S. entry into the war at a low point for the Allies and takes the war through the final desperate German offensives and ultimate Allied victory.

Part 6, "Lost Generations," covers the Treaty of Versailles and tells how the peace following the "war to end all wars" created the conditions that made World War II all but inevitable. The final chapter discusses the great influenza pandemic that engulfed the world following the war and also addresses the profound cultural and social changes brought about by the American war experience.

At the back of the book, you'll find appendixes devoted to who was who in the war, a glossary of relevant terms, and suggestions for further reading.

Extras

Throughout *The Complete Idiot's Guide to World War I,* you'll find four types of sidebar-style features to enhance your knowledge and understanding of the Great War.

Combatants

This feature presents biographical sketches of the most important military, political, and cultural figures of World War I.

From the Front

This sidebar gives concise facts and statistics of the war and the warriors.

Words of War

World War I created a vocabulary all its own. Here are definitions of the key terms of the era.

Voices of Battle

The Great War produced heartbreaking eloquence and stunning eyewitness accounts. Here is a sampling of quotations, including material from diaries, speeches, songs, memoirs, and verse.

Special Thanks to the Technical Editor

The Complete Idiot's Guide to World War I was reviewed by an expert who double-checked the accuracy of what you'll learn here, to help us ensure that this book gives you everything you need to know about the first world war. Special thanks are extended to Mr. Harris Andrews.

Harris J. Andrews is a resident of Annandale, Virginia. He was born in southern Virginia and graduated from Randolph-Macon College with a BA in History in 1971. A professional researcher, writer, and editor, he is an active student and collector of the Great War, and military history in general. A member of the Company of Military Historians, he is co-author of *Photographs of American Civil War Cavalry,* and a regular contributor to *Military Heritage Magazine.* He was editor of Time-Life Books' *Echoes of Glory: Arms and Equipment of the Civil War.*

Trademarks

All terms mentioned in this book that are known to be or are suspected of being trademarks or service marks have been appropriately capitalized. Alpha Books and Macmillan USA, Inc., cannot attest to the accuracy of this information. Use of a term in this book should not be regarded as affecting the validity of any trademark or service mark.

Part 1
The Lamps Go Out

In 1914, Europe was a civilized, prosperous, mostly content place. Then, following an assassination in an obscure capital of an obscure Balkan province, it suddenly started blowing itself up and tearing itself down. Here is the story of what happened, how it happened, and why it happened. It is a story of international politics crossing the line into world madness and collective suicide.

Chapter 1

The Great War

In This Chapter

➤ Overview of the causes of the war

➤ Entangling alliances

➤ The impact of technology

➤ Deadlock follows advance on the Western Front

➤ War of grand movement on the Eastern Front

➤ Armistice and a doomed peace

Soldiers, sailors, and airmen involved worldwide: 65,038,810. Military deaths worldwide: 8,020,780. Civilian deaths worldwide: 6,642,633. Military wounded world wide: 21,228,813. Approximate monetary cost in early twentieth-century dollars: $281,887,000,000.

This was the Great War. It's hard to imagine a catastrophe greater or more devastating, yet the conflict of 1914–1918 is no longer called by its original name, the "Great War"—it's now referred to as World War I, to distinguish it from the even more catastrophic orgy of global bloodletting that followed a little more than 20 years later. It staggers the imagination to realize that the carnage of World War II eclipsed that of World War I. But it did, and, in part for this reason, most of us know far less about the first war than about the second.

There is another reason for the remarkable obscurity of so cataclysmic an event as World War I. Its causes seem to us much more vague and ill-defined than those of

World War II. That second war was, in the truest sense possible, a struggle of good against evil—an evil, moreover, dramatically personified in such figures as Hitler of Germany, Mussolini of Italy, and Tojo of Japan. The causes of World War I, as we will see, are not terribly complex, but they are far more difficult to comprehend.

So, for us at the start of the twenty-first century, the war that opened the twentieth century is a strangely shadowy conflict. Yet, without it, there would have been no *second* world war. Without it, the last century would have been vastly different. And without an understanding of World War I, a full understanding of the twentieth century is impossible. The chapter that follows begins the story of World War I with an overview of this terrible seminal event.

How Did It Start?

The Swiss historian Jean Jacques Babel has estimated that 5,500 years of recorded history present a meager total of 292 years without armed conflict somewhere on the planet. So, to say that the years immediately preceding the outbreak of World War I were peaceful is very much a relative statement. True, there had been wars: In 1905, Russia and Japan went to war over territorial matters. In 1911, Italy declared war on Turkey and carved out Libya from the Ottoman Empire's African holdings. In 1912 and again in 1913, war broke out in the Balkans. In the 1912 war, Serbia, Bulgaria, and Greece fought the Turks and obtained most of the Turkish territory in Europe. In the 1913 war, Bulgaria fought her own Balkan neighbors in a doomed effort to grab a bigger share of what had been torn from the Turkish grasp the year before. France, of course, still smarted from the humiliating defeat it had suffered at the hands of Prussia in the Franco-Prussian War of 1870–1871. But Europe as a whole was at peace, and there had been no general European war since the days of Napoleon I at the beginning of the nineteenth century.

Voices of Battle

"One sees many wounded soldiers with broken noses, the result of having held their guns improperly while firing."

—Herr Wangenheim, the German ambassador to the Ottomans, on the incompetence of the Turkish army during the Balkan War of 1912

As 1914 dawned, the nations of Europe did business with one another, travelers freely passed from one country to another, and the arts and industry flourished. Europe appeared to be the epitome of civilization.

Wants and Needs

In fact, the quiet was deceptive. As we will see, Europe had been poised for a general war for years. Since the brief Franco-Prussian War, all the major nations had developed substantial arms industries, and all—except for Great Britain—had instituted programs of compulsory military service so that they could mobilize large forces quickly. All the major powers had developed elaborate war plans, which differed greatly from one another but did have two assumptions in common: that war *would* come, and that, when it came, all Europe would be involved.

The motives for this apparently inevitable war were really very simple:

➤ Germany, only recently formed as a whole nation from a collection of smaller states and principalities, wanted to become more influential among its European neighbors and, like the most powerful of them, wanted to amass a colonial empire.

➤ In contrast to new Germany, the Austro-Hungarian Empire was an ancient and doddering relic. It consisted of a collection of peoples who really had very little in common, and it was subject to intense nationalist pressures from its Balkan provinces, which wanted to break away. Although Austria-Hungary had some ambition for new territorial acquisitions, its main goal was simply to survive as an empire.

➤ France wanted to recover Alsace-Lorraine, the eastern provinces that it had lost to Prussia (now part of Germany) as a result of the Franco-Prussian War. Even more than this, the proud nation wished to exact revenge on its Germanic adversaries.

➤ Russia, like the Austro-Hungarian Empire, was boiling over with revolution and the threat of revolution. The czar, Nicholas II, was hoping to keep the Romanov dynasty alive. Ways to do this included restoring the prestige that Russia had lost in the Russo-Japanese War of 1904–1905, gaining territory at the expense of its age-old rival Turkey, and presenting itself to the world and to its own discontented citizens as the spiritual, cultural, and military champion of all Slavic peoples everywhere.

➤ Great Britain had no territorial designs in Europe, nor did it have a score to settle with the Germans, but it was deeply concerned with maintaining and exploiting the vast empire that it had built in Africa, India, and Asia during the nineteenth century. The continuation of this empire required a stable Europe. Insofar as upstart Germany threatened the European status quo, military intervention against that nation might not only be necessary, but desirable.

➤ Great Britain was involved in a naval arms race with Germany beginning in the 1890s. The rapid expansion of the German High Seas Fleet seemed, to the British, to be aimed at them.

From the Front

On the eve of World War I, the United States may have thought of itself as safely isolated from Europe, but it was, in fact, intimately connected to that continent by an ever-increasing influx of immigrants. The vast majority of the 8,795,386 who were admitted between 1901 and 1910 were from the nations about to be engulfed in war.

➤ More than the other nations, Italy and Turkey watched and waited. They saw nothing to gain from initiating conflict, but they were prepared to enter an ongoing war on whatever side promised the greatest reward. Italy saw the prospect of territorial gain. For Turkey, the prize was regaining some of its recently lost lands and much of its vanished prestige.

➤ As for the United States—well, in 1914, who here could envision *any* reason for fighting in a European war?

A Wrong Turn

Sarajevo. The name of this war-torn capital of Bosnia, a province of the former Yugoslavia, is all too familiar today. Early in the twentieth century, however, few Americans had heard of what was then a backward provincial capital in the Balkans. In 1908, the Austro-Hungarian Empire annexed Bosnia and Herzegovina from the long-tottering Ottoman Empire. The Serbs, neighbors of Bosnia-Herzegovina, saw the region as vital to their nationalist interests; influential officers in the Serbian military created a secret society, called the Black Hand, which trained anti–Austro-Hungarian resistance fighters in Bosnia and Herzegovina.

Combatants

Gavrilo Princip was born in West Bosnia on his father's farm on June 13, 1894. The parish priest mistakenly entered the birthdate as July 13, 1894, in the civil register. Austrian law prevented execution for a crime committed when under the age of 20, so Princip escaped death after he assassinated Archduke Franz Ferdinand and his wife, the Archduchess Sophie, on June 28, 1914.

"I do not feel like a criminal," Princip said at his trial, "because I put away the one who was doing evil. Austria as it is represents evil for our people and therefore should not exist .... The political union of the Yugoslavs was always before my eyes, and that was my basic idea. Therefore it was necessary in the first place to free the Yugoslavs ... from Austria."

Sentenced to 20 years in prison, Princip's tuberculosis worsened, and he died on April 28, 1918. On the wall beside his bunk, he scrawled: "Our ghosts will walk through Vienna/ And roam through the palace/Frightening the lords."

Into this troubled region, in June 1914, ventured Franz Ferdinand, Archduke of Austria, inspector general of the Austro-Hungarian army and heir apparent to the imperial throne. Accompanied by his wife, Sophie, Duchess of Hohenberg, he decided to make a state visit to his empire's most recent acquisition. The archduke harbored the ambition to add a "third crown" to the dual monarchy of Austria-Hungary. He saw himself becoming king of the Slavs as well as Emperor of Austria and King of Hungary. This self-aggrandizing plan would lead to administrative changes within the Austro-Hungarian Empire that would surely undermine Serbian influence over the empire's Slavic population. Franz Ferdinand was eager to visit his prospective kingdom.

The archduke and duchess arrived in Sarajevo on June 28, 1914, coincidentally their 14th wedding anniversary. Along the route of their procession, the couple survived the explosion of a small bomb, but when their driver took a wrong turn into a blind alley and then backed out, Gavrilo Princip, a sickly youth wracked by tuberculosis, found himself alongside the open car at pointblank range. He leveled his pistol and fired a shot into the carotid artery of Franz Ferdinand and another into the gut of Sophie. Both were dead within minutes.

A Tangled Web

Did the Serbian government play any role in the assassination? Probably not officially, but no one knows for sure. In any case, absence of proof did not stop Austria-Hungary from deciding to teach Serbia a lesson. It drew up a list of demands that effectively nullified Serbia's sovereignty. Surprisingly, Serbia was willing to agree to most of them, although it asked for international mediation on some points.

But Austria-Hungary refused mediation. It became clear that Austria-Hungary did not want simply to avenge the death of the heir to the Hapsburg throne. It *wanted* to go to war. To attack and defeat little Serbia would crush a nationalist movement and secure for Austria-Hungary a firmer foothold in the Balkans. The decision to refuse mediation and conciliation triggered a chain of events that proceeded with an almost mechanical mindlessness.

Ever since the Franco-Prussian War had upset the balance of power in Europe by making Germany a force to be reckoned with, the nations of Europe had been bound to one another by a web of alliances, some public and some secret. These will be explored in detail in Chapter 2, "Family Affairs"; for now, it is enough to take a quick, preliminary glance at this infernal political machinery.

➤ Austria-Hungary declared war on Serbia on July 28, 1914, a month after the assassination in Sarajevo.

➤ Russia, bound by treaty to Serbia, mobilized its vast but unwieldy army.

➤ Germany viewed the Russian mobilization as an act of war against its ally Austria-Hungary and so declared war on Russia.

➤ France, bound by treaty to Russia, declared war on Germany and, by extension, its ally Austria-Hungary.

Words of War

An **entente** is an agreement between two or more nations for cooperative action. It is somewhat less binding and more limited than a full-scale alliance.

Words of War

Poilu was the World War I nickname bestowed on the French soldier; it translates roughly as "hairy one." A **kepi** is the traditional visored cloth cap worn by French soldiers since the mid-nineteenth century. The caps worn by enlisted troops during the American Civil War were modeled on the French kepi. The **Pickelhaub,** or spiked helmet, was the traditional German headgear, used in parade as well as in combat. Even the American army copied this style from the Prussians for its dress uniforms during the late nineteenth century.

➤ Great Britain was more loosely bound to France by an *entente*—an understanding—which did not absolutely oblige it to join the fray. But Britain's sympathies clearly lay with the French and against the Germans, who presented a competitive threat to Britain's colonial empire. As a motive for war, Britain seized on the issue of protecting Belgian neutrality, as it was bound to do by a long-standing treaty with that nation. When Germany invaded Belgium, Britain declared war on Germany.

➤ Three weeks after Britain's declaration, Japan declared its military alliance with Britain.

For now, both Italy (although it was part of the Triple Alliance with Germany and Austria-Hungary) and the United States remained neutral. Italy would enter the war in 1916, and the United States would become involved the year after.

Red Pants and Spiked Helmets

The armies that marched off to war during August 1914 looked like quaint forces of the nineteenth century rather than the twentieth century. Cavalry helmets were surmounted by ostrich plumes, and sabers glinted in the summer sun. The French *poilus,* as the soldiers were called, wore dark blue coats and bright red pants. Helmets were considered superfluous among the French; instead, soldiers sported rakish cloth caps known as *kepis*. German troops did wear helmets, but these *Pickelhauben* were surmounted by an ornamental spike that gave them either a medieval or a comic opera appearance, depending on how one liked to look at such things. (Once off the parade ground and in the field, ostrich plumes were shed and the shiny spiked helmets were camouflaged with special gray-green cloth covers. French troops, however, were still clad in blue coats and scarlet trousers, even in battle.)

Summer of Six Million

Even in countries that staffed their armies largely through conscription, voluntary enlistment was high in the beginning. Crowds cheered men who believed that they were on their way to a great adventure that called to mind the bygone days of crusades and chivalry.

All sides were confident that it would be a short war. In August, Kaiser Wilhelm II sent the first waves off with the promise that they would "be home before the leaves have fallen from the trees."

In that summer of 1914, six million men marched —jauntily—to combat.

Big Plans

Although the parading armies looked like relics of the previous century and the emotions that drove them smacked of romanticized, naively old-fashioned patriotism, politicians were persuaded that modern war, even a big modern war, would be brief. In contrast to the feudal powers of old, they reasoned, modern industrial nations simply would not and could not finance a long war.

Voices of Battle

"All over Europe, young men went to war just as they would go on an unexpected holiday, delighted to escape the daily boredom of their clerking."

—James H. Meisel, *Counter-Revolution: How Revolutions Die* (1966)

For their part, the military leaders willingly fed this political illusion. Yes, they said, the war would be brief—and productive, too. As we will see in Chapter 3, "Blueprints for a Bloodletting," they had planned carefully for the day Europe would erupt:

➤ The German General Staff had been developing, honing, and tinkering with its Schlieffen Plan since the end of the Franco-Prussian War. The Schlieffen Plan was nothing less than a formula for fighting a two-front war, against France in the west and Russia in the east, with lightning speed that would bring these allies to their knees.

➤ The French had Plan XVII. It was based on recent historical precedent, the experience of the Austro-Prussian War (1866) and the Franco-Prussian War (1870–71), conflicts of sweeping mass movement. The French hoped that a series of coordinated offensives would place them in control of Alsace-Lorraine. Yet Plan XVII was, in fact, more in the nature of a collective national mythology than a fully formulated military plan. It called for the

Words of War

The term *élan*—or *élan vital*—was used by the philosopher Henri Bergson (1859–1941) to describe a "life force" that he believed the French possessed in abundance.

9

defense of the nation by means of a continual offensive, a push into Germany propelled by a secret weapon the French called *élan:* a vital force fueled by a mixture of spirit and guts believed to be uniquely French.

The Last Man on the Right

Something else about a modern war might have persuaded the planners and politicians that it would all be over quickly. Weaponry was far more efficient than it had ever been. Explosives were more powerful than ever before, the machine gun had been perfected, and artillery hurled shells with unprecedented velocity and accuracy. And, in the course of the war, scores of other new weapons—most notably the airplane, the tank, and poison gas—would come into their own. In short, technology had made it possible to kill more people in less time than ever before.

Indeed, the Germans counted heavily on the new technology to enable them to swing like a great scythe through Belgium and France, mowing down in short order all that came before them. Speed was of the essence in Germany's Schlieffen Plan. The idea was to devote the bulk of the German forces to war in the West and to defeat France before the great, lumbering Russian army had even mobilized. With France crushed in a matter of weeks, the troops could be swiftly transported from the Western Front to the Eastern Front, ready to meet the Russian onslaught, once it finally got under way.

What nobody had counted on, however, is that the technology of defensive weaponry had advanced faster and farther than the technology of offensive weaponry. This hard fact would not make for a short war, but rather, ensured a long one— at least if the German scythe lost its initial momentum.

Advance

At first, that great scythe, guided by the Schlieffen Plan, worked with a terrible swiftness and efficiency. During the first August of the war, a vast army of German troops cut a 75-mile-wide swath of death through Belgium and down into France, where, still according to plan, the German army enveloped the French left flank. Again and again, the French forces fell back, battered.

Count Alfred von Schlieffen, author of the plan, had emphasized that the advancing army was to proceed in a great wheel, moving counterclockwise through Belgium in an arc across northern France so that the "sleeve of the last man on the right" would "brush the English Channel." This great envelopment, Schlieffen believed, would surely crush the French army.

And it very nearly did. German forces came within 30 miles of Paris itself when, with his troops exhausted, and fearing that his vastly overextended lines of supply were vulnerable to attack, the German commander-in-chief, Helmuth von Moltke, gave the order to halt. Deep within France, the Germans had suddenly switched from an offensive to a defensive strategy. In response, the French made a stand at the Marne

River, where, after a monumentally destructive week-long battle involving two million men, they succeeded in pushing the previously undefeated Germans northward to the Aisne River.

Race to the Sea

At this point, the two armies desperately tried to outflank each other, with the opposing lines moving westward and then northward in what came to be called the "race to the sea." In short order, however, the futility of these movements became apparent. Once the sea had been reached, there was no more room for maneuver, no way to get around the opposing army. The result, by the autumn of 1914, was a stabilized Western Front that extended for some 600 miles from the Belgian coast along the English Channel down to the border of neutral Switzerland.

Trenches and Graves

And it was a front like no other in history. It consisted of the opposing armies dug into a system of trenches, which were a crucifixion of misery for the soldiers. Cold, wet, and always filthy, they were home to men and rats alike. The trenches were packed with troops, on average one soldier for every 4 inches of front. The crowded tedium of existence along this front was regularly punctuated by attacks and counterattacks that might or might not result in a few yards of territory gained or lost, but that certainly resulted in plenty of deaths. On an average day, 2,533 men died on the Western Front, 9,121 were wounded, and another 1,164 were missing—which typically meant that they had been blown apart and were no longer identifiable as individuals, or even as members of the human race.

From the Front

By 1915, four million young men were living in trenches. In the first year of the war, France had lost 1.5 million men, out of a total population of 40 million.

No Man's Land

The German hesitation 30 miles outside Paris at the end of the first month of the war sacrificed any chance for a quick conclusion to the conflict. It transformed a war of swift movement in the west into four years of static slaughter, inescapable proof that, during 1914–1918, the weapons of defense were far more effective than those of offense.

As the months and years dragged by, men seemed to forget what they were fighting for. Or, rather, the object of any given battle had become nothing more than taking possession of the bleak, cratered, dead extent of territory separating the opposing trenches: *no man's land.*

Western Front

In some of the chapters that follow, we will trace the course of the war on the Western Front, the battles at Ypres, Artois, the Somme, Verdun, and elsewhere. We will also look at the war as it was fought on the sea as well as under the sea and, beyond the confines of Europe, in the Middle East, Mesopotamia, Africa, and even Asia.

But it was in France, Belgium, and Flanders (encompassing part of Belgium and part of the Netherlands) that the greatest, longest slaughter took place. There, armies attempted to end the war with mostly fruitless forays out of the trenches and with new weapons, including poison gas, aircraft (used for reconnaissance, for aerial bombardment, and for air-to-air combat), new and more powerful artillery, new and more efficient machine guns, and tanks, which were touted hopefully as the only land vehicles that could break the stalemate of trench warfare by traveling over and across the trenches and through the barbed wire and other obstacles that scarred the landscape of France and Belgium.

Words of War

No man's land, one of the most enduring phrases produced by World War I, originally described the contested territory between the trenches of the opposing armies.

Eastern Front

In contrast to the static combat in the West, the Eastern Front was characterized by the grand movement of large forces. The German strategy had been to crush France quickly so that the full attention of the army could be turned against the Russians. The Germans believed that it would take the Russian army many weeks to mobilize; the Germans knew that communication technology in the czar's armies was slow and that the Russian rail system was poorly developed, so troop transport would be even slower. But the Germans also feared the might—the sheer numbers—of the Russian army once it did get into the field. A "steamroller" is what both Russia's allies and enemies called the czar's army.

Despite the Schlieffen Plan, however, France was not defeated, and the Germans had to face the Russians with far fewer troops than they had intended to deploy. Nevertheless, the Russian military leaders proved phenomenally inept, and although the army was brave, it was inadequately supplied and poorly trained. In 1914, the Russians suffered a devastating defeat at the Battle of Tannenberg. In 1915, Serbia was crushed. In 1916, Romania, which had joined the Allied cause, was also defeated in combat among the Carpathian Mountains. This freed up German troops to pound Italy, a latecomer to the war, in 1917.

The New War

By 1917, the war was bleak for all sides, but bleaker for the *Allies* than for the *Central Powers*. On the Western Front, the French had replaced the superannuated and corpulent Joseph Joffre—"Papa Joffre," as he was called—as commander-in-chief with the dashing young Robert Nivelle. He ordered an "unlimited offensive," which failed horribly, producing not only an accelerated harvest of French dead, but also an epidemic of mutinies throughout the French ranks.

With the French reeling, Britain was called on to launch an offensive in Flanders. Like the French efforts, however, it, too, failed.

The Russians Leave

Deepening the crisis for the Allies, 1917 also brought the Russian Revolution, which toppled the Romanov dynasty and was followed later in the year by the Bolshevik Revolution. This ushered in a Communist government that quickly made a "separate peace" with Germany. The war in the east ended, and a million German troops were now available for combat in the west.

It was a new war.

The Americans Arrive

But, in their darkest hour, the Allies gained a whole new army. During his first term in office, President Woodrow Wilson had struggled to maintain United States neutrality in the "European War." It wasn't easy. German U-boats, prowling the Atlantic, sank Allied ocean liners such as the *Lusitania* (in 1915), on which many Americans lost their lives. Although the Germans, for a time, agreed to respect U.S. neutrality on the high seas by calling off unrestricted submarine warfare, they soon resumed the practice.

On February 3, 1917, the *Housatonic,* a U.S. Navy warship, was torpedoed and sunk without warning. This prompted President Wilson to sever diplomatic relations with Germany. The next month, Wilson made public a document known as the Zimmermann Note or Zimmermann Telegram.

Words of War

The **Allies** were Great Britain, France, and (until it dropped out of the war late in 1917) Russia. Japan played a minor Allied role, and Italy joined in 1916. The United States joined the Allies in April 1917. The **Central Powers** were chiefly Germany, Austria-Hungary, and Turkey.

Voices of Battle

"The world must be made safe for democracy."

—Woodrow Wilson, message to Congress, asking for a declaration of war, April 2, 1917

It was a coded message, sent on January 19, 1917, that had been intercepted by British intelligence from Germany's foreign secretary Alfred Zimmermann to his nation's ambassador to Mexico. The telegram proposed a German-Mexican alliance against the United States. The Zimmermann Telegram galvanized public opinion, and on April 2, 1917, Woodrow Wilson asked Congress for a declaration of war. It was approved on April 6.

Creating a wartime trans-Atlantic expeditionary force out of the peacetime American army and navy is one of the great stories of World War I. Although the American commander-in-chief, General John J. Pershing, arrived in Paris as early as June 14, 1917 (laying a ceremonial wreath at the grave of the Marquis de Lafayette, the liberty-loving French aristocrat who had come to Washington's aid during the American Revolution), and although the first American Expeditionary Force troops followed on June 26, it was not until October 1917 that substantial units were committed to battle. Finally, in the spring of 1918, American involvement became massive, with some two million troops.

Between June 6 and July 1, 1918, the "Yanks" recaptured for the Allies Vaux, Bouresches, and—after a particularly bitter battle—Belleau Wood. The Americans also managed to hold the critically important Allied position at Cantigny against a great German offensive during June 9–15. At the Second Battle of the Marne (July 18–August 6, 1918), 85,000 American troops broke the seemingly endless deadlock of the Western Front by defeating another major German offensive. The Second Marne was, at last, a turning-point victory.

The American triumph at the Marne was followed by Allied offensives at the Somme, Oise-Aisne, and Ypres-Lys during August—actions in which Americans fought alongside the British and French. During September 12–16, in action against a German strongpoint called the St.-Mihiel salient, they fought alone. Some 1.2 million United States soldiers pounded and then cut the German supply lines between the Meuse River and the Argonne Forest. It was a spectacular success. In conjunction with the massive British offensives at Amiens on August 8, 1918, it did nothing less than bring about the end of the war. But action in the Argonne was also terribly costly to American units; on average, the Americans suffered a casualty rate of 10 percent.

Voices of Battle

"Lafayette, we are here!"

—proclaimed on the arrival of the first American contingent in Paris, often attributed to General John J. Pershing, but actually spoken by Major Charles E. Stanton, paymaster of the American Expeditionary Force

Armistice

The fighting skill and spirit of the American troops was formidable enough, but what ultimately overwhelmed the German forces were the health and energy of these fresh men. It was also clear that the United States was willing to pour in as many troops as it would take to win the war. Moreover, the industrial might of the United States was matchless. Faced with inevitable defeat, Germany sued for peace and agreed to an armistice, a cessation of hostilities to be concluded precisely at the dramatic 11th hour of the 11th day of the 11th month of 1918.

Requiem at Versailles

President Wilson traveled to Europe to play a major role in negotiating a final peace, which he hoped would make the Great War the war he had promised to the American people: "a war to end all war." Although Wilson proposed an idealistic set of conditions for peace and for creating a world in which war would no longer figure as an option for solving disputes among nations, the other major Allies—Britain, France, and Italy—were interested mainly in avenging themselves against Germany and punishing that country so severely that it would never be able to make war again.

The Long Truce

The result, the mercilessly punitive Treaty of Versailles, created in Germany the hopeless social, political, and economic conditions that sealed the doom of fledgling democracy there and virtually guaranteed the rise of a militaristic dictatorship. Intended to end the German threat forever, Versailles gave the German people a reason to rearm and to follow a clique of evil leaders into a new, even more terrible war.

The Treaty of Versailles brought to Europe and the world nothing more than a 20-year truce. World War I, the war to end all war, became the war that spawned war.

The Least You Need to Know

➤ The causes of World War I can be traced to a misguided struggle to restore the balance of European power upset by the emergence of Germany as a nation.

➤ The outbreak of war was triggered by the assassination of the archduke and archduchess of Austria-Hungary, which set into motion a series of binding alliances among the major powers of Europe.

➤ Each major belligerent had a plan to end the war quickly; none of them worked, in large part because the technology of defensive weaponry outstripped that of offensive weaponry, thereby creating conditions that virtually guaranteed costly stalemate.

➤ Although World War I was fought all over the globe, the principal action was on the Western Front (in France, Belgium, and part of the Netherlands) and on the Eastern Front (in eastern Prussia, Poland, and the borderlands of Russia).

➤ The United States remained neutral until 1917, when German violations of U.S. neutrality on the high seas and the exposure of a plot to form a German-Mexican alliance propelled America into the war.

Family Affairs

In the rearview mirror of history, the landscape is all too clear. In the second decade of the twentieth century, Europe was poised for—was *spoiling* for—a major war. One can see Europe, with the approach of 1914, as two armed camps. There was the Triple Alliance of Germany, Austria-Hungary, and Italy versus the Triple Entente of France, Russia, and Great Britain. Each nation in either alliance had motives for war, and because each nation believed that any war would be quick and, therefore, cheap, those motives didn't have to be particularly pressing. Gaining an economic or nationalist advantage or settling an old score—these were motive enough.

Yet squint into that rearview mirror a second time. Europe is not marching across the threshold of the twentieth century, but, rather, strolling through it. The nations and their leaders look a lot less like armed camps and warriors than like members of one big family. And so they were. But as anyone who watches today's tabloid television programs knows, family feuds are the bitterest of all.

Combatants

Wilhelm II (1859–1941) would be Germany's last kaiser. Son of Crown Prince Friedrich Wilhelm (later Kaiser Friedrich III) and grandson of Wilhelm I, he primarily was influenced in his youth by his mother, Victoria, daughter of England's Queen Victoria. She raised him to be as much an English gentleman as a stern Prussian aristocrat, although Wilhelm I did much to minimize her influence.

Wilhelm II became kaiser in 1888 after the three-month reign of his father, who succumbed to cancer. Immediately, the new kaiser, who wanted to restore the monarchy to the absolute power it had enjoyed under Frederick the Great, clashed with Bismarck, whom he dismissed in 1890. Unfortunately, Wilhelm II proved inept at foreign policy, progressively alienated the British, and increasingly yielded power and authority to the German military. By 1914, Wilhelm II, like everyone else in the German civil and military government, had enslaved himself to the Schlieffen Plan and, despite his own misgivings, let his nation be drawn into World War I.

Late in 1918, with Germany plunging toward defeat in the war, Chancellor Prince Max of Baden announced Wilhelm II's abdication—without having consulted the kaiser. When army commander-in-chief Paul von Hindenburg then informed Wilhelm II that the military would no longer support him, the kaiser fled to the Netherlands. The Dutch declined to extradite him to the victorious Allies, who wanted to try him as a war criminal. Until his death on June 4, 1941, he remained in exile there—out of world politics, an all but mute witness to the rise of Germany under Adolf Hitler and the Nazi regime in the 1930s.

A Historian Remembers a Funeral

The great American historian Barbara Tuchman portrayed the family aspect of turn-of-the-century Europe most memorably in one of the best books ever written about World War I. In her 1962 *The Guns of August,* Tuchman opens on the "spectacle of the May morning of 1910 when nine kings rode in the funeral of Edward VII of England." At the very center of the front row of mourners was England's new king, George V. On his right was, as the *London Times* reported, a person to whom "belongs the first place among all the foreign mourners," a foreign leader who "has never lost his popularity amongst us": Wilhelm II, *kaiser* of Germany. Out of respect to Edward, his maternal uncle, Wilhelm wore not the Prussian blue tunic of a German officer, but the scarlet uniform of a British field marshal.

Some years earlier, the kaiser had written home after spending a night in Windsor Castle, in what had been the apartment of his mother. "I am proud to call this place my home," he wrote, "and to be a member of this royal family." And, shortly before Edward's funeral, Wilhelm had described the late king's successor, George V, to Theodore Roosevelt as "a very nice boy."

The family feeling that Edward inspired extended well beyond Kaiser Wilhelm II. Edward's nickname, the "uncle of Europe," was partly a figurative description of the affection he inspired among the nine kings and the other high-ranking representatives of some 70 nations who attended the funeral. Partly, the sobriquet was literal. Edward was not only the German kaiser's uncle, but, through his wife's sister, he was uncle to Czar Nicholas II. His own niece was Alexandra, the czarina, wife of Nicholas. Edward's daughter Maud was queen of Norway; his niece Ena was queen of Spain; and Marie, yet another niece, was about to ascend the throne as queen of Romania. Edward's wife was the daughter of the Danish royal couple; her family had not only mothered Nicholas II, but also supplied the kings of Greece and Norway. If one looked a bit more deeply into the royal courts of Europe, even more relatives of Edward VII would be found.

Words of War

Kaiser is the German equivalent of "emperor." Phonetically, it reflects the classical Latin pronunciation of *caesar*, the ancient Roman title for emperor. The Russian word *czar* is another version of the Latin "caesar."

Empires

Yet all was not happiness and warmth in this politically and geographically extended family. In 1907, Kaiser Wilhelm II had occasion to vent his rage after Russia concluded an agreement with England to bring it into the Franco-British alliance to create the Triple Entente of Britain, France, and Russia. Wilhelm accused Edward of plotting to encircle him and, in a dinner speech in Berlin, said of the English king, "You cannot imagine what a Satan he is!"

The Old World

Wilhelm was right. He *was* being encircled. But the second part of the kaiser's assessment of his uncle was not necessarily true. For Edward was no more a Satan than the other monarchs of Europe, who were not so much devils as they were chess players with the continent of Europe—and even much of the world that they had colonized—as their vast board. Encirclement, containment, perpetual check—these were the moves of diplomacy as expressed in complex alliances periodically punctuated by war.

During the Middle Ages, Europe had been less a continent of nations than of fiefdoms run by feudal rulers—some called lords, some princes, and some even kings and queens. Whatever the title, their power was limited and the sense of nationhood that they created was commensurately weak. Economic, technological, and cultural changes wrought during the Renaissance, beginning in the fifteenth century, started to make it both feasible and desirable for Europe's rulers to consolidate their authority. This, in turn, created national armies that were big, able to travel, and motivated by patriotic themes orchestrated by a central government.

By the later Renaissance in the 1600s, Western Europe consisted of modern nation-states, the mightiest being France, Spain, England, and Italy. On a regular basis, these nations warred with one another and struck alliances with one another, always jockeying for power in what British diplomats of the nineteenth century would come to call "the great game."

In the east, the transformation of feudal and tribal entities into nation-states moved much more slowly and irregularly. Vast Russia, for example, is not recognizable as a nation, in the modern sense, until the early eighteenth century, when Czar Peter the Great began consciously to forge an empire along the lines of western examples.

In middle Europe, the transformation was even slower and sketchier. The Balkans, for example, remained a collection of tiny realms, almost tribal in nature, and were eyed greedily by the loosely constituted Austro-Hungarian Empire. (Austria-Hungary was formally created in 1848.) Germany was also a latecomer to nation status, but when its transformation came, it was swift, sure, and dramatic.

The creation of the German Empire from a collection of smaller kingdoms and principalities was the work of Otto von Bismarck (1815–1898), who was prime minister of Prussia and then first chancellor of the German Empire he had created. Bismarck pulled together the disparate German states through a combination of internal politicking and war waged against France. The Franco-Prussian war not only gained territory for the new empire, but, in January 1871, it also served to unite the southern German states with what was then called the North German Confederation to create the German Empire.

Voices of Battle

"Let us put Germany in the saddle, so to speak—it already knows how to ride."

—Otto von Bismarck, speech, 1867

Suddenly, a new and very strong European power had emerged; by 1914, it would be the single greatest economic and military power on the continent. The creation of the German Empire instantly wrecked the balance of power in Europe. And Germany's influence did not stop with Europe. The new empire played vigorous catch-up by expanding in the Pacific and especially Africa in a bid to become a major colonial power.

The creation of Germany in 1871 did as much to shake up the Old World as had the discovery of America in 1492. Germany wanted to grab more of a share of European capital, power, prestige, and real estate, and it wanted more of the colonial world as well. The "great game" was a zero-sum game. For every winner, there was a loser. For every item gained by one nation, some other nation lost something. Germany was hungry, ambitious, and greedy.

Twilight of the Kings

The emergence of Germany was not the only shudder that shivered the Old World. Revolution was in the air, threatening the old monarchies. Napoleon III of France had fallen after his ignominious defeat in the Franco-Prussian War of 1870–1871, his government replaced by a republic. Alfonso of Spain, Manuel of Portugal, Ferdinand of Bulgaria—all of these would soon lose their thrones, too.

The two most important imperiled monarchs were the Russian czar, Nicholas II, who had been fending off revolution since 1905, after Russia's stunning defeat in the Russo-Japanese War, and Franz Josef, the aging and doddering emperor of aging and doddering Austria-Hungary. He was clearly incapable of containing the centrifugal force of the jarring nationalities and ethnic groups that made up his empire.

Their precarious positions made these monarchs desperate. Russia would go to war to gain prestige in a hopeless bid to bolster the Romanov dynasty, to gain territory at the expense of yet another tottering empire (Turkey), and to attempt to claim or reclaim its position as defender of the Slavic world. Austria-Hungary was most eager among the nations for war, but it wanted a strictly local conflict with Serbia, hoping thereby to end Serbian pan-Slavic agitation, which threatened the continued existence of the Hapsburg's "Dual Monarchy." Additionally, the heir apparent to the Austro-Hungarian throne, Archduke Franz Ferdinand, hoped to add a Slavic kingdom to what would become his realm, transforming the Dual Monarchy into a triple one.

Voices of Battle

"It is true that liberty is precious—so precious that it must be rationed."

—attributed to Vladimir I. Lenin

Secrets and Lies

Any brief encyclopedia article worth reading on World War I mentions the two hostile systems of alliance that dominated Europe at the start of the twentieth century: the Triple Alliance of Germany, Austria-Hungary, and Italy, and the Triple Entente of France, Russia, and Great Britain. Seems neat, clean, and clear enough. But these great overarching alliances were rooted, like monstrous plants, in a complex of lesser alliances with the smaller European nations.

Romania, for example, was wedded to Germany by a separate alliance, so that, say, an attack on Romania would bring Germany into the fight, which, in turn, would drag along the other members of the Triple Alliance. Once these powers went to war, those of the Triple Entente would almost certainly be obliged to join in. The same held true, say, for an attack on Serbia, which was allied to Russia. Start a war against that small nation, and Russia would come into it, hauling the other members of the Triple Entente in tow.

Bismarck's Diplomacy

A basic, encyclopedia-article understanding of the Triple Entente and the Triple Alliance is necessary to understand the causes of World War I. But the subject is far from basic. Behind these great alliances was the hand of Otto von Bismarck. After he had reshaped Europe in 1871 by creating a unified Germany, he turned from bold innovator to archconservative. Having achieved his objective of building a brand-new empire, he now wanted nothing more than to preserve the status quo, to protect what he had gained.

Territorially, his biggest gain had been the coal-rich Alsace-Lorraine region, which had been the eastern frontier of France and which, as a result of the Franco-Prussian War, was now the western frontier of Germany. Possession of this land, Bismarck understood, created a lasting enmity between France and Germany. The chancellor was confident that German military might could deal with whatever France might throw at it—provided that France faced Germany alone. In the 1870s, Britain had adopted a policy of *"splendid isolation,"* so Bismarck believed that he had little to fear from that nation.

For Bismarck, the key was to isolate France by tying both Russia and Austria-Hungary to Germany. In 1873, he negotiated the Three Emperor's League, binding the three powers to assist one another in time of war. In 1878, Russia withdrew, and Germany and Austria-Hungary signed the Dual Alliance in 1879. The agreement bound the signatories to aid one another if either were attacked by Russia. If either signatory were attacked by any other country, a military alliance was optional, but, at the very least, the signatories would remain benevolently neutral to one another. However, if the attacking country were aided by Russia, the mandatory military alliance would kick in. It was a powerful bond that endured up to and through World War I.

The Triple Alliance, concluded among Germany, Austria-Hungary, and Italy in 1881, was another Bismarck creation. Germany and Austria-Hungary agreed to aid Italy if it were attacked by France, while Italy would aid Germany if it were attacked by France. If one of the signatories became involved with two or more powers, the others would come to its aid. Most provocative of all was the provision that, if one of the

Words of War

Splendid isolation described British foreign policy during the last third of the nineteenth century, a policy that ended when England concluded the Triple Entente with France and Russia in 1907.

signatories launched a "preventive attack" on another power, the others would remain benevolently neutral. (When the war began, Italy would effectively withdraw from the alliance, ultimately siding with the Allies of the Triple Entente.)

In 1883, Bismarck negotiated an alliance between Austria-Hungary and Romania, with Germany as an adherent. Then, in 1887, the chancellor negotiated a secret "Reinsurance Treaty" between Germany and Russia. By this document, the two nations agreed to remain neutral if either became involved in a war with a third power—unless Germany attacked France, or Russia attacked Austria-Hungary. With this secret treaty, Bismarck hoped to keep Germany from facing a two-front war against France and Russia, but the alliance lapsed in 1890.

Combatants

Otto von Bismarck was born in 1815 in Prussia, the son of a landowner of modest means. He studied law but left the university to enter the Prussian civil service and, in 1849, entered politics as a representative in the Prussian Chamber of Deputies, gradually emerging as an intense advocate of German nationalism. In 1859, he served as Prussian ambassador to Russia and then, in 1862, as ambassador to France. Later that year, Kaiser Wilhelm I appointed him both prime minister and foreign minister.

Bismarck maneuvered brilliantly to unite the disparate German states under the leadership of Prussia. He engineered war with Austria in 1866 over dominion of Schleswig-Holstein. Defeating Austria in a mere seven weeks, Prussia not only acquired new territory but also ousted Austria as the dominant force among the German states, thus becoming the center of a new North German Confederation. Next Bismarck readily goaded Napoleon III into the Franco-Prussian War of 1870–1871, which resulted in Prussia's acquisition of Alsace and Lorraine and brought all the German states, except for Austria, under the umbrella of the new German Empire, with Bismarck as its chancellor. He forged key alliances with Austria-Hungary and Italy, dividing Europe into two opposed armed camps and setting the stage for what would be World War I.

Wilhelm II ascended the German throne in 1888. The new kaiser did not want to share power with the "Iron Chancellor" and brought about his dismissal in 1890. Bismarck died eight years later.

The Entente

As Russia fell away from the German-dominated fold, it attached itself to France. The August Convention of 1891 bound the two nations to consult each other for a joint response if either were threatened or if the peace of Europe were endangered. In 1893–1894, France and Russia concluded a Franco-Russian Military Convention, which was intended specifically to counter the Triple Alliance. If either signatory were attacked by a Triple Alliance power, the other would come to its aid. Moreover, if any member of the Triple Alliance *mobilized*, both France and Russia would instantly mobilize in response.

Next, France concluded a secret agreement with Italy, which—despite its obligations under the Triple Alliance—agreed to remain neutral if Germany attacked France or if France attacked Germany to protect its "national honor." This secret agreement effectively drew Italy out of the Triple Alliance, even though it remained a member on paper.

Words of War

To **mobilize** is to put a nation on a war footing, calling up reservists to active service and putting regular forces on high alert. In nations with compulsory military service, conscription is typically commenced.

By the beginning of the twentieth century, Britain was rousing itself out of its splendid isolation. After all, Germany was vying for a place among the great colonial powers, of which none was greater than Britain. In 1902, Britain concluded a military alliance with Japan in a move to check German colonial advances in the Pacific and Asia. In 1904, it signed the Entente Cordiale with France, which resolved colonial disagreements between the two countries. No specific military alliance was included in the Entente Cordiale, but the agreement opened the way for close cooperation between the two nations in diplomatic matters. The Entente Cordiale between France and Britain was followed in 1907 by the Anglo-Russian Entente, which was likewise directed toward the resolution of colonial conflicts. Together, the Entente Cordiale and the Anglo-Russian Entente formed the Triple Entente.

Technically, the Triple Entente was not a military alliance, although there was a presumption of a "moral obligation" among the allies to come to one another's aid in the event of attack. However, in 1912, Britain and France concluded the Anglo-French Naval Convention, whereby Britain pledged to protect the French coast from German naval attack, and France promised to defend the Suez Canal. The signatories also agreed to consult if either were attacked on land.

The World as a Trap

The nations of Europe concluded public alliances and secret treaties for what they thought was their advancement and protection. In fact, they had bound themselves together like prisoners on opposing chain gangs. A move by one signatory pulled the others in the same direction. The world was transformed from the immense chessboard of the "great game" into a universal snare, a deathtrap for nations.

A Set of Wars

Although most of Europe was at peace—and, indeed, enjoying prosperity—during many of the years leading up to World War I, a set of wars served as the overture to the Great War that would begin in 1914.

Seven Weeks in 1866

A first step toward creating the empire Bismarck envisioned was to overcome Austria-Hungary's dominance of what in 1866 was the collection of states known as the German Confederation. In place of Austria-Hungary, Bismarck would put his native Prussia. Over the objections of his own king, Wilhelm I, Bismarck provoked war with Austria-Hungary by occupying the Austrian-administered duchy of Holstein. Prussia, with its superb army, quickly defeated the Austro-Hungarians. In a peace mediated by the French emperor Napoleon III, Austria-Hungary was excluded from German affairs, and Prussia was given control of Schleswig-Holstein, Hanover, Hesse, Nassau, and Frankfurt. The former German Confederation became the North German Confederation, with Prussia—and Bismarck—at the helm. Thus, the basis of the German Empire was created. Defeated—except against Italy—Austria-Hungary would not again seriously vie for dominance among the German states.

The Shame of Sedan

Having attained victory over Austria, Bismarck next began to draw the independent southern German states into union with the North German Confederation. The vehicle of this union would be an alliance against the French. All that was needed was a convenient war, and Bismarck was determined to furnish one.

In 1870, Bismarck's government attempted to put a Hohenzollern prince—a relative of the royal house of Prussia—on the throne of Spain. France's Napoleon III took alarm at this, fearing that France would face the prospect of a war on two fronts, from Spain to the south and from Prussia to the east. Seeking to provoke war, on July 14, 1870, Bismarck published the so-called Ems Telegram, a communication between the Prussian king and himself. He edited the published telegram to insult both Prussia and France over their failed talks to resolve the issue of the Spanish throne.

For his part, Napoleon III had been persuaded by his army's high command that nothing could defeat French soldiers. The army, he was told, would welcome a war—and so would the French nation, which was in the throes of republican radicalism. A war would restore glory to the throne and dispel all talk of revolution. On July 19, Napoleon III declared war.

The French army attacked to the east, only to be beaten back by a Prussian onslaught. French troops made a stand at the Battle of Gravelotte on August 18, 1870, inflicting some heavy losses on the Prussians, who nevertheless prevailed, pushing the badly mauled French army to its fortress at Metz. This Prussian victory was led by Count Helmuth von Moltke, one of the most brilliant commanders Prussia ever produced. His nephew, also named Helmuth von Moltke, would lead the initial assault on France in 1914.

From the Front

Defeat in the Franco-Prussian War was a French national disgrace. The French army, however, retained its pride, largely through the heroism of the defenders of "Belfort the Invincible," a fortress held against a 105-day German siege at the cost of 4,800 French casualties. Only after the war was over, and on direct orders from the French General Assembly, did the battered garrison finally capitulate.

The French emperor personally led his nation's forces at the Battle of Sedan, which proved disastrous. Napoleon III surrendered and was deposed in a concurrent civil war that installed the Third French Republic. In the meantime, Prussian forces laid siege to Paris from September 1870 to January 1871, forcing the city to surrender as starvation threatened. As a result of the defeat, France relinquished Alsace and Lorraine to Prussia and was forced to pay an indemnity equivalent to a billion dollars; the nation would remain occupied until the indemnity was paid.

As Bismarck had hoped, the Franco-Prussian War brought the southern German states into union with Prussia and the northern German states, creating the German Empire. Peace reigned in a Western Europe that was no longer dominated by France, but France now simmered with a desire for vengeance and the restoration of its honor.

Rising Sun

Another nation that felt its honor stained before the start of World War I was Russia. In 1903, the czar's government rebuffed a Japanese proposal that the two nations recognize one another's "special interests" and "economic privileges" in Manchuria and Korea. To this rebuff, the Japanese responded with a naval attack on Russian warships at Inchon, Korea, and in Port Arthur, China. Having quickly achieved superiority at sea, Japan staged a land invasion of Korea and Manchuria. Korea was instantly overrun, and, by September 1904, the Russians had been driven as far north as Mukden in Manchuria. The main Russian naval and military installation at Port Arthur was surrounded. It fell on January 2, 1905, after a bitter siege.

Other major battles followed, both on land and at sea. In the two-day Battle of Tsushima (May 27–28, 1905), the entire Russian fleet was wiped out, while the Japanese lost only two torpedo boats—minor vessels.

U.S. President Theodore Roosevelt offered to mediate peace between Russia and Japan, and the belligerents met in Portsmouth, New Hampshire, where they concluded a treaty on September 5, 1905. Russia gave up part of Sakhalin Island, recognized Japanese economic interests in Korea, transferred to Japan territory that it had leased from China, granted certain valuable fishing rights to Japan, and even paid Japan for the costs of having maintained tens of thousands of Russian POWs.

The Russian defeat was stunning on at least three counts. First, it was the world's first look at the new technology of naval and artillery warfare. Japan's fleet and guns were of the latest design, while Russia's were antiquated. The effect of the new weaponry was devastating, and it spurred the nations of Europe to upgrade their forces accordingly. Second, the Russo-Japanese War was the first modern defeat of a European nation by an Asian one. Whatever this boded for the rise of Japan, it certainly had an impact on the myth of Russian invincibility—although not everyone took the lessons to heart. The nations of the Triple Alliance, especially Germany and Austria-Hungary, no longer assumed that Russia would figure in the next war as the "steamroller" it was touted to be. Their fear of this enemy—and, consequently, their fear of a two-front war with France and others on the west, and Russia on the east—was diminished.

In contrast, the Russo-Japanese War did not diminish the enthusiasm of France for a Russian alliance. With something of the same capacity for self-delusion that had prompted Napoleon III to march heedlessly into battle against Prussia in 1870–1871, France chose to continue to think of Russia as unbeatable, even though it had been defeated.

The third stunning result of the war was the blow to Russia itself. The costly and tragic humiliation severely weakened the already imperiled Romanov government. The war triggered the Russian Revolution of 1905, which resulted in an incongruous and destabilizing mixture of genuine reform and intensified repression. The days of the czarist government were numbered, creating in Nicholas II and his advisers a desperation to regain lost honor and authority. In 1914, that desperation would help propel Russia into war.

Balkan Tragedies

After the Franco-Prussian War of 1870–1871, Western Europe was deceptively peaceful. It was a different story in the Balkans, however.

In 1911–1912, Italy and Turkey went to war over some of Turkey's African possessions. The result

From the Front

The siege of Port Arthur exhibited to the world the fierce determination of the Japanese soldier. The Japanese victory came at the staggering cost of 59,000 Japanese killed, wounded, or missing (another 34,000 succumbed to illness) versus Russian casualties numbering 31,000.

Words of War

The **Young Turks,** mostly junior Turkish military officers, were members of a military-political movement that overthrew the centuries-old rule of the sultans and sought to reform and modernize Turkish government and society.

was that Turkey lost Libya, Rhodes, and the Dodecanese Islands to Italy. No sooner had Turkey concluded peace with Italy than it found itself at war with Greece, Serbia, and Bulgaria, which, later joined by Montenegro, fought Turkey over possession of territories on the Balkan peninsula. The war was ended by intervention from the "great powers" of western Europe, which essentially forced Turkey to relinquish Crete and all of its European possessions.

This First Balkan War had begun in 1912 and ended in 1913. Later that year, however, a Second Balkan War erupted when the so-called *Young Turks* (Turkish army officers who had overthrown the ancient and corrupt rule of the sultans) denounced the peace and when Bulgaria attacked its recent allies in an effort to grab more of Macedonia, ceded by Turkey as a result of the first war. The Balkan allies quickly beat back Bulgarian forces in a series of bloody battles between May and July 1913. During July and August, Romania declared war on Bulgaria, invaded that country, and took its capital, Sofia. For their part, the Turks also prevailed against the Bulgars, reoccupying Adrianople, which had been lost in the first war. Bulgaria surrendered on August 10.

Nations and Tribes

The Balkan Wars resolved none of the tensions that had been mounting in this part of Europe. If anything, the wars encouraged and intensified the nationalist emotions of the small countries that had been torn between Turkey and Austria-Hungary for so long. The nationalist passions were energized by ancient loyalties based on age-old tribal and ethnic affiliations. These same affiliations drove and pulled the Balkan nations in two directions. Individual countries sought independence, yet they also sought a "pan-Slavic" identity, a solidarity with one another and with Russia, which, eager to regain lost prestige, presented itself as the spiritual, cultural, political, and military defender of all Slavic peoples. In this way, the seeds of a world-engulfing war had been planted in one of the world's most obscure recesses.

The Least You Need to Know

➤ At the beginning of the twentieth century, Europe was ruled mainly by a family of monarchs, who felt many of the loyalties and enmities that figure in all extended families.

➤ Bismarck created the German Empire, which upset the delicate balance of power in Europe and resulted in a series of entangling alliances that transformed the continent into two armed—and opposed—camps.

➤ Five important wars served as military and political preludes to World War I: the Seven Weeks' War between Prussia and Austria, the Franco-Prussian War, the Russo-Japanese War, and the two Balkan Wars.

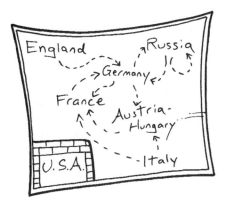

Blueprints for a Bloodletting

Bound by competing alliances, some public and others secret, and armed to the teeth, the European family of nations was highly dysfunctional. As with any dysfunctional family, the potential for a tragic explosion was great.

This chapter sets out the economic and military assets and liabilities of the nations about to go to war, together with their plans for that war.

European Balance Sheet

On May 23, 1916, a French lieutenant at Verdun gazed in stunned disbelief at the carnage, filth, and ruin about him and wrote in his diary, "Humanity ... must be mad to do what it is doing."

Some people believe that all war is madness, but most, if closely questioned, concede that sometimes war is actually reasonable: in response to oppression or attack, for example, or perhaps in a bid to gain independence and liberty.

None of these motives were pressing in 1914, at least not among the nations of the West. Western Europe was more prosperous than it had ever been. For more than four decades, it had largely enjoyed the blessings of peace. True, Russia, Austria-Hungary, Turkey, and the Balkans were rife with injustice and hardship. But, from a Western point of view, to engulf all Europe in a war, at this time, under such generally happy circumstances, would indeed be madness.

Yet prosperity created the economic and industrial wherewithal to man and equip great armies and navies and to prepare them for what they were meant to do: make war. And prosperity also created a hunger for more and greater prosperity, even at the expense of another nation. Given these two facts, Europeans—including those in the fortunate West—would find reasons to fight.

Allied Advantages

In the coming war, the nations of and associated with the Triple Entente—France, England, Russia, and their lesser allies—would be called the Allies. They enjoyed substantial material advantages over the two major nations of the Triple Alliance, Germany and Austria-Hungary, which, together with their lesser allies, would be called the Central Powers.

The Allies possessed greater economic and demographic resources than the Central Powers, and they had far more access to the sea coasts, which were vital for trade (with neutral countries, especially the United States) and supply.

From the Front

In 1914, the population of the Central Powers was 115.2 million; the Allies numbered 265.5 million. In terms of military strength, the Central Powers could field 146 divisions in August 1914, versus 212 for the Allies. The Central Powers possessed 20 modern dreadnought battleships, whereas the Allies had 39. However, steel production, an important gauge of industrial capacity, was greater among the Central Powers—an annual production of 17 million metric tons versus 15.3 million for the Allies.

A Matter of Self-Sufficiency

Of the Allies, only England regularly imported food. Agriculturally, the island nation was not self-sufficient. Of the Central Powers, populous Germany also relied on imports to supplement its domestic food production. This rendered both of these major powers vulnerable to *blockade* and other disruptions of trade.

Industrially, Great Britain could outproduce Germany and, therefore, had the edge on self-sufficiency in this regard. However, German industry was highly advanced, especially in the production of chemical products. German industrialists could create a whole range of *ersatz*—artificial, or substitute—products for goods that might be in short supply.

Haber's Miracle

With regard to war, the most important ersatz product Germany possessed was a process for synthesizing ammonia from atmospheric nitrogen, the nitrogen in the very air that Germans (and everyone else) breathed. The invention of the great German chemist Fritz Haber, this so-called Haber Process had been developed to manufacture nitrogen fertilizer, which traditionally had been made from nitrate material imported from Chile. The demand for nitrogen fertilizer far exceeded the supply of Chilean nitrate, so Haber's process, perfected on an industrial scale in 1909, was of tremendous importance both to the German chemical industry and to German farmers.

Words of War

A **blockade** is the use of military forces, especially warships, to forcibly intercept goods and persons attempting to enter or depart from a particular place or an entire nation.

The Haber Process was also of critical importance to the German military machine. Nitrogen-rich ammonia was an essential ingredient not only in fertilizer, but also in explosives. In fact, it was the lifeblood of war. Intending to create a process for helping to feed Germany and the world, Haber had also created the means by which Germany could attain self-sufficiency in the business of dealing death.

Words of War

Ersatz is a German word, also borrowed into English, meaning "replacement" or "substitute"; it is a synonym for "artificial."

Nations at Arms, 1914

The military forces that would face each other in 1914 were vastly changed from those that had taken to the field in the Franco-Prussian War 44 years earlier. They were bigger and better equipped, the beneficiaries of economic prosperity as well as technological advances not only in weaponry, but also in transportation. Since 1870, the network of European railways had been greatly extended and stood ready to transport and supply large numbers of troops quickly and efficiently.

If the military use of railroads was a lesson taught by the American Civil War, the Second (Great) Boer War (fought between the British and the Boers—descendants of Dutch settlers—in South Africa) and the Russo-Japanese War demonstrated the lethal effects of newly developed automatic weapons. The weapons the armies of Europe had in 1914 were far more destructive than those of any earlier era.

Combatants

Fritz Haber (1868–1934), the son of a chemical merchant, became one of Germany's leading chemists, a great teacher, and the author of important theoretical works. A scientist of tremendous versatility, he applied his theoretical genius to solve the practical problem of finding a process for manufacturing all-important nitrate fertilizer without using scarce and costly nitrate from Chile. With the chemist Carl Bosch, he developed the Haber Process, by which ammonia is synthesized from atmospheric nitrogen. Not only did this free Germany from dependence on imported nitrate for the manufacture of fertilizer, but it also created a synthetic source of a principal ingredient in high explosives.

While the Haber Process ensured Germany a supply of ammunition in World War I, Haber also worked during the war to develop poison gas as a weapon. An intense German patriot, Haber was heartbroken by Germany's defeat and set out to find a way of extracting gold from seawater to help his country pay the enormous indemnity levied against it by the Treaty of Versailles. Although this effort failed, it did result in a number of results important for chemical research. In 1918, Haber was awarded the Nobel Prize for Chemistry for his work on the Haber Process.

Until the rise of the Nazi Party in 1933, Haber enjoyed authority and honor in Germany. Denounced by the Nazis as that "Jew Haber," the great chemist left Germany for England, where he taught at University of Cambridge. He succumbed to a heart attack in Switzerland while on holiday.

France Versus Germany

In 1914, the French army numbered 4.5 million men, most of them conscripts (draftees). Germany mustered even more: 5.7 million, again, the great majority conscripted. Both countries had instituted peacetime compulsory military reserve service, which created a vast pool of trained men who were liable to serve for a certain period of time—28 years in France and 23 years in Germany, although the span of active compulsory service was much less in the armed forces of both countries.

On the water, France had 14 modern *dreadnought* battleships and 15 of the earlier pre-dreadnought class of battleships. In addition, the French navy had 76 submarines and a variety of other surface vessels. The German navy had 13 dreadnoughts and 30 older battleships, as well as 30 submarines and many other surface craft, including 152 destroyers (small but fast and agile vessels) versus France's 81 destroyers.

Words of War

Dreadnought described a revolutionary new style of battleship—bigger, faster, and more heavily armed. The prototype of this class of vessel was HMS *Dreadnought*, launched in 1906. Through the end of World War I, "dreadnought" was used as a synonym for any modern battleship.

British Volunteers

In contrast to both France and Germany, England had not instituted a program of compulsory military service. In 1914, its British Expeditionary Force (BEF) was a superbly trained body of professional soldiers, volunteers all, but it numbered a mere 160,000 men. Backing up the BEF was a Territorial Army, a poorly trained and poorly equipped home-defense force that could not even be sent—without its consent—to fight overseas.

Traditionally, the island nation of Great Britain had depended more on its navy than its army. England had 24 modern dreadnought-class battleships, far more than any other power possessed, and it also had 38 pre-dreadnoughts. In addition to 76 submarines, the Royal Navy fleet included a mighty array of surface vessels. The battle cruiser had much of the size and firepower of a dreadnought, but was more lightly armored to decrease weight and allow greater speed. England had 10 of these, Germany had a half-dozen, and France had none. The cruiser, a vessel that combined some of the firepower of a battleship with greater speed and maneuverability, figured importantly in the British inventory. The Royal Navy had 47 heavy cruisers and 61 light cruisers, far more than in any other nation's navy. Although the German navy had an impressive 152 destroyers, the Royal Navy had 225.

The Russian "Steamroller"

The muster rolls of the Russian army in 1914 showed 5.3 million men—more than any of the other great powers except for Germany. But with a population of 77 million, compared to 41 million for Germany, the nation had an enormous reserve of manpower from which to conscript an even bigger force.

In view of these numbers, the Allies referred with comforting confidence to the irresistible force of the "Russian steamroller." German military planners were certainly impressed with the Russian numbers, but they also had a more realistic view of the nature of this army. It was poorly trained (manned mainly by uneducated peasants), poorly equipped (with antiquated weapons), and poorly led. Moreover, the Russian infrastructure was not nearly as well developed as that in Germany or the rest of Central and Western Europe. Whereas German soldiers could be carried swiftly by rail, the Russian rail network was thin and inefficient. Even where rail service was available, Russia was plagued by rail lines of differing gauges (the width between the rails), so frequent and time-consuming changes of train were required.

Nor was the Russian navy especially impressive, having been decimated in the Russo-Japanese War. The czar's navy had only 4 dreadnoughts, a single battle cruiser, and 7 pre-dreadnoughts. In addition, there were 8 heavy cruisers, 5 light cruisers, and 36 submarines. Destroyers were plentiful at 106, but that was still substantially fewer than the 152 that Germany possessed.

The Dual Empire

In 1914, Austria-Hungary's army was large—some 2.3 million men, about half the size of the French army or the Russian army—but the force was poorly organized and, for the most part, poorly led. Reflecting the dozen very different and often jarring ethnic groups living within the empire's borders, it was hardly a cohesive or dependable force. For example, there was no telling how a predominantly Slavic unit would perform against Serbians or Russians, who were, after all, fellow Slavs.

Compared to other major powers, the Austro-Hungarian navy was modest: three dreadnoughts, no battle cruisers, a dozen pre-dreadnought battleships, three heavy and four light cruisers, a mere 14 destroyers, and 14 submarines.

Deadly Innovations

By 1914, three major innovations had been introduced into warfare: the machine gun, advanced artillery, and the dreadnought battleship. A fourth innovation, the airplane, was becoming increasingly available to armies but had yet to serve in combat. As we will see, the airplane would play an increasingly significant role as the war dragged on (see Chapter 19, "Winged Knights"). Another innovation, the tank, would also come to figure importantly (see Chapter 12, "Deadlock"). But neither of these counted for much in 1914.

The Machine Gun

Hiram Maxim, born in Maine in 1840, was apprenticed to a carriage maker but showed an early genius for invention. His first patent was awarded in 1866—for a hair-curling iron! After a stint as chief engineer for United States Electric Lighting Company, the world's first electric utility, and after a string of inventions, Maxim moved to London to work on the problem of automatic weapons. In 1884, he produced the Maxim gun, the first modern machine gun and the world's first truly *automatic weapon*.

Maxim's invention differed from the multibarreled, hand-cranked *Gatling gun* in that it had a single barrel and fired as long as the trigger was squeezed. The Maxim gun could fire much faster and much more accurately than its multibarreled predecessor. By 1914, several manufacturers, in addition to Maxim's company, were producing the weapon that was by then universally called the machine gun.

The machine gun had been used with great effect in the Russo-Japanese War of 1904–1905, but strangely, military analysts failed to appreciate the true significance of the weapon in that conflict. For it had done nothing less than change the nature of land war from an offensively focused enterprise to a defensively directed one. With a machine gun, a small number of defenders could hold off a substantially superior number of attackers. That is, the machine gun made attack difficult—even suicidal—if the defenders were well covered.

Words of War

An **automatic weapon** is any firearm that continuously fires as long as the trigger is squeezed and as long as it is supplied with ammunition.

The lesson of the Russo-Japanese experience was that the machine gun was not only a great leap forward in the technology of defense, but a leap that left the technology of offense well behind. Accordingly, nations should have anticipated that future wars would be essentially defensive and, therefore, long. Instead, they ignored the lesson and planned, as nations have always done, for a swift offensive war. It was a tragic error, based on an emotionally charged, utterly irrational reading of reality.

More than any other single factor, the machine gun transformed what could have been a war of rapid advance and conquest into an endless struggle of defense. It barred the possibility of "glorious" bayonet charges and dictated instead a squalid nightmare fought grimly in the filth of trenches.

Words of War

The **Gatling gun** was a predecessor of the machine gun, with a cluster of barrels that were fired in sequence as the cluster was crank-rotated. It was patented in 1862 by Richard Jordan Gatling (1818–1903).

The New Artillery

The *artillery* of 1914 was lighter, more mobile, and more accurate than the guns of the nineteenth century. The great masterpiece of modern light artillery was the French 75 (named for the caliber of its shell, a base diameter of 75 millimeters). Its signal advantage was a shock-absorbing hydropneumatic recoil system that allowed it to fire at a rate of 16 rounds per minute without getting out of alignment and having to be "relaid" (aimed again) on target.

Words of War

Artillery, used as both singular and plural, is the generic term for large-caliber weapons, such as cannons, howitzers, mortars, and so on. It also denotes the combat arm that uses such weapons.

Voices of Battle

"After a thunderous crash in our ears, a young boy began to cry for his mother in a thin, boyish voice. 'Mam, mam ....' He had not been hit but was frightened and crying quietly. Suddenly he started screaming again, screaming for his mother with a wail that seemed older than the world."

—W. Griffith, British soldier recalling the effects of an artillery barrage (*Up to Mametz*, published 1931)

The other armies had similar light field pieces, but none nearly as good. Still, all were lethal—and they would become far more lethal. In concentrating on the lighter field pieces, the French had neglected to develop heavy guns. The Germans entered the war with better heavy artillery than the French, but, as early as the second year of the war, 1915, all of the armies were calling for heavier, less mobile, much more powerful artillery pieces that were better suited to trench warfare and artillery combat against strongly fortified and reinforced positions. As we will see, by the end of the war, both sides were creating huge guns, some capable of hurling giant projectiles many miles. As the military historian Ian V. Hogg wrote, "The war of 1914–1918 became an artillery duel of vast proportions," and it became a duel whose sheer destructiveness no one had even dimly imagined at the outset of the war.

The Dreadnoughts

In 1906, the British Royal Navy commissioned the HMS *Dreadnought*. Displacing 21,845 tons, clad in 11-inch belt armor, and bristling with ten 12-inch guns (that is, guns firing shells 1 foot in diameter) as well as many smaller defensive guns, the new vessel also had a top speed of 21 knots. It was a leviathan compared to the common battleship of its time, which typically displaced 15,000 tons, had four 12-inch guns and a number of smaller guns, and was capable of no more than 18 knots.

The construction of this single vessel, the *Dreadnought*, instantly rendered all other battleships obsolete. The major powers rushed to build fleets of dreadnought-class battleships, most even bigger than the prototype. Indeed, the word "dreadnought" became a synonym for battleship during the period leading up to World War I.

Spoiling for War

Fully armed and manned, the armies of Europe were spoiling for war. Beginning in the late nineteenth century, the major powers had been drawing up, modifying, and generally tweaking master plans for a war that they assumed would involve most of Europe. These were the plans that would be activated in 1914.

French Élan: Plan XVII

Following the disaster of the Franco-Prussian War of 1870–1871, French military planners concentrated on war strategies aimed at recovering the lost territory of Alsace-Lorraine. Plan XVII, the principal master plan that was developed, was entirely offensive in nature and called for an immediate and overwhelming concentration of force against the Alsace and Lorraine region. No thought was given to a defensive war—which, as it turned out, would be precisely the nature of World War I.

Plan XVII called for four major forces to advance into Alsace-Lorraine on either side of the Metz-Thionville fortresses, which had been occupied by the Germans since 1871. Originally, the plan foolishly ignored the possibility of a German advance through neutral Belgium, but a last-minute alteration did deploy troops to check such an advance.

It was a simple plan that relied far more on a combination of military and cultural mythology as well as a liberal helping of wishful thinking than it did on sound strategy. French commanders believed that the French soldier was animated by an overpowering patriotism amounting to a kind of Gallic life force that they called *élan vital* or simply *élan*. It was a concept borrowed from the prominent French philosopher Henri Bergson, and planners managed to persuade themselves that this spiritual force would prove irresistible on the field of battle. French generals believed that a charge into German territory would utterly disrupt German war plans and send the invaders running back to their homeland.

The mystical belief in élan was not the only fatal flaw of Plan XVII. The plan had been formulated on the basis of a gross underestimation of German troop strength. The French knew the total size of the German army accurately enough, but they calculated that the Germans would mobilize only their first-line troops, not their reserves. Because they had no faith in the prowess of their own reserves, French generals planned to mobilize only their own first-line forces and assumed that the Germans would do likewise. It was a tragic miscalculation and meant that, from the beginning, the French would find themselves outnumbered and overwhelmed.

German Speed: The Schlieffen Plan

Like the French Plan XVII, the German war plan, formulated at the start of the twentieth century by Count Alfred von Schlieffen, the chief of the General Staff, relied first and foremost on offense. Unlike the French plan, however, it also included a strong defensive component—even more important, the plan had been meticulously, even obsessively, thought out.

Schlieffen understood that Germany would have to fight on two fronts, against the French to the west and the Russians to the east. He reasoned that the French, with a more modern and better-led army, were the greater of the two threats because they could mobilize quickly. In contrast, the Russians, though numerous, were poorly equipped and poorly led. It would take them at least six weeks to mobilize effectively. Therefore, Schlieffen developed an offensive plan against France and a defensive plan against Russia.

The objective was to invade France with overwhelming force and at lightning speed, while simultaneously holding off a Russian invasion of eastern Prussia. The plan turned on a precisely formulated timetable, whereby France would be effectively neutralized within a matter of weeks so that forces could then be transferred from the Western Front to the Eastern Front. At that point, the defensive war against Russia could be transformed into an offensive war on what would now be a single front, the Russian Front. And Schlieffen was confident that the Russians, without the support of the French, would be beaten.

Schlieffen's plan for the advance into France was much more thoughtful than the French plan to attack Alsace and Lorraine. The French contemplated a direct frontal assault, a bold strategy that satisfied the generals' desire for dash and glory, but one that was always a dangerous gamble. Schlieffen, in contrast, planned a "great wheel:" a wide, turning movement through Flanders Plain northeast of French territory, and then into France from the north.

Voices of Battle

"When you march into France, let the last man on the right brush the channel with his sleeve."

—Alfred von Schlieffen

Words of War

In the language of military organization, an **army** is the largest administrative and tactical unit into which a national army is organized.

Five principal German armies would make their thrust, covering a huge swath of France, from the Alsace-Lorraine all the way west to the English Channel. Indeed, commenting on how his plan should be executed, Schlieffen quipped that the sleeve of the last man on the right should brush the English Channel. This great wheel was intended to *outflank* the French forces, hitting them where they were most vulnerable, mainly from the rear. Moreover, the maneuver would ensure that all the fighting was done in France, not in German territory, and would therefore wear down the French infrastructure, and would menace French civilians. Finally, the Schlieffen Plan gave the Germans room to retreat, if necessary, but to do so farther into the French territory, not German land.

In many respects, it was a brilliant plan, intoxicating in its ingenuity. And therein was its first weakness: It was such a beautiful scheme that it became a kind of object of worship among the German high command as well as among German political leaders. As the French had been seduced by the allure of élan, the Germans were mesmerized by the precision of the great machine they had designed. Seeing no reason to look beyond the Schlieffen Plan, they did not. If a machine is perfect, why tamper with it?

But that brings up the plan's second great weakness. Armies are not machines; they are people. The Schlieffen Plan called for complexly coordinated movements over great distances and in adherence to a strict timetable. If anything went wrong, the entire plan could collapse. Moreover, the "great wheel" put incredible distances between the advancing combat soldiers and their necessarily slower lines of supply. The longer an army's lines of supply, the more vulnerable those lines become—an army may find itself stranded and low on ammunition, food, and other supplies.

As we will see in Chapter 6, "The Marne: Massacre and Miracle," there was a third weakness as well. The overall commander of the German advance into France would be Helmuth von Moltke, nephew of the general of the same name who had led the Prussian armies to an overwhelming victory against France in 1870–1871. The younger Moltke had come of age in the long and intimidating shadow of his uncle. In fact, he was a highly competent officer, but he lacked his uncle's confidence, will, and sheer brilliance. He was a self-doubter and was chronically depressed, and these qualities would be sufficient to color, taint, and ultimately doom the execution of the Schlieffen Plan in August 1914.

Austro-Hungarian Flexibility: Plan B

Austria-Hungary, whose military would ignite the war in the first place, had far more modest plans than France or Germany. It would follow Plan B, which assumed that the war would be confined to Serbia. This plan called for three Austrian *armies* to invade Serbia and three to watch the border with Russia and to stand ready to defend against an attack from that quarter.

Of course, circumstances would rapidly overrun the confines of Serbia and outrun the provisions of Plan B. Another plan, Plan R, called for more of Austria-Hungary's forces to be concentrated against Russia, in the south, in coordination with German action in the north. This plan, however, never got off the ground because the demands of the Schlieffen Plan prevented the Germans from committing sufficient forces against Russia at the outset of the war.

And the Russian Alphabet

The Russians also had their military master plans. The first, Plan G, assumed that Germany would commit most of its troops against Russia, not France—precisely the opposite of what Germany actually did. Essentially, Plan G exploited the vastness of Russia, a resource that had defeated no less a conqueror than Napoleon in 1812. Plan G allowed the Germans to invade until the Russian armies could amass the combat power to launch an overwhelming counteroffensive and drive the invaders out.

Russia's French allies were appalled by the sacrificial and wholly defensive nature of Plan G and pressured the Russians to develop Plan A, which assumed that the Germans would throw the bulk of their forces against France rather than Russia. In this case, the Russians were to advance simultaneously into East Prussia and Galicia (an area in central Europe encompassing southeast Poland and the western Ukraine).

From here, the Russians would advance into Silesia (the region encompassing south-western Poland and northern Czechoslovakia), ultimately concentrating in southern Poland.

Having two alternate plans to cover two vastly different scenarios was a good idea. The problem was the impracticality of shifting rapidly from one plan to the other to meet actual circumstances as they developed.

In fact, this was the great flaw common to all the plans. The celebrated nineteenth-century military theorist Karl Maria von Clausewitz (1780–1831) wrote of the "fog of war" and the "friction of war." The first was a description of the inevitable confusion generated by actual combat, especially the difficulty of efficient communication in the heat of battle. The second encompassed the myriad things that go wrong whenever large numbers of people move into action: Mistakes are made, wagons break down, the weather turns bad, weapons don't work as expected, and soldiers get sick or tired. War requires planning, Clausewitz declared, but the nature of warfare tends to defeat plans. At the very least, a great gulf stretches between the plan and its execution, and much is lost in that gulf.

None of the great powers girding for war in 1914—*itching* for war in 1914—took this wisdom sufficiently to heart, despite all their plans and planning. They marched ahead on the double-quick, willingly and willfully blindfolded.

The Least You Need to Know

➤ Europe's prewar prosperity brought a period of relative peace, but it also supplied the economic wherewithal for massive national armament programs.

➤ The Allies had the edge in terms of demographics, trade, and industry, but the Central Powers had large standing armies. Germany had an especially advanced industrial base that was well suited to the needs of war.

➤ The German army was the largest and best equipped among all the powers.

➤ Technological advances, especially the machine gun, improved artillery; the dreadnought battleship ensured that war would be more destructive than ever.

➤ Each of the major powers had formulated master war plans, which became another force propelling Europe toward combat.

The Black Hand

The small nations of the Balkans knew a history of poverty and oppression, pushed and pulled by the larger powers that surrounded them—Austria-Hungary, Russia, and Turkey. In the mid-nineteenth century, a secret society, the Omladina (a Serbian word meaning "youth") practiced terrorist tactics in an effort to bring about the downfall of the Serbian government and push Serbia toward a union with other Balkan states, plus parts of Poland, Moravia, Silesia, and Romania. This union would form a single great Slavonic nation. Omladina members shot Serbian Prince Michael in 1868, kidnapped Serbian Prince Alexander shortly afterward, organized an unsuccessful rebellion against Serbian King Milan (who subsequently abdicated), and finally murdered his successor, the 27-year-old King Alexander Obrenovic, and his wife.

Few people outside of the Slavic world took much notice of the activity of the Omladina. After all, what did the affairs of obscure Serbia, deep in the obscure Balkans, have to do with anything in the European mainstream?

On June 28, 1914, the world would begin to find out.

Union or Death

The Omladina was active through the end of the nineteenth century. In 1909, it became the National Defense Society, which soon developed into a secret society that

called itself *Ujedinjenje ili Smert*—"Unity or Death"—and sometimes, more simply, the Black Hand.

The Black Hand consisted of Serbian army officers and was run by a former officer, Colonel Dragutin Dmitrievich, who called himself Apis, "The Bull." He had earned this sobriquet back in 1903 after participating in the assassination of King Alexander Obrenovic and Queen Draga of Serbia. Police officers had shot Dragutin, riddling him with bullets and leaving him for dead. But he recovered, went underground, and founded the Black Hand.

The Assassins

The Black Hand was less a political organization than it was a band of young assassins, most of whom were students, some of whom were afflicted with tuberculosis, endemic early in the twentieth century, and therefore destined to short lives. Colonel Apis personally trained the young men in the deadly art of assassination.

Words of War

The **Black Hand** was the popular name for a secret society, founded in 1909, consisting of Serbian military officers and dedicated to the overthrow of Austro-Hungarian rule throughout the Balkans. The Black Hand sponsored the assassination of Archduke Franz Ferdinand in Sarajevo in 1914, thereby triggering World War I.

A Sick Boy

Gavrilo Princip was born on his father's farm in West Bosnia June 13, 1894. The parish priest entered that birthdate in the parish register but then slipped up in transcribing it to the civil register, making it July 13, 1894. A minor slip, it would have a profound effect. Austrian law prevented a criminal from being condemned for a crime he committed when under the age of 20. When Princip killed Archduke Franz Ferdinand and his wife Sophie on June 28, 1914, he was legally nineteen years old. Thousands would perish in the great war Princip's act triggered, but the assassin himself would be spared execution.

Although he grew up as a shepherd boy, Princip was given a good education, at the insistence of his mother. A decent student, he nevertheless earned a reputation as one quick with his fists, particularly irritable and sensitive to any kind of insult, real or imagined. After his elementary education, Princip left home to attend a business school. He boarded in the house of Danilo Ilic, a committed revolutionary, and emerged after three years dedicated to the cause of overthrowing the Austro-Hungarian yoke of oppression.

In 1912, Princip had tried to enlist in the Serbian army but was rejected as too small and weak. He lived a miserable life in Belgrade, begging food, sleeping in doorways, and avoiding work, but he became actively engaged in talk of anarchy and revolution. He formed a friendship with 19-year-old Nedeljko Cabrinovic, with whom he fantasized about killing the Archduke Franz Ferdinand, the heir apparent to the Austro-Hungarian throne.

When Princip learned that the archduke would be visiting Sarajevo, capital of Bosnia-Herzegovina, Princip and Cabrinovic recruited one of Princip's boyhood friends, Trifko Grabez, and sought out Milan Ciganovic, a Balkan War hero known to be a radical terrorist. Ciganovic brought Princip and the others to the attention of Apis, who gave Ciganovic four Browning revolvers and ammunition, six bombs, and some capsules. The capsules, Apis explained, contained cyanide, which was to be swallowed by the assassins if capture seemed imminent.

The fact is that the capsules contained nothing more than a harmless watery substance. Clearly, Apis did not really believe that the youths—whom he hadn't even met—would ever get close enough to the archduke to kill him. But Apis understood that the boys were fanatics, who believed they had nothing to lose.

Voices of Battle

"There is an outside chance that they just might blunder into a success. We might as well give them a try at it as any other."

—Dragutin Dmitrievich ("Apis"), after authorizing Gavrilo Princip and others to assassinate Franz Ferdinand

The Archduke and His Lady

Franz Ferdinand von Sterreich-Este was every inch the typical Hapsburg autocrat: elegant, bigoted, and completely out of touch with most of the empire whose throne he was slated to ascend when his uncle, the aged Emperor Franz Josef, should die.

In 1900, the archduke fell in love with Countess Sophie Chotek von Chotkova, daughter of an obscure Czech noble. Franz Josef objected that his nephew was marrying beneath him, but the archduke held firm. He would marry the woman he loved. The old emperor relented but compelled Franz Ferdinand to renounce the right of his children to inherit the throne. As for Sophie, she was officially snubbed by Franz Josef and the members of his court.

The official mistreatment of his wife embittered the already intolerant and ill-tempered archduke, who vented his spleen against Jews and against Serbians, whom he counted as members of a hostile Magyar race bent on the destruction of the Hapsburgs. His personal hatred of the Serbs energized his will to suppress all signs of Serbian nationalism.

A Blind Alley in Sarajevo

Franz Ferdinand looked forward to appearing in Sarajevo on June 28, 1914—St. Vitus' Day, the great Serbian national day of *Vidovan*—precisely because it would put Serbia in its place. Serbia wanted Bosnia-Herzegovina to be part of a grand Slavic state, but Bosnia-Herzegovina was now a province of the Austro-Hungarian Empire—a fact the archduke's official visit would underscore. Moreover, the military had scheduled important maneuvers in Bosnia-Herzegovena, and the archduke would oversee them in his official capacity as inspector general of the Austro-Hungarian army. This official visit would give Franz Ferdinand an opportunity to have his much-maligned wife appear as his equal, riding with him in an open car at his side. She would be officially recognized as royalty.

Waiting for the archduke and his wife on the streets of Sarajevo would be a number of assassins. In addition to the three principal conspirators, Princip, Cabrinovic, and Grabez, there was Danilo Ilic, the young man with whom Princip had boarded after he left his father's farm. Ilic brought three more assassins into the plot, so seven in all were prepared for attempts on the archduke's life. If Princip, Cabrinovic, and Grabez failed to score a kill, Ilic would use the others to finish the job.

The limousine route of the royal couple was well publicized and would include a drive to the Sarajevo town hall for a formal reception, a sight-seeing tour, and then lunch at the Governor's Palace. After this, there would be brief visits to a museum, the local mosque, and army headquarters.

Ilic stationed his assassins along a 300-yard stretch of the principal avenue of Sarajevo, the Appel Quay. The first assassin was armed with a bomb at the Cumuria Bridge. The second, with a bomb and a Browning revolver, was stationed farther along the road. Next came Cabrinovic, with a grenade, then Ilic himself and another assassin with revolvers, and then Princip, armed with only a Browning revolver. He was the second-to-last in line, just before Grabez. Princip expected that at least one of the other assassins would score a hit and that he would not even be called on to act.

Despite warnings about the danger of assassination, security was lax. The archduke had ordered his crack military units to stay out of Sarajevo because he didn't want to give the impression that he was trying to intimidate the population. His only protection was a small coterie of elite guards.

The royal couple arrived by train and boarded a waiting limousine. It was an open car, designed to display the archduke in his full general's uniform, including a hat with green plumes, and plump Sophie in her finery, a white silk dress with a red sash, an immense picture hat, and a cape adorned with ermine tails. As the motorcade reached the Cumuria Bridge, the first assassin fumbled with his bomb, panicked, and failed to hurl the device. The second assassin, Cabrinovic, threw his grenade, which bounced off the back of the archduke's car and rolled in front of the car following it. The resulting explosion damaged that vehicle and sent shrapnel in all directions, injuring several spectators as well members of the entourage. Sophie's own cheek was bruised by a small flying splinter. Cabrinovic tried unsuccessfully to drown himself in the River Miljacka but was apprehended.

"Who are you?" a plainclothes detective demanded.

"A Serbian hero!" Cabrinovic responded.

When they saw the archduke's car speed past them, Ilic and the assassin that he had stationed with himself were too stunned to act. They did nothing. Neither did Princip nor Grabez. Having failed in his duty, Princip walked off dejectedly to a table at an outdoor cafe and ordered a cup of coffee, the revolver still weighing down his coat pocket.

The archduke and his wife went to the reception at the town hall as scheduled, after which Franz Ferdinand called for a change of plan. He wanted to visit the local military hospital to look in on those who had been injured by the bomb blast. He tried to dissuade Sophie from accompanying him, but she insisted.

The chauffeur was unfamiliar with the route to the military hospital. At the corner of the Appel Quay and Franz Josef Street, the chauffeur suddenly turned. A military aide shouted to him: "What's this? We've taken the wrong way!" At this, the driver braked and tried to turn around. But crowds behind the car caused him to slow to a crawl.

The car came to a halt in front of Moritz Schiller's cafe and delicatessen, 5 feet from where Gavrilo Princip was sipping his coffee.

Voices of Battle

"Mr. Mayor, what is the good of your speeches? One comes here for a visit and is received with bombs. Mr. Mayor, what do you say? It is outrageous!"

—Archduke Franz Ferdinand to Fehim Effendi Curcic, mayor of Sarajevo, after surviving a first assassination attempt

June 28, 1914, 11:15 A.M

"I recognized the heir apparent," Princip told police. "But as I saw that a lady was sitting next to him, I reflected for a moment whether I should shoot or not. At the same moment I was filled with a peculiar feeling and I aimed at the heir apparent from the pavement—which was made easier because the car was proceeding slower at the moment. Where I aimed I do not know. But I know that I aimed at the heir apparent. I believe I fired twice, perhaps more, because I was so excited. Whether I hit the victims or not, I cannot tell, because instantly people started to hit me."

Princip aimed at pointblank range. A policeman spotted him, but as he rushed Princip, an unemployed actor named Pusara leaped forward to shove the policeman out of the way. This allowed Princip to get off his shots. He fired three times.

When the policeman regained his balance and lurched after Princip, who had turned to flee, one Ferdinand Behr punched the cop in the stomach. Instead of running, however, Princip stood frozen; another man, named Velic, knocked the revolver from his hands. At this, spectators descended on Princip, punching and kicking him.

Princip's first shot had penetrated the car door to hit Sophie in the stomach. The second shot hit the archduke in the neck, severing his carotid artery and lodging in his spine. Blood was everywhere. A third shot rang out, but found no target.

"For God's sake," Sophie turned to her husband, "what has happened to you?" Then she collapsed against the archduke's chest and into his lap. The stricken man cradled her head.

"Soferl, Soferl, don't die! Stay alive for our children!"

But she was already dead.

A Count Harrach, who had climbed from the front seat into the back, took hold of the archduke. "Are you suffering, your highness?"

"It is nothing, it is nothing, it is nothing." With this, Archduke Franz Ferdinand died.

Crime and Punishment

Informed that he had killed the archduke and his wife, Princip admitted the crime, allowing only that he was "sorry that I have killed the Duchess of Hohenberg, for I had no intention of killing her." Then he declared that he had "aimed specifically at the archduke because he ... is an enemy of the Slavs in general but especially of the Serbs."

Austro-Hungarian officials would seize on this statement as a cause for war against Serbia. Princip amplified it at his trial:

> I do not feel like a criminal because I put away the one who was doing evil. Austria as it is represents evil for our people and therefore should not exist .... The political union of the Yugoslavs was always before my eyes, and that was my basic idea. Therefore it was necessary in the first place to free the Yugoslavs ... from Austria. This ... moved me to carry out the assassination of the heir apparent, for I considered him as very dangerous for Yugoslavia.

From the Front

Twenty-five Serbians were tried for conspiracy in the assassination. Ilic and two others were executed. Cabrinovic and Grabez received 25-year sentences, and two other conspirators were sentenced to lesser terms. The others were found not guilty. By 1916, Cabrinovic and Grabez were dead of malnutrition and tuberculosis. Princip succumbed to tuberculosis in 1918.

Princip, thought to be under the legal age for execution, was sentenced to 20 years in prison. The young man's tuberculosis rapidly worsened, spreading to one of his arms, which had to be amputated. He wasted away in solitary confinement. On April 28, 1918, as the world war was consuming a fourth year, his jailers found Princip curled in a tight ball on his bunk. On the wall beside the bunk, he had scratched these lines:

> Our ghosts will walk through Vienna
> And roam through the palace
> Frightening the lords.

Austro-Hungarian "Diplomacy"

Decades before that Sarajevo June morning in 1914, Otto von Bismarck, whose diplomacy had erected the complex of alliances that now bound Europe, had remarked that war would erupt some day because of "some damn foolish thing in the Balkans."

That there was no evidence of Serbian complicity in the killing of the archduke and his wife did not stop Count Leopold von Berchtold, Austria-Hungary's foreign minister, from assuming Serbia's guilt. By punishing Serbia, Berchtold saw an opportunity to squelch Bosnian nationalism and the pan-Slavic movement while simultaneously regaining some of the prestige that the corrupt and senescent Austro-Hungarian Empire had been steadily losing. Far from wanting to avert war, Berchtold looked for a means of fomenting a quick, sharp, decisive local war to teach Serbia a lesson.

The Kaiser's Pledge

But in the Europe that Bismarck had created, there could be no *local* wars. Indeed, as Berchtold called for the mobilization of the Austro-Hungarian army, he sent a message to the German government, asking if he could count on its support. Kaiser Wilhelm II responded to Berchtold at lunch in Berlin on July 5, 1914. Germany would back Austria-Hungary, he said—even if it meant war with Russia.

It was an almost impulsive, thoughtless declaration. In any case, the kaiser did not think that anything would come of it. Surely, Serbia would accede to whatever demands Austria made.

Ultimatum and Response

With assurances from Germany, Austria-Hungary dispatched Baron Vladimir von Giesl, ambassador to Serbia, to deliver 10 demands to the government at Belgrade. The most important demands stressed prosecution of the conspirators, with Austrian officials to be put in charge of the investigation; furthermore, Austrian officials were to operate within Serbia to root out sources of anti-Austrian agitation and propaganda. These and other terms called for Serbia to make a humiliating sacrifice of its sovereignty. After delivering the ultimatum at 6:00 on the evening of July 23, the ambassador announced that Serbia would have 48 hours to reply.

On the next day, Serbia's premier, Nicholas Pashich, consulted with Russian officials, who promised, "For Serbia, we shall do everything." However, they also advised acceding to all of the demands that did not require completely relinquishing national sovereignty. In the meantime, Britain's foreign secretary, Sir Edward Grey, indignantly remarked that the ultimatum is "the most formidable document that was ever addressed from one state to another." He called for Britain, France, Germany, and Italy to mediate.

On July 25, within the 48-hour deadline, a Serbian official delivered his government's response to Austria-Hungary. All of the demands had been

Voices of Battle

"Austria–Hungary, with the bellicose frivolity of senile empires, determined to use the occasion [of the assassination] to absorb Serbia as she had absorbed Bosnia and Herzegovina in 1909."

—Barbara Tuchman, *The Guns of August*, 1962

accepted, except for one. Serbia would not grant authority for Austrian officials to operate in Serbia.

The rejection of this single item was deemed a cause for war. As he had been instructed to do, Giesl summarily severed diplomatic relations with Serbia. He and his staff had already packed their bags. Berchtold would get his war—and much more.

Combatants

Leopold von Berchtold (1863–1942), whose full name—Count Leopold von Berchtold von und zu Ungarschita—reflected his aristocratic origins, had the dark, oily look of a melodrama villain. Certainly, it was the villain's role he played in fomenting World War I, by deliberately construing the assassination of Franz Ferdinand as a cause for war.

Berchtold joined the diplomatic corps in 1894, and although he demonstrated nothing in the way of diplomatic talent, he possessed courtly manners in abundance as well as a flawless pedigree, which gained him rapid promotion to the highest government offices. During the Balkan Wars of 1912–1913, his policy as foreign minister seemed weak and vacillating. As if to make up for this perceived deficiency, he took an unyielding and irrational position against Serbia, which made war inevitable. After almost single-handedly causing World War I, Berchtold went on to fumble relations with Italy, ensuring that it would ultimately leave the Triple Alliance to join the Allied cause. Berchtold resigned as foreign minister in 1915, never to enter public life again.

The Kaiser Comes Home to a War

On July 27, Kaiser Wilhelm II returned from a holiday that the crisis had forced him to cut short. In his absence, his government had already rejected Edward Grey's call for mediation. On the next day, Emperor Franz Josef signed Austria-Hungary's declaration of war against Serbia. In response, the Russian government ordered a partial mobilization of Russian army forces near the Austrian border.

In Berlin, some semblance of sanity remained. Theobald von Bethmann-Hollweg, Germany's chancellor, telegraphed Austria's Berchtold: "Serbia has in fact met the Austrian demands in so wide-sweeping a manner that if the Austro-Hungarian government adopted a wholly uncompromising attitude, a gradual revulsion of public opinion against it in all of Europe would have to be reckoned with."

Berchtold made no reply. On the next day, July 29, the chancellor sent him a stronger telegram, warning that Germany would refuse to be drawn into war because Austria "has ignored our advice." Even the kaiser admitted that Serbia's conciliatory reply to the ultimatum "dissipates every reason for war."

First Mobilizations

But it was too late. In the absence of reason and good faith from anyone involved, events had taken on a life and energy of their own. Even as the German chancellor chided Austria, warning that its support could not be counted on, he made a bellicose "offer" to Sir Edward Grey, telling him that if England remained neutral, Germany would not annex any of mainland France. (On July 31, Grey would reject this offer as "infamous.") Bethmann-Hollweg also warned Russia that its partial mobilization was inflammatory, and Germany now mobilized its navy in the North Sea. In response to this, Winston Churchill, First Sea Lord, mobilized the British Grand Fleet.

From the Front

The Austro-Hungarian declaration of war was the first ever delivered by telegram.

On this most eventful day, Austrian river gunboats began to shell Belgrade. If Princip's three shots were the first of the Great War, the shelling was the conflict's initial bombardment. War had begun.

In Lockstep to Armageddon

Austria-Hungary and Serbia had mobilized on July 28, and the chronically indecisive Czar Nicholas II had ordered a partial mobilization. On August 30, he allowed himself to be persuaded that the national honor of Russia as a Slavic nation demanded full mobilization. Hearing of the general mobilization, Helmuth von Moltke, chief of staff of the German army, picked up a telephone and called Field Marshal Franz Conrad von Hötzendorff, his counterpart in the Austro-Hungarian army.

"Mobilize at once against Russia," Moltke barked. This meant a shift from Austrian Plan B, calling for a local war against Serbia, to Plan R, general war against Serbia and Russia (see Chapter 3, "Blueprints for a Bloodletting").

It is significant that Moltke, a general, not a statesman, had ordered a move to expand the war. He, like the other German leaders, was trapped by the only plan he had, the Schlieffen Plan, which conceived of no scenario in which Russia would not play a part. The plan committed Germany to war against France and Russia; with a tragic absence of imagination, the German high command as well as the politicians assumed that the war plans of all the major powers made identical assumptions.

Germany issued an ultimatum to Russia, demanding that it cease general mobilization. To France, Germany issued another ultimatum, threatening it with war if it began to mobilize at all. Russia rejected the German ultimatum; its mobilization would continue. France stated nothing more than that it would consult its "own interests." Germany took this as a negative reply as well.

On August 1, 1914, Germany ordered general mobilization and began execution of the Schlieffen Plan. On August 2, Germany demanded free passage through Belgium. By the time King Albert of that nation refused the demand, German divisions were already marching through Flanders.

The Great War was now under way on the Western Front. On August 3, at 3:00 in the afternoon, Edward Grey addressed the British Parliament on the nation's obligation to protect Belgian neutrality: "If ... we run away from these obligations of honor and interest as regards the Belgian Treaty ... I do not believe for a moment that, at the end of this war ... we should be able ... to prevent the whole of the West of Europe opposite us from falling under the domination of a single power ... and we should, I believe, sacrifice our respect and good name and reputation before the world." With this, Grey pledged to defend Belgium.

That evening, the evening of August 3, 1914, Germany declared war on France. As daylight dissolved into twilight and twilight into night, Edward Grey remarked to a friend: "The lamps are going out all over Europe; we shall not see them lit again in our lifetime."

At dawn, Germany declared war on Belgium, having already invaded it, and England joined the other powers of Europe in a headlong rush to deal death and to die.

The Least You Need to Know

➤ Gavrilo Princip, a youthful Bosnian nationalist, joined a secret society dedicated to the overthrow of Austro-Hungarian rule in the Balkans.

➤ Princip's assassination of Archduke Franz Ferdinand and his wife, Sophie, sparked an international incident that Austria-Hungary fanned into war.

➤ Austria-Hungary's declaration of war on Serbia set into motion the interlocking alliances that brought all of Europe's great powers into war.

Part 2

Home Before the Leaves Fall

Winston Churchill wrote of World War I that its outcome "was decided in the first 20 days of fighting, and all that happened afterwards consisted in battles which, however formidable and devastating, were but desperate and vain appeals against the decision of Fate."

This part narrates the first few weeks of the war, focusing on the initial German drive through Belgium and France, the unremitting failure of the Allies, and then the end of the German offensive and the beginning of four years of stalemated slaughter. Simultaneously, on the Eastern Front, Germany, menaced by the "Russian steam-roller," responded with brilliance and dealt Russia blows at Tannenberg and the Masurian Lakes from which it would never recover.

Battle of the Frontiers

The Great War had begun. If you think you've missed something—the momentous cause of the war, the great wrong to be righted, the outrageous invasion to be repelled, the Fort Sumter or Pearl Harbor of this terrible conflict—be assured, you have not. War began, as Bismarck had predicted it would, over "some damn foolish thing in the Balkans." The great British mathematician and pacifist Bertrand Russell put it even more precisely—and more bluntly: "All this madness, all this rage, all this flaming death of our civilization and our hopes," he wrote in a letter to the London *Nation* on August 16, 1914, "has been brought about because a set of official gentlemen, living luxurious lives, mostly stupid, and all without imagination or heart, have chosen that it should occur rather than that any one of them should suffer some infinitesimal rebuff to his country's pride."

The first month of the war would be the single most important period of the conflict. As Winston Churchill later wrote, "The War was decided in the first 20 days of fighting, and all that happened afterwards consisted in battles which, however formidable and devastating, were but desperate and vain appeals against the decision of Fate."

"The Guns of August"

The Schlieffen Plan was the product of 18 years of study, work, and revision. German leaders regarded it as the ultimate expression of what the great military theoretician Karl von Clausewitz had written in 1833: "War is … a political instrument, a continuation of political relations … by other means." Yet the plan had actually straitjacketed Germany because it lacked flexibility. Its detailed timetables, its mobilization schedules, and even its precise prescriptions for training troops assumed a two-front war. German leaders had no alternate plans for anything short of a general war against the West and the East. Responding to the crisis that Austria-Hungary had precipitated with Serbia, the Germans were incapable of seeing any other option than starting a war that would involve all of Europe.

Across the Belgian Threshold

Kaiser Wilhelm II signed general mobilization orders at 5:00 on the afternoon of August 1, 1914. At this point, what historian Barbara Tuchman has called "the guns of August" commenced firing.

The kaiser's order meant that German armies would march through Luxembourg and Belgium, the neutrality of which was guaranteed by both British and French treaties. Mobilization was a declaration of war against Britain and France.

From the Front

"Wireless communication" had been patented by Guglielmo Marconi in 1900. Within a very few years, nations and armies were communicating by radio. Despite this innovation, events in the opening weeks of World War I consistently outran the means of communicating them. As a result, political and military decisions often followed actions instead of preceding and determining them.

But even after signing the mobilization order, Wilhelm himself was dubious about committing Germany to total war. He had received a cable from Prince Karl Maxmillian Lichnowsky, Germany's ambassador to Great Britain, stating that England would remain neutral and would attempt to restrain France from declaring war on Germany. Helmuth von Moltke explained to the kaiser that the advancing armies now had a momentum of their own and that an infantry company had already crossed the Luxembourg border. Nevertheless, Moltke returned to his headquarters to begin the process of halting the German advance that had just begun. Then, at 11:00 on the evening of that first August evening, he was again summoned into the kaiser's presence. Wilhelm had just received a new cable. Lichnowsky had misunderstood Edward Grey's remarks. England would most certainly *not* remain neutral and would *not* restrain France.

"Now you can do what you like," Wilhelm told Moltke.

With that, the world lost its very last chance to avert the Great War. Moltke ordered the advance to continue, and German regiments streamed into Belgium during the night and early morning of August 3 and 4.

An Orgy of Declarations

Great Britain had no interest in Serbia, and many Britishers doubtless had only the vaguest notion of where Serbia was. Nor did Britain have an absolute obligation to fight either for Russia or for France, although the Triple Entente did imply certain "moral" obligations to do so. But one tie was diplomatically binding. Britain had committed itself by treaty to defend Belgium. On August 4, therefore, England declared war against Germany, Belgium's invader.

On August 5, Austria-Hungary responded to the Russian mobilization along its border by declaring war against Russia. Serbia declared war against Germany on August 6. Montenegro, another of the Balkan countries, declared war against Austria-Hungary on August 7 and against Germany on August 12. France and Great Britain declared war against Austria-Hungary on August 10 and on August 12, respectively. Japan joined in against Germany on August 23, and Austria-Hungary responded with a declaration of war against Japan on August 25, and then against Belgium on August 28. On February 26, 1914, Romania had renewed with the Central Powers a secret anti-Russian alliance that it had originally concluded with Germany in 1883. For the present, however, it chose to remain neutral.

Italy Avoids War—For Now

Italy also chose temporary neutrality. As recently as December 7, 1912, it had confirmed the Triple Alliance with Germany and Austria-Hungary. But now the Italian government found reasons to disregard it. To begin with, Italy was not obliged to support its allies in a "war of aggression," and it deemed both Austria-Hungary's attack on Serbia and Germany's invasion of Luxembourg and Belgium the opening salvos of such a war. Second, the original treaty of alliance, concluded in 1881, had expressly specified that the alliance was not against England. Furthermore, Italy had also concluded a secret agreement with France, agreeing to remain neutral if Germany attacked France, or if France attacked Germany, to protect its "national honor" (see Chapter 2, "Family Affairs").

Treaty of London

On September 5, 1914, Russia, France, and Great Britain built on the Triple Entente by concluding the Treaty of London, by which each promised to refrain from making a *separate peace* with the Central Powers. From this point forward, the three nations would refer to themselves as the Allied (or Entente) Powers or, more simply, the Allies.

Words of War

A **separate peace** is an armistice or treaty of peace made between warring nations regardless of other alliances in force. In 1918, Russia, though bound in alliance with France and Britain, would conclude a separate peace with Germany.

Like an Unexpected Holiday

"You will be home before the leaves have fallen from the trees," the kaiser told departing troops in the first week of August.

This is one of those wrongheaded statements that history buffs love, much like the response a deckhand made to a passenger's query about the safety of the *Titanic*—"God himself could not sink this ship!"—or the 1977 remark of Digital Equipment Corporation's president that "there is no reason for any individual to have a computer in their home." But the kaiser's promise reflected his perception of the gospel according to the Schlieffen Plan, which scheduled the conquest of France before autumn. The statement also reflected the perception of most citizens of Europe. They believed that modern technology would make war quick, cheap, and neatly decisive, and that this was a good thing since, in any case, no modern nation could afford to finance a long war.

And all sides were confident of victory. Germany had already beaten France in 1870–1871 and saw no reason why it couldn't do so again. France had the will and fighting spirit of the French soldier, gorgeously clad in a dark-blue greatcoat and scarlet trousers, marching off to battle singing songs about "going home to Alsace and Lorraine." Russia had faith in its sheer numbers. And in England, despite Edward Grey's sepulchral pronouncement about the lamps going out all over Europe, the war came as nothing more than a mild interruption of comfortable routine. On the day Britain declared war, August 4, the small-town Bradford *Daily Argus* suggested that "it will be in the kitchens that the pinch will be chiefly felt, but that difficulty may be overcome by deleting the more dainty dishes." Another village paper, the Catford *Journal,* reported 10 days later that "what with the war and the rain, last Saturday was a most depressing day for the Catford cricket club."

In none of the major powers were there demonstrations of hatred for the enemy. In England, for example, newspapers still advertised fine German cameras and even tourist excursions to Germany, and German nationals were actually permitted to return home to join the German army. "To be really at war I ought to burn with hatred," a letter in the Catford *Journal* of August 21 declared. "But the only two Germans I have ever spoken to were two of the nicest gentlemen I have ever met. We may be at war in the technical sense with the German emperor, but with the German people—never. We must fight; honour demands it. But we must not lose our tempers."

Voices of Battle

"To me those hours seemed like a release from the painful feelings of my youth. Even today I am not ashamed to say that, overpowered by stormy enthusiasm, I fell down on my knees and thanked Heaven from an overflowing heart for granting me the good fortune of being permitted to live at this time."

—Adolf Hitler, in *Mein Kampf* (1924), recalling his reaction to news that World War I had started

In a way, this was typical of attitudes throughout Europe: *We have to fight. We don't really know why. But we have no choice, so let's get on with it.*

Some sanity prevailed. The irascible playwright George Bernard Shaw suggested in a letter to the *Statesman* that troops on both sides should shoot their officers and return home. But, as the historian James H. Meisel observed, "All over Europe, young men went to war just as they would go on an unexpected holiday, delighted to escape the daily boredom of their clerking."

Bottleneck at Liège

On the Western Front, the span from August 2 to August 26, 1914, is usually referred to as the Battle of the Frontiers because it was the period during which national boundaries were crossed as Germany advanced into France.

Belgium had been a neutral power since 1839, and its neutrality was guaranteed by a multilateral international agreement. Although, in the years before the war began, Belgium's King Albert had come to believe that Germany presented a grave threat to his nation, he dared not coordinate military planning with Britain or France, lest that be interpreted as an act violating neutrality. For its part, France stubbornly rejected any notion that its *frontier* with Belgium was vulnerable. Some years before the war, French General Augustin E. Michel was dismissed from a top command post for even suggesting that France should shift some of its forces from the Franco-German border to the Belgian frontier in order to defend the northern border or, if necessary, even make a peremptory attack through Belgium. France did not want to appear to threaten Belgium, so Belgium was left to defend itself.

Words of War

For Americans, the word **frontier** connotes the borderland between settled country and the wilderness; in Europe, however, the word denotes the border and the border region between nations.

Belgium's army was tiny—only 100,000 men—but it had invested heavily in the construction of one of the most formidable system of fortresses in Europe. The strongest of these impressive fortifications was at Liège, a fortress-city surrounded by a ring of six pentagonal-plan main forts supplemented by six triangular secondary forts. The main forts were interconnected by a system of tunnels, which also contained ammunition magazines, crews' quarters, food storage, and the like.

The Liège fortifications covered the Meuse River at a highly strategic point. Germany was willing to violate Belgian neutrality, but it did not want to be sidetracked by war with the Dutch, so it resolved to preserve the neutrality of the Netherlands. Thus, the German First and Second Armies, which, according to the Schlieffen Plan, were to be the northernmost of the five German armies invading France, had no choice but to pass through the area dominated by Liège.

The Germans formulated a plan to get them through this bottleneck. To begin with, German high command knew that the fortress had certain weaknesses. Rifle trenches had been planned to protect the intervals separating the outer forts, but they had never been prepared. Even more important, the forts' guns were of an obsolete design. New ones, ordered from Krupp Arms Works, the great German artillery factory, had not arrived before the commencement of the war. The Germans prepared a special task force of 30,000 elite troops under General Otto von Emmich to cross the Belgian border and make a night attack on the forts.

In the meantime, on August 2, German forces invaded Luxembourg, securing vital railheads into France and Belgium. On the same day, the German ambassador to Belgium delivered an ultimatum demanding free passage through Belgium. King Albert refused and began blowing up bridges and rail routes into his country. Two days later, German troops crossed the Belgian frontier at Gemmerich, sweeping aside the border *gendarmes*.

On the night of August 5–6, General von Emmich's task force began its assault and was stunned by the ferocity of the Belgian response. Belgian General Gerard M. Leman, handpicked by King Albert to defend Liège, had been ordered to hold the position to the last. He intended to do just that.

German cavalry sealed off the area from reinforcement while the infantry attempted to infiltrate the weak points between the forts. Although the Belgian infantry was outnumbered five to one, it inflicted heavy losses on the Germans. However, by August 6, the German 14th brigade had managed to attain the high ground overlooking the main citadel of the Liège fortification system. Leman, wanting to preserve his infantry from destruction or capture, ordered it to retreat to join the main portion of the Belgian army. In the meantime, he decided to fight on from the isolated forts that ringed the main citadel.

Words of War

In France, the **gendarmes** are members of the national police force; in Belgium, circa 1914, they were a national police force with specific paramilitary duties.

Words of War

A **staff officer** is attached to headquarters and typically acts as a liaison or link between top command and **field commanders,** the officers at the front who actually execute the strategy and orders of top command. Staff officers ensure that orders are executed and strategy is realized.

Big Bertha and the Zeppelin

The commanding officer of the German 14th Brigade had been killed early in the initial assault on the Liège forts, and his place was taken by a visiting officer, no less than Major General Erich Ludendorff, chief of staff of the German Second Army. Ludendorff was a *staff officer,* not a *field commander,* but he took to his emergency assignment with intense initiative. Using the mobile field guns he had, Ludendorff shelled the main citadel at the center of the fort system. When that proved ineffectual, he called in a new weapon, the *zeppelin.*

The first zeppelin, LZ-1, brainchild of the retired army officer and inventor Count Ferdinand von Zeppelin (1838–1917), flew in 1900. It was a cigar-shaped craft, 420 feet long and 38 feet in diameter, built on an aluminum frame and powered by two 16-horsepower engines. Filled with hydrogen, it attained speeds approaching almost 20 miles per hour. By 1914, a German commercial airline was operating scheduled zeppelin service to a number of German cities and, despite the highly explosive nature of hydrogen, compiled an admirable safety record. The German military took notice, and no less a figure than Helmuth von Moltke, the German chief of staff, saw the potential of airships as bombers. One German contemporary commentator declared, "England will cease to be an island."

The zeppelin that Ludendorff now called in dropped bombs on the citadel and on the city of Liège. The bombs had little effect on the heavily reinforced citadel, but in the city, nine civilians died. This was the first indication to Belgium and to the world that this war would bring new forms of death to combat and that it would bring that combat to ordinary citizens as well as soldiers.

Although neither the field guns nor the zeppelin produced much effect on the citadel, it became apparent that the main fortress was actually offering remarkably little resistance. Ludendorff concluded that the citadel had been largely abandoned, and he ordered his brigade to advance to the gates of the facility. Ludendorff personally banged on the gates to demand surrender.

It was August 7. The citadel of Liège had fallen to the Germans, but the outlying forts still commanded the area. Having failed to penetrate this system by ordinary infantry tactics, Ludendorff called on new artillery, which had been manufactured by the venerable German arms firm of Krupp explicitly for the mission of reducing the Belgian forts.

In contrast to the other European powers, Germany avidly heeded a key lesson of the Russo-Japanese War: that heavy weapons, despite their relative lack of mobility, were essential to crushing major fortifications. The biggest of the guns in the

Words of War

Named for its inventor, Count Ferdinand von Zeppelin (1838–1917), the **zeppelin** was a hydrogen-filled airship constructed on a rigid frame and driven by propellers. Later, the zeppelins were called *dirigibles*, a word derived from the Latin *dirigere*, meaning "to direct" or "to steer"; zeppelins were, in effect, steerable balloons.

Words of War

A **howitzer** is any short cannon that delivers its shells in a high trajectory. The word is derived from an old German word for "catapult."

early part of the war was a 420-mm siege *howitzer* christened "Big Bertha" (in German, *"Dicke Bertha,"* "Fat Bertha"). Together with 305-mm guns manufactured by the renowned Skoda works and borrowed from Austria-Hungary, it was transported by rail to the Liège area. On August 12, the guns began firing their huge projectiles, which had hardened heads, designed to penetrate concrete, and delayed fuses, which caused them to explode only *after* penetration rather than on impact. The new shells were fired at a very high angle so that they dropped like bombs, and they were fired incessantly.

One by one, the stunned, shaken, and deafened soldiers of the outer forts capitulated, and the last fort fell on August 16. The remainder of the Belgian army retreated to Antwerp, where it was sufficiently effective at menacing the invaders' right wing so that the Germans had to detach troops from the front. This somewhat compromised the timetable of the Schlieffen Plan. In all, the Germans were put behind schedule by at least two days.

Combatants

Joseph Jacques Césaire Joffre (1852–1931) saw his first military service during the defense of the siege of Paris (1870–1871) and then served in the French colonies. On recommendation of his mentor, Joseph Simon Galliéni, he was appointed chief of the General Staff (Grand Quartier General) in 1911. In this capacity, he and the General Staff developed Plan XVII.

During World War I, Joffre took overall charge of the French war effort for the first 30 months of the conflict. The qualities of calm and resolute refusal to panic, which had impressed his superiors in earlier days, were valuable during the darkest days of the war. Yet Joffre was also perceived by many as slow-witted and either unable or unwilling to see beyond the limitations imposed by Plan XVII.

When the German offensive at Verdun (February 21–December 18, 1916) caught Joffre thoroughly unprepared, he was ultimately relieved of command on December 13, 1916, although he was subsequently honored with the title of Marshal of France. During 1917, Joffre served as head of the French military mission to the United States. He then retired from military and public life after the war.

Papa Joffre's Decision

In addition to delay, the experience at Liège should also have gained another important advantage for the Allies: It announced in a spectacular manner where the main German attack was centered. But General Joseph J.C. Joffre, in overall command of the French armies, refused to acknowledge this fact. Half affectionately and half contemptuously, the rotund 62-year-old general was called "Papa Joffre" by his immediate subordinates as well as by the men of the entire army. Very much of the old school, Joffre was a passionate advocate of Plan XVII and its doctrine of offensive "à l'outrance" (attack "to the utmost").

The problem was that Plan XVII failed to account for the reality of the situation. First, the plan grossly underestimated the strength of the German Army in the west at a maximum of 68 infantry divisions instead of the 83 $\frac{1}{2}$ divisions actually mobilized. To compound this, French intelligence estimated that the Germans would not even use 68 divisions, but would limit the attacking force to regular, first-line troops only. The notion that reservists would be included in the initial assault was discounted.

The second problem is that Plan XVII assumed that the main German attack would be made through the Ardennes, not through Belgium. This assumption blinded Joffre, who insisted that the attack on Liège was nothing more than a feint to decoy French forces away from the Ardennes. He even ignored reports of a large German force amassing at the Belgian border. Accordingly, Joffre decided to execute Plan XVII faithfully. The First and Second French armies would thrust toward the Saar River into Lorraine; to the north (the French left), the Third and Fifth armies would stand prepared to launch an offensive between Metz and Thionville or to strike from the north at the flank of any German drive through the Ardennes.

All this deployment was well to the south of the Belgian border, the actual location of the great German offensive. Unwittingly, the French were setting themselves up to be attacked on their left flank and rear. Not that Joffre totally ignored Belgium: He dispatched cavalry on a reconnaissance mission into that country on August 6. As luck would have it, the foray was too early and missed sighting the main German force. Reassured that he was acting wisely, Joffre simply ordered the Belgian allies to hold fast until French and British troops could be spared.

The Great Wheel

The British declared war on August 4 and mobilized quickly and efficiently. Field Marshal Sir John D.P. French, in overall command, proposed altering the original plan of directly aiding French forces and suggested instead deploying to Antwerp to aid the Belgians. He was overruled by his own government, however, and the BEF, which had arrived on the continent on August 9, marched toward Mons in northwestern France. Once again, an opportunity to check the main German advance had been lost.

The Schlieffen Plan in Motion

After the Liège bottleneck had been broken, the German right wing—the two north-ernmost armies, under General Alexander von Kluck (First Army) and General Karl von Bülow (Second Army)—marched swiftly through Belgium as the outermost rim of the great wheel movement that would take them deep into France and behind the main positions of the French army. The advancing armies faced problems of com-mand, for they were far from the supreme headquarters, the *Oberste Herresleitung* (or OHL). The OHL had been set up well to the rear to accommodate the kaiser, who insisted on being located near headquarters, but who had to be protected from the hazards of the front. The army also was faced with difficulties of supply and commu-nication. Nevertheless, it pushed on relentlessly.

At various points, the Allies hastily put up defensive lines. This would temporarily halt the advance. Inevitably, when this happened, the Allied defenders would switch to the offensive mode called for by Plan XVII. Interestingly enough, the Germans, who were the invaders and the attackers, always strongly emphasized defensive as well as offensive techniques. Again and again, by the time the Allies mounted an of-fensive run, the Germans had dug in and were prepared to defend themselves. The result, again and again, was slaughter. Joffre's troops charged gallantly, and German machine gunners aimed at the line of bright scarlet French trousers, quickly cutting down the attackers. Forced into retreat, the Allied attackers suffered pursuit by the Germans, who pressed hard in a mostly successful effort to prevent the French and British from consolidating new defensive positions.

This pattern of Allied defense followed by Allied attack and German defense, followed by Allied retreat and German pursuit, was repeated many times during August. With each iteration, the Schlieffen Plan advanced and the French yielded more of Belgium—and, soon, their home territory as well. By the close of August, German troops were a mere 30 miles outside of Paris.

The casualties piled up, and still Joffre refused to de-ploy more of his army to the Belgian frontier.

Through all this, the people of Belgium suffered horri-bly. Soldiers and civilians alike continued heroically to resist the German invasion, even after the fall of Liège had made such resistance hopeless. Ordinary Belgians became snipers. They laid ambushes for the advancing soldiers, and they destroyed or sabotaged bridges, rail-ways, and telephone lines. For their part, the Germans responded with outrageous cruelty. Anyone caught act-ing against a German soldier was summarily executed; when the guilty could not be caught, mass reprisals—summary shootings, mostly—were made on hostages arrested at random from the general population.

Voices of Battle

"Wounded; wounded every-where, maimed men at every junction; hospitals crowded with blind and dying and moaning men."

—Philip Gibbs, British war corre-spondent, on the first months of combat, 1914

In a climate of continual reprisal, the individual German soldier was given—or took—license to act with utmost brutality against the conquered population. Theft, vandalism, arson, and rape became commonplace and were reported by the press. Fueled by German atrocity stories, the Allied propaganda machine went into high gear, depicting the invaders as subhuman "Huns." These stories not only goaded the Allies into pressing the fight even in the face of mounting losses and increasing discouragement, but they also deeply affected neutral nations, especially the United States. Although it would be three years before America entered the war, reports of the agonies of "poor little Belgium" were already turning American public opinion against Germany.

Lorraine Erupts

On August 8, General Paul Pau led the French Army of Alsace to Mulhouse, in German territory, not far from the Swiss border. This was followed farther north, during August 14–22, by a full-scale offensive led by General Auguste Dubail (First Army) and General Noël de Castelnau (Second Army) against the German Sixth Army led by Crown Prince Rupprecht of Bavaria and the Seventh Army commanded by General Josias von Herringen. Both of these forces withdrew under attack before converging and bouncing back in a fierce and brilliantly executed counterattack, according to the typical German tactic of luring the French into a futile and costly attack on a strong defensive position, then counterattacking and pursuing the retreating French column.

The offensives of Dubail and Castelnau were thrown back west to Nancy. General Ferdinand Foch, in command of the French XX Corps, played a heroic role in holding Nancy against the German onslaught. Nevertheless, the French right wing, consisting of the First and Second armies, had suffered a grave setback.

Offensive in the Ardennes

The next French position north of the First and Second Armies, in the Ardennes region, was held by the Third Army under General Pierre Ruffey and, behind him, in reserve, the Fourth Army, commanded by General Fernand de Langle de Cary.

The French forces advanced and met head on the German Fourth and Fifth armies, under Duke Albrecht of Würtemberg and Crown Prince Wilhelm, respectively. These two German armies were at the center—the pivot—of the Schlieffen Plan's "great wheel" and therefore were vital to execution of the plan. The French, badly outnumbered, put up a furious fight during August 20–25 before they were pushed back to the Meuse River and the great fortress of Verdun, having suffered shocking losses.

Sambre and Mons

As early as August 7, General Charles L.M. Lanrezac, commanding the French Fifth Army—on the left flank (extreme north) position of the French forces—had been vigorously warning Joffre that the Germans were moving into Belgium in great strength. Because these warnings concerned events not contemplated by Plan XVII, Joffre and the General Staff discounted them as exaggerations. Nevertheless, Lanrezac was so insistent that Joffre finally felt compelled to slightly modify the execution of Plan XVII, arranging for British and Belgian forces at Namur, Belgium, to join with Lanrezac in battle to the north. Joffre saved face—and his faith in Plan XVII—by insisting that the action was really in support of the attack into the Ardennes.

On August 9, Lanrezac sent a reconnaissance force into Belgium and quickly concluded that he would be trapped in the Ardennes if he proceeded with the attack that Joffre demanded. At last, on August 15, Joffre agreed to send the Fifth Army north to Namur, at the confluence of the Sambre and Meuse rivers. Here, on August 21, Lanrezac collided with Bülow's Second Army.

At this point, something seems to have died in Lanrezac. He had warned Joffre that the true German menace was to the north, and here it was. Now, in the face of superior numbers, he discarded Joffre's instructions to "attack to the utmost" and instead dug in for defense. Yet he failed to instruct his subordinate commanders adequately on just where and what to defend. As a result, the defensive lines were weak and uncoordinated.

Not that the absence of initiative was entirely Lanrezac's fault. Joffre's initial orders to him had consisted of vague instructions to "act in concert" with the British and Belgians. By the time Papa Joffre clarified his orders, Lanrezac was desperately uncertain of the state of his left flank. Nor did he know the intentions of his British and Belgian allies. Defending the high ground along the Sambre must have seemed to him a reasonable alternative.

The Battle of the Sambre commenced on August 21 and continued, in its first phase, through the 22nd. The result was a bloody slugfest: The French were indecisive and lacked guidance, and the Germans held their position—for Bülow had been ordered to await reinforcement from General Freiherr Max von Hausen. By August 22, however, when Bülow had succeeded in pushing back all French attacks, he decided to counterattack without Hausen. Recognizing this, Lanrezac planned to send his I Corps against the German left flank. Just as his subordinate, General Louis Franchet d'Esperey, was about to execute this attack on August 23, Hausen and his Third Army arrived at the French rear. General d'Esperey was forced to cancel the attack on Bülow to defend against Hausen.

To compound the difficulty of the French situation on the Belgian front, the German advance, having pushed back Lanrezac, now hammered away at the Belgian defenders of the fortress at Namur. On the same day that d'Esperey and Hausen fought, Namur fell to the Germans, and the Belgian survivors retreated behind the French lines.

By August 23, the BEF was in position at Mons, Belgium, about 8 miles west of where Lanrezac was engaged with Bülow and Hausen. Lanrezac simply ignored the BEF, made no attempt to coordinate an attack or defense with that force, and instead withdrew in the night. On the morning of August 24, when Bülow and Hausen resumed their converging attacks, Lanrezac and his Fifth Army were gone. There was no one for the two German armies to fight.

In the meantime, Bülow, having been given operational control of Alexander von Kluck's First Army, ordered that unit to move south to support the Second Army's attack on Lanzerac's left flank. This unexpectedly brought Kluck into collision with the BEF under Field Marshal Sir John French at Mons.

British and German cavalry elements were the first to make contact, on August 22, so that the main body of the outnumbered British had time to dig into favorable defensive positions that commanded a broad *field of fire.*

For his part, the aggressive Kluck mounted a full-scale attack, beginning on August 23 with an intensive artillery barrage intended to disrupt the defensive lines of the British. This preparation was completed at about 9:30 in the morning, and Kluck hurled his infantry against the British, whose withering rifle fire soon broke the tightly compacted advancing columns. So rapid and accurate was the British fire that the Germans assumed it came from machine gunners. In fact, it was the work of highly trained riflemen.

The German attackers pulled back, planning to regroup that night. The British defenders wearily prepared to resume defensive operations on August 24, in anticipation of gaining some relief from Lanrezac. Disaster would have been total for the British if Field Marshal French's liaison officer had not reached the commander with the news that Lanrezac had withdrawn and would offer no support. At this news, Field Marshal French resolved to withdraw as well, in an effort to coordinate with Lanrezac. But Kluck pursued him, inflicting 7,800 casualties on the British rear guard (a force of 40,000 men) at the Battle of Le Cateau on August 26. The rest of the BEF now joined the French Fourth and Fifth armies in a general retreat.

Words of War

A **field of fire** is the area that a weapon or group of weapons may cover effectively from a given position.

From the Front

The British rifleman was among the elite of European soldiery. He was trained to fire 15 accurately aimed rounds per minute at a range of 600 yards.

"Hardly Satisfactory"

On August 22, General Langle de Cary, commanding the French Fourth Army, wrote a battle report: "All corps engaged today. The whole result hardly satisfactory."

Applied to the entire French offensive of August 1914, it was a grim understatement. The offensive had failed at the cost of more than 300,000 of France's best troops and additional great losses among the other Allies.

From August 27 to September 4, the defeated Allies withdrew deeper into France. Yet all was not well with the victorious Germans, either. As they thrust farther into France, supply and communication lines stretched thin. Fatigue was general. Combat losses were not replaced, and many of the wounded and sick were treated inadequately or not at all.

For his part, Joffre was at last disillusioned as to the magic of Plan XVII. Surely, he must have been depressed and horrified. The blame for much of the disaster—perhaps all of it—could be laid at his feet. Yet, to his credit, he remained rock steady in defeat, projecting a confident optimism that was calm and composed rather than forced.

On August 24, he reported to Minister of War Adolphe Messimy, stating that the French army was now "condemned to a defensive attitude." Despite the vehemence of the verb *condemned,* it was really a healthy admission of reality. The old, slow-moving Joffre showed himself capable of shifting the basic French strategy from the offensive frame of mind that had dominated it since 1871 to the defensive mode that this new, terrible war now dictated. He also secured Messimy's approval to replace the inept among his field commanders; "eliminate the old fossils without pity," Messimy concurred.

Joffre resolved to inaugurate the new "defensive attitude" by forming a line along the Somme River, using this as a position from which he could make one more all-out counterattack. Rapidly changing circumstances would force him to change this plan, too.

The Least You Need to Know

➤ The comprehensive Schlieffen Plan, adhered to unswervingly, committed Germany to a two-front war that encompassed virtually all of Europe.

➤ French high command's adherence to its war plan, Plan XVII, blinded decision-makers to the realities of the German invasion strategy; as a result, the invaders penetrated deep into France at great cost to the defenders.

➤ Belgium, as the portal to France, was the first victim of German aggression in World War I; the atrocities inflicted on its civilian population inspired the Allies and turned public opinion in neutral America against Germany.

➤ Throughout August 1914, the Allies retreated, with heavy losses, through Belgium and France.

Chapter 6

The Marne: Massacre and Miracle

> **In This Chapter**
>
> ➤ French government in chaos
>
> ➤ The defense and salvation of Paris
>
> ➤ The Allies achieve strategic victory in the First Battle of the Marne
>
> ➤ Trench warfare begins
>
> ➤ The Western Front is deadlocked

We cannot know what depths of despair Papa Joffre felt after the loss of a third of a million men and the collapse of the offensive on which France had pinned its hopes. It is easier to imagine the elation Helmuth von Moltke must have experienced with the extent of the German victory. Barely a month into the war, and German armies were already thrust deep into the heartland of France.

Yet we must also realize that any elation was, to a large extent, unfounded. Moltke was headquartered far from a front that he had never visited firsthand. His lines of communication were stretched out and faulty. He believed that the Battle of Lorraine had been decisive. He believed that the Ardennes and Sambre had been decisive as well. He believed that the French Army was on the verge of destruction.

And, believing all this, Moltke began to depart from the Schlieffen Plan, opting to capitalize on what he believed were decisive victories instead of following through with Schlieffen's strategy for the right wing—the armies of Kluck and of Bülow—which should have been used as hammer blows against the vulnerable flank and rear of the hard-pressed French Army.

This chapter tells how Moltke faltered and, in so doing, threw away victory in the Great War.

The Fortified Camp of Paris

If Joffre projected an air of calm in the face of disaster, the French government was in a frenzy. According to Minister of War Adolphe Messimy, the deputies (elected representatives) were in a "panic that painted a livid mask of fear upon their faces." What they saw behind Joffre's emotionless reports was the grim truth: The nation had been invaded, the Alsace had not been regained but, rather, irretrievably lost, and the army had been defeated.

They had even more to fear. Minister Messimy received a report from the chief military engineer, pointing out that Paris was utterly vulnerable to attack and siege. Before the war had begun, plans were laid to construct fortifications, including barricades and entrenchments, around the city. These were supposed to have been ready by August 25, but Joffre had been so persuasive that the French offensive would succeed that the deadline had been put off to September 15. Yet even this deadline was unrealistic. The fact is that authorities had been reluctant to begin the demolition necessary to construct entrenchments and to clear fields of fire: Houses had to be razed, and trees had to be felled. In many places, no orders to begin this demolition had been issued. With the Germans rapidly approaching, only about half of the preparations had been made, and this did not include provisioning the city for a siege. Provisioning had hardly begun at all.

Messimy summoned to his office General Joseph-Simon Gallieni, a 65-year-old veteran of the Franco-Prussian War, who could always be counted on for straight talk.

Gallieni reported to Messimy on August 25, "Briefly you may expect the German armies to be before the walls of Paris in 12 days. Is Paris ready to withstand a siege?"

Messimy admitted that it wasn't, and then he immediately secured approval to appoint Gallieni as military governor of the menaced city. In the meantime, Joffre was actually ordering troops out of Paris to reinforce positions at the front.

The night he was appointed military governor, Gallieni declared to Messimy:

> They do not want to defend Paris. In the eyes of our strategists Paris is a geographical expression—a town like any other. What do you give me to defend this immense place enclosing the heart and brain of France? A few Territorial (home-guard) divisions and one fine (colonial) division from Africa. That is nothing but a drop in the ocean. If Paris is not to suffer the fate of Liège and Namur, it must be covered for 100 kilometers around, and to cover it requires an army. Give me an army of three active corps and I will agree to become Governor of Paris; on this condition, formal and explicit, you can count on me for its defense.

The war minister gratefully embraced Gallieni and then set out to find him an army. In the French system of government at this time, it was General Joffre, not the minister of war, who wielded final authority over the army. Joffre would never be persuaded to release so many men to the defense of what he saw as a position in the "zone of the rear."

In any case, Messimy had little time to bring about his powers of persuasion. As the defeated French armies continued to retreat, calls came demanding his resignation—the major industrial town of Lille, France, was declared an *open city* on August 27 and was abandoned to the Germans. Messimy's refusal to resign forced the entire government—all of the ministers—to resign. The French premier, René Viviani, frantically reshuffled his cabinet, appointing five new ministers, including Étienne-Alexandre Millerand to replace Messimy as minister of war. As for Messimy, he resumed the military rank of major that he had held before his own appointment, and he joined the army at the front.

Words of War

An **open city** is one that is declared demilitarized during war and, by international law, is therefore immune from attack.

While the French government imploded, Joffre's deputy, General Belin, dismissed Messimy's order to send troops to Paris: "What does Paris matter!" he exclaimed. Millerand's messenger was given a similar reply.

As long as Joffre persisted in thinking of Paris as occupying the "zone of the rear," he would not be persuaded to part with frontline troops. In the meantime, Gallieni worked tirelessly to transform Paris, "the city of light," into an armed camp. His purpose, however, was not to hunker down in Paris, which, as had been learned in 1871, could not stand up to a siege. Instead, he planned to use the city as a genuine military camp, a base of operations for battles that would be fought on the outskirts of the city.

From the Front

Among those who rushed to the defense of Paris was the former Captain—now Major—Alfred Dreyfus, the figure who had been at the center of the infamous "Dreyfus Case," which tore France apart in the 1890s. Dreyfus had been wrongfully convicted of treason in 1894 and had been sent to Devil's Island. A worldwide firestorm of protest, stirred by the radical novelist Emile Zola and others, ultimately freed Dreyfus, who was shown to have been the victim of trumped-up charges motivated by anti-Semitism. He then performed heroically as an officer of artillery.

Gallieni oversaw construction of a system of deep and narrow trenches on the far periphery of Paris, positions protected by earthen mounds, logs, and barbed wire, and manned by machine gunners. These trenches would interconnect strong artillery positions.

To the people of Paris, Gallieni was unsparingly frank. For while he had no faith in the French politicians, he had immense faith in the French people. Preparations were made for mass demolition of buildings to provide fields of fire, and bridges to impede German progress. Gallieni recruited bakers, butchers, and greengrocers to stockpile provisions, and farmers brought their cattle into the city to graze on the elegant Bois de Boulogne. In a rush to gather stores of ammunition, Gallieni pressed into service every transport vehicle available, including the city's legion of taxicabs.

Moltke's Unsure Hand

Moltke overestimated the finality of his army's victories even as he doubted the ability of the army to continue its advance into France in strict accordance with the Schlieffen Plan. Stationed far from the front and plagued by poor communication, he was assailed by second thoughts. As the shadow of his glory-covered uncle and namesake, the total victor of the Franco-Prussian War, closed over him, Moltke's hand became increasingly unsteady.

Moltke was also distracted by events on the Eastern Front. On August 25, he ordered the withdrawal of two German corps from the Western Front to reinforce the East. This strategic flinch would help bring about the failure of the German right flank and thereby contribute to the collapse of the Schlieffen Plan.

From the Front

The World War I "Tommy," as the British soldier was familiarly called, marched to battle saddled with pack crammed with extra clothing, a rifle, 100 rounds of ammunition, entrenching tools, a greatcoat, bedroll, and rations totaling just under 60 pounds.

British Peril

At Le Cateau (August 25–27), the BEF fought off envelopment by the entire strength of Kluck's army. On the 29th, Joffre at last ordered the French Fifth Army to the relief of the British. He directed that the army make a 90° turn back to the west to attack Kluck's flank. This first French attack was futile, but General Louis Franchet d'Esperey swiftly led the I Corps of the Fifth Army up from a reserve position to attack Bülow's Second Army at Guise. This move managed to check Bülow's advance and was the very first French tactical victory in the Battle of the Frontiers. Bülow was forced to call on Kluck for help. How that general responded to this call would alter the course of the next four years.

Kluck Takes a Turn

In contrast to Moltke, the German chief of staff, Alexander von Kluck, the general of the First Army, was single-mindedly aggressive and never given to second thoughts. Impatient for victory, he wrote off the British as finished. Ignoring the French Sixth Army, which was assembling to the west—the extreme left of the French forces—he concluded that the *Fifth* Army was the extreme left flank of the French forces.

Unable to communicate with the distantly located Moltke, Kluck took it upon himself to abandon altogether the already compromised Schlieffen Plan. Schlieffen had instructed that the sleeve of the last man on the right should brush the English Channel so that the right wing of the German army would make a great sweeping movement of encirclement. Now, instead, Kluck turned his First Army, the German right wing, abruptly to the southeast to hit what he believed was the vulnerable left flank of the entire remainder of the French army.

The Front Is Paris

Joffre saw Kluck's sudden turn as nothing less than a miracle. To this point, the French army had been rolled over by the juggernaut of the Schlieffen Plan. Suddenly, the entire German right wing was turning so that it would pass east of Paris instead of west and around the capital. How close was the German army? Just 30 miles outside the city of light.

Joffre now gave Gallieni everything he wanted, and more—an entire army. He ordered the Sixth Army—the force that constituted the true French left wing—to concentrate in the Paris area. This meant three things: first, that Joffre had to abandon his plan to take a defensive stand behind the Somme River and launch a counterattack; second, that the French Fifth Army would not be flanked and encircled as Kluck intended; and finally, that Paris was now at the war's Western Front.

From the Front

Joffre was made aware of Kluck's turn by reports from aerial reconnaissance. The first important use of airplanes in the war was not for fighting or bombing, but for observation.

Kitchener Intervenes

Just as Joffre was about to get a reprieve from the Germans, he had another crisis to face, this time from his British allies. Sir John French, commanding the BEF, wrote to Lord Horatio Kitchener, field marshal and secretary of state for war, essentially to tell him that he considered the French army beaten and was ready to return home. In the meantime, he intended to withdraw from the front—to desert the French in the hour of their greatest need, as Kitchener saw it, and in violation of the Triple Entente and treaties flowing from it.

After consulting with the cabinet, Kitchener set off for Paris, where he met with Premier Viviani, Joffre's representatives, and Sir John French. Kitchener managed to persuade Sir John French to cooperate with Joffre and not to abandon him.

Combatants

Horatio Herbert Kitchener, 1st Earl Kitchener of Khartoum (1850–1916), was Britain's foremost general at the beginning of the twentieth century. He had seen service as a volunteer in the Franco-Prussian War (1870–1871), in North African colonial wars (1883–1898), and in the Great (Second) Anglo-Boer War (1899–1902). He had been instrumental in defeating the forces of the anti-British insurgent Mahdi in the Sudan and then in forcing the surrender of the Boer guerrillas in South Africa.

Kitchener returned to England as a national hero in July 1902 and set about radically reorganizing the army during 1902–1909, molding it into an efficient colonial force. In 1909, he was promoted to field marshal, then became Viceroy of Egypt and the Sudan, where he served from 1911 to 1914.

Kitchener was back in England, on leave, when World War I broke out. With reluctance, he accepted an appointment in July 1914 as Secretary for War and called for full-scale mobilization, which included expansion of British industry as well as the creation of a vast conscripted army. Accustomed to taking full charge of all efforts, he refused to delegate authority and was soon swamped. Kitchener's policies in the recruitment of the "Kitchener Army" in 1915–16 led to the sacrifice of many of Great Britain's best and brightest citizens. In November 1915, the British Cabinet ended Kitchener's strategic authority. Disgusted, Kitchener nevertheless remained a patriot and stayed on in the Cabinet. Dispatched on a mission to Russia, he perished when the cruiser H.M.S. *Hampshire* struck a mine and sank off the Orkney Islands on June 5, 1916.

Taxis to the Marne

The consequences of overextended lines of communication combined with sharply differing command personalities now began to derail the German advance.

The German Advance Falters

Worried that what he took to be the fleeing French forces would elude him, Kluck had driven his First Army with great speed far in advance of the Second Army. He was unaware of the buildup of the French Sixth Army in and around Paris. Back at headquarters, Moltke had learned of that buildup and, accordingly, ordered Kluck to protect the right flank of the Second Army. Yet, unaccountably, Moltke did not explain the reason for his order—namely, that the German Second Army was menaced by the French Sixth. Without this explanation, Kluck was aware only that following Moltke's instructions would mean idling the First Army for two precious days. This, Kluck reasoned, would certainly allow the defeated French to escape final destruction. He therefore concluded that he could disregard the *letter* of Moltke's order and still obey its *intention* by continuing to move south to assure that the French, whom he believed beaten and disorganized, were driven well to the southeast of Paris, where they could not menace the Second Army.

So Kluck departed even farther from the coordination demanded by the Schlieffen Plan. He marched across the Marne River, exposing his own right flank just east of Paris—where, unknown to him, the French Sixth Army had assembled.

Counterattack on the Marne

On September 4, Joffre issued his orders. The Sixth Army would attack eastward, toward Château-Thierry, just to the northeast of Paris; simultaneously, the BEF would move against Montmirail, farther east. The Fifth and Ninth armies would conform to these actions as the developing situation required. The Fourth Army would hold on along the Marne, well to east of these positions, ready to advance when ordered. The Third Army, stationed at the fortress of Verdun on the Meuse River, would strike westward. Properly coordinated, these attacks would result in the double envelopment of the German right wing.

Kluck's turn had presented nothing less than an opportunity to save France.

Battle of the Ourcq

Under temporary command of Gallieni, the Sixth Army advanced from Paris to the Ourcq River, where Kluck had left exposed his right flank. A skilled German corps commander, General Hans von Gronau, acted quickly against this advance on September 5 and managed to extricate the German right wing from entrapment.

At first, Kluck, still operating on his conviction that the French were essentially finished, believed that the attack on his right was nothing more than a feint. But after the Battle of the Ourcq raged for two days, Kluck finally realized that although the French were badly battered, they were not a beaten army. He also realized that by having advanced south of the Marne, he was exposing his own force to destruction. Quickly, he reversed himself and pulled his troops back north of the river. Then, with his customary drive, he turned to the west and unleashed a series of savage counterattacks.

Paris Saved

The French were now sent reeling under Kluck's pounding, and they fell back toward Paris during September 7–9. Once again, Gallieni leaped into action. He rushed to the Marne the last troops stationed within Paris proper, pressing into service a string of buses and, most famously, Paris taxicabs, which presented an incredible sight as they drove up to the front lines.

Victory—of Sorts

The German forces were very much intact and viable, but between Kluck's First Army and Bülow's Second was a 50- or 60-mile-wide gap. The BEF and the French Fifth Army (now under General Franchet d'Esperey, after the faltering Lanrezac had been relieved of command) penetrated this gap, striking at the flank of the German Second Army.

Southeast of this combined French and British action, the French Ninth Army, under General Ferdinand Foch, attacked at St.-Gond. Foch was battered by the other end of the German Second Army while the German Third Army struck at his right. On September 8, soldiers of the Third Army launched a spectacularly violent bayonet attack, which threw the French into confused panic. Foch nevertheless stood fast and ordered an immediate renewal of his attack. Stunned by this resilience, the Germans halted their advance.

Voices of Battle

"My center is giving way, my right is falling back, situation excellent, I attack."

—Ferdinand Foch, message from St.-Gond, during the Battle of the Marne

Elsewhere along the lengthy Marne front, the fighting raged intensely, yet indecisively. At the river town of Vitry-le-François, the French Fourth Army of Langle de Cary slugged it out with the Duke of Württemberg's Fourth Army and a portion of the Third. Farther east, in the Argonne Forest, the French Third Army (now commanded by Maurice Sarrail, who had replaced the ineffectual "fossil" Pierre de Ruffey) arrested the advance of the German Fifth Army led by Crown Prince Wilhelm. At Nancy and all along the Alsace frontier, the French First and Second armies held their ground, continuing to command the heights, despite successive attacks from the German Sixth and Seventh armies. Schlieffen had specifically warned against making such wasteful frontal attacks along this southerly portion of the frontier.

Moltke at last dispatched a staff officer, Lieutenant Colonel Richard Hentsch, to inspect the front personally. What he saw was the German right flank being turned under pressure from the French Fifth Army. Bülow was commencing a retreat. Kluck, ever the aggressor, was making progress, but his left flank and rear were highly vulnerable to the BEF. Hentsch approved Bülow's retreat and, acting on Moltke's behalf, ordered the incorrigibly pugnacious Kluck to withdraw as well.

When these orders had been executed, Moltke realized that the grand German offensive had failed, and he ordered a general withdrawal to the Aisne River.

The End of Moltke

Although Helmuth von Moltke had never personally visited the front during the first weeks of the war, he was a casualty of battle nonetheless. Personally defeated by the failure of so promising a campaign, he voluntarily resigned executive responsibility for the German armies on September 14, turning over command to General Erich von Falkenhayn. He retained the title of chief of the General Staff until November 3 before he was reassigned to the post of deputy chief of staff in charge of rear-echelon affairs. It was a cruel slap, and Moltke fell into a profound depression. Within two years, he was dead of a heart attack, having lived quite long enough to witness the death and devastation caused by his failure to force a decision within the first month of the war.

Trenches on the Aisne

Erich von Falkenhayn was as self-assured as Moltke had been self-doubting. He immediately set about reviving the Schlieffen Plan, at least on a modest basis, by amassing strength on the right flank to attack the Allies' left. This strategy resulted in what historians have called the "race to the sea": a movement toward the North Sea coast as each army tried to outflank the other by moving progressively farther north and west. As the two armies maneuvered in this way, they dug into a series of trench lines that would come to characterize the war on the Western Front for the next four years.

The high ground that the Germans occupied just north of the Aisne River was a strong position. The German armies were deployed from west to east, beginning with the First Army (Kluck), the Seventh Army (under Josias von Heeringen), and the Second Army (Bülow); the Third, Fourth, Fifth, and Sixth German armies stretched from this point eastward to the Swiss frontier. Against the First, Seventh, and Second armies, beginning on September 14, Joffre hurled the Sixth Army (under Michel Joseph Maunoury), the BEF (with Sir John French commanding), and the Fifth Army (under d'Esperey). To the east, the French Ninth, Fourth, Third, Second, and First armies were positioned.

Despite the determination of massed Allied attacks, the German defenses were too strong and could not be breached. On September 18, Joffre called off the offensive.

Ypres

In addition to heavy Allied casualties, Aisne created two results. First, it marked the transition from a war of movement to a static war of trench lines, the increasingly elaborate system of filthy ditches that the soldiers of the Western Front would call home for the next four years. Second, Aisne marked the start of the flanking and outflanking pattern that extended the trench lines northward in the so-called "race to the sea."

By the beginning of October, the Allies reached the North Sea at Niuwpoort, Belgium. German forces drove the Belgian army out of Antwerp and sent it fleeing to the coast and then south from the coast to Ypres. The BEF took over the line from Ypres, Belgium, south to La Basée, France, while the seven French armies entrenched themselves from this point—which was now the Allies' extreme left—all the way down to the Swiss border. This long line of entrenchments would be the Western Front.

On October 14, Falkenhayn sent his Fourth and Sixth armies against Ypres. The resulting battle was drawn out through the first three weeks of November.

The first phase was a German offensive that lasted nine days and was halted only by a massing of French reinforcements and the deliberate flooding of the Belgian front. Belgian troops opened the sluice gates of the dikes holding back the sea from the low country. By this time, however, 35 percent of the Belgian army had been lost.

On October 20, French General Foch hurled a vigorous counterattack against the Germans, but to no avail. Both sides were discovering that trench warfare greatly favored defenders and made offensive action extraordinarily costly. Foch called off his offensive on October 28, and Falkenhayn counterattacked—without decisive success. The heavy rains and snows that closed in by the middle of November brought the First Battle of Ypres to a close.

The BEF held Ypres and a *salient* extending from Ypres 6 miles into the German front. But this stand had come at a terrible cost. Dead, missing, or wounded were 2,368 British officers and 55,787 enlisted men—some 80 percent of the BEF committed in this region and the very flower of the British professional volunteer army. French casualties numbered perhaps 50,000, while the Germans had lost at least 130,000 men.

Voices of Battle

"The nations were caught in a trap, a trap made during the first 30 days out of battles that failed to be decisive, a trap from which there was, and has been, no exit."

—Barbara Tuchman, *The Guns of August*, 1962

Words of War

A **salient** is a battle line that projects into territory nominally held by the enemy.

From the First 30 Days to the Next 5 Years

In the first three months of fighting, France had seen 380,000 men killed and about 600,000 wounded. German losses were only slightly less.

What had been purchased at this horrific price?

Ugly scars in the earth: a system of trenches, long, undulating, dug-in defenses extending from the North Sea down to the Swiss border. In Flanders, the "low country," the trenches were shallow, always filling with stagnant groundwater. Farther south, where the soil and elevation were more favorable, trenches were dug deep and included elaborate tunnels, dugouts, and covered "galleries."

Following the wisdom of military engineers, the trench-makers zigzagged their trench lines so that the enemy could not get a clear line of fire down the length of any given trench. Nevertheless, trenches were vulnerable to hits by explosive artillery shell (which might bury any number of men alive) and to attacks by poison gas (which, heavier than air, collected and concentrated in the trenches). They also were breeding grounds for myriad diseases and for vermin, were cold and wet, and were productive of general subhuman misery.

Neither side had planned to dig trenches. In fact, the high command of both sides was horrified by them. They came about in part because the armies possessed better defensive weapons, machine guns and artillery, than offensive weapons—chiefly, the rifle. The defensive weapons were most effectively used from the cover provided by the trenches.

But the trenches also were the result of naked, primitive instinct. To survive a ceaseless rain of fire, the human animal started to dig. Members of a civilization who had erected the great cathedrals and other towering monuments of human achievement now desperately scratched and burrowed into the mud, where they lived and died for four years.

The Least You Need to Know

➤ The speed and extent of the German invasion of France threw the French government into panic and collapse, but General Joffre, while guilty of many disastrous errors, kept his battered army intact and functioning.

➤ A combination of poor communication and the self-doubting nature of Helmuth von Moltke brought about departures from the Schlieffen Plan that forfeited Germany's chance for a quick victory.

➤ The First Battle of the Marne was a strategic victory for the Allies, but it hardened the Western Front into a static line of opposing trenches, from which the combatants would engage in futile slaughter for the next four years.

Chapter 7

The Sun Sets in the East

In This Chapter

➤ Misguided confidence in Russia's military might

➤ The Russian army

➤ Eastern Front strategies

➤ First blood at Stallupönen

➤ A draw at Gumbinnen

➤ The first battles between Austria-Hungary and Russia

Historians think of World War I as a conflict fought on many fronts, but two fronts were the most important: the Western Front, mainly in France and Belgium, and the Eastern Front, mainly in East Prussia and "Russian Poland," the westernmost part of the Russian Empire that was enclosed to the north by East Prussia, to the west by German Poland (Poznania) and Silesia, and to the south by Austrian Poland (Galicia). In writing about World War I, Winston Churchill took a somewhat different view from his fellow historians, suggesting that the Western Front and the Eastern Front were virtually two different wars. If, he observed, "for a space we obliterate from our minds the fighting in France and Flanders, the struggle upon the Eastern Front (emerges as) incomparably the greatest war in history."

We can look at the Eastern Front not only as a war in itself, a titanic and staggeringly costly struggle, but also as a war in which, as Churchill concluded, "nothing was gained by any." This chapter covers the opening of the war on the Eastern Front.

The Myth of the Russian Steamroller

The influential nineteenth-century military theorist Karl von Clausewitz developed the strategic doctrine of what he called "total war"—that is, war in which combat is not waged between armies alone, but also by armies upon the civilian population, with the object of breaking the enemy economically as well as psychologically and culturally. Such a war, the philosopher Karl Marx observed, would sweep the world like "fresh air let into a tomb." Marx believed that essentially healthy societies would survive and perhaps even thrive in total war, whereas those that were decayed from within would crumble into dust.

This is precisely what World War I did to Russia. The corrupt, oppressive, and politically bankrupt Romanov dynasty disintegrated under the pressure of total war, and the Communist Revolution swept in to fill the void.

If few of the politicians and military leaders believed that war would be the long nightmare of unprecedented destructiveness that it proved to be, probably none saw its potential for fomenting revolution. Instead, Russian officials and their Western allies saw Russia in war as nothing less than monolithic and single-minded, a great "steamroller" that could mobilize millions of troops to sweep over any adversary in Europe by sheer numbers.

From the Front

During the course of the war, 12 million men would wear the uniform. More than half this number, 6.7 million men, would be killed or wounded before the revolutionary Communist government made a separate peace with Germany at the start of 1918.

When Numbers Lie

And those numbers were impressive. Before the war, the Russian army numbered 1.4 million men. Immediate mobilization added another 3.1 million to this figure.

But the vast numbers of Russian army resources were deceptive. After the debacle of the Russo-Japanese War, Russia instituted a system of mandatory military service in which all able-bodied men were assigned to army units and were to be given annual training. Although the assignments were made, training was rarely conducted. Thus, the reserve units, which constituted the bulk of the millions of men recorded on the rolls of the Russian army, consisted mainly of untrained civilians in uniform. At that, most of these men were peasants, woefully uneducated and many of them wholly illiterate and virtually untrainable.

The officers who commanded the regular army as well as the reserves were almost universally incompetent, especially at the senior levels, where advanced age compounded incompetence. Reflecting the strict class divisions within the nation itself, officers remained aloof from the men they commanded, turning over most of the work of leadership to the noncommissioned ranks. If the officers were notorious for being remote from their troops, the noncoms were infamous for treating the common soldier with great brutality and sadistic cruelty.

The weapons of the Russian army were generally comparable to those of the Western forces, although the standard infantry rifle, the Mosin-Nagant Model 1891, was somewhat obsolescent and plagued by a difficult safety catch, yet so tough and generally reliable that it would serve not only in World War I, but in World War II as well. The real problem was less in the quality of the equipment than in the quantity. In the first mobilization of 1914, at least one-third of the soldiers committed to battle lacked rifles and were told to pick up weapons from fallen comrades. It is recorded that, at least on one occasion, Russian troops were sent on a suicidal charge against German machine-gun emplacements wielding nothing deadlier than axe handles.

The Russian army was also under-supplied with field artillery and woefully lacking in heavy artillery. While the Russians did deploy the sturdy Maxim machine gun, they did so in insufficient numbers and lacked proper doctrine for its use. Another problem was a chronic shortage of rifle and machine gun ammunition. In 1914, throughout the entire Russian Empire, there were only three factories capable of manufacturing small arms ammunition. Additional sources were not developed until late 1916.

Voices of Battle

"Russian resources are so great that in the long run, Germany will be exhausted without our helping Russia."

—Sir Edward Grey, British foreign secretary, to Raymond Poincaré, president of France, 1914

Lessons of the Russo-Japanese War

As unreliable as the Russian army was in 1914, it had actually improved since the Russo-Japanese War of 1904–1905, which exposed so many of the force's weaknesses. Most important among the changes ushered in by that war was the introduction of a new generation of officers. To be sure, they were outnumbered and outranked by the incompetent and senescent lot that preceded them, but they did introduce certain reforms.

The Czar's Problems

Unfortunately, the military reforms advocated by the new officer corps were tied to politically progressive views just this side of revolutionary. Effective military reform, they argued, could not be achieved without extensive political restructuring. This meant that the czar would have to yield some degree of his absolute authority to an increasingly representative form of government. The young officers argued that the entire Russian aristocracy was mired in a medieval epoch incompatible with a modern, technically advanced military force.

The czar, Nicholas II, was by no means an evil man, but neither was he an imaginative or even very bright man. With his broad goatee beard and magnificent moustache, he looked the part of a Romanov aristocrat, but he lacked the iron will, resolve, and vigor of a leader. He was overwhelmed by the revolutionary movements simmering and boiling over throughout his nation, and he allowed himself to be persuaded by the old-line autocrats surrounding him that change must not be actively engaged, but rather, should be entirely avoided. This meant ignoring it wherever possible and stamping it out where it couldn't be ignored.

In 1909, Nicholas II, urged by his courtiers, authorized a wholesale purge of the reformed army, in which "unreliable"—that is, politically liberal—officers were removed. At the top, the quite able minister of war, A.A. Rediger, was replaced by the doddering, incompetent, and highly pliable Vladimir Sukhomlinov.

Manpower Russia had. However, equipment was in chronic short supply. And effective political and military leadership was almost totally absent.

Voices of Battle

Of General Vladimir Sukhomlinov: "It was very difficult to make him work, but to get him to tell the truth was well-nigh impossible."

—Russian foreign minister Sazonov, quoted in Barbara Tuchman, *The Guns of August*, 1962

Strategy for the Eastern Front

The contested region, what would be called the Eastern Front, was Russian Poland. On the one hand, it posed a threat of invasion to East Prussia. On the other hand, it was highly vulnerable to invasion by Germany from the northwest and by Austria-Hungary from the southwest.

What the Germans Counted On

The Germans, historically never shy about their appetite for new territory, certainly saw the desirability of acquiring real estate in Russian Poland, especially as a permanent buffer between them and Russia. But the Schlieffen Plan called for crushing France before embarking on an offensive war against Russia. The Germans needed time to achieve their goals in the West before tackling the Eastern Front in earnest.

They counted on their estimation that it would take an inordinate amount of time for the dispersed and poorly led Russian army to mobilize. Not only was this built-in delay a function of an antiquated and inefficient command structure, but it also was the product of a poorly developed infrastructure. Communication was inadequate, and, most important, rail transportation was poor—especially in Russian Poland. (Indeed, as German planners saw it, the lack of adequate rail transport would not only slow the Russian mobilization, but it also would impede a *German* invasion of Russia. Thus, it was a double reason to avoid moving prematurely on this front.)

The German strategy for the Eastern Front, then, was to fight a defensive war, using its reserve divisions, to stave off invasion until France was neutralized and troops could be released from the Western Front to the Eastern Front for an offensive thrust into Russian territory.

What Austria-Hungary Feared

Russian Poland extended far to the west, between East Prussia and the Austro-Hungarian region of Galicia. Its western tip was a mere 200 miles from Berlin. Nevertheless, Austria-Hungary was even more vulnerable to attack from the east and therefore looked upon the Eastern Front very differently from its German ally. Much more of the Austro-Hungarian frontier with Russia was farther east than Germany's. The eastern fringes of the Austro-Hungarian Empire were populated by Slav minorities, who felt a much greater affinity for the Russians than for the Austrians. A Russian offensive would be enthusiastically received by these minorities, and the integrity of an already tremulous empire could easily be shattered.

Austrian military and political leaders wanted immediate action to check any Russian offensive. They persuaded Helmuth von Moltke to agree to an Austro-Hungarian advance northeastward into Russian Poland. Moltke allowed himself to be convinced that this would help keep Russia occupied while Germany concentrated on France.

What the Russians Hoped For

The Austrians were quite right to assume that Russia was most interested in operating in regions populated by Slavs. In fact, a war in the name of Slavic unity was seen by many czarists as just the remedy required to cure Russia of its revolutionary discontent. On the eve of the war, within the court at St. Petersburg, there was a pride and optimism about Russia's military prowess. Of course, the feeling was unrealistic and not shared by most military men, but it was compelling nonetheless. However, it did not extend to war with Germany, for very little would be gained by such a conflict. Indeed, the Russians almost willingly played into the Schlieffen Plan. Their wish was to concentrate all immediately available forces against Austria-Hungary and to leave the German Front alone until mobilization was complete.

What the French Demanded

The trouble was, of course, that the nations of Europe had relinquished much of their free will and national sovereignty by entering into a host of entangling alliances. Germany would have preferred that Austria-Hungary help defend its border with Polish Russia, but it had to allow Austria-Hungary to protect its own frontier area. Russia would have preferred to focus an offensive against Austria-Hungary, but its ally France insisted on action against Germany to relieve some of the pressure on the Western Front.

France persuaded the pliable Czar Nicholas II to authorize an offensive involving two great Russian armies against the Germans in East Prussia, while another four armies were deployed against the Austro-Hungarians in Galicia.

A Divided Army

What the French were asking Russia to do was well beyond its capability. With all its faults, the Russian army was a formidable force on account of sheer manpower alone. But its inherent slowness called for a highly cautious strategy, directed against one objective at a time. What France was asking for required a highly mobile, agile, thoroughly organized, and extraordinarily efficient force. These qualities Russia could not offer.

Against East Prussia

In prewar planning conferences, France had insisted that Russia be able to move with 900,000 men by the 14th day after the mobilization order—called, in military jargon, M+14. *Stavka*, the Russian General Staff, replied that such an offensive could not be mounted until M+20. After much discussion, the Russians agreed that M+15 was reasonable.

In fact, the Russian Northwest Army Group, under General Yakov G. Jilinsky, began its westward march on August 13, 1914—even earlier than the M+15 promised. Unfortunately, the march was premature. Although infantry and cavalry units were at least approaching full strength at this time, the all-important supporting units—supply and communication—had not even been assembled yet. The army was on the move without adequate supplies or communications.

On August 17, the First Russian Army, under General Pavel V. Rennenkampf, crossed into East Prussia. The Second Army, under Alexander V. Samsonov, was supposed to keep pace with Rennenkampf's command so that the two armies could converge in an attack on the German Eighth Army, a force that it outnumbered almost three to one.

On paper, the plan looked good. In the field, however, the inadequately supplied, poorly trained, and ineptly led armies faltered over difficult terrain.

CHARGE!!

Words of War

The **Stavka** was the Russian supreme military headquarters during czarist days, including the period of World War I.

Opposing the Russian invasion was the overwhelmingly outnumbered German Eighth Army, under General Max von Prittwitz. Prittwitz was headquartered in the fortress of Königsberg on the Baltic coast, and his army was widely dispersed from the Baltic some 90 miles south to Frankenau. His difficult mission was to trade space for time, delaying the Russian advance into East Prussia, and exact a cost in casualties from the

Russians until the Western Front was sufficiently stabilized to allow troops to be transferred east for a definitive offensive against the Russian invaders.

Prittwitz was not a great general, and Moltke was uneasy at his appointment to lead the Eighth Army, especially in so difficult a mission. The Germans rightly believed that they were better trained and better equipped than the Russians, but they had also heard horrifying tales of Russian brutality and ferocity. Intentionally confronting a superior force was difficult enough. The rumors of "Russian barbarism" and "Cossack cruelty" made the task seem terrifying.

Encounter at Stallupönen

The first combat came at Stallupönen, about a hundred miles east of Eighth Army headquarters and near the East Prussian frontier with Russian Poland. There one of Prittwitz's most aggressive corps commanders, the energetic and dashing Hermann von François, disobeyed standing orders to avoid decisive engagement by launching an offensive against Rennenkampf's center.

François tore into Rennenkampf, inflicting 3,000 casualties and pushing the Russians back across the frontier into Russian Poland. His action, however, had been risky. If the Russians had been better led, they could well have encircled François's corps and annihilated it. The cautious Prittwitz was appalled and immediately sent his chief of staff to François with orders that he break off the engagement immediately. It was too late, however, because the engagement had already been fought and won.

The Battle of Stallupönen had little effect in immediate and direct military terms; however, it stunned Rennenkampf, who had not expected anything so ferocious from the Germans in the east. Rennenkampf resolved to proceed with greater caution, and he greatly slowed the pace of the advance of his First Army. This would have dire consequences for the soldiers of the Second Army in the coming Battle of Tannenberg (see Chapter 8, "A Suicide").

Triumph and Failure at Gumbinnen

François' victory had another effect. It bolstered Prittwitz's uncertain resolve, and the intense François, whose distant ancestors had been Huguenots—bold rebels and agile survivors—persuaded his commanding officer to launch another offensive.

Eighth Army headquarters had made a key discovery about Russian communications. The Russian soldiers, including junior and middle-level officers, were so poorly trained and the level of literacy so low that the army had given up the practice of transmitting wireless (radio) messages in code. The process of encryption and decryption was just too complex for most of the Russian troops to handle. Instead, the army broadcast orders and instructions "in the clear" for everyone—including the Germans—to hear. Prittwitz and his officers received Russian orders simultaneously with the Russian officers.

From the Front

In the days long before computer encryption, coding and decoding messages was time-consuming, even for well-trained personnel. Wherever possible, field telephones, which relied on wire, were used instead of radio. In this way, messages could be safely sent "in the clear" (unencrypted) because (at the time) it was virtually impossible to tap the enemy's phone lines. The Russians, however, had mobilized so hastily that they had neither the time nor the equipment to string telephone wire, so they had to rely on highly vulnerable radio communication.

Prittwitz decided to attack with three corps at the village of Gumbinnen on August 20. The corps led by the redoubtable François smashed into Rennenkampf's First Army on its right flank. Relentlessly, François pushed over five miles, driving the flank back.

The other two German corps were not successful, however, and the main part of Rennenkampf's force, the center, held fast. The Battle of Gumbinnen was a draw, perhaps even marginally a Russian victory.

When Prittwitz learned that two of the three corps engaged had been repulsed at Gumbinnen and that 13 divisions of Samsonov's Second Russian Army had now crossed the southern frontier of East Prussia—thereby posing a threat to the German Eighth Army rear—he blanched and instantly reverted to his customary fainthearted-ness.

He proposed a general retreat, to which his staff loudly objected. One of his staff officers, Lieutenant Colonel Max Hoffmann, made a counterproposal of an attack on Samsonov's left flank in the vicinity of Tannenberg, near East Prussia's southern frontier with Galicia. Pressed by the others, Prittwitz tentatively approved. The mission that had been assigned him, in accordance with the Schlieffen Plan, had been one of delay and gradual retreat—which was fine with Prittwitz. Instead, however, he now found himself nervously preparing for another offensive.

Against Austria

Austria-Hungary had conducted the very first operations of World War I with the July 29 bombardment of Belgrade, capital of Serbia. This attack was not followed up on until August 12–21, when Austro-Hungarian forces numbering 200,000, under the command of General Oskar Potiorek, invaded Serbia across the Save and Drina rivers, from the west and the northwest.

The Austrians were in for a shock. They were met by an almost equal number of Serbs, inadequately equipped, but fierce and determined after becoming honed and hardened by the just-concluded Balkan Wars. Under Marshal Radomir Putnik, the Serbs counterattacked vigorously on August 16, delivering a series of punishing blows that sent the Austro-Hungarian army reeling back across the River Drina. It would be early September before the Austrians renewed the invasion.

In the meantime, in Galicia (Austrian Poland), General Count Conrad von Hötzendorf, the Austro-Hungarian chief of staff, prepared on August 23 to lead the First, Fourth, and Third Austrian armies (positioned from west to east) northward to invade the so-called Polish Salient. This thick tongue of Russian Poland projected westward below East Prussia and above Galicia, thus driving a broad wedge between Germany and Austria-Hungary. It presented a threat to both of these allies, but conversely, it was also vulnerable to a *pincers attack* from both. With the Germans busy fighting the Russians above the Polish Salient—and too committed on the Western Front to send more troops east—it would be, for now, up to the Austro-Hungarians to invade this region on their own.

Words of War

A **pincers attack** is a military tactic whereby an attacking force closes in on the enemy from two sides, so that the defending troops are "squeezed" as by a giant pincers.

The three Austro-Hungarian armies deployed along a 200-mile front north and east from Lvov (then called Lemberg), Poland, and met headlong the Southwestern Russian Army Group (consisting of the Third, Fourth, Fifth, and Eighth armies) southwest of the Pripet Marshes, some 400 miles to the northeast of the Ukraine and deep inside Russian Poland. Here the Battle of Krasnik was fought during August 23–24. As a result, the northern flank of the Army Group—the Russian Fourth Army—was driven back by the Austrian First Army.

The battle ended without full resolution, however, and, in fact, the conflict spread throughout the colliding forces. From August 26 through September 1, the Battle of Zamosc-Komarów erupted and raged. In bitter fighting, the Austrian Fourth Army hammered at the Russian Fifth, driving it well back.

In the meantime, at the southern flank of the engaged forces, the Austrian Third Army (together with some elements of the Second, which arrived from the Serbian front) suffered a setback at the Battle of Gnila Lipa (August 26–30). The combined Russian Third and Eighth armies drove this outnumbered force back to Lvov. Here, the Austrians organized a hasty defense but were penetrated by the Russian Fifth

Army as a result of the Battle of Rava Ruska during September 3–11. Despite their initial successes, the Austrians were now forced to fall back a full hundred miles to the Carpathian Mountains, leaving behind only a garrison at the fortress of Przemysl.

Combatants

Paul Ludwig Hans von Hindenburg (1847–1934) was the son of a Prussian military officer and was raised in an atmosphere steeped in his nation's military traditions. He fought in the Austro-Prussian (Seven Weeks') War of 1866 and the Franco-German War of 1870–1871 and secured a post on the staffs of German field marshals Helmuth von Moltke (uncle of the Moltke of World War I) and Alfred von Schlieffen (author of the Schlieffen Plan) in 1878.

Hindenburg retired from the army in 1911 but was called out of retirement to assume command on the Eastern Front in 1914. In collaboration with Erich Ludendorff, he formulated the plan that decisively defeated the advancing Russian armies at the Battle of Tannenberg in August 1914 and then at Masurian Lakes the following month. Victory in Poland at the Battle of Lodz led to Hindenburg's appointment as chief of the General Staff in 1916, replacing Moltke.

Hindenburg attempted to formulate a strategy to defeat France and England before the neutral United States joined the conflict. He advocated a campaign of submarine warfare against Great Britain, intended to blockade and starve that nation into surrender. The effect, however, was to propel the United States into the war.

The German people never blamed Hindenburg for defeat in World War I, and in 1925 they elected this popular hero to two terms as president of the second Weimar Republic. The aging Hindenburg could not reconcile the factions of a country plagued by punitive peace terms, torn by political unrest, and worn down by the economic effects of a worldwide depression. In desperation, he looked to the charismatic Adolf Hitler for support, appointing him chancellor of his second cabinet in 1933. With Hindenburg by this time senescent, Hitler became de facto leader of Germany and, after Hindenburg's death the following year, absolute dictator.

Austria-Hungary had incited war to punish Serbia and thereby secure its own faltering grasp on the disparate peoples of its creaky empire. Now, however, Galicia—Austrian Poland—had fallen into Russian hands, and the Austro-Hungarian army had lost a quarter-million men killed and wounded, with perhaps another 100,000 taken prisoner by the Russians. With characteristic inefficiency, Russian officials did not bother to count their own casualties, but, doubtless, they were comparable. Heartened nevertheless, the Russians were poised for an advance into the Carpathians.

The New Commander

Back at the German Eighth Army, Colonel von Hoffmann had given Prittwitz a plan for an effective recovery from the disappointment at Gumbinnen. At general headquarters, however, Helmuth von Moltke sensed Prittwitz's undercurrent of panic. After all, at the very first setback he had announced his intention to withdraw all the way to the Vistula River. To his credit, although Moltke was embroiled in the fast-moving action of the Western Front, he saw opportunity in the east. It was time to stop entrusting this front to a marginally competent commander and turn it over to someone of proven ability. Moltke called out of retirement Paul von Hindenburg to assume command of the Eighth Army, and he assigned the brilliant Erich Ludendorff, the hero of Liège (see Chapter 5, "Battle of the Frontiers") as his chief of staff. This command team would prove to be the most effective in the entire war.

On August 22, Ludendorff formulated a plan that, quite coincidentally, duplicated what Hoffmann had proposed to Prittwitz. Elements of the Eighth Army would attack Samsonov's Russian Second Army while other elements remained farther east to delay Rennenkampf's First Army. If these two forces could be kept from joining, they could be defeated in detail. It was a tactic as old as Caesar—and probably much older: divide and conquer. That both Rennenkampf and Samsonov were proving themselves Russian officers of the old school—that is, fumbling and incompetent—would greatly aid Ludendorff's strategy in the coming titanic Battle of Tannenberg.

The Least You Need to Know

➤ The Allies placed inordinate and unthinking confidence in the "Russian steamroller," counting on the sheer numbers of the Russian army to defeat any enemy.

➤ Despite reforms after the disastrous Russo-Japanese War of 1904–1905, the Russian army was rife with corruption and incompetence—its men were poorly trained and inadequately equipped.

➤ Russia's early encounters with the Germans boded ill for Russia's military fortunes, although some important gains were made against Austria-Hungary and its forces.

Chapter 8

A Suicide

> **In This Chapter**
>
> ➤ The Germans intercept key Russian battle plans
>
> ➤ General François: difficult hero of Tannenberg
>
> ➤ The Russians' unrealistic objectives
>
> ➤ The Russian Second Army is destroyed
>
> ➤ Battle of the Masurian Lakes

The Battle of Tannenberg would wipe out an entire army. More than 30,000 Russian soldiers would perish or be wounded. Another 92,000 would be taken prisoner. By any measure, it would be one of the greatest military disasters in history.

The reason for the disaster? In part, a combination of brilliant German military leadership and inept leadership on the Russian side. In part, the superior training of German versus Russian troops. But in part, too, this most terrible defeat and destruction of human life was the product of a feud between the two Russian commanders.

The sheer numbers of men who were ordered about, who moved from place to place, who killed, and who were killed makes it all too easy to forget that World War I was not exclusively the work of the impersonal forces of history, but also of individuals, each with his own set of desires, memories, grudges, goals, motives, prejudices, insights, and blind spots. For the Russians, Tannenberg was a fiery furnace fueled by human passion, human folly, social injustice, and political oppression.

Prelude to a Russian Tragedy

Newly arrived on the Eastern Front, Erich Ludendorff instantly grasped the situation. He could feel the hot breath of Rennenkampf's army at his back, so he knew that he had limited time in which to deal with the vulnerable army of Samsonov. Accordingly, he ordered François' I Corps to attack at Usdau on August 25. Irascible as he was aggressive, François replied that he would do no such thing. His troops were still arriving from Gumbinnen, and not only were they exhausted, but they were not yet fully supplied; their artillery and ammunition was still on wagons. Ludendorff took this reply as insubordination and personally drove to François' headquarters.

"If the order is given," François told Ludendorff, "of course I shall attack, but my troops will be obliged to fight with the bayonet."

So be it. Ludendorff, the stern Prussian officer, reissued the orders without change.

Ludendorff drove off from this meeting in one car, while Colonel Hoffmann drove in another to the railroad station at Montovo. There German signal officers had been busily intercepting Russian radio traffic, which, as always, was transmitted "in the clear"—unencrypted. (Even when the Russians did bother to encrypt their messages, they did so using an elementary cipher, which the Austro-Hungarian military quickly cracked and rendered transparent.) Hoffmann was handed two intercepts, one sent by Rennenkampf at 5:30 that morning and the other by Samsonov a half-hour later.

The Rennenkampf message was nothing less than the marching orders of the Second Army. It revealed the distance between the Second and First armies, and it further revealed that Rennenkampf would not, in fact, pose a threat to the German position for at least another day.

Samsonov's message was even more revealing. The day before, August 24, he had engaged the German XX Corps at the Battle of Orlau-Frankenau. Moving without advance reconnaissance, Samsonov had stumbled into the XX Corps, which was deeply entrenched. Despite heavy fighting, Samsonov's center could not get past the German lines. On the 25th, the Russians rested while XX Corps withdrew from Orlau-Frankenau to Tannenberg. Samsonov's intercepted message revealed his belief that the withdrawal signaled a full German retreat, and he gave exact directions and times of movement for his planned pursuit of the enemy that he believed he had defeated.

From the Front

Thanks to the inadequacy of Russian war industry and the indolent incompetence of War Minister Sukhomlinov, Russia went to war with terrible shortages of equipment. Each Russian gun was allotted a mere 850 shells, compared with the 2,000–3,000 shells per gun used by the Western armies. Each Russian infantry division had 7 field-gun batteries, compared with 14 in the German division. In the entire Russian army, there were only 60 heavy artillery batteries, compared with 381 for the Germans.

The Generals Decide

Hoffmann was gleeful at the bounty that had fallen into his hands. His immediate superior, however, Major General Grünert, began to look this gift horse in the mouth.

"He kept asking me anxiously over and over if we should believe them," Hoffmann later recalled. "I myself believed every word of them on principle."

That "principle" was a certain item of information that Hoffmann possessed about Rennenkampf and Samsonov: They hated one another far more than either hated the Germans.

Combatants

Aleksandr Vasilievich Samsonov (1859–1914) was all too typical of the Russian army's officer corps. A graduate of the cavalry school at St. Petersburg, he saw his first combat service during the Russo-Turkish War of 1877–78, received regular promotions, and, at the outbreak of World War I in August 1914, was made commander of the Second Army along the River Narew in Poland. He was new both to the territory and to his command, but was nevertheless ordered to invade East Prussia from the south. Unfortunately, he was assigned to work in coordination with the First Army, invading from the east, which was commanded by General Pavel Rennenkampf, a bitter personal rival. The two generals hated one another more than any foreign enemy and did little to communicate, let alone cooperate.

Samsonov obeyed orders from the high command to advance deep into East Prussia, even though Rennenkampf, with whom he was to attack in concert, had halted after the Battle of Gumbinnen on August 20. As a result of this incoordination, Samsonov was surprised by the German Eighth Army, which virtually annihilated his entire force at Tannenberg during August 26–31, 1914.

When Samsonov realized just how badly he had lost, he cut off his communications with the rear and rode to the fore in order to take personal command. It was too late. During the disorderly retreat that came on August 30, he committed suicide.

Many of the world's nations had sent military observers to the distant battlefields of the Russo-Japanese War of 1904–1905. Hoffmann had been one such observer, and what he saw was a private quarrel explode between the two Russian generals. Samsonov's Cossacks had gained at great cost the Yentai coal mines in Manchuria, only to have to relinquish them because Rennenkampf's cavalry division had refused to come to their aid at a critical juncture, despite Samsonov's repeated entreaties. Hoffmann had heard that, later, Samsonov and Rennenkampf came to blows in the

Mukden railway station and that Samsonov had knocked Rennenkampf to the platform.

Hoffmann explained to General Grünert that this incident strongly suggested that Rennenkampf would indeed be in no hurry to come to Samsonov's aid at Tannenberg. Persuaded, Grünert pulled Hoffmann back into their car and instructed the chauffeur to catch up with Ludendorff and Hindenburg. In a moment of high drama, their car overtook that of the two commanders, and Hoffmann handed over the messages while both vehicles, abreast, sped ahead. Either Ludendorff or Hindenburg signaled to pull over, and all four officers got out of their vehicles to ponder the situation.

The situation was this: The attack against Samsonov planned for August 25 could proceed without fear of exposure to Rennenkampf. Both Hindenburg and Hoffmann believed that the situation was so favorable that François could even afford to postpone his role in the attack—the brunt of which would be borne by two corps under General August von Mackensen and Otto von Below—until all of his men and materiel were available. More out of a desire to yield nothing of his command authority than from tactical necessity, Ludendorff insisted that François carry out the original order.

So much for the plans of August 25. Now Ludendorff and Hindenburg pressed forward with additional plans for the 26th. These involved exploiting the absence of Rennenkampf to accomplish the *double envelopment* of Samsonov's Second Army. General Friedrich von Scholtz, who had already tangled with Samsonov at Orlau-Frankenau, would hit from the center; Mackensen and Below would attack Samsonov's right wing. François, in the meantime, would strike the Russian's left.

Words of War

A **double envelopment** is executed by forces moving around both flanks of an enemy to attack those flanks or objectives to the rear of the enemy.

Nerves

On the morning of August 26, Ludendorff experienced a shudder of anxiety. Generals are human, and Ludendorff, a particularly imaginative officer, vividly pictured the disastrous result if Rennenkampf, after all, converged with his colleague. Rennenkampf's army, Ludendorff declared, "hung like a threatening thunder cloud to the northeast."

But Hindenburg reassured Ludendorff, and, as Hindenburg observed, "we overcame the inward crisis."

That was all well and good, but Ludendorff soon discovered that François was still awaiting his artillery and, therefore, had not begun the battle. Ludendorff demanded that the fight commence by noon, and the two generals fell to bickering—while François continued to play for time.

Then came proof that Ludendorff was not the only nervous general in the German command. The telephone at his headquarters rang. It was Moltke at supreme headquarters with news that three corps and a cavalry division were about to be sent from the Western Front to reinforce the Eastern Front.

Ludendorff was flabbergasted. Had he been a lesser and more self-centered officer, he would have greeted this as nothing more or less than very good news. Fresh from the Western Front himself, however, he understood that the Schlieffen Plan had included precise calculations on the "density of manpower per square mile of offensive"—just how many men were needed, per unit of space, to carry out the grand offensive. He knew that none could be spared, particularly on the all-important right wing, the flying column that was to encircle the French army from well to the north and then the west of Paris.

Ludendorff demurred, telling headquarters that the reinforcements were not "positively" needed. Clearly, however, Moltke had begun to fret about the weakness of the Eastern Front. He was willing to compromise the Schlieffen Plan. The kaiser himself had remarked before the war had even begun that "all the success on the Western Front will be unavailing if the Russians arrive in Berlin."

The Russian Position, August 26, 1914

The new troops would not figure in the Battle of Tannenberg. The Belgians had destroyed their own railroads precisely to impede German mobility. And so the reinforcements had to march through Belgium to reach railway stations in Germany. They would not arrive in the east for several days.

If Ludendorff had the jitters, Samsonov was all confidence as he prepared to resume the battle that had seemed to begin so promisingly. He deployed on his extreme right (the northeast end of the Russian Second Army) his VI Corps, leaving that unit entirely isolated as he pushed the main body of his army westward for an assault on the Germans. Not only did this movement leave VI Corps vulnerable, however, but it also drew the Second Army farther from, not closer to, Rennenkampf's First Army. Still, Samsonov glued his eyes to the map and decided that this course of march would place him between the Vistula River and what he believed was the retreating German army; moreover, it would take him to the main German railway, by which, he declared, "it would be easier to advance into the heart of Germany."

Samsonov's intentions were unrealistic on many levels. To begin with, of course, he was simply—and tragically—mistaken: The German army was not retreating in defeat. But even if it had been, the Russian mobilization was so poorly executed that rations and other supplies were not coming up to the front. As the Second Army pulled farther from Russia, less and less reached the troops, who were exhausted and starving. Normally, an army in this condition attempted to live off the land—to *forage*—but the population, fearing the invasion of "Cossack brutes," had deserted, leaving little or nothing behind them.

Words of War

For an army, to **forage** is to live off the land of the enemy, appropriating whatever food and supplies can be stolen.

On the 26th, Samsonov's hungry VI Corps on the right was 50 miles from I Corps (and other elements) on the left. Between these, Samsonov had arrayed the rest of his army. The information he had about the position of the German army came chiefly from Rennenkampf, who had not been in contact with the enemy since the Battle of Gumbinnen (see Chapter 7, "The Sun Sets in the East"); in any case, as Samsonov well knew, Rennenkampf was hardly trustworthy. Accordingly, Samsonov dispatched a cavalry reconnaissance, although it did its job so poorly that the general was entirely unaware that two German corps under General Mackensen and General Below, having retreated from Gumbinnen, had regrouped and were now approaching the isolated right flank of his army.

Tannenberg

Slowly, Samsonov was roused from his fantasy vision of riding the rails into the heart of Germany. Belatedly realizing that his right flank was vulnerable, and with a growing sense that the Germans had not fled but were massing about him, he issued an order for VI Corps to hold fast to protect the army. Then he changed his mind. The advance would continue after all, and VI Corps was ordered to move toward the center to support the advance. At the last minute, however, on the morning of the 26th, Samsonov countermanded his order once again, telling VI Corps to remain on the right after all.

From the Front

By 1915, some Russian troops were being sent into battle unarmed. Some authorities believe that, at times, as many as one-third of Russia's soldiers lacked rifles.

It was too late. Those troops were already moving toward the center, leaving the right flank of the entire Russian Second Army naked.

If the optimism was just beginning to shatter in Samsonov's mind, it had by this time completely evaporated among his superiors. Russian High Command had lost all confidence in the ability of the army to win this war, and the grossly negligent Russian minister of war, Vladimir Sukhomlinov, didn't even bother to order the construction of new arms factories. He just didn't see the need for it; indeed, defeatism spread like a cancer throughout the *Stavka* (Supreme Headquarters).

The German Guns Speak

As the Russian VI Corps marched toward Samsonov's center—unaware that this order had been changed—its commander received word that German forces had been sighted six miles behind it, to the north. Under the prevailing misapprehension that the Germans were defeated and in retreat, a commander of one of VI Corps' divisions ordered his column to reverse its march—countermarch—and attack.

What the division ran into was Mackenson's corps. Far from retreating, they were advancing precisely to attack the isolated and badly outnumbered Russian unit.

The Germans fell upon the Russians with efficient ferocity, and the Russians immediately found themselves fighting for survival and losing ground—fast. The divisional commander called for help from another division, which, already exhausted, marched 19 miles to join its beleaguered comrades. At the end of the day, however, it ran up against General Below's division and also found itself in a fight for its life.

Flight and Pursuit

With VI Corps split in two and suffering devastating casualties, its commander, a General Blagovestchensky, was incapacitated by panic. He issued a series of garbled orders and counterorders, which made a desperate situation completely chaotic. By the morning of August 27, the remnants of VI Corps would be less an army than a disorganized, terrified mob. With its *rout*, the right wing of Samsonov's army collapsed as the Germans pressed the pursuit toward the center.

Words of War

A **rout** is the disorganized withdrawal of a military force from the line of battle; it contrasts with a **retreat,** which is an orderly—and, therefore, militarily effective—withdrawal.

The Russian Center Resists

On August 26, Samsonov, unaware of the ongoing collapse of his right flank, ordered the center of his army, two and a half corps, to take the offensive. Predictably, confusion reigned.

While the Russian center tangled with the Germans, a division of the XXIII Corps, just to the left, collapsed and exposed the left flank of the entire corps. In the meantime, the Russian XIII Corps, on the right, advanced to Allenstein, a town on the railway that Samsonov had intended to ride into Germany. Learning that the army's center was in trouble, however, the XIII Corps' commander ordered it back to assist, assuming that Allenstein would be occupied by the Russian VI Corps. What the commander did not know is that VI Corps was fighting for its life and would never show up. A great yawning gap was left at Allenstein.

While this was occurring late on August 26, General Samsonov was enjoying dinner with his chief of staff and the British military attaché at Second Army Headquarters in Neidenburg, several miles behind the front lines. Suddenly, a great tumult was heard in the street outside. Survivors of XXIII Corps were running, shouting, screaming.

Samsonov and his chief of staff hurriedly buckled on their swords, rushed out, and beheld the exhausted, terrified rabble that had once been a military formation.

It now dawned on Samsonov that he was in no position to envelop and finish off a defeated enemy. He understood now, at this late hour, that it was *his* army that was in the process of envelopment. Instead of breaking off the battle, however, Samsonov decided to reengage the next day with the object of holding off the Germans with his center corps until Rennenkampf arrived to turn the tables— Rennenkampf, who had proved himself unreliable in the Russo-Japanese War and who had given no indication of performing any differently in this war.

Voices of Battle

"To see the enemy where he does not exist is cowardice. I will not allow General Samsonov to play the coward. I insist that he continue the offensive."

—Yakov Grigorievich Jilinsky, chief of the Russian General Staff and commander of the North-west Army Group, in response to General Samsonov's warning that his army was about to be sur-rounded

Against the Russian left at this point, the German I Corps, under the dauntless François, was about to pound away. Samsonov issued an order to the Russian I Corps, which formed the Russian left wing: "Protect the flank of the Army … at all costs …. Not even a greatly superior enemy can break the resistance of the famous I Corps!"

At 4:00 A.M. on August 27, François commenced an artillery barrage against the Russian I Corps at Usdau. Offensives typically began with such a barrage to "soften up" the enemy for the infantry advance that would follow. In this case, however, "the famous I Corps," hungry, weary, and afraid, abandoned the field by eleven o'clock after a bombardment that had lasted seven hours. The battle had been won by artillery alone.

Yet Samsonov's army wasn't finished. Its two center corps, though battered, were still a formidable force. If Rennenkampf's First Army showed up, it would be the Germans whose situation would be suddenly desperate.

Incredibly, however, Yakov Grigorievich Jilinsky, chief of the Russian General Staff and commander of the Northwest Army Group, which included the First and Second armies, failed to appreciate the disaster that was unfolding at Tannenberg. Until late on the 27th, the second day of battle, he persisted in the belief that the Germans were retreating to the Vistula. Finally, when it was all too clear that they were attacking, not retreating, Jilinsky telegraphed Rennenkampf, informing him that the Second Army was heavily engaged and that he should render assistance "by moving your left flank as far forward as possible."

It was, in fact, a very stupid order. The objectives that Jilinsky gave Rennenkampf were hardly positioned to be of much help to Second Army. Moreover, Jilinsky put no urgency behind his order, failing even to call for forced marches. For his part, Rennenkampf made little effort to obey the order, inadequate though it was.

Encirclement

August 27–28 witnessed one of the most violent battles in the history of modern warfare. By this point, 300,000 men were fully engaged in combat. At any given time, the fighting was confused but was consistently at the expense of the Russians. On August 28, François opened up another fearful artillery barrage. He was determined to lead his I Corps in the final encirclement of the Russian left flank. Ludendorff, anxious that the German center should not collapse in the process, ordered François to break off this attack and support the center. With his customary single-minded insubordination, François ignored this order and continued to drive eastward, determined to keep the enemy from breaking out.

Ludendorff fretted over this as he agonized over the prospect of Rennenkampf's arrival. Surely his army must be on the march by now?

But, by the end of the day on the 28th, the news, confused and fragmentary at first, began to come in loud and clear. General Mackenson continued to crush the Russian right wing, even as General Below was exploiting the gap at Allenstein to hit the Russians—harder and harder—in the center. Ludendorff issued a new order to François: Continue the attack on the left. (Doubtless, François had never considered doing otherwise.)

Voices of Battle

"All the success on the Western Front will be unavailing if the Russians arrive in Berlin."

—Kaiser Wilhelm II, on the necessity of victory against Russia, remark recorded shortly before 1914

The End of Samsonov

For Samsonov, the horrific vision of the end came with the news that the "famous I Corps" had collapsed on the left, as had VI Corps on the right. Like the proverbial drowning man, Samsonov had held fast to the straw that was I Corps. Now it was broken, and both flanks of his army had been turned.

At nightfall on the 28th, in his headquarters, Samsonov distinctly heard the ever-closer approach of François's guns. He dispatched a telegram to General Jilinsky in Russia, informing him that he was leaving headquarters—not for the safety of the rear, but for the front. With this, he ordered his personal baggage to be sent back to Russia, and he cut communications with the rear.

Samsonov mounted his cavalry horse and bade farewell to the British attaché. Admitting that the situation was critical, he said that his place was at the front. Then he smiled at the attaché.

"The enemy has luck one day, we will have luck another," he said.

Reaching the front, Samsonov could do little more than order the general retreat of what remained of the Russian Second Army.

War is rarely a gentlemanly game, and World War I was as far from gentlemanly as any war ever gets. Retreat from battle does not neatly and chivalrously end the killing. Indeed, in retreat, an army is typically even more vulnerable than it is in attack. To retreat is to expose to the enemy the weakest part of an army: the rear. In the two-day Russian retreat from the Battle of Tannenberg, on August 29–30, the Germans took full advantage of every weak point. Of all Samsonov's units, the two corps of the center had fought longest, most bravely, and most effectively. They had led the advance, and now they were the last to withdraw, so they became the most fully enveloped in the great German net. All semblance of battle had been lost. War had become slaughter, nothing more, nothing less.

From the Front

Among the 92,000 Russian prisoners that the Germans captured were men of all ranks, including General N.N. Martos, commander of one of Samsonov's valiant center corps. General Ludendorff, whose Russian was fluent, took pleasure in taunting him with the prospect and promise of a German invasion. Hindenburg approached his prisoner differently, holding his "hands for a long time, begging me to calm myself," as Martos later recalled. Taking his leave of Martos, Hindenburg promised the return of his sword, bowed to him, and said, "I wish you happier days."

Some 30,000 Russians perished or were wounded at Tannenberg (compared to between 10,000 and 15,000 German casualties), among the last of which was General Alexander Samsonov. On the night of August 29, he and a few other officers were huddled in the woods, just seven miles from the Russian frontier. The Germans were all around them, so the group decided to proceed through the marshes—on foot, because the ground was too swampy for the horses.

The Russian officers stumbled and groped their way through the pitch-dark forest, holding hands to keep from becoming separated. Samsonov, an asthmatic, began to wheeze heavily. The group rested at one o'clock on the morning of August 30.

"The czar trusted me," Samsonov gasped out. "How can I face him after such a disaster?"

The general quietly rose. He walked off into the darkness. Then there was the crack of a single gunshot.

His faithful officers searched vainly in the dark, looking for their commander's body. It was no use. The search would have to wait until dawn, but with dawn came the Germans, and the officers were forced to abandon the search and continue their trek to the safety of the Russian frontier.

Defeat at the Masurian Lakes

The Masurian Lake district comprises 20,000 square miles of the southwestern corner of East Prussia (today, northeastern Poland), just to the south of the Baltic Sea and down to the Vistula River. It is a region of some 2,000 separate lakes in marshy ground punctuated by sand dunes. In this country, the First Army of Pavel Rennenkampf was deployed, well north of the disaster at Tannenberg.

By the start of September, when the German Eighth Army was marching to meet Rennenkampf after having crushed Samsonov, it had been reinforced by the three corps that Moltke had released from the West. Rennenkampf had been inching his way toward Samsonov when he heard of the Second Army's collapse; he reversed course and pulled back to the Masurian Lakes. He set his left flank among the lakes and strung out a defensive cordon north to the Baltic coast.

On September 5, in prelude to the battle proper, the German Eighth Army began hammering the southern end of the Russian First Army. In response, Rennenkampf ordered a general withdrawal on September 9.

Once again, it was Hermann von François who spearheaded the hard-driving German attack. His I Corps bore down on the retreating Rennenkampf, covering 77 miles in four days. To protect his left flank from this lightning drive, Rennenkampf counterattacked the German center on September 10. This spoiled the advance of the main portion of the Eighth Army, halting it for at least 48 hours and buying the Russians enough time to escape the fate of double envelopment that had destroyed the Second Army at Tannenberg.

Still, Rennenkampf's escape was hardly a victory. He had lost a number of men equal to what Samsonov had sacrificed at Tannenberg, about 125,000 killed, wounded, missing, or captured.

From the Front

A German patrol later found the body of Alexander Samsonov. Recognized as a Russian general officer, he was given a military burial at Willenburg. In 1916, with the aid of the International Red Cross, the general's widow recovered his body, which was reburied in Russia.

From the Front

In retreat from François, Rennenkampf proved that he could move quickly—at least, when his life depended on it. Some retreating First Army forces covered 55 miles in 50 hours.

German losses may have numbered as many as 40,000, although some authorities think this figure is too high. Most important, the First Battle of the Masurian Lakes had finished clearing the Russian invaders out of East Prussia.

At *Stavka,* the Russian Supreme Headquarters, General Jilinsky was removed as chief of staff and was replaced by Nikolai Russki, who had enjoyed success against the Austrians in Galicia. In the long run, the change in command would make little difference. Although Russia would fight on, the army would never recover from Tannenberg and the Masurian Lakes.

To Russia's allies, France and Britain, barely saved from destruction by a strategic victory at the First Battle of the Marne, the defeats on the Eastern Front came as cruel blows. In a matter of a few terrible days, the myth of the "Russian steamroller" had been shattered. By contrast, German spirits had been raised to a great height—a height sustained, however, by delusion. The stunning victories in the east obscured the terrible significance of the failure of the Schlieffen Plan in the west.

The Least You Need to Know

➤ Although outnumbered, the German army was staffed by officers and men who were better equipped and better trained than their Russian counterparts.

➤ The Russian practice of transmitting uncoded messages alerted the Germans to their plans—in detail—ensuring a terrible Russian loss at Tannenberg.

➤ Hermann François, difficult and even insubordinate, proved to be an officer of unbounded initiative whose vigor was responsible for much of Germany's success on the Eastern Front.

➤ The twin Russian disasters at Tannenberg and the Masurian Lakes were the result of poor training, inadequate supplies, poor leadership, faulty communication, and an astonishing lack of cooperation between the two commanding generals, Samsonov and Rennenkampf.

➤ The Russian defeats on the Eastern Front dismayed France and Britain, but gave the Germans an inflated confidence.

Chapter 9

Duel of Doomed Empires

In This Chapter

➤ Austria-Hungary's costly defeat in Galicia

➤ Austro-German cooperation

➤ Germany shifts its emphasis to the Eastern Front

➤ The Carpathian campaign

➤ The Germans unleash poison gas

➤ The Second Battle of the Masurian Lakes

The Battle of Tannenberg was the horrific and tragic outcome of an encounter between a waning empire and one that was on the rise. The battles between Russia and Austria-Hungary were different from those between Russia and Germany; both the realm of the Romanovs and the empire of the Hapsburgs were in decline and were surviving only on borrowed time. The leaders of both doomed empires saw the war as an opportunity for reinvigoration at best, or, at the very least, continued survival. They were in for a cruel surprise. The war that Austria-Hungary brought on did nothing to avoid the final destruction of both empires.

Austrian Priorities

Austria-Hungary was slow to respond to the realities of the war it had created. According to the Dual Empire's Plan B, the war was supposed to be limited to an offensive against Serbia, with three Austrian armies held in readiness to defend the Russian frontier. Austria-Hungary saw Serbia as its no. 1 adversary, with Russia as a secondary problem to be dealt with after Serbia had been taught its lesson in subjugation.

That was the plan.

The reality was that Austria-Hungary's first invasion of Serbia failed dismally (see Chapter 4, "The Black Hand"), and the Russians invaded East Prussia much sooner than expected. This initially deprived Austria-Hungary of Germany's support on the Eastern Front. Moreover, the Austrians had counted on two potential rivals, Italy and Romania, joining the cause of the Central Powers. Neither, however, decided to enter the war on the side of Austria-Hungary and Germany, which meant that both became yet another threat. Finally, Russia assembled large forces between Lublin and the Dniester River, menacing Galicia (Austrian Poland).

All of these factors dictated a shift from Plan B to Plan R, which required the transfer of an entire army from Serbia to Galicia. If the Austrians had enjoyed the benefit of early German support, they might have been able to concentrate more effectively on one front—either Serbia or Galicia. But the early support was not forthcoming, and the Austrians had to divide their forces. The time and energy required to shift from one plan to the other was draining.

Still, there were compelling reasons to expand the war so drastically. First, it was tactically important to defeat Russia in Galicia, north of the Carpathian Mountains, where there was more room to maneuver than there was in the mountains themselves. Second, the initial defeat at the hands of the Serbs was a terrible blow to Austro-Hungarian prestige; a successful offensive against the Russians in Galicia would bring an emotional recovery. Third, Austria-Hungary did want to cooperate with its German ally by relieving pressure on East Prussia.

As we saw in Chapter 7, "The Sun Sets in the East," however, the Galician offensive failed totally. In one of their few successes in the war, the Russians soundly defeated the Austrians at the Battle of Gnila-Lipa at the end of August. Although the Austrian Fourth Army responded vigorously with an attempted double envelopment of the Russian Fifth Army early in September, effective coordination among the Austrian commanders could not be achieved, and the Russians pushed the Austro-Hungarian forces further south, toward the Carpathians.

Desperate for room to maneuver, Austrian field marshal Franz Conrad von Hötzendorf ordered his Fourth Army to break off contact with the Russian Fifth Army and attack the Russian Third Army, which was pounding on the retreating Austrian Third Army. The result, on September 5, was the Battle of Rava-Russka—and

Voices of Battle

"We are ready, and the sooner the better for us."

—Austrian field marshal Conrad von Hötzendorf, to Germany's Baron Eckhardstein, on the eve of World War I

From the Front

Austrian losses in the Galician battles were more than a quarter million killed and wounded. About 100,000 Austro-Hungarian troops became prisoners of war. Russian losses were almost certainly similar.

yet another Russian victory. The Austrian Fourth Army managed to save itself, but the Austrian Third Army was being ground into dust. Field Marshal Conrad had no choice but to order a general retreat.

During September 12 through 26, the battered Austro-Hungarian forces withdrew a hundred miles, halting about 50 miles east of Cracow, Poland, having relinquished Galicia to the Russians. Now the Austro-Hungarian forces held only a narrow corridor between the Vistula River and the Carpathian Mountains and were encircled at the Przemsyl fortress.

Combatants

Count Franz Conrad von Hötzendorf (1852–1925) served as field marshal—the overall commander—of Austro-Hungarian forces during World War I, a role in which he was spectacularly unsuccessful.

Conrad was the son of an army officer and a graduate of the military academy who served in the Balkans and taught at the War Academy until his friendship with Archduke Franz Ferdinand helped him achieve promotion to Chief of Staff in 1906.

Conrad vigorously promoted the conflict that led to World War I, hoping primarily to squash rebellion in the Austro-Hungarian empire by punishing Serbia. When fighting developed on a large scale, however, Conrad proved wholly inadequate to lead his nation's forces. By 1915, Conrad was forced to subordinate himself to German command, and the following year he formally turned over the Austro-Hungarian forces to Paul von Hindenburg. By the end of the war, Conrad had been reduced to the rank of colonel in the Austrian Imperial Guard.

What had begun for Austria-Hungary as a war of aggression was now a desperate struggle for national survival. If the Russians moved quickly, pressing the pursuit of the retreating Austro-Hungarian armies, the two sides would be fighting for the very passes into the interior of Austria-Hungary itself.

A New Army Materializes

Except for the besieged fortress of Przemysl, Galicia was in Russian hands. Defeated by Serbia, defeated by Russia, badly battered, and displaying a morale that had sunk into a bloody abyss, the Austro-Hungarian armies were nevertheless still intact. And the Germans, having crushed the Russian Second and First armies at Tannenberg and the Masurian Lakes (see Chapter 8, "A Suicide"), were not about to abandon their ally. Besides, Silesia—present-day southwestern Poland, but at the time a province of Germany—was now vulnerable to Russian invasion. The new German chief of staff, Erich von Falkenhayn, decided to create a new army to bail out the Austrians. Units were withdrawn from the Eighth Army to create the Ninth Army, which was dispatched southward in a gigantic rail movement involving 750 trains. The new force would be under the direct command of General Hindenburg.

➢ Guessing the Russian Game

At about the time that the new German Ninth Army was en route to its staging area, on September 22, the Russian supreme headquarters, *Stavka*, decided to exploit its success in Galicia by launching an offensive from the so-called Polish Salient around Warsaw and Lodz into Silesia.

It was just as the Germans had guessed. But Hindenburg knew that before the Russians could launch their offensive, they would have to realign their armies, shuffling them about to relieve crowded conditions in Galicia and improve supply. Also, more strength would be required, and it would take some time for the Russians to build up sufficient numbers.

Hindenburg resolved to strike preemptively, before the Russians could organize their offensive. On September 28, he led the Ninth Army in a drive aimed at seizing the Vistula River crossings from Warsaw to the San River and, in the process, doing as much damage as possible to the Russian Northwest Army Group.

On September 30, the Ninth Army, supported by the Austrians on the south, hit the Russians west of the Vistula and fought relentlessly through October 9, by which time the Germans had attained the river south of Warsaw. But, as usual, Hindenburg was greatly outnumbered, pitting 18 German divisions against 60 Russian. By October 12, the Russians' superior numbers had succeeded in checking the German advance. Hindenburg then proved himself as skilled in retreat as he was in attack. He withdrew the Ninth Army in good order, leaving behind a swath of destruction—wrecked roads and railroads, leveled villages, burnt farms—that impeded the Russian pursuit. Not that a Russian pursuit ever amounted to much. The usual logistical problems and bureaucratic fumbling slowed the lumbering forces of the czar.

The Austro-German Advance Stalls

For their part, the Austrians had contributed predictably little to the offensive in southwest Poland. On paper, the Austro-Hungarian army looked very good. It was functionally diversified, possessing a good mix of infantry, cavalry, and artillery units, and it carried modern equipment into battle. But it suffered from two grave weaknesses. The first, mentioned in Chapter 3, "Blueprints for a Bloodletting," was the ethnic diversity of the forces, which reflected the ethnic and nationalist fragmentation of the disintegrating Dual Empire. This made communications difficult, and often deeply divided loyalties and compromised resolve.

The second problem was the inadequacy of training of officers as well as enlisted men. In contrast to the rigidly functional military culture of the Prussian-dominated German army, the Austro-Hungarian military served as much a social and decorative role as it did a combat function. Officers attained rank not through training and proof of competence, but through inheritance and birthright. High military rank was passed along much as the title of duke or prince might be.

Although the German as well as Austro-Hungarian armies had withdrawn to their original lines by late October, they were hardly defeated. The engagements they fought had cost the Russians heavily and had seriously delayed the Russian offensive into Silesia.

Hindenburg's performance was rewarded by Falkenhayn and the kaiser on November 1 with an appointment as commander-in-chief of the entire Austro-German Eastern Front. With the Western Front clearly hardened into stalemate by this time, however, there were no additional troops to spare for the Ninth Army, and Hindenburg was told to expect no reinforcements.

Hindenburg knew that he would have no chance against the strong Russian concentration southwest of Warsaw. In collaboration with Ludendorff, and with consummate skill, Hindenburg executed a strategy that substituted deft movement for numbers. He shifted northwest to the vicinity of Posen and Thorn, in the process searing another swath of devastation to bedevil and delay the Russians.

Battle at Lodz

The shift to the northwest had put the German Ninth Army in position to exploit a weakness in the Russian deployment. The Grand Duke Nicholas, in command of the Russian Northwest Army Group, had disposed the First and Second armies on the northern flank of the army group in preparation for the massed offensive. The German Ninth Army (which, after Hindenburg's elevation to command of the entire front, was now under the immediate leadership of the very able August von Mackensen) thrust itself between the Russian First and Second armies in the protracted Battle of Lodz, which began on November 11 and raged until December 6.

The First Army—still commanded by Rennenkampf, who had failed Samsonov at Tannenberg and who led his own force to disaster at the Masurian Lakes (see Chapter 8)—was utterly crushed, while the Second Army found itself in the embrace of a double envelopment. This maneuver, however, was ultimately foiled by a prompt *counterattack* by the Russian Fifth Army from the south and a hastily

Words of War

Counterattack is an offensive response to an enemy attack. It is not merely a defense against attack.

assembled mixed Russian force from the north. Although the counterattack arrested the German offensive, General Reinhard von Scheffer-Boyadel, who commanded the XXV Reserve Corps which had penetrated the gap between the two Russian armies, saved his force from encirclement by breaking through the vastly superior Russian counterattackers. Not only did he bring his soldiers through this trap, but he also managed to capture 16,000 Russian prisoners in the process, together with 64 Russian heavy guns.

Words of War

A **tactical victory** describes the attainment of short-term objectives in a given battle. A **strategic victory** describes the attainment of long-term, overall objectives. It is possible to attain a short-term objective at the cost of a long-term objective, and thereby lose a campaign or an entire war.

Because the Russians had halted the German offensive at great cost to themselves, Lodz had to be accounted a *tactical victory* for the forces of the czar; however, the battle also resulted in the Russians entirely abandoning their Silesian offensive. This made the battle a German *strategic victory*. Moreover, although German losses were high, at 35,000 killed or wounded, Russian losses were staggering, as usual. Although records were not kept, most military historians believe that at least 90,000 Russian soldiers were wounded or lost their lives. The actual number is probably even higher.

New Orders from the Kaiser

As 1914 drew to a close, thinking among the German High Command underwent a drastic revision. For nearly two decades, the kaiser as well as his commanders had been wedded to the Schlieffen Plan, which prescribed a quick victory in the west and therefore cast the east into a secondary role. But now that trench warfare had congealed the Western Front into deadly stalemate, a growing number among the German General Staff were thinking of the Eastern Front as the decisive theater of the war. In contrast to the west, warfare on this front was characterized by grand movements, and great gains were possible. Moreover, the Russians had proven to be a very different enemy from the French and the British. Their commanders had shown next to no regard for the realities of combat. Time after time, they ordered massive head-on charges against well-prepared defenses and superior firepower.

Hindenburg, Ludendorff, Colonel Hoffmann, and General Mackensen all passionately advocated launching a major strategic effort across the Vistula River to defeat Russia once and for all—to knock it out of the war. Falkenhayn, together with the commanders of the Western Front, argued for keeping the Eastern Front secondary.

In the end, actions, not arguments, spoke most convincingly. Hindenburg produced measurable positive results in the east, while in the west, the only results were casualties. By the end of 1914, the kaiser issued orders instructing Falkenhayn to make the Eastern Front the "theater of decision."

Carpathian Snows

The opening of 1915 saw a reorganization of German forces on the Eastern Front in conformity with the new emphasis on the east. At the direction of Falkenhayn, another new German army, the Southern Army, was created and placed under the command of General Alexander von Linsingen. The split that had developed between Falkenhayn and Hindenburg over the Western Front versus the Eastern Front was now renewed over the question of whether to concentrate on the north end of the Eastern Front or the south. Falkenhayn felt obliged to buoy up the faltering Austrians, so he created a *Southern* Army. Hindenburg worried that Russia would again advance into East Prussia, so, on his own authority, he created another new army, the Tenth Army, using four corps that had recently arrived from the Western Front.

As usual, the remarkable Hindenburg had analyzed the situation with great accuracy. That very winter, the Russians were creating a new Twelfth Army, which they intended to unite with the Russian Tenth Army in a fresh invasion of East Prussia. They did this with no knowledge of the army Hindenburg was forming at Königsberg.

In the meantime, the Southern Army, collaborating with the Austrians, was battling Russians in the snow-covered Carpathians from January through March 1915. The Russian objective was to march through the Carpathian passes onto the great Hungarian plains. The Austro-German objective was to prevent this and to relieve the fortress at Przemysl.

Fighting in the frozen mountains was exhausting for both sides. The Russians were commanded by the exceptionally capable General Aleksei A. Brusilov, certainly the best commander the Russians fielded during the war. For their part, the Austro-Hungarians showed remarkable tenacity in holding the mountain passes. However, as an offensive, the Austro-German operation failed, and Przemysl surrendered to the Russians on March 18.

When this happened, there was no longer any reason to fight the Russians in the mountains. Instead, the Austrian contingent established defensive positions on the Hungarian plains. This was sufficient to discourage a Russian invasion. As for the troops who remained dug into the Carpathians, the battle quickly reached a stalemate not unlike that of the Western Front. The difference was that troops here seemed to sense that slaughtering one another from entrenched positions was not productive. The offensive, therefore, simply petered out in frustration after a half-hearted Russian counteroffensive ending in April.

The Winter Battle

While armies struggled in the mountains to the south, Hindenburg and Ludendorff were planning to prove their contention that victory on the Eastern Front would be had in the north, not the south. Schlieffen, the late nineteenth-century German chief of staff who had formulated the now-abandoned war plan, was both a practical soldier and a respected military theorist. All German officers read and reread his *Cannae Studies*, a work devoted to the celebrated Battle of Cannae, which had been fought on August 3, 216 B.C.E. during the Second Punic War between Roman legions and the Carthaginian army of Hannibal.

From the Front

An early version of the Hague Convention—an attempt to outline the rules of "civilized" warfare—outlawed the use of "*armes poisonnees*" (poisoned weapons), which certainly included poison gas. A later version retracted this prohibition, so at the time of the war, there was no international prohibition against the weapon. After World War I, the Geneva Convention once again prohibited the use of "poisonous or asphyxiating gas" in war.

For centuries, the battle had been studied by military men as a perfect example of the double envelopment. Hannibal allowed the Romans to push back his center, and then, like some giant Venus flytrap, he slammed the jaws of the Carthaginian army upon the flanks of the advancing Roman legion. The result was the worst defeat a Roman army ever suffered—50,000 dead (including many of high rank) and another 4,500 captured, versus a mere 5,700 casualties for Hannibal.

Now Hindenburg and Ludendorff, who enjoyed on the Eastern Front what had been denied the generals on the Western Front—vast spaces in which to maneuver—proposed a double envelopment of the Russian Tenth Army on the model of Cannae.

A New Weapon

As Hannibal had lured the Romans to attack his center, so the Germans used their Ninth Army, east of Warsaw, to draw the Russians to Bolimov, about 30 miles west of the Polish capital. With the Russian attention concentrated here, the German Eighth and Tenth armies assumed positions for the main offensive in the region of the Masurian Lakes.

At Bolimov, by way of experiment, the Germans unleashed a new weapon: xylyl bromide (code named *T-Stoff*), a lachrymatory (tear producing) agent in specially modified artillery shells lobbed over to the Russians in an artillery barrage on January 31. Although some 18,000 poison gas canisters were fired, their effect was so inconsequential that the Russians didn't even report the innovation to the other Allies. Although xylyl bromide could be deadly if inhaled in sufficient concentrations, the Germans intended it more as harassment than as a lethal weapon. Presumably, too, the frigid temperatures on the battlefield prevented the gas from diffusing in the air or even affecting the men. In other battles, on the Western Front, the effects of more lethal forms of gas would be far more devastating (see Chapter 12, "Deadlock"), and "poison gas" would be remembered as one of the worst horrors of World War I.

Second Battle of the Masurian Lakes

The debut of poison gas in the Great War may have been less than spectacular, but the artillery barrage, together with a determined attack by the German Ninth Army toward the Sucha River, had succeeded in drawing Russian troops away from the Masurian Lakes area so that main German offensive preparations were completed in great secrecy. (The cost to the Ninth Army was high. Turned back by desperate Russian resistance, it lost over 20,000 killed.)

The Second Battle of the Masurian Lakes began on February 7. It would also be called simply "The Winter Battle" because it began in a brutal, blinding snowstorm, with the Germans hitting the Russian Tenth Army's left flank hard. On the next day, the German Tenth Army struck the Russian right flank, rolling it up.

The totally surprised Russians mounted a vigorous but hopeless defense and retreated 50 miles southeast to the Augustow Forest. On February 21, the Russian XX Corps, surrounded and battered, surrendered. Its heroic defense, however, had spoiled German hopes for another Cannae; the defense had occupied the Germans sufficiently to allow three other Russian Tenth Army corps to escape. Yet the defeat, if not total, was nevertheless devastating. The Russian Tenth Army suffered about 200,000 killed or wounded, and some 90,000 Russian soldiers were made prisoners.

The next day, February 22, the newly formed Russian Twelfth Army, under General Wenzel von Plehve, counterattacked Hindenburg's own right flank, bringing the German advance to a standstill after approximately 70 miles.

A Breakthrough

The Hindenburg offensive was no failure, but it hardly achieved the definitive victory that Hindenburg and Ludendorff had promised, and it certainly fell far short of being another Cannae. Come spring, Falkenhayn left headquarters to take personal overall command of the southern sector. While Hindenburg kept the Russians busy north of Warsaw, Falkenhayn dispatched the German Eleventh Army, under Mackenson and supported by several Austrian units, to attack Russian positions between the towns of Tarnow and Gorlice, to the southeast of Cracow and just north of the Carpathian foothills.

Beginning on May 2, after a four-hour artillery "preparation" (the military euphemism for a bombardment), the Austro-German forces punched through the Russian Third Army along a broad 28-mile front. This put the first crack in the Polish Salient, and the Austro-German forces continued to hammer away at that crack. On June 3, the fortress at Przemysl was retaken, and then the town of Lvov (Lemberg) was captured and occupied on June 22. During June 23–27, the Dniester River, to the southeast of Przemysl, was crossed.

The Long Retreat

Once cracked, the front that Russia had held quickly disintegrated. North of Warsaw, the new German Twelfth Army, under Max von Gallwitz, advanced toward Warsaw, sweeping the Russians before it. During August 4–7, the city was abandoned by the Russians, signaling the total collapse of the Russian front. The Polish Salient, which had projected far between East Prussia on the north and Galicia on the south, now melted away as the Russian armies, in complete disarray, retreated to the Bug River, a hundred miles east of Warsaw, by August 18.

And still the Austro-German forces pushed eastward. Brest Litovsk fell on August 25, followed by Grodno, to the north, on September 2. The ancient town of Vilna, in what is today Lithuania, was occupied on September 19. It marked the farthest extent of the German advance, a spectacular 300 miles since June.

A New Eastern Front, a New Commander

The summer and fall of 1915 capped the many disasters that had befallen Russian arms since 1914. During the first half of 1915, Russia lost about one million men, killed or wounded, and another million were captured.

From the Front

Total German and Austrian Eastern Front casualties for 1915 were about half those of the Russians: 500,000 killed or wounded—still a staggering number.

Voices of Battle

"God will provide."

—Russian Czar Nicholas II's customary reply when confronted with military losses or other crises

The Germans, under the leadership of Hindenburg and Ludendorff, had performed with brilliance even though they always had been outnumbered, and their armies had fought with bravery and great determination. In sharp contrast to the stasis on the Western Front, the armies in the east moved swiftly, despite poorly developed railways and primitive roads. Both sides endured the punishing rigors of brutal winter combat.

Although chronically outnumbered, the Germans had everything else the Russians lacked: excellent leadership, a high degree of training and discipline, superb weaponry, accurate intelligence and reconnaissance, and an ability to move quickly, precisely, and with the coordination of disparate units. Lacking leaders of genius and manned by diverse peoples with divided loyalties, the Austro-Hungarians fared far less impressively than the Germans, but once they began operating in support of the Germans, they proved useful.

The new Russian front was 300 miles east of where it had been at the beginning of 1915. Grand Duke Nicholas, in overall command of the Russian armies, miraculously managed to stave off the massive encirclement—the ultimate Cannae—that Hindenburg and Ludendorff had hoped to achieve. But Czar Nicholas II did not see the Grand Duke as the savior of the army. The czar removed him from command of the Eastern Front and banished him to the secondary Caucasus front to fight the Turks. In his place, he nominated a new overall commander: himself. With this, he opened a new chapter of Russian disaster and the last chapter of his own reign as czar of all the Russias.

> ### The Least You Need to Know
>
> ➤ No single nation was more responsible for the start of war than Austria-Hungary, which sowed its own destruction by its bellicose actions.
>
> ➤ In view of Hindenburg and Ludendorff's victories against the Russians, the German high command temporarily shifted much of its focus from the Western Front to the Eastern Front.
>
> ➤ Austro-Hungarian forces fared poorly against the Russians until they began coordinating operations closely with the Germans.
>
> ➤ After the Second Battle of the Masurian Lakes ("The Winter Battle"), Czar Nicholas II, incompetent as a military as well as a political leader, assumed personal command of the Russian army—a move that sealed its doom.

Chapter 10

The Sick Man and Serbia

In This Chapter

➤ Why Turkey entered the war

➤ Turkey's ill-fated Caucasus campaign

➤ Austro-German victory against Serbia

➤ The fall of Serbia

➤ The Greek role in the war

In 1914, Turkey was still called the Ottoman Empire and its government was the Sublime Porte, grandiose names that dated from the fifteenth- and sixteenth-century heyday of the empire. In those days, it had encompassed most of southeastern Europe to the very gates of Vienna and included the region of present-day Hungary, Serbia, Bosnia, Romania, Greece, and Ukraine. In the Middle East, the Ottoman realm included Iraq, Syria, Israel, and Egypt; in North Africa, it reached as far west as Algeria. In addition, it took in most of the Arabian Peninsula.

The empire began its long decline by the end of the sixteenth century. Under a succession of despotic, corrupt, and incompetent sultans, many infamous for a degenerate sadism that was eclipsed only by their naked greed, the Ottoman Empire existed in a state of perpetual disintegration. By the nineteenth century, it was routinely referred to as the "Sick Man of Europe," and what was left of its imperial holdings tended to fall into the hands of whatever major European power was nimble enough to catch it.

This chapter tells the story of Turkey's entry into the war and how it affected the war's Balkan Front.

The Turkish Connection

Throughout its long history, the Ottoman Empire had been periodically swept by reform movements, most of which quickly failed until the Young Turk Revolution of 1908. This reform effort installed progressive-minded young men, most of whom were military officers, into influential positions within the government. They increasingly sought connections with the great powers of Europe and, being military men, eagerly gravitated into the German orbit.

Young Turks

Within a year of the 1908 revolution, the Turkish government was chiefly under the control of the Young Turks. Germany seized this opportunity to gain an increasingly powerful influence over Turkey. The Turkish army employed a large number of German military instructors, and Enver Pasha, the Turkish officer who emerged as the leader of the Young Turks, became avid in his belief that an alliance with Germany would serve Turkey well. He especially sought the protection that it would provide against the continual threat posed by Turkey's ancient enemy, Russia, which now menaced the Dardanelles.

The Dardanelles, a narrow strait in northwestern Turkey linking the Aegean Sea with the Sea of Marmara, has always been of tremendous strategic and economic importance, not only as the portal to Istanbul, but also as a means of passage between the Black Sea and the Mediterranean Sea. For Russia, it was the only *warm-water outlet* to the rest of the world.

It was Enver Pasha who persuaded the grand vizier, Said Halim Pasha, nominal head of the Ottoman government, to make a secret treaty with Germany. It bound Turkey to a military alliance if Germany had to take Austria-Hungary's side against Russia. This represented a great diplomatic achievement for Germany because both Austria-Hungary and Russia had frequently warred with Turkey, and both coveted Turkish possessions. The idea of Turks and Austro-Hungarians fighting as allies was novel, to say the least.

> **CHARGE!!**
>
> **Words of War**
>
> In northern countries subject to frozen winters, a **warm-water outlet** or **warm-water port** is one open year round.

The Flight of the Goeben *and the* Breslau

During that fateful August of 1914, when England suddenly and unexpectedly seemed about to enter the war, the Turks briefly questioned the wisdom of the secret alliance they had just concluded. England had long served as a kind of unofficial protector of Turkish interests on the sea, especially where routes to India, Asia, the Mediterranean, and the Suez Canal were concerned. However, a British action erased any lingering Turkish doubts about the alliance.

Before the war, Turkey had contracted with British shipyards to build two dreadnought-class battleships. Financed through voluntary donations by the Turkish people, the ships were powerful symbols of a new Turkish pride. On August 3, 1914, just as the vessels were nearing completion, the British government commandeered them. To compound the diplomatic damage caused by this action, Britain declined to offer any apology or definitive payment—save for a vague promise to provide compensation at some later date.

The very next day, August 4, brought the British ultimatum to Germany concerning the neutrality of Belgium. With Germany's defiance of the ultimatum, Britain was propelled into the war. On that day, the German battle cruiser *Goeben* and the light cruiser *Breslau* were cruising in the Mediterranean, closely followed by a British battle cruiser squadron. At nightfall, the two German vessels managed to steal away from the British. However, the commanding officer of the *Goeben*, Vice Admiral Wilhelm A.T. Souchon, realized that ultimate escape from the Mediterranean was impossible. Accordingly, he decided to seek refuge with Germany's Turkish ally—and, on the way to the Dardanelles straits, he took the opportunity to shell the French North African ports of Bone and Philipville, from which French colonial soldiers were embarking for transfer to the Western Front in Europe.

The ships reached the Dardanelles on August 10, in direct violation of international treaties forbidding warships from transiting the straits. The German government then ceremoniously presented the *Goeben* and the *Breslau* to the Turkish navy—and not just the ships. Admiral Souchon and the crews formally joined the navy of Germany's ally and thus continued to man the vessels.

Voices of Battle

"I can recall no great sphere of policy about which the British Government was less completely informed than the Turkish."

—Winston Churchill, on the situation in the Middle East, 1914, quoted in Barbara Tuchman, *The Guns of August*, 1962

Turkey's "Declaration"

At this point, Turkey had not yet entered the war. A majority of the cabinet wanted Turkey to remain neutral—at least until it became clear which side looked like the winner. Enver Pasha, now Turkey's minister of war, saw opportunity for himself and his country in taking an active part in the conflict. In October, he authorized the *Goeben* and the *Breslau* to lead the Turkish fleet across the Black Sea to bombard the Russian ports of Odessa, Sevastopol, and Theodosia without warning. The attacks during October 29–30 also sank several Russian ships.

This assault constituted Turkey's declaration of war. Enver Pasha had maneuvered his nation into a position from which there was no escape. On November 1, Russia responded with a formal declaration of war against Turkey. The western Allies briefly and ineffectually bombarded the outer forts of the Dardanelles on November 3 and then formally declared war against Turkey on November 5.

Strictly as a military force, Turkey did not seem to present a great threat to the Allies. Since the beginning of the twentieth century, Turkey had fought three wars—and had won none of them. The troops, poorly fed and erratically paid (the paymaster was at least six months in arrears), were, many of them, physically unfit and showed low morale. German military instructors had done much to train junior officers, but the instructors did not reach the upper ranks, and these officers were almost universally incompetent. Nevertheless, the loss of the Dardanelles was a serious blow to the Allied cause. Without it, Russia was isolated, cut off from badly needed western sources of supply.

Combatants

Enver Pasha (1881–1922) was an organizer of the Young Turk Revolution and played an instrumental role in deposing Sultan Abdülhamid II. In 1911, when Turkey went to war with Italy, Enver organized the Ottoman resistance in Libya. He led a coup in Constantinople in January 1913 and became chief of the General Staff of the Ottoman army, leading it to defeat in the Second Balkan War.

In 1914, now minister of war, Enver Pasha engineered the alliance that brought Turkey into World War I on the side of Germany. His ultimate objective was to unite the Turkic peoples of Russian Central Asia with the Ottoman Turks. This ambition prompted Enver's disastrous Caucasus campaign, in which he lost most of the Third Army, a defeat from which Turkey never fully recovered. Nevertheless, Enver himself regained a large measure of prestige after the Allied forces withdrew from the Dardanelles in 1916 (see Chapter 14, "The Gallipoli Disaster").

With the defeat of the Central Powers in 1918, Enver fled to Germany, where he met the Bolshevik leader Karl Radek and subsequently traveled to Moscow, where he sought aid in overthrowing Mustafa Kemal (Atatürk), known as the father of modern Turkey. The Soviets turned down this plan, but they did endorse an expedition to Turkistan, where Enver was to help organize the Central Asian republics. In 1921, Enver Pasha turned about face and joined a rebellion against the Soviets. He was killed in action against the Red Army.

Action in the Caucasus

Enver Pasha saw the war as a golden opportunity for dealing with Turkey's traditional foe, Russia, once and for all. Enver had figured prominently in Turkey's three twentieth-century wars, and the fact that none of these had resulted in victory did not discourage him now. He planned a campaign against Russia in the Caucasus Mountains, the natural border between Turkey and Russia. Although Turkey's long-time German military adviser, General Otto Liman von Sanders, counseled against the Caucasian invasion, Germany raised no official objection to it. From the German point of view, anything—no matter how ill-conceived—that would occupy Russian troops and draw them away from the Eastern Front was welcome.

Enver assumed personal command of 95,000 poorly equipped and poorly trained troops during November and December. His objective was to destroy the Russian Caucasian army and to expose south Georgia to invasion. Enver believed that Turkish victory here would trigger a widespread Muslim uprising throughout Russia's southern provinces.

The campaign had little going for it and much going against it. The Caucasian terrain was most forbidding, with an average elevation of 6,500 feet and many peaks reaching 16,000 feet. Six months out of the year, the Caucasus were totally snowbound. Supply was impractical, and living off the rugged, often frozen landscape impossible. Although it was true that the Russian soldier was generally as ill-prepared as the Turkish, the Russian leadership in the Caucasian theater was uncharacteristically adept. Enver Pasha was outgeneraled.

On December 29, the Battle of Sarikamish resulted in the arrest of the Turkish advance over the mountains. The defeat came with severe losses. Of the 95,000 men who had marched with Enver Pasha, only 18,000 returned to Erzurum. Most of the Turkish casualties had been incurred during the disastrous retreat back through the icy mountain passes.

The Turkish army would never fully recover from the doomed Caucasian campaign, and its effectiveness as an offensive force was compromised for the remainder of the war.

From the Front

At the Battle of Sarikamish, the Turks suffered an 81 percent casualty rate. Conventionally, a 10 percent casualty rate is considered tantamount to disaster.

Serbia Resists

Of course, World War I was triggered by the action of Serbian nationalists—the assassination of Archduke Francis Ferdinand and his wife in Sarajevo, Bosnia—but Serbia itself went to great lengths to avoid war. To Austria-Hungary's ultimatum following the assassination, Serbian officials made a downright servile response (see Chapter 4, "The Black Hand"), but to no avail. As the Dual Monarchy saw it, Serbia was neither more nor less than a fitting object for punishment, which would discourage the nationalist movements that were tearing apart the ethnically varied Austro-Hungarian Empire.

If Austro-Hungarian politicians failed to see Serbia as a fiercely proud and determined little nation, the Austro-Hungarian military was even more dismissive. General Oskar Potiorek, commander of the Austro-Hungarian troops slated to invade Serbia, declared that the conquest of Serbian "pig farmers" would be a quick and simple matter. As we saw in Chapter 7, "The Sun Sets in the East," however, the initial Austrian invasion was repulsed.

In early September 1914, a second offensive was mounted; by December 2, Austrians occupied Belgrade, the Serbian capital. Despite chronic shortages of ammunition, the Serbs fiercely counterattacked on December 3, driving the Austrians out of Belgrade and, by December 15, out of Serbia altogether.

It was a most ignominious defeat for the Austro-Hungarian army, and Oskar Potiorek was relieved of command.

Bulgaria Joins Austria and Germany

The respite for Serbia would be brief. After Turkey joined the war on the side of the Central Powers, the Allies recognized that Serbia was not just a pawn in a deadly game of international chess, but occupied what was now a highly strategic location astride the land route to Turkey. With the British navy largely in control of the Mediterranean supply routes, the Central Powers were determined to seize Serbia to open an overland supply artery to its ally.

From the Front

Bulgaria mobilized a total force of 650,000 troops when it entered World War I. This was 12 percent of the nation's total population—almost a quarter of the male population.

The Central Powers' plan to subjugate Serbia was greatly aided on September 6, 1915, when Bulgaria threw in its lot with Germany and its allies. Bulgaria had been holding itself neutral in the war, nervously waiting to see which side would offer it the greater advantage. The victories of Hindenburg and Ludendorff in Poland were highly persuasive, as was, conversely, the Allied failure to open the Dardanelles (see Chapter 14). Bulgaria, which felt cheated of territorial gain in the two Balkan Wars of 1912 and 1913, eyed Serbia as a potential acquisition. After joining the Central Powers, then, Bulgaria contributed four divisions to a tripartite force of 330,000 Germans, Austro-Hungarians, and Bulgarians poised to invade Serbia.

Serbia's western allies, France and England, urgently advised Serbia to offer Bulgaria territorial concessions in Macedonia, an appeasement that would likely stave off the attack. By this point, however, Serbia had invested too much blood in defending itself to yield now. The country was determined to fight it out as best it could.

The invasion was put under the overall command of German General August von Mackensen. In its broad strokes, it was a simple plan. Two armies, the Austrian Third and German Eleventh, would attack Serbia across the Save and Danube Rivers. Shortly after this, another two armies would attack from Bulgaria.

The Austro-German contingent crossed the rivers on October 7, 1915, and marched into Belgrade just two days later. In the face of this advance, the Serbian army made an orderly retreat into the interior, pursuing a *scorched earth policy* as it went, destroying depots, roads, and bridges to deprive the enemy of their use.

Words of War

Scorched earth policy describes the practice of deliberately destroying crops, food supplies, and other facilities to prevent an invading enemy from using them.

Combatants

August von Mackensen (1849–1945) was one of Germany's very best field commanders. Although not of a military family (he was the son of a land agent, whose ancestors were Scots), Mackensen joined the elite Death's Head Hussar regiment in 1869 and served with distinction during the Franco-Prussian War of 1871. He was appointed to the General Staff in 1882 and fought in all the major engagements on the Eastern Front in World War I. His final campaign of the war was the consolidation of German control over Romania during December 1916–January 1917.

Mackensen retired from the army in 1920 and became involved in the Nazi Party and government in 1933. He was not active in the German government during World War II, which he lived through in retirement.

The Bulgarian First Army was to squeeze the Serbian forces between itself and the Austro-German armies, while the Bulgarian Second Army swung round from the south to block any reinforcement that might be forthcoming from Greece—which, however, had thus far proved reluctant to help. The Second Army was also supposed to prevent French and British contingents, which landed at Solonika on October 5, from coming to the aid of Serbia.

From the Front

From the perspective of the Western Allies, the Serbian Front was a kind of military exile. French General Maurice P.E. Sarrail was sent there because of his extreme political views. After Joffre relieved him of command on the Western Front, Sarrail went to Paris, where he spread his radical socialist gospel and fomented something approaching political rebellion. More to get him out of the picture than for any other reason, the French high command dispatched him to the Serbian Front.

The Western Allies Far from Home

Two small Allied contingents had arrived at the Greek-controlled Macedonian port of Salonika but ultimately contributed nothing to the fight. General Maurice P.E. Sarrail's French force marched up the Vardar Valley but was turned back by superior Bulgarian forces. Bryan T. Mahon, commanding a British contingent, reached the Bulgarian border and was beaten back. These Allied gestures of aid were too little too late. As a result, Allied troops remained bottled up in Salonika for the rest of the war.

Words of War

Typhus, an infectious, debilitating, and often fatal disease caused by bacteria transmitted primarily by lice, was among the most common afflictions of World War I soldiers. Of the 65 million troops mobilized between 1914 and 1918, about 8 million were killed in battle, and an additional 2 million succumbed to disease.

Doom and Defeat of Serbia

The Serbs were left to fend for themselves, and while Serbian Field Marshal Radomir Putnik managed to keep his army from being enveloped by the massively superior invasion forces, he could do nothing to fend off two even deadlier enemies: exhaustion and *typhus*—although the Allies did send hospital units to help the Serbs combat the latter.

The ever-dwindling number of survivors sought to evade capture by withdrawing into the mountains of Montenegro and Albania. There, however, in mid-November, they found themselves among ancient tribal enemies who attacked with a ferocity even greater than the political enemies who had invaded the country. Putnik lost 100,000 men killed or wounded. An astounding 160,000 had been captured. The handful who escaped either of these fates and the ravages of disease found their way to Allied ships, which ferried them to the island of Corfu. Here they were interned in squalid refugee camps. They remained there until they were re-formed to join the Allied ranks in Salonika, where they would fight in the Salonika campaign (see Chapter 14).

By the end of 1915, Austria occupied both Serbia and Montenegro.

The Greek Situation

Throughout 1914 and 1915, Greece maintained a murky and tenuous neutrality, which typified the confusion that reigned in this corner of the war. King Constantine was personally in favor of joining the war on the side of the Central Powers, but his prime minister, Eleutherios Venizelos, was strongly pro-Allied. Venizelos pointed out that Greece was bound by a mutual defense treaty to support Serbia if it was attacked by Bulgaria. The king countered that the treaty required Serbia to provide 150,000 men to fight Bulgaria. Beleaguered by the Austro-German forces, Serbia was hardly in a position to commit that number of troops, so the treaty could not be activated.

It was Prime Minister Venizelos who gave the French and British permission to use Solonika, the Macedonian port controlled by Greece, to move units from Gallipoli (see Chapter 14) to march to the aid of the Serbians. Two days after this was done, however, on October 7, Venizelos was forced to resign for violating the Greek king's official neutrality policy.

Not to be daunted, Venizelos established a rival government in Thessaloniki in October 1916. In June 1917, the Western Allies then engineered the ouster of King Constantine and installed Venizelos as prime minister of an officially reunited—but still, in fact, bitterly divided—Greece. Acting on the Allies' promise of territorial gains from Turkey, Venizelos then ended Greek neutrality and brought his nation into the war on the side of the Triple Entente.

For now, however, in 1915, the outlook on the Balkan and Turkish fronts, as on the Eastern Front, was especially grim for the Allies. While the war was bitterly stalemated on the Western Front, the Central Powers were steadily gaining ground in the East.

The Least You Need to Know

➤ The new "Young Turk" regime ruling the Ottoman Empire saw an alliance with Germany as a way to revive and strengthen the nation long called the "Sick Man of Europe," and Germany was eager to use Turkey as a base of naval operations in the Mediterranean.

➤ War Minister Enver Pasha led the Turkish army to disaster against the Russians in the Caucasus campaign. The Turks suffered a crushing defeat from which they would never recover.

➤ Austria-Hungary suffered a series of humiliating defeats against Serbia; once Austria-Hungary was joined by Germany and Bulgaria, however, Serbia was doomed, and its army was all but destroyed.

➤ Greece's King Constantine tried to keep his nation neutral in the war, but his prime minister, Eleutherios Venizelos, engineered a coup that sent Greece into the Allied camp.

A World War

We have seen how a political assassination in an obscure corner of the Balkans triggered a conflict that engulfed all the major powers of Europe—and many of the minor powers, too. But the conflict immediately became even wider because the world of 1914 was a world of colonial empires. All the major European powers had far-flung imperial possessions, which were now transformed into distant battlefields.

The colonies were tied to their European possessors by sea routes, which were defended by navies, so World War I became a naval war as well as a land war. This chapter covers the early years of the colonial struggle as well as the opening of the war at sea.

Sea Power

Over the centuries, Britain's geographical status as an island nation served as a stalwart defense against invasion. But physical isolation also had a downside. Britain could not be self-sufficient agriculturally or in terms of many of the raw materials required by its highly developed industries. The country was heavily dependent on imports and international trade to sustain its economy and to feed its people. For this reason, Britain developed a great commercial fleet and the most formidable navy in the world.

At the outbreak of war, Britain had 29 *capital ships* in service, with an additional 13 under construction. Its closest rival was Germany, with 18 ready and 9 in the works. Both powers wanted to avoid a major sea confrontation until more of their fleet was ready for service.

British Objectives

At the start of the war, the British deployed their navy to protect key trade routes. Given the island's vulnerability to strangulation by blockade, it was a sound strategy. Until overwhelming superiority could be achieved, Britain held offensive operations in check.

German Strategy

The Germans hoped to avoid a confrontation between surface capital ships. Their navy would be used to lay mines in key enemy harbors and their submarines would attack merchant ships as well as Royal Navy vessels in an effort to chip away at Britain's numerical superiority. After a prolonged program of such attacks, it was hoped, a major surface confrontation could take place on more equal terms.

Words of War

A **capital ship** is the largest and most powerful warship of any given era in naval history. The capital ship of World War I was the battleship.

Battle at Helgoland Bight

Even early in the war, the British did not entirely rule out offensive operations. On August 28, 1914, British light cruisers ventured into German home waters to provoke a fight. German cruisers took the bait and bore down on the British ships. At this point, a battle cruiser squadron under Admiral Sir David Beatty appeared and opened fire. Four German light cruisers were sunk, and a thousand German sailors were killed or captured. The British suffered substantial damage to one ship and lost 35 sailors.

The U-Boat War Begins

Beatty's action succeeded in bottling up the German surface fleet, which dared not venture beyond its home waters. Instead, emphasis was put on U-boat—submarine— operations. For sailors, the submarine service was the most hazardous in the navy, as well as the most arduous and uncomfortable. Yet it was also the most effective.

On September 22 a single German submarine, the *U-9*, operating off the Dutch coast, sank three British cruisers, the *Aboukir*, the *Hogue*, and the *Cressy*, in a single hour. Then, on October 7, came a strike much closer to home. A U-boat sailed into the anchorage of Loch Ewe, on the west coast of Scotland, damaging several craft. A few days later, on October 15, the British cruiser *Hawke* was torpedoed and sunk.

The Germans mounted a U-boat raid on Scapa Flow at the northern tip of Scotland. No British vessels were lost, but the British Grand Fleet had to be transferred to an alternate station while vast submarine nets, underwater structures intended to block passage of U-boats, were installed at Scapa.

The principal weapon of the U-boat was the *torpedo*, a long, cigar-shaped, self-propelled projectile that was launched from the submarine while submerged. The submarine didn't even have to surface to take aim on its prey. U-boats were equipped with periscopes, with which the captain could sight an enemy vessel and take aim against it.

In addition to firing torpedoes, specially equipped submarines could deploy contact mines. These were typically laid in key anchorages and harbors and would explode when struck by a surface vessel. On October 27, the British battleship *Audacious* was sunk by a mine that had been laid by a U-boat.

The very advantage of the U-boat, its stealth, would also prove its greatest liability. The idea of striking without warning was repugnant to belligerent as well as neutral nations. In the United States, submarine warfare increasingly turned public opinion against Germany. This intensified when a policy of *unrestricted submarine warfare* was instituted against merchant and passenger vessels entering a defined war zone. International naval conventions permitted attacks on enemy merchant and passenger vessels, provided that warning was given first so that passengers and crew could safely abandon ship. Under the policy of unrestricted submarine warfare, no such warning was given. To Americans—and others—this seemed a singularly immoral and barbaric practice. Ultimately, it would be instrumental in propelling the United States into the war on the side of the Allies.

Words of War

A **torpedo** is a self-propelled underwater projectile equipped with an explosive charge. It can be launched from submerged submarines as well as from surface vessels and even aircraft. **U-boat** is an abbreviation of the German *Unterseeboot* (undersea boat) and is a synonym for submarine.

Words of War

Unrestricted submarine warfare describes the naval war policy instituted by Germany during much of World War I; it gave German U-boat captains a mandate to torpedo Allied merchant and passenger craft without prior warning.

High Seas Fleet Breakout

While the submarine war raged, Admiral Franz von Hipper decided to break out of home waters with the battle cruisers of the German High Seas Fleet for a lightning sortie (advance in force) across the North Sea to raid the British coast. The towns of Scarborough and Hartlepool were shelled, resulting in the loss of many civilian lives.

The Battle of Dogger Bank

Hipper hit and ran, getting his cruisers safely back to his home port. Encouraged, he made another sortie in January 1915 but was intercepted on the 24th at Dogger Bank, midway between England and Germany. The British navy had intercepted German radio traffic, and British admiral Beatty sailed with five battle cruisers to meet Hipper's three. Both squadrons were accompanied by various lighter vessels.

Voices of Battle

"Fear of a break (with the United States) must not hinder us from using this weapon (the U-boat) that promises success."

—Henning von Holtzendorf, German admiral, to German government officials, 1917

The German commander attempted to flee, but Beatty, whose ships were faster, overtook him, sinking the cruiser *Blücher* and damaging the two other cruisers, including the admiral's flagship, *Seydlitz*. After Beatty's own flagship, *Lion*, was damaged, a failure in communication caused the British to break off the attack, allowing Hipper to escape.

Although two of the three German cruisers survived to fight another day, the engagement did result in an order from the kaiser to avoid all further risks of losing major surface ships.

The East Asiatic Squadron

The Germans' most formidable surface force was not on the Atlantic, but on the Pacific, in the form of the East Asiatic squadron, which was equipped primarily with modern fast cruisers, including the heavy cruisers *Scharnhorst* and *Gneisenau,* and the light cruisers *Nürnberg, Emden,* and *Leipzig* under the general command of Admiral Graf Maximilian von Spee. The British were slow to respond to the threat posed by the squadron, and for the first four months of the war, Spee preyed upon merchant shipping on the British trade routes as well as troopships on their way to Europe or the Middle East from India, New Zealand, or Australia.

From August to November 1914, the *Emden,* under Captain Karl von Müller, was detached from the East Asiatic squadron for service in the Indian Ocean. The *Emden* sank merchant vessels in the Bay of Bengal; bombarded Madras, India, on September 22; and harassed the approaches to Sri Lanka (then called Ceylon). By the time the Australian cruiser *Sydney* finally damaged it so severely that Captain Muller ordered it scuttled to avoid capture off the Cocos Island on November 9, the *Emden* had sunk 15 Allied ships.

While the *Emden* was wreaking havoc in the Indian Ocean, Spee's main squadron, now augmented by the light cruisers *Leipzig* and *Dresden,* steamed toward the Chilean coast. Unknown to Spee, Admiral Sir Christopher Cradock had sailed out from the Atlantic, with two obsolescent heavy cruisers, the *Monmouth* and *Good Hope,* and one light cruiser, *Glasgow,* in addition to a cruiser hastily converted from a merchant vessel, to hunt down the East Asiatic squadron. Cradock also had a predreadnought battleship, *Canopus,* but against admiralty orders, he did not sail with it, believing that the slow old ship would only impede his pursuit.

The squadrons sighted one another at Coronel, off the southern coast of Chile. What happened next, on November 1, 1914, was a hard lesson in the cold mathematics of war. In terms of numbers, the British and the Germans were fairly matched, but the older British vessels were outgunned by the much newer German ships. Cradock's biggest guns were a pair of 9.2-inchers on his flagship, the *Good Hope,* whereas Spee's *Scharnhorst* and *Gneisenau* had sixteen 8.2-inch guns between them. Although the British collectively had more light guns than the Germans had, these were never brought to bear because Spee, with great skill, foiled Cradock's every effort to get close enough to use them. In the meantime, from beyond the Britishers' range, Spee battered Cradock's squadron with the big guns of his two heavy cruisers.

The toll on the British was terrible. Two heavy cruisers sank with all hands, including Cradock. Only the light cruiser the *Glasgow* and the auxiliary cruiser (converted from the merchant ship) the *Otranto* escaped.

German Disaster at the Falklands

Flushed with his success, Spee steamed toward Port Stanley, in the Falkland Islands, to raid the British wireless facilities and coaling stations there. Unknown to the German admiral, however, a British squadron—including the battle cruisers *Invincible* and *Inflexible,* each fitted with eight mammoth 12-inch guns, and six other cruisers, all under the command of Vice Admiral Sir F. D. Sturdee—was just now refueling there.

Spee attacked on December 8. His ships as well as his crews were battle-weary and, in any case, were outgunned as well as outperformed by the newer, faster British ships. Sturdee gave chase, firing his big guns at very long range. The *Scharnhorst,* with Spee on board, was sunk first. The *Gneisenau, Nürnberg,* and *Leipzig* followed her to the bottom.

The British ships had fired from well beyond the range of the German vessels. Twenty-five British sailors suffered injury. No British ships were significantly damaged. Twenty-two hundred German sailors died.

Only the light cruiser *Dresden* escaped Sturdee, remaining at large for three months before its captain ran up the white flag off the Juan Fernández Islands on March 14, 1915, evacuated his ship, and scuttled it by blowing up its main ammunition magazine.

Lusitania Lost!

The Battle of the Falklands put an end to commerce raiding on the high seas by German surface ships. For the British, this was a tremendous naval achievement. However, the German U-boat fleet was just beginning to intensify its efforts.

Combatants

Graf (Count) Maximilian von Spee (1861–1914) joined the Imperial German Navy in 1878 and by 1914 had attained the rank of vice admiral. During 1887–1888, Spee was commander of the port of the Cameroons, a German colony. He later held key positions in weapons development and in 1908 became Chief of Staff on the North Sea Command. In 1912, he was given command of the German East Asian Cruiser Squadron.

The victory that Spee achieved against Sir Christopher Cradock off Coronel, Chile, in November 1914 stunned the British, who were amazed not only by the awesome effectiveness of Spee's gunnery and seamanship, but also by his ability to fight so well so far from home. After the Coronel battle, Spee became the object of the British Admiralty's personal vendetta. At the Falkland Islands, on December 8, 1914, Spee lost the *Scharnhorst*, the *Gneisenau*, the *Nürnberg*, and the *Leipzig*. The admiral perished in this battle, along with his two sons and 2,200 other German seamen. In 1934, the Germans named a modern pocket battleship, *Graf Spee*, in his honor.

Both the German and the British navies devoted more effort to disrupting one another's high seas commerce than they did to directly fighting each other. With the outbreak of war, Britain set up a blockade of Germany. That nation was served by only two trade routes: via the English Channel and the Dover Straits, or around the northern tip of Scotland. The British laid a minefield in the Dover Straits, allowing a very narrow lane of passage that made interception easy. The region north of Scotland, however, was vast and required a full-time patrol.

After the German surface raiders were sunk at the Battle of the Falklands, U-boats were widely assigned to attack the British merchant marine. On October 20, 1914, the British steamship *Glitra* was torpedoed. Other sinkings followed. On January 30, 1915, two Japanese liners, the *Tokomaru* and the *Ikaria,* were sunk. Whereas the early attacks on the British vessels had been preceded by warnings so that passengers and crew could evacuate, the attacks on the Japanese ships came without warning.

On February 4, 1915, the Germans announced that they would regard the waters around the British Isles as a war zone in which all Allied merchant ships were to be destroyed, and in which no ship, whether enemy or not, would be immune. This included the ships of neutral nations, such as the United States.

Not that U-boats always escaped scot-free. Countermeasures were soon developed: Antisubmarine nets erected in harbors were very effective at trapping and even disabling the boats, and innocent-looking merchant ships were often armed with newly developed depth bombs or depth charges, which could destroy a U-boat if exploded sufficiently close to it. And while it was true that U-boats were invisible once they submerged, British scientists developed hydrophones, underwater microphones that could locate a U-boat by the sound of its engine and the churning of the water by its "screw," or propeller.

Worst of all, unrestricted submarine warfare was a propaganda disaster that turned the public opinion of neutral nations against Germany. This was demonstrated spectacularly on May 7, 1915, when the British liner *Lusitania,* bound from New York to Liverpool, was torpedoed and sunk. Of its nearly 2,000 civilian passengers, 1,198 people perished, including 128 U.S. citizens.

This single incident pushed the United States to the brink of war, but President Wilson demurred and preserved neutrality by sending nothing more than some strongly worded protests to Germany.

Even after the *Lusitania* was sunk and war with the United States was only narrowly averted, Germany persisted in attacking Allied passenger shipping. On August 17, the *Arabic* was sunk, resulting in more American deaths and a new U.S. protest. The Germans now promised to ensure the safety of passengers before sinking any more liners, but it then torpedoed and sank the *Hesperia,* on September 18, again without warning. After this, at the insistence of German diplomats, the navy agreed to suspend U-boat activity in the English Channel and west of the British Isles.

Empires Far Flung

That 36 nations would ultimately be involved in combat justifies calling the Great War a world war. Although the colonial possessions of the principal powers were also caught up in the conflict, most of the fighting in World War I was confined to the European continent and did not—as it would in World War II—extensively involve colonial possessions. Nevertheless, the *peripheral fronts* did see action as battles were fought in Asia, Africa, and the Pacific.

From the Front

The British government claimed that the *Lusitania* was a civilian ship on a nonmilitary cruise. It was later revealed, however, that in addition to passengers and nonmilitary cargo, the ship also carried 173 tons of ammunition bound for the Western Front.

Words of War

The **peripheral fronts** in World War I included all the colonial fronts, as well as the so-called Turkish Fronts (mainly the Dardanelles and the Caucasus).

Voices of Battle

"Unrestricted U-boat war would in any event mean the breaking of diplomatic relations with the United States, and, if American lives are lost, would finally lead to war .... If we take up unrestricted U-boat warfare, the attitude of all neutral Powers will be changed against us and we shall have to calculate upon establishing new fronts. Germany will in such case be looked upon as a mad dog against whom the hand of every man will be raised for the purpose of finally bringing about peace ...."

—German Secretary of State Gottlieb von Jagow, arguing with the admiralty in 1914 against instituting unrestricted submarine warfare

The great powers undertook operations on the peripheral fronts in the belief that fighting in the colonies would shorten the war. This became a motive of increasing importance as soon as it became apparent that the Western Front was stalemated. In this tragic and frustrating war, however, the peripheral action actually had the effect of prolonging the war because it drew troops and materiel away from the decisive theaters.

The Conquest of Togoland

At the outbreak of war, the British understood well that Germany would be largely unable to defend most of its colonial possessions. From the very beginning, therefore, the British began planning for the capture of all the German colonies throughout the world. Ostensibly, this action was planned to prevent German warships from gaining access to ports and to protect Allied colonies from German aggression. In reality, the British attacks on the German colonies were among the biggest dividends that Britain hoped to realize from prosecuting this war. At the very least, captured colonies would serve as bargaining chips during postwar negotiations. More important, however, they would simply enlarge the already far-flung British Empire.

In Africa, German colonies included Togoland, the Cameroons, and German South-west Africa on the continent's west coast, and German East Africa on the east coast. On August 7, just three days after England declared war, four companies of British-led native troops from the Gold Coast (modern Ghana) and a unit of French-led native troops from Dahomey (now Benin) acted without instructions to invade Togoland. After 20 days of sporadic combat, German colonial officials surrendered the colony.

It proved to be an important victory because Togoland harbored wireless (radio) stations that regulated the operation of German surface vessels raiding in African waters. Without the wireless stations, operations there were greatly curtailed.

War Comes to the Cameroons

Allied forces, including French, British, and Belgian colonial troops, invaded the Cameroons on August 20 from the south, the east, and the northwest, and also attacked from the sea in the west. Here the Germans put up a stiffer resistance than in Togoland. The German Cameroonian Army, a small force of 12 companies, withdrew to a stronghold at Mora and held out against attacks through February 18, 1916.

Theater: South Africa

On August 10, 1914, by official order, all British regular troops were withdrawn from South Africa for duty on the Western Front. Immediately, the white civilian residents of South Africa formed four irregular units and invaded German South West Africa (present-day Namibia), beginning in September 1914. Although these British forces enjoyed considerable superiority of numbers and quickly gained control of all the ports, the invasion was delayed by an uprising of pro-German South Africans who had fought against the British during the Second (Great) Boer War of 1899–1902.

By January 1915, the ranks of the British forces had swollen to 50,000, and this vastly superior force put down the rebellion by February. In Cameroons, many Germans continued to fight, however, in a guerilla war of sporadic skirmishes. The colony officially capitulated on July 9, 1915.

German China and the German Pacific

By the start of the twentieth century, Germany had acquired minor colonial footholds in China and in the Pacific, including Tsingtao, an important harbor town in the Chinese province of Kiaochow. In the North Pacific, the Marianas, the Caroline Islands, and the Marshall Islands were all German possessions. In the South Pacific, Germany held Western Samoa, Neu-Pommern (present-day New Britain), and a portion of New Guinea.

Enter Japan

Japan entered the war at the end of August 1914, honoring an alliance with Britain. Beginning in September, it launched an attack on Tsingtao, which was later supported by Allied warships. The port fell on November 7.

North Pacific Battles

While Tsingtao was under attack, Japanese forces also invaded the Marianas, the Caroline Islands, and the Marshalls, which fell in October, having offered little resistance because Spee's naval squadron was no longer there to defend them.

133

Allied Triumphs in the South Pacific

The German colony of Western Samoa yielded to a force of New Zealanders, supported by Australian, British, and French warships, at the end of August 1914 without resistance. In September, Australian troops invaded Neu-Pommern (New Britain) and took over all of German New Guinea in a matter of weeks.

The German Genius of East Africa

In western Africa, in China, and in the Pacific, the weakly defended German colonies toppled easily. German East Africa (comprising present-day Rwanda, Burundi, and continental Tanzania) would be a sharply different story, thanks mainly to Paul von Lettow-Vorbeck, a German military officer with a genius for guerrilla warfare who had the good fortune to command a force of *askaris*, as the very capable local, European-trained African troops were called.

Lettow-Vorbeck Takes the Offensive

Lieutenant Colonel Lettow-Vorbeck was sent to East Germany early in 1914. A lesser commander would have written off the situation as hopeless. The *askaris* he commanded were equipped with obsolete weapons, and Lettow-Vorbeck had no illusions about being able to obtain supplies once war had commenced. Nevertheless, with limited supplies and very limited manpower, he resolved to strike preemptively.

With the commencement of hostilities in August 1914, Lettow-Vorbeck hit the ground running with a series of raids against the British railway in Kenya. Next, he launched an attempt to capture Mombasa. Although he was driven back by September, he successfully defended against a British amphibious attack on the port town of Tanga in northeastern Tanzania (then called Tanganyika) during November 2–3, 1914. He made this invasion attempt especially costly for the British, inflicting heavy losses and also capturing a large cache of badly needed arms and ammunition.

Lettow-Vorbeck continued to strike at the British, who were themselves poorly supplied and who had been ordered to maintain a defensive posture only. Even after the Royal Navy sank the German cruiser *Koningsberg* in the Rufiji River delta, the ship on which Lettow-Vorbeck depended heavily for support, he did not give up, but instead set about salvaging most of the stricken vessel's guns. He even commandeered the *Koningsberg*'s crew for use as land troops.

The Smuts Offensive

In February 1916, Lettow-Vorbeck faced a massive invasion from the north composed of British and colonial troops under the command of South African General Jan Christian Smuts. It was coordinated with a Belgian invasion from the west and with an independent British invasion from Nyasaland in the south.

Combatants

Paul Emil von Lettow-Vorbeck (1870–1964) was the son of a prominent Prussian army officer and was himself a graduate of the prestigious Kriegsakademie in 1899. After serving on the General Staff (1899–1900), he was dispatched to China in 1900 with the German East Asia Corps as part of an international expedition to punish the so-called Boxers, Chinese nationalists who rebelled against European interests in their country. Following the conclusion of the Boxer Rebellion in 1901, Lettow-Vorbeck served in German Southwest Africa (present-day Namibia), fighting the Hereros during 1904–1908. Lettow-Vorbeck was wounded in an ambush in 1906 and was sent to a hospital in South Africa. Returned to Germany, he was promoted to lieutenant colonel and, early in 1914, was sent back to Africa as commander of forces in German East Africa.

During World War I, Lettow-Vorbeck led an extraordinarily effective defense of the German colony, which exacted a heavy toll on Allied resources. He did not surrender until several days after the Armistice and, at that time, his small 4,000-man army was undefeated.

Following the end of World War I, Lettow-Vorbeck remained in Africa to arrange for the repatriation of German soldiers and POWs. When he returned home in January 1919, it was to a hero's welcome and a promotion to *generalmajor*. Enormously popular, he became a right-wing extremist. He served in the Reichstag (German parliament) from May 1929 to July 1930. Although a rightist, he opposed the Nazis but, finding that opposition to them was a lost cause, retired from politics and from public life generally. He lived out the remainder of his long life quietly in Hamburg.

The hopelessly outnumbered Lettow-Vorbeck met this new threat with brilliant patience and a tactical approach that made the climate and terrain his strong allies. He fought nothing more than delaying actions designed to wear down the Allied troops. In the end, tropical diseases did far more damage than German bullets.

Despite their losses, the British continued to pour men and resources into the invasion. Lettow-Vorbeck responded by gradually yielding to the advance, exacting from the invaders the highest price he could. Whenever possible, he turned on his pursuers and lashed back, frequently surprising the British. At Mahiwa, during October 15–18, 1917, he cost the British forces—which outnumbered his four to one—1,500 casualties while he incurred a mere 100.

A Fight Beyond the Finish

Supremely tenacious, Lettow-Vorbeck was no fanatic. It was clear to him that the British would ultimately drive him out of German East Africa. Rather than make a useless stand in defense of a lost cause, he took the audacious step of invading the Portuguese colony of Mozambique in December 1917. By raiding Portuguese garrisons there, he supplied his 4,000-man army sufficiently to enable him to raid as far south as Quelimane on the coast during July 1–3, 1918. From here, he turned north again and reentered German East Africa during September-October.

Of course, the war was all but over in Europe, but Lettow-Vorbeck was so isolated that he had no knowledge of the ill fortune of his countrymen on the Western Front. He launched an invasion of British-held Rhodesia (present-day Zimbabwe) and took the principal city of Kasama (in modern Zambia) on November 13, 1918—two days after the Armistice had officially ended the war.

After this, Lettow-Vorbeck began to hear vague rumors of the German capitulation in Europe. They were sufficient to prompt him to open negotiations with the British. On November 23, he surrendered his undefeated army to them at Abercorn (Mbala, Zambia). His nation may have lost World War I, but the ranking commander in East Africa retired victorious.

The Least You Need to Know

➤ Both Britain and Germany directed most of their naval effort not at one another's warships, but at disrupting trade.

➤ Despite the daring and brilliance of such German admirals as Graf Spee, the Germans were largely outclassed by British surface vessels; increasingly, therefore, Germany turned to its large U–boat fleet.

➤ Germany's policy of unrestricted submarine warfare menaced Allied trade and supply, but never decisively so; for Germany, the policy was a strategic blunder that served ultimately to end United States neutrality.

➤ Germany quickly lost its poorly defended colonial possessions in Africa, Asia, and the Pacific; the exception was in East Africa, where the brilliant Lettow-Vorbeck used a small force of mostly native troops to harass and tie down large numbers of Allied soldiers.

Part 3

We Are the Dead

The second two years of the war, 1915 and 1916, presented the belligerents with a bloody puzzle: how to stop killing and dying, and start winning. Here are the desperate attempts to break the stalemate of trench warfare, including the heartbreaking Allied offensives on the Western Front, the German attempt to "bleed the French army white" at Verdun, the disastrous attempt at an "indirect" solution at Gallipoli and the Dardanelles, the forlorn hope offered by Italy's entry into the war, and the action on fronts in the far-flung corners of the world.

Chapter 12

Deadlock

> ### In This Chapter
>
> ➤ Deadlock on the Western Front
>
> ➤ Uniforms: from dreams of glory to recognition of reality
>
> ➤ Machine guns, artillery, and tanks
>
> ➤ Life and death in the trenches
>
> ➤ Gas warfare

The First Battle of the Marne, September 5–10, 1914 (see Chapter 6, "The Marne: Massacre and Miracle"), arrested the great German juggernaut into France and established the battle lines on the Western Front that would endure, largely unchanged, through the Armistice of November 11, 1918. Although the Marne had been a strategic victory for the Allies, it was not really a defeat for the Germans. The most accurate statement one can make about the result of this battle is that it doomed both sides to four years of inconclusive slaughter.

By the end of 1914, the fantasies of military glory spawned by Germany's Schlieffen Plan and France's Plan XVII had been pounded into so much bloody dust. It was now clear to both sides that the Western Front was deadlocked, and it was up to each government and general staff to find a way to break out of it.

This chapter describes the nature of the deadlock, something of life—and death—in the trenches of the Western Front, and the strategies each side adopted to cope with a war that produced nothing but death.

The Technology of Stalemate

As mentioned in Chapter 3, "Blueprints for a Bloodletting," at the outbreak of World War I, there was a deadly disconnect between the awesome effectiveness of modern armaments and the *doctrine of war* generally adopted by the Allies and the Central Powers. It was as if both sides stubbornly refused to heed the leading lessons of the two most recent large-scale conflicts, the Second (Great) Boer War in South Africa (1899–1902) and the Russo-Japanese War (1904–1905). These had dramatically demonstrated how far the technology of defensive armament had outstripped that of offensive armament. Frontal attacks by infantry or cavalry on well-prepared defensive positions were shown to be utterly futile. Gallant troops on the charge were instantly and invariably transformed into nothing more than machine-gun targets or were blown to bits by artillery fire of unprecedented rapidity and accuracy.

Words of War

A **doctrine of war** is a set of principles by which military forces guide their actions in support of particular objectives.

These lessons were written all too legibly in human blood, but few military leaders chose to read and comprehend them. After all, generals do not achieve glory by shrinking into a defensive posture. Historically, victorious armies attack. Few leaders had the imagination, the mental flexibility, or even the will to follow through to its conclusion the new logic of the machine gun and rapid-firing field artillery as well as increasingly massive heavy artillery: These weapons would force armies to choose between two terrible alternatives—inglorious, squalid, seemingly ceaseless, and often pointless combat in muddy trenches; or rapid death, destruction, and defeat.

The German Edge

At the outset of war, both the French and the Germans suffered from doctrinal delusions, albeit in varying degrees. French military leaders chose almost completely to ignore the experience of South Africa and of the Russo-Japanese War. In August 1914, French doctrine still stubbornly called for "attack to the utmost" and was founded on the tactic of headlong bayonet charges, even against entrenched positions defended by efficient rifle fire, machine guns, and rapid-firing artillery.

In the French military mind, logic had yielded to visions of glory driven by *élan*, the supposedly indomitable French will to achieve victory.

The Germans also believed in a will to win, but they made certain key concessions to the realities of modern war. The Schlieffen Plan assiduously avoided frontal assaults and was based instead on a strategy of maneuver that would put the German armies in position for deep, decisive flanking attacks. Moreover, the Germans devoted far more attention than the French to training officers and enlisted men in defensive tactics using machine guns, barbed wire, and fortifications.

Germany's greater understanding and acceptance of the nature of modern war gave its army the edge on the Western Front, allowing it to advance far into French territory and to exact a terrible toll on the Allied armies. Yet, the Germans also failed to recognize just how dominant the technology of defensive war would become. The available means of supply and communication were insufficiently developed in 1914 to ensure the success of the deep invasion that Schlieffen's plan called for. And once the plan was compromised and then aborted altogether, the Germans had little choice but to fall back on a strong defense.

A Change of Uniform

The French army had marched off to war in uniforms that, as high command saw it, embodied the glory of France and instilled patriotic fervor in the troops. Enlisted men wore long, blue-gray overcoats and bright red trousers. Instead of helmets, officers as well as men wore red *kepis*, soft caps. The sole effort at camouflage was a blue-gray cloth cover for the *kepi* and for cavalry helmets. As far back as 1905, some officer recommended more practical field uniforms, but neither military leaders nor the French public wanted any part of it. Thus, the French high command continued to dress the French soldier for the glory of the attack, not for the practicalities of defensive concealment.

The early fighting quickly demonstrated the folly of this attire. The scarlet pants made excellent targets for German machine gunners. Over the protests of many old-line officers, who bellowed that "the red trousers *are* France," new uniforms were issued. A new single-breasted tunic was made available, but most soldiers preferred the traditional greatcoat—albeit in a light blue-gray, called "horizon blue," designed to blend in with the earth and the sky. Gone for good were the scarlet trousers, replaced by blue-gray breeches and puttees (leg wrappings). In 1915, enlisted men were issued steel helmets, known as "adrians"—officially called the "Casque d'Adrian"—after their designer. Although officers were also issued helmets, many felt that to cower under the protection of one was unseemly. They retained their *kepis* (now in horizon blue)—at least when they weren't hunkered down in the trenches. Away from the front lines, *kepis* were gradually replaced by the soft, flat "overseas cap."

Before 1910, the basic German uniform was a handsome medium-dark blue known as Prussian blue. But the German soldier and officer alike marched off to World War I in a more practical drab, grayish-green uniform of a color called *feldgrau*, "field gray." The one carryover from the days of earlier glory—the era of the Franco-Prussian War—was the *Pickelhaub*, a heavy black polished leather helmet with brass or silver metal trim. This highly ornamental headgear included a decorative crest on the front, which varied depending on regiment or state. The spike as well as the helmet surface was shiny, so, as early as 1910, troops were issued *feldgrau* cloth covers which concealed the helmet as well as its spike. To modern eyes, the appearance of the covered helmet is distinctly comical.

The *Pickelhaub* covered only the top of the head, above the ears. In 1916, troops were issued the "coal scuttle" style of steel helmet, the sides of which swept down to afford greater protection, especially to the neck. It was essentially the same headgear that German troops would wear into World War II.

National variations notwithstanding, World War I uniforms soon became universally dull, drab, and anonymous. Insignia and badges of rank were all but hidden. The object became one of blending in with the terrain. The purpose, of course, was survival in what was—on *both* sides—a defensive war, but it all somehow seemed an admission of the shame and humiliation of the fruitless and deadly activity in which the combatants were engaged.

From the Front

Authorities agree that, from the beginning of the war, the British had the most practical uniform. Made of khaki-colored serge, it had been developed from decades of experience in colonial service and included a unique all-webbed load-carrying system, in which fabric webbing belts replaced much of the leather belting. This was far more efficient for carrying field packs and other equipment. In the trenches, in 1916, soldiers were issued the "basin" style of helmet, with a flangelike visor all the way around.

Machine Guns

As mentioned in Chapter 3, the machine gun, developed in the 1880s and 1890s, profoundly altered the nature of war. The models available by 1914 could fire 600 rounds per minute at a range of more than 1,000 yards. A pair of machine gunners— one man to feed the weapon, the other to fire it—could operate from the relative safety of a trench and simply sweep away all exposed attackers.

Artillery

Chapter 3 also explained the development of new field artillery. The two principal improvements in artillery were more efficient breech loading mechanisms, which made for much more rapid firing, and the development of efficient brakes or recoil mechanisms. An artillery piece lacking a good recoil mechanism lurches out of position each time it is fired and must be re-aimed ("relaid") after each round. The French 75 (named for the 75-millimeter shell it fired) was equipped with an especially elegant recoil mechanism that allowed it to remain essentially motionless during repeated firing. Because it was not necessary to continually readjust the aim, firing could be more rapid and, therefore, more deadly.

The combination of machine guns, rapid-firing artillery, and increasingly powerful heavy artillery when placed within deep trenches protected by barriers of barbed wire, was very difficult to assault successfully. Not only were attackers exposed to withering fire, but, with their advance slowed by a profusion of barbed wire, they also made slow-moving targets. Any commander foolish enough to order a frontal assault against such weapons in such *emplacements* doomed his men to death. The particular horror of this war is that there seemed no end of foolish commanders.

But what was the alternative to attacking entrenched positions? Throughout 1914, the only alternative appeared to be an effort to hammer the enemy with endless artillery barrages. Throughout the war, both sides worked to develop increasingly heavy artillery of greater and greater range.

The first development was a move away from *shrapnel rounds* to *high-explosive (HE) rounds*. Most of the field guns in 1914 were loaded with shrapnel rounds. Shells packed with steel balls, shrapnel rounds were equipped with time fuses and were designed to explode not on impact, but in the air, sending the shrapnel flying, like shot from some horrible airborne shotgun.

Shrapnel is an antipersonnel weapon and is deadly against troops in the open. However, it is far less effective on entrenched troops and wholly ineffective against fortifications. Very soon, the armies began to rely increasingly on the high-explosive rounds, known as HE. High explosives were all about producing the maximum concentrated blast possible. Not only could these shells penetrate fortifications, but they also could obliterate trenches. Exploded above entrenched positions, they produced a concussion or blast wave that was deadly over a large area. By the end of World War I, the technology of the shrapnel round and the HE was combined into a high-explosive shell that also produced a great deal of fragmentation. Those troops who did not succumb to the blast wave might be cut down by the shrapnel.

By 1916, artillery would come to dominate combat on the Western Front. Frustrated commanders on both sides used heavy guns to pound the enemy almost indiscriminately. The prevailing philosophy was summed up by the slogan "Artillery conquers, infantry occupies." The most common offensive tactic became artillery preparation: bombardment

Words of War

An **emplacement** is a prepared position for one or more weapons or other pieces of equipment to afford protection from hostile fire.

Words of War

Shrapnel rounds are artillery shells designed to detonate in the air, showering personnel with deadly fragments. **High-explosive (HE) rounds** employ powerful explosives that do their damage primarily by generating an intense blast wave rather than creating shrapnel fragments.

of the enemy for a sustained period, followed by an infantry attack on the objective thus "prepared."

The first example of this tactic was the British attack at Neuve Chapelle on March 10, 1915. In the greatest artillery bombardment up to that time, 363 British guns shelled German positions for 35 minutes straight. The heavy artillery was directed at the trenches, while the lighter field guns were concentrated against barbed-wire obstacles.

Neuve Chapelle initiated an era of increasingly longer artillery preparations, lasting not minutes or hours, but days and even weeks. It was believed that every HE shell lobbed against the enemy made the job of infantry that much easier. In truth, the long "preps" finally served only to strengthen the deadlock.

From the Front

In July 1916, the British started its attack at the Somme with a seven-day artillery preparation in which 1,537 guns fired 1,627,824 rounds. This was typical of tactics used in the war.

To begin with, an extended preparation tipped the attacker's hand, revealing exactly where his attack was coming from. The element of surprise was entirely sacrificed. Second, the longer the preparation, the more time the defender had to prepare for the coming infantry onslaught. Often, the defender would quietly withdraw from the area under bombardment and then return in force once the bombardment ceased and the infantry attack began. Third, the massive bombardments tore up the terrain of no man's land, making it harder for the attacking infantry to advance. Finally, massive and sustained use of artillery was expensive. HE shells were costly to manufacture, and the logistical drain they created bled the national economies of all the nations involved. If anything, artillery only made the war longer.

Enter the Tank

If technology had largely created the Western Front deadlock, Winston Churchill—at the time First Lord of the Admiralty—saw a way in which technology might also be used to break the deadlock.

In January 1915, Churchill wrote to Prime Minister H. H. Asquith with a recommendation that a "committee of engineering officers and other experts" collaborate on the development of "special mechanical devices for taking trenches." Just six months later, in June, a lieutenant colonel of engineers, Ernest D. Swinton, came up with a set of requirements for an armored fighting machine designed to overcome entrenched machine guns. Swinton specified that the machine must be able to climb a 5-foot ledge, span a 5-foot trench, have a range of 20 miles, weigh about 8 tons, and accommodate a 10-man crew to operate two machine guns and one field gun.

Swinton was an army man, but despite his early—and vital—contribution, the tank, initially called a "landship," would be developed primarily under British *navy* sponsorship. That the army had little faith in it is not surprising. After all, the world of 1915 was largely horse-drawn. The automobile had made its debut in 1885 as a three-wheel vehicle invented by Germany's Karl Benz, but it was not until 1908 that America's Henry Ford devised practical methods of mass-producing commercially appealing automobiles. Only from this point did the vehicles begin to make a significant impact on the world landscape. Now, just seven years later, engineers were being asked to create nothing less than a self-propelled fighting machine.

The first tank, dubbed Little Willie, was cobbled together by the British firm of William Foster & Co. and made its appearance on September 19, 1915. It failed its initial tests, but by this time, a new design was in the works. Because of its naval sponsorship, the larger tank was christened in ship fashion, H.M.S. *Centipede* but, more familiarly, was known as Big Willie and also, strangely enough, as Mother. The prototype worked reasonably well and went into mass production as the Mark I. It first saw action on the Somme in September 1916.

Equipped with caterpillar-style tracks instead of wheels, the tanks could indeed lumber across many obstacles and could span most trenches; those it could not span, it usually could descend and climb. The bulkily armored Mark I was much heavier than Swinton had specified—30 tons rather than 8—and it moved at a slow walking speed. However, it was impervious to machine gun fire—unless it was struck in its vulnerable fuel tanks.

Throughout the war, the British tanks were improved, culminating in the smaller, lighter, faster, and more maneuverable Whippet of 1917 and the larger Mark V in 1918.

From the Front

The Mark V and the Mark V Star were the most successful tanks of the war, produced in quantities of 400 and 642, respectively. The Mark V Star weighed 36 tons and could span a 14-foot trench. It was produced in a so-called "male" version, with two 6-pounder guns and five machine guns, and in a "female" version, which carried machine guns only—seven of them. The tank's top speed was 4.6 miles per hour.

The French also developed tanks, producing the Schneider "cheese box" in 1916, which sported two machine guns and a 75-mm cannon, and the St. Chamond, again equipped with a 75-mm gun, but also bristling with four machine guns. Both of these tank types were plagued by mechanical problems, and the French began to rely more on lighter tanks manufactured by the Renault automotive firm. Manned by a crew of two and carrying only a 37-mm gun or an 8-mm machine gun, the Renault was very lightly armored and therefore was more vulnerable to armor-piercing rounds, even those fired from rifles. However, the 17-ton vehicle was highly maneuverable and could attain the impressive speed of 6 miles per hour.

The Germans lagged behind both the British and the French in tank development, fielding only a single tank model, the A7V—an impressive giant, 11 feet high, 24 feet long, and 10 feet wide, built by Daimler Motor Company. Powered by a pair of Mercedes-Daimler 150-horsepower engines, the 33-ton tank could race ahead at 8 miles per hour, carrying an 18-man crew, and was equipped with a 57-mm cannon as well as six machine guns. The tank did not appear on the battlefield, however, until March 21, 1918, quite late in the war.

At Cambrai, in August 1918, British tanks had a powerfully demoralizing effect on German troops and the high command alike. Nevertheless, despite Churchill's hopes, the tanks alone were not sufficient to break the deadlock on the Western Front. They were too slow and mechanically too unreliable. They were never produced in the vast quantities that would have been necessary to make a profound impact on the course of the war. Moreover, armies were laggardly in the development of effective tank tactics, including the coordination of tank operations and the use of tanks to support infantry assaults. In World War II, for example, tanks would be used to punch through enemy defenses so that the breaches created could be exploited by foot soldiers.

From the Front

In a twist of fate, the tanks of World War I had the greatest doctrinal effect on the Germans. Slow to develop the weapon in the Great War, the Germans nevertheless took note of it and, by World War II, had developed some of the most formidable tanks—and tactical armored doctrine—in the world.

Words of War

A **war of attrition** is one in which victory depends on wearing down the enemy rather than destroying him outright.

The New German Strategy

While the advocates of artillery and the advocates of tanks looked for technological solutions to the deadlocked Western Front, the German commander-in-chief who had succeeded Helmuth von Moltke in September 1914, Erich von Falkenhayn, began to formulate a new strategy. Falkenhayn clung to the belief that the final decision in the war would be reached in the West, but, by the end of 1914, he had also determined that Germany could not expect immediate success there. Therefore, he reluctantly concluded that the "theater of decision"—at least in the short term—was on the Eastern Front, as we have seen in Chapter 9, "Duel of Doomed Empires."

But this hardly meant giving up on the Western Front. Instead, Falkenhayn decided to continue to prosecute war on this front vigorously, but in a defensive mode, designed to wear the enemy down in a *war of attrition*.

Falkenhayn set his commanders to work to develop increasingly effective methods of field entrenchment. He directed the expansion of the German military rail system so that reserves could be moved more efficiently. He saw to it that munitions production was greatly increased. Indeed, throughout the war, the Germans never suffered from the acute shortages of supply that periodically plagued the Allies. Despite the increasing effectiveness of Britain's naval blockade of Germany, the nation had reached a high level of self-sufficiency. Although its civilian population suffered many shortages, the army continued to be well supplied.

While German armies moved boldly and decisively in the East, they dug in defensively in the West (except for the costly offensive against Verdun), creating a great wall against which the Allies fruitlessly hurled their bodies.

Combatants

Erich von Falkenhayn (1861–1922) replaced Helmuth von Moltke as German Chief of Staff in September 1914, after the German failure at the First Battle of the Marne. Born into an impoverished family of Prussian aristocrats, Falkenhayn served in the Far East and was an officer during the Boxer Rebellion of 1900. Kaiser Wilhelm II recognized Falkenhayn as a promising young officer and sponsored his rapid promotion through the ranks. By mid 1913, Falkenhayn was a lieutenant general and had been appointed minister of war for Prussia.

After Moltke faltered, it was to Falkenhayn that the kaiser turned. Falkenhyan found himself faced with the insurmountable problems of fighting a two-front war, which prompted him to make compromises that failed to provide quick, decisive victories on either the Western or Eastern fronts. In 1916, he wagered everything on an all-out assault against the fortress city of Verdun, believing that France would pour all of its resources into this position and could thus be (as he said) "bled white."

The Verdun strategy failed, and Falkenhayn was removed from overall command and given assignments in Romania and Turkey. He was about to launch an offensive in Mesopotamia, when he was relieved of command and sent, briefly, to Lithuania. He retired at the end of the war.

Allied Arguments

In the face of deadlocked battle, the principal commanders among the western Allies fell to arguing among themselves about strategy. Papa Joffre, most of the French general staff, and British field marshal Sir John French advocated continuing the assaults on German entrenchments—despite the appallingly high rate of casualties. Needless to say, this was not an inspired, innovative, or very promising strategy. As we have just seen, Churchill and others favored a technological solution, which resulted in the development of the tank. Still others argued that a breakthrough should not be sought on the *Western* Front at all, but in the Balkans or perhaps even by a massive amphibious assault on Germany's Baltic coast.

Ultimately, Joffre and his supporters prevailed, although a modified version of the alternate front strategy was adopted in the disastrous campaign to capture the Gallipoli Peninsula and the city of Constantinople (see Chapter 14, "The Gallipoli Disaster").

Trench Life

The Allies' failure to decide upon an alternative to continued battle on the Western Front doomed most troops on both sides to a miserable life—and often a squalid death—in the trenches.

Trench warfare was not new. It had been an occasional feature of many wars, most notably the American Civil War and the Russo-Japanese War, but never before had an entire theatre of war been dominated by trenches.

The first trenches of the war were simple slit-trenches—nothing more than ditches, really. In low-lying areas, where flooding was a problem, soldiers elaborated the ditches with earthen walls, berms, or parapets. As the deadlock hardened, trenches became increasingly complex, bringing into play the collected wisdom of some three centuries of military engineering for siege warfare. The Allies pushed their trench lines as far forward as possible in the belief that the more ground they could claim and control, the better. However, this sometimes put them at a disadvantage because the farthest forward position did not always offer the most advantageous terrain. In contrast, the Germans were willing to sacrifice some of no-man's land to site their trenches on the best available terrain.

Allied trenches were laid out in three sets of lines. At the front was an outpost line, which was usually a set of unconnected trenches several hundred yards in advance of the main line. The main line was an elaborate trench system typically consisting of three or more sets of parallel trenches. Behind this was a reserve line. About two-thirds of the troops were concentrated in the main line trenches.

In contrast to the Allied systems, the Germans developed more sophisticated and flexible defenses, which were more varied in pattern than the Allied trenches and could be held by fewer soldiers.

Words of War

Enfilading fire rakes the enemy with gunfire in a lengthwise direction. This is also called "raking fire."

Common to both Allied and German trenches was a basically zigzag layout or, when time and conditions permitted, a crenellated pattern, like a row of square teeth. Either layout minimized the blast effect of a shell impact, and it also prevented an enemy raiding party from setting up *enfilading fire,* in effect using a straight trench as a lengthwise shooting gallery.

Perpendicular to the main trench lines were communications trenches, which connected the lines. The trench system was entered from the rear by an access trench that lay well behind the enemy's line of sight.

The typical main line trench was slightly deeper than the average height of a man. A *fire-step* was built into the forward wall so that soldiers could gain sufficient height to fire at the enemy. The best trenches were reinforced with "revetments" constructed of wooden beams and sandbags, and the floors of trenches were covered with wooden slats called duckboards.

Even the best trenches, however, were nothing more or less than elaborated ditches. They were filthy and poorly drained. They bred misery, depression, and disease, including frostbite from constant exposure to freezing water, ice, or snow; trench foot, a condition resembling frostbite, caused by constant immersion in water—if untreated, it could result in gangrene, amputation, and even death; trench mouth, a severe bacterial infection of the throat and the mouth; and dysentery and typhus, both of which were extremely debilitating and often fatal. Soldiers shared the trenches with rats, fleas, garbage, human waste, and the remains of decaying corpses.

Words of War

The **fire-step** was a platform built into the forward wall of a trench from which soldiers could take aim and fire over the rim of the trench.

Voices of Battle

"Soldiers are dreamers; when the guns begin
They think of firelit homes, clean beds, and wives.
I see them in foul dug-outs, gnawed by rats,
And in the ruined trenches, lashed with rain,
Dreaming of things they did with balls and bats,
And mocked by hopeless longing to regain
Bank-holidays and picture shows, and spats,
And going to the office in the train."

—from "Dreamers," by Siegfried Sassoon, British poet and soldier

At night, supplies would be brought up through the access trench. Food was generally canned and entirely unpalatable. Dawn brought the greatest danger of enemy attack, which might take the form of a trench raid, as enemy infantry swarmed over the trench. For these occasions, soldiers depended on the archaic weapons of hand-to-hand combat: knives, billy clubs, blackjacks, brass knuckles (which the British called knuckle dusters), and even the medieval-style mace, a club bristling with spikes.

More commonly, an attack came in the form of artillery shelling. The mortar, a short cannon that fires at a very high trajectory, could lob high-explosive shells directly into a trench, killing or wounding hundreds at a time. Hand grenades, hand-thrown explosive devices with delayed fuses, were routinely hurled into the trenches. The flame-thrower, shooting a jet of flaming jellied gasoline, produced its own special brand of horror—if an attacker could get close enough to a trench to use one.

Words of War

Over the top referred to an advance out of the trenches ("over the top" of the trench) to venture into no man's land for an attack on the enemy.

Getting close enough to attack the enemy's trench was not easy. No-man's land—typically a space anywhere from 50 to 3,000 yards between the opposing trench lines—was littered with obstacles and cratered by shell holes. Vicious tangles of barbed wire were thickly strung all along no man's land to prevent or to slow the advance of enemy troops. Of course, the barbed wire also impeded any break out *over the top* by one's own soldiers as well.

Poison Gas

If the ubiquitous trench came to stand as the most enduring symbol of World War I, poison gas emerged as its archetypal weapon, an emblem of the overwhelming inhumanity of this war.

As we saw in Chapter 9, gas was introduced by the Germans on the Eastern Front, but to negligible effect. Its debut on the Western Front was very different—and much more terrifying.

A Yellow-Green Cloud at Ypres

At sunset on April 22, 1915, French Algerian troops holding a section of the line at Ypres, Belgium, saw a greenish-yellow cloud advancing from the German lines. The gas was chlorine, 168 tons of it boiling up from 6,000 cylinders opened by German soldiers on the rim of their trenches and carried to the Allied positions by the prevailing winds.

Heavier than air, chlorine hugged the ground, seeping into burrows, shell holes, and especially trenches. The Ypres attack released a cloud that covered four miles of French trench lines, affecting 10,000 troops. Half of this number died within

10 minutes, in an agony of coughing and asphyxiation. Others, temporarily blinded by the strongly irritating gas, panicked and stumbled wildly about. Two thousand confused troops were thus snapped up as prisoners of war.

If the terrible effect of the gas assault shocked its Allied victims, it also surprised the German attackers, who advanced into the abandoned French positions timidly. They had not even assembled reserves to exploit the breach in the French line, so they ultimately failed to hold what they had gained.

Masks On!

Germany's chemical genius Fritz Haber, who had given his country the means of creating a limitless supply of high explosives (see Chapter 3), spurred the development of a sophisticated chemical warfare industry. Following the Ypres attack, however, the Allies were quick to manufacture and deploy their own poison gas weapons.

The British unleashed an attack at Loos, Belgium, on September 25, 1915—but when the wind suddenly changed direction, they quickly learned the lesson of this weapon's great drawback: It was difficult, even impossible, to control. Many British tommies were lost in the attack. Nevertheless, all the principal belligerents—including the Americans, when they joined the war—used gas.

Except for the British, the Allies moved rather slowly to develop effective countermeasures against gas. The first expedient was typical of the squalor of trench warfare. British soldiers were advised to soak socks in urine and hold them over their faces because the ammonia neutralized the chlorine. Soon, however, British as well as German soldiers were issued cloth masks soaked in triosulphate, another substance that counteracted the effects of chlorine. Next came gas helmets—cloth hoods soaked in a special chemical and equipped with eye lenses, which offered protection against asphyxiation as well as blinding eye irritation. The early helmets, leaky and inefficient, were followed by the SBR, the small box respirator. This unit was worn over the face, and air was breathed through a tube that led to a box containing a soda lime and charcoal filter. Integral goggles protected the eyes, and the nose was held closed with a clip. Although this was very uncomfortable and awkward to put on, British troops trained in using this mask were very well protected against gas of almost any kind.

Curiously, the other Allies were slow to follow the British example in developing and issuing adequate countermeasures. The French M2 gas mask was a treated canvas face mask containing gauze pads soaked in antigas chemicals. It was never entirely effective, and it was not until late in the war that the French improved this protection. As for the Russians and the Italians, they didn't even bother to issue adequate masks.

When they entered the war, the Americans were also slow to respond, making do with British masks and inadequate French masks. The American military developed no gas mask of its own, and neither were American troops trained in techniques of chemical war defense. After suffering severe gas casualties, U.S. equipment and training were both upgraded.

For their part, the Germans had quickly developed a sophisticated mask of rubberized cloth (later made of leather, due to wartime shortages), and they also employed large quantities of powdered bleach to decontaminate areas and equipment that had been saturated by gas.

Voices of Battle

"Gas! Gas! Quick, boys!—An ecstasy of fumbling,
Fitting the clumsy helmets just in time,
But someone still was yelling out and stumbling
And flound'ring like a man in fire or lime.
Dim through the misty panes and thick green light,
As under a green sea, I saw him drowning."

—from "Dulce et Decorum Est," by Wilfred Owen, British poet and soldier killed on the Western Front, one week before the Armistice

New Poisons

As most of the combatants developed at least marginally effective masks, a race began to create a gas that would "break" the masks. In this, the Germans took the lead. In December 1915 they introduced phosgene, a lethal choking agent that carried with it the deceptively inviting smell of new-mown hay. Many a homesick farm boy sniffed the aroma with pleasure, took in a deep breath, and choked to death as the gas became hydrochloric acid in his lungs.

Another innovation was chlorpicrin, or vomiting gas. This agent defeated most of the early gas-mask neutralizers, including even the charcoal filters of the more sophisticated masks. It was not especially deadly in and of itself, but when a soldier helplessly tore off his mask to vomit, he would often inhale other, far more lethal agents mixed with the chlorpicrin.

Nevertheless, further improvements in gas masks and training proved adequate against chlorpicrin; in July 1917, again at Ypres, the Germans deployed yet another terrible poison called mustard gas. In low concentrations, its presence was hardly noticeable; it was pleasant, with a scent reminiscent of lilacs in bloom. But in higher concentration, it caused first- and second-degree chemical burns on whatever it contacted: skin, eyes, or the lining of the nose, throat, and lungs. Worst of all, it was an atomized liquid rather than a true gas, which meant that it soaked everything, lingering with full potency for weeks, especially in shell holes, dugouts, and trenches. Long after a mustard gas attack, a soldier might seek refuge from enemy machine-gun fire in a shell hole, only to find himself smothering and burning.

Gas was a truly terrible weapon that nevertheless failed to break the deadlock on the Western Front. Perhaps a half-million men on both sides were affected by poison gas, but the overwhelming majority quickly recovered (although many would suffer some form of chronic respiratory disease for the rest of their lives).

Yet the mythology surrounding poison gas was disproportionately powerful during the war and continues to loom as a symbol of that war's particular cruelty. It was a terror weapon, its emotional impact out of proportion to its tactical as well as strategic effect. But perhaps it is a fitting symbol of the war after all. Poison gas was the product of an ultimate mean-spiritedness, a cold disregard for human life and human suffering, and an abandonment of any notion, however illusory, of honorable combat. It was a weapon of indifferent and even gratuitous viciousness, very much a piece of a war of unremitting slaughter that might have been avoided if any major participant had shown simple humanity or even the most rudimentary goodwill.

From the Front

Poison gas accounted for no more than 30,000 combat deaths in all of World War I— out of a total of 4,888,891 battle deaths.

The Least You Need to Know

➤ The Western Front was deadlocked by opposing armies that had both settled into a defensive war of attrition; for four years, the combatants vainly looked for a way to break the deadlock.

➤ Allied strategy for breaking the deadlock consisted of essentially fruitless assaults on hardened German lines. The result was bloody stasis.

➤ Both the Allies and the Central Powers looked to technology to bring about a final decision on the Western Front. Both the tank and poison gas were seen as weapons that could overcome the tyranny of the trench; while the tank was sometimes highly effective, neither it nor gas proved decisive.

➤ The trench and poison gas emerged as the two most prominent symbols of World War I combat; although poison gas created great terror and much suffering, it actually caused fewer deaths than other weapons and had an almost negligible effect on the outcome of the war.

Chapter 13

A New Year and No Hope

In This Chapter

➤ The First Battle of Champagne

➤ The missed lesson of Neuve Chapelle

➤ Aerial bombardment of London and other English cities

➤ Poison gas at Ypres

➤ The Allied offensives of summer and fall 1915

➤ The British get a new commander

By 1915, both sides should have realized that this war would have no winners, only losers. Typically, at any given point in a conflict, at least one side feels that it is winning. In 1915, however, both sides felt only frustration.

The German chief of staff, Erich von Falkenhayn, clung to the belief that the outcome would ultimately be decided on the Western Front. Yet he also recognized that the struggle on this front would be long and drawn out and that, for the present, the only opportunities for immediate gain lay in the East. It was an odd and demoralizing position, this notion that victory had to be achieved in the West but that, at least in the short term, productive action was possible only in the East.

The Allies were even more frustrated and discouraged than the Central Powers. There was little unity of command between the French and the British, and there were very deep divisions within the British hierarchy. This chapter focuses on the grim realities of the Western Front in the second year of the war.

A Crisis of Priorities

In view of the bold promise of rapid victory represented in the Schlieffen Plan, it is remarkable how readily the German military, government, and people now accepted the prospect of a long war. German officials recognized that a protracted war of attrition required careful husbanding of raw materials, supplies, and provisions. Accordingly, they instituted a stringent program of rationing and distribution, as well as the development of ersatz (substitute) commodities for supplies cut off by the British naval blockade.

In contrast to Germany's attitude of acceptance and positive action, the subject of supply and provisioning created a bitter and divisive crisis among the Allied leadership. Turkey's entrance into the war (see Chapter 10, "The Sick Man and Serbia") had cut off Russian access to supplies from France and England. This was bad for the Russians, of course, but also hard on the armies of the Western Allies; from their point of view, the function of Russia had been to occupy as many German and Austrian troops as possible, thereby making them unavailable for service on the Western Front. Moreover, the western Allies also depended on the Ukrainian grain fields to help ensure that their people and armies were fed. Turkey's entry had cut off access to this source of supply.

To restore access to Russia, the young First Lord of the Admiralty, Winston Churchill, advocated an immediate and concerted campaign to seize from Turkish control the Dardanelles, the strait affording passage between the Black Sea and the Mediterranean. Churchill and his adherents argued that this was essential not only to aid the Eastern ally, but also to ensure a steady source of supply for the long haul ahead.

Others, including British War Minister Field Marshal Horatio H. Kitchener and France's Papa Joffre, believed that diverting resources from the Western Front to address the Dardanelles was sheer folly. They insisted that it was still possible to achieve victory on the Western Front and that everything should be concentrated there toward that goal.

In the end, an amphibious operation against the Dardanelles was grudgingly approved, but in part because the resolution to act was half-hearted—and was carried on simultaneously with a decisive offensive in the west—the assault was doomed, as we shall see in Chapter 14, "The Gallipoli Disaster."

500 Yards for 50,000 Men

At the end of 1914, Joffre mounted a general Allied offensive from Nieuport on the Belgian coast of the English Channel all the way southeast to Verdun in the Argonne Forest. From December 14 to December 24, British and French forces beat against German lines that were being rapidly entrenched and fortified. The door was slamming shut on any possibility of maneuver.

The Battle of Champagne

On December 20, the First Battle of Champagne commenced and expanded with the new year into an Allied offensive spread throughout the Champagne and Artois regions. Joffre focused on the so-called Noyon salient, a vast pocket of Germans bulging into central France between Reims and Verdun.

Progress was measured in yards. The First Battle of Champagne gained 500 yards for the Allies—at the cost of 50,000 Allied troops. In response, the Germans made only limited counterattacks along the La Bassé Canal and near the town of Soissons during January 8 through February 5. But these were sufficient to arrest the pathetically small and monumentally costly French advance.

Joffre regrouped and made another foray in March, but got nowhere.

From the Front

Combat in the Champagne and Artois regions resulted in some 400,000 French casualties. British and German losses were also heavy.

An Experiment at Neuve Chapelle

As mentioned in Chapter 12, "Deadlock," Neuve Chapelle, just below the Lys River in northwestern France, was the site of a new approach to offensive combat. British general Sir Douglas Haig began an assault by his First Army with an intensive 35-minute "artillery preparation." This was part of a very carefully planned assault that, in contrast to the vast and massive efforts of Joffre, was surgically concentrated in a very narrow front of a mere 2,000 yards. The object was to reduce the small salient (German strong point) near Neuve Chapelle and use this breach as a way to break out with a second offensive onto the plain of Douai. This area offered a rare opportunity for productive maneuver and a chance to disrupt German supply and communication lines.

Because it was a thoughtful approach (Haig made extensive use of aerial reconnaissance photographs) to a modest but valuable objective, Neuve Chapelle had a real chance for success. Haig massed 40,000 men supported by 62 light artillery batteries against a much smaller force of German defenders and began the attack at 7:30 on the morning of March 10.

At first the operation went very well, but then got bogged down. In several places the British troops broke through the German lines into the rear areas. Although the planning had been impeccable, management of execution was poor, communication broke down, and the attackers even had to wait for their own supporting artillery to cease fire. Hesitant leadership and poor communication led to battalions milling around behind the lines on the assumption that they were to regroup and assault a second line of trenches—which, in fact, did not even exist.

The British advance was delayed until late in the afternoon, by which time the Germans, whose system of backup troops was always highly flexible, had managed to bring up large numbers of reserves. By the time the assault resumed in earnest, at 5:30 in the afternoon, German machine guns and artillery beat back the advance. In the later stages of the battle, the British artillery was unable to support continued infantry attacks because nearly all of the ammunition had been spent in the battle's early phase.

Voices of Battle

"… a bullet pierced the exact centre of the helmet of the man on my right as he walked forward with his head down. He spun round as he fell with a stream of blood spurting out of a circular hole in the top of his head, and he scrambled back for about ten yards then rolled over. A short, white-haired lad rushed screaming, right along our line with an eye shot away. Another near neighbour was hit in the groin and lay in the ditch at the foot of the slope screaming."

—British soldier recalling his experience at Neuve Chapelle, quoted in Denis Winter's *Death's Men: Soldiers of the Great War* (1978)

Haig's frustration over the collapse of his offensive was intense. He had come *so* close to achieving a breakthrough! What had gone wrong?

In the opinion of the Allied generals, the attack had failed because artillery preparation and subsequent artillery support had been inadequate due to a shortage of ammunition. The answer for the future, they concluded, was to stockpile more ammo for longer "preps."

In fact, by concentrating on the reasons for the failure of the offensive instead of on the reasons for its near success, the Allied commanders missed the real lesson of Neuve Chapelle. Success came within grasp because Haig had managed to preserve much of the element of surprise—a rare commodity on an entrenched front, where enemies continually look one another in the eye. By deciding to stress artillery preparation in the future, however, the commanders completely sacrificed surprise (for there is no louder announcement of intention than an artillery bombardment), neglecting the very key to a success that had been narrowly missed.

The real frustration of Neuve Chapelle was not so much that a modest offensive had failed, but that the commanders had failed to draw from it the correct tactical lesson.

Fire from the Sky

In Chapter 5, "Battle of the Frontiers," we saw how a German zeppelin was used to bomb the Belgian fortress town of Liège during the opening days of the war. During January 19–20, 1915, zeppelins were deployed by the German navy to bomb English cities. Little damage resulted, and Londoners reacted not so much with panic as with rage. Eighteen such attacks occurred during 1915, including several directed against London. Naval captain Heinrich Mathy bombed the capital extensively on September 8, and even more damage was caused by multiple airship attacks on October 13. After this raid, a London coroner's inquiry returned indictments for "willful murder" against Kaiser Wilhelm II.

It is arguable that airship attacks did more harm to the German cause than to their British targets. The attacks stirred English patriotism and created outrage against Germany, not only among the people of Britain, but also among various neutral nations, including the United States.

Not that British authorities stood idly by during the attacks. Defensive measures were quickly put into place. Searchlight and antiaircraft artillery batteries were installed in and around major cities. The guns were loaded with *incendiary shells,* designed to ignite the highly explosive hydrogen with which the zeppelins were inflated. Approximately 110 fighter aircraft were also stationed near target cities and were dispatched to shoot down attacking airships. By 1916, such defenses were proving highly effective, although the Germans continued to conduct zeppelin raids periodically through the end of the war. The increasing success of British aircraft, however, forced the Germans to operate from higher altitudes, which made their bombing far less effective.

From the Front

Zeppelins created terror and outrage among the civilian population of England, but they actually caused little damage. German airships dropped 196 tons of bombs on England, killing 557 and wounding 1,358 civilians. Total property damage was estimated at £1.5 million. (To put this in perspective: In 1915, rats caused British property owners an estimated £70 million in damage.)

Words of War

An **incendiary shell** is an artillery shell loaded with highly flammable material, such as magnesium and phosphorous, intended to start and spread fire when detonated.

159

Woëvre and Ypres

Along the Western Front were various bulges or incursions of German strength, the two most prominent of which were the Noyon salient and the St.-Mihiel salient. The latter, located between Verdun and Toul, projected well beyond the main German lines and loomed throughout the war as an inviting target for Allied offensives.

During April 6 to April 15, French units repeatedly attacked the northern face of the St.-Mihiel salient at the Battle of Woëvre. The Germans held fast, and the French withdrew with very heavy losses.

From the Front

The attack at Ypres was the first use of *lethal* poison gas in the West. Earlier in the war, both the French and the Germans had occasionally lobbed nonlethal tear gas grenades and even tear gas artillery shells at one another.

Voices of Battle

"23 April

"Terrible day, no food or water, dead & dying all around."

—Diary of Sgt. S. V. Britten, 13th Battalion, The Royal Highlanders of Canada, April 23, 1915, at Ypres

Far to the north of this action, the Allies prepared for a second attempt at an offensive against Ypres, Belgium. We saw in Chapter 12 that, while preparation was underway, the Germans launched the first poison gas attack on the Western Front.

The attack caused at least 5,000 Allied deaths and created great panic along a four-mile stretch of front. This probably wouldn't have happened if the attack had not come as a surprise. And it should *not* have come as one. Back in March, German prisoners of war had supplied French intelligence officers information about the storage of the gas and the intended method of discharge. Somehow the French intelligence service failed to pass on this information to the commanders in the field. The troops were entirely unprepared for the gas.

The Germans themselves seemed to have little confidence in the effectiveness of gas as a weapon. Falkenhayn deployed it at Ypres primarily to distract Allied commanders from the large movement of forces that was underway as he transferred troops from the Western Front to the east to participate in the Gorlice-Tarnow offensive (see Chapter 9, "Duel of Doomed Empires"). The German commanders did not expect that the gas would create a breach worth exploiting, so no reserve troops were made available to occupy the territory vacated by the panic-stricken French soldiers. Without troops to hold their new positions, and harried by fierce British and Canadian counterattacks, the Germans retreated, and the Allies soon regained the positions they had lost.

Thus the Second Battle of Ypres ended, as did virtually all the battles on the Western Front, in continued deadlock.

Allied Offensives

To the southeast of Ypres, in northwestern France, the British staged an offensive in May, gained scant territory, and then were stopped cold at Festubert, southwest of Neuve Chapelle, by May 26.

Vimy Ridge

Just south of the Britishers, the French launched a vigorous offensive against Vimy Ridge, seeking to push the Germans off this commanding piece of high ground. This battle, near the French town of Souchez, stretched from May 16 to the end of June, when the exhausted Allies finally broke off the attack, utterly spent.

From the Front

At Second Ypres, German casualties numbered 35,000 killed and wounded; British, 60,000; French, 10,000.

Vimy Ridge was to be the last major Western Front offensive of the summer. The exhausted and thoroughly demoralized Allies withdrew to their trench lines to rest, to reorganize, and to reinforce.

For their part, the Germans were in no position to press their advantage. They, too, had suffered heavy casualties and were drained by having fended off so many attacks. They used the summer lull to reinforce the west with troops released from operations in the east.

By the early summer of 1915, another commodity was in short supply on both sides: ammunition. The Allies as well as the Germans were deep into their ammo reserves by now, and they had little choice other than to wait for production to catch up with demand.

Artois and Champagne

The Artois and Champagne regions had already been the scenes of extended—and quite futile—French offensives. With the coming of fall, Joffre decided to renew the Allied offensive and determined to hit the German line in the Champagne region yet again. From September 25 to November 6, the fighting was some of the most intense of the entire war. The Second Battle of Champagne resulted in 75,000 German casualties—a catastrophic number, until you look at the French casualty roles: 100,000 men wounded or killed.

From the Front

The death toll for the Western Front, 1915, was nothing short of appalling: 612,000 German soldiers killed or wounded; 279,000 British troops killed or wounded; and 1,292,000 French troops killed or wounded. Beyond the loss of life, nothing had changed since the autumn of 1914. The Western Front remained a long, motionless scar from the English Channel coast to the frontier of Switzerland.

During September 25 to October 30, at the Third Battle of Artois, the French once again chipped away at German positions on Vimy Ridge. They made minor territorial gains at the cost of another 100,000 casualties.

Loos

While the French battered themselves against Vimy, the British, a few miles to the north, attacked Loos (September 25–October 14). Again, they managed to achieve small gains in territory, but at a disproportionately heavy loss: 60,000 casualties. German losses from the Artois, Vimy Ridge, and Loos battles totaled about 65,000 killed and wounded.

Combatants

British General Sir John Denton Pinkstone French, 1st Earl of Ypres (1852–1925) served with great distinction in the Second (Great) Boer War, but led the British Expeditionary Force to its early disasters in World War I. Born in Kent, the son of a naval officer, French served first in the Royal Navy before transferring to the army in 1874. After distinguished service in North Africa, French was promoted to brigadier general, and was dispatched to a cavalry command against the Boers in South Africa, ultimately achieving promotion to lieutenant general.

With the conclusion of the war in Africa, French returned to Britain, was promoted to general in 1907, and was appointed inspector general of the army. In 1912, he was named chief of the Imperial General Staff and, the following year, promoted to field marshal. When World War I began in August 1914, it was French who was chosen to lead the British Expeditionary Force (BEF).

French directed all BEF operations in France and Belgium during the disastrous opening months of the war. The dismal Allied performance at Ypres I (October 19–November 22), Ypres II (April 22–May 25, 1915), and the Loos offensive (September 25–November 4) was in significant measure due to French's irascible refusal to coordinate his actions with those of the other commanders. On December 15, 1915, French was relieved as BEF commander and replaced by Sir Douglas Haig. Although removed from combat command, French was created a viscount, was named commander in chief of home forces, and, in 1918, given the office of Lord Lieutenant of Ireland.

A Changing of the Guard

After thousands of British lives had purchased nothing, high command decided to make a change. Sir John French, who had led the BEF into combat, was a brave commander, but he was also quirky, mercurial in temperament, subject to intense mood swings, and mired in nineteenth-century concepts of warfare. He argued bitterly with his superiors—especially Lord Kitchener—and with his subordinates as well, especially Sir Douglas Haig.

At Loos, Haig, encouraged by local successes, had wanted to call on all reserve forces to press the attack to a conclusion. However, Field Marshal French refused to release them. The result was an offensive failure to make much headway against the German line. Realizing this only after the fact, French altered the record of the orders he had given to make it appear that he had indeed made the reserves available. This transparent fraud was discovered, and King George V personally prevailed on Prime Minister H.H. Asquith to relieve the commander. Asquith offered French the more honorable alternative of resignation, and on December 17, 1915, the field marshal stepped down to be replaced by Sir Douglas Haig.

Before the war, Haig had been described by R.B. Haldane, Secretary of State for War, as "the most highly equipped thinker in the British Army." He was regarded as aggressive, decisive, and highly skilled, and he was popular with his subordinates as well as with politicians and the general public. The British—and the French—looked upon his appointment with great hopefulness. His name, they believed, would be linked with glorious deeds that might yet be wrested from the death grip of the deadlocked Western Front. In fact, the name of Douglas Haig would be forever wedded to the two campaigns, the Somme of 1916 and Passchendaele of 1917, that piled up British corpses in record numbers.

The Least You Need to Know

➤ The year 1915 opened with both sides frustrated by the deadlock on the Western Front.

➤ By 1915, the Germans were resigned to maintaining a defensive posture in the West as they continued to make great gains in the East; for their part, the British and the French were deeply divided on what strategy to pursue.

➤ The Battle of Neuve Chapelle introduced the tactic of artillery preparation—which often turned out to be more of a liability than a means of promoting the success of an offensive.

➤ Despite almost complete lack of success and staggeringly high casualties, the Allies continued to hurl one futile assault after another against the German defensive lines.

➤ At the end of 1915, a frustrated British government and high command replaced the doddering Sir John French with the dynamic Sir Douglas Haig as commander-in-chief of the British Expeditionary Force.

Chapter 14

The Gallipoli Disaster

In This Chapter

➤ Churchill's proposal

➤ The failure of the all-naval assault

➤ The first amphibious campaign

➤ Churchill's downfall

➤ The second amphibious campaign

The Great War had no shortage of brave men. Simply to endure for a single day the squalor of the trenches, the shriek of the artillery shells, the impact of the shrapnel, the searing of the mustard gas, and the sight of so many corpses that were strong young men—any one of these is a greater test of courage than most people undergo in a lifetime.

Yet the Great War had few indisputable heroes—at least, not at the command and decision-making level.

Where is the Hannibal, the Caesar, the Charlemagne, the Washington, the Napoleon, the Wellington, the Nelson, the Lee, or the Grant of this war? Or the MacArthur, the Bradley, or the Patton? The forceful and highly competent American General John J. Pershing comes close (see Chapter 22, "Over Here and Over There"), and Joseph Gallieni performed mightily in the defense of Paris (see Chapter 6, "The Marne: Massacre and Miracle"), as did Henri-Philippe Pétain at Verdun (Chapter 16, "'They Shall Not Pass!'"). On the German side, Hermann von François was an outstanding tactician, and Erich Ludendorff and Paul von Hindenburg were exceptional strategists, but none of these qualify as great men or inspiring leaders. For the most part, however, the commanders in key positions—Joffre, Jalinsky, Samsonov, Rennenkampf, Moltke, Falkenhayn, and French—were deeply flawed or even worse.

An exception to the prevailing mediocrity promised to be Winston Spencer Churchill, the man who, during the *second* world war, would prove himself one of the titans of the twentieth century. In World War I, as First Lord of the Admiralty (the equivalent of secretary of the navy), he proposed a bold plan to break the terrible deadlock of the Western Front. This chapter tells what that plan produced.

To Break the Deadlock

Winston Churchill had been born in 1874 at Blenheim Palace, venerable seat of his most illustrious ancestor the Duke of Marlborough. As a youngster, Churchill was less than impressive. A poor student, he barely gained entry into Sandhurst, the British service academy, but he did attend; there, he persevered, graduated, and obtained an officer's commission.

Churchill served well, if not brilliantly, in military assignments in India and Africa before resigning to take up a career as a journalist. In this he suddenly excelled, gaining fame for his firsthand coverage of the Second (Great) Boer War—he was even briefly captured by the Boers—and then entered politics. From 1900 to 1904, he served as a member of Parliament and then obtained the important cabinet post of undersecretary for the colonies. It was in 1911 that he was appointed First Lord of the Admiralty, a position from which he oversaw the buildup of Britain's naval power before the outbreak of the war. Thanks in part to Churchill, the nation stood in August 1914 as the most formidable seagoing force in the world.

Yet, the performance of the Royal Navy at the outset of the war, especially in the Battle of Coronel (see Chapter 11, "A *World* War"), was hardly spectacular: German Admiral Spee sank three British cruisers with two torpedoes—and killed senior British Admiral Cradock in the process. Although subsequent action at the Falklands, Heligoland, and Dogger Bank did much to redress the early failures, the magnificent weapon embodied in the ships and men of the Royal Navy was by no means being wielded to best advantage. And accusing fingers began pointing to the First Lord of the Admiralty.

Target: Dardanelles

It is no wonder that Churchill, pugnacious and aching to prove himself, pushed so hard for the Dardanelles campaign.

Not that Churchill was solely out for self-glorification, and not that he was alone in advocating the campaign. He, First Sea Lord Admiral John Fisher, and David Lloyd George—at the time Chancellor of the Exchequer (the equivalent of secretary of the treasury)—were united in their belief that, given the stalemate on the Western Front, Britain needed at this point to take an indirect approach to the war.

The benefits, they argued, were many:

➤ Seizing control of the Dardanelles would open up an avenue of aid to beleaguered Russia, which would then draw off German troops from the Western Front to the Eastern Front.

➤ Opening up the Dardanelles would give the West access to the vast grain fields of the Ukraine, an important advantage in this war of attrition.

➤ Defeating a lesser power than Germany—an Austria or a Turkey—would greatly boost British and Allied morale. As politician Lloyd George well appreciated, the people were clamoring for *results*.

Initially, France's Joffre and England's Kitchener vigorously opposed drawing any resources from the Western Front to fight on a peripheral front. But then Kitchener gave the Dardanelles project support by expressing his view that the German trench line in France was too strong to be broken until more heavy artillery and a sufficiently vast stockpile of ammunition were available to pound it mercilessly. Producing and delivering this materiel would take time. If gains were to be made in the near future, therefore, they would have to be made outside of Western Europe.

Voices of Battle

"This is one of the great campaigns of history. Think what Constantinople is to the East. It is more than London, Paris, and Berlin, rolled into one, are to the West. Think how it has dominated the East. Think what its fall will mean. Think how it will affect Bulgaria, Greece, Romania, and Italy .... You cannot win this war by sitting still."

—Winston S. Churchill, in a speech supporting the Dardanelles campaign

Allied Naval Assault

Yet Joffre and Kitchener remained adamant that troops could not now be spared from the Western Front. Undaunted, Churchill and his supporters proposed an exclusively naval operation. This flew in the face of repeated studies that had been made by the Admiralty as well as by the Imperial General Staff before the war. The strategic importance of the Dardanelles was well appreciated, and much thought had been given to how this key passageway might be seized and controlled in the event of conflict. The conclusion of all studies by both the navy and the army was that a purely naval operation against the Dardanelles could not succeed. A joint army-navy amphibious operation was the only answer.

Churchill was not one to be thwarted by prewar plans and studies. On January 3, 1915, he cabled Vice Admiral Sackville Carden, commander of the Royal Navy forces in the Aegean, to ask if his ships, unsupported by land troops, could force the straits. Carden replied that there was no way to "rush" the Dardanelles, but he submitted a plan for a slow, methodical assault on the Turkish defenses. The idea was to pound the Turkish forts with the big guns of the Aegean fleet's aging battleships while *minesweepers* worked the straits to clear them of mines. Carden estimated that it would take at least a month to reach Constantinople and begin bombarding it.

In truth, it was a very vague plan—but it was exactly what Churchill and his circle wanted to hear. They prevailed on the British War Cabinet to direct "a naval expedition in February to bombard and take the Gallipoli Peninsula with Constantinople as its objective."

To anyone even rudimentarily skilled in military affairs, the order would have seemed absurd. Although it was certainly possible for a naval expedition to bombard a target, *taking* the objective required troops—and troops were not slated for this particular mission. Never mind. The operation *would* go forward. As Churchill remarked, "You cannot win this war by sitting still."

Leading an Anglo-French naval squadron of a dozen predreadnought battleships plus the *Queen Elizabeth*, one of the newest *super dreadnoughts*, and various auxiliary ships, Admiral Carden proposed to level the forts at Cape Helles at the southern tip of the Gallipoli Peninsula and Kum Kale on the Asiatic shore. At the narrows, where the passage between the straits was only a mile wide, no fewer than 20 enemy forts were massed. Here is where the attack had to be concentrated.

Based on its performance in the Balkan Wars and the Caucasus campaign, the British and French had grossly underestimated the Turkish army. At Gallipoli, the Turks were actually reinforcing the forts with considerable skill, deploying mobile artillery batteries along the shore and adding to the underwater mines that extended across the straits. They were making an already formidable objective far more forbidding.

On February 19, after three weeks of preparation—which entirely sacrificed the element of surprise—Carden opened fire against the forts at Cape Helles. When no fire was returned, Carden was convinced that the Turks had hastily decamped, and he closed his squadron to within three miles of shore. Suddenly, shore batteries opened fire, and a surprised Carden hastily withdrew.

Storms delayed the admiral's return until February 25, but the squadron succeeded in silencing the outer forts within 48 hours. After parties of marines landed to destroy the guns, the entire squadron steamed into the straits.

Words of War

A **minesweeper** is a ship designed to locate and safely detonate explosive marine mines. Most World War I minesweepers were converted from fishing-type vessels that worked two abreast, dragging a cable between them to snag the mooring lines of mines. The mooring line would be cut, and the mine would bob to the surface, where it could be safely detonated by gunfire.

Words of War

The **super dreadnought** was the biggest battleship class of the war. The British **Queen Elizabeth,** for example, displaced 31,500 tons, had 13-inch belt armor, mounted eight 15-inch guns, and cruised at 24 knots; the earlier *Dreadnought*, at 21,845 tons, had 11-inch armor, fired ten 12-inch guns, and logged a top speed of 21 knots.

It proved to be slow, tough going against bad weather and remarkably accurate Turkish artillery fire, which wreaked havoc among the British minesweepers, many of which were nothing more than converted North Sea fishing trawlers, whose wooden hulls were vulnerable to fire from small arms, let alone artillery. Moreover, the British minesweeper flotilla with the Aegean Fleet was manned by Royal Navy reservists who, while certainly brave men, lacked the training and discipline necessary for the job. On March 10, a seven-boat minesweeper flotilla entered the Dardanelles at night, only to be turned back by searchlight-directed Turkish gunners. One minesweeper was sunk. The Turks were careful to support their minefields with artillery batteries, which made it nearly impossible for the Royal Navy to sweep the mines.

It was March 18 by the time the British were ready to mount a major assault to break through the final Turkish defenses. But on the eve of the planned action, Admiral Carden suddenly resigned, suffering from a severe ulcer and reportedly on the verge of a total nervous breakdown. He was replaced by Rear Admiral John de Robeck, who immediately pressed ahead with the attack.

In the confusion caused by Carden's collapse, the British and French commanders failed to discover that a Turkish *minelayer,* the *Nousret,* had deposited a line of new mines parallel to the shore. The attack proceeded in the belief that the area straits had been entirely cleared of mines. There was, in fact, no basis for this belief, because the minesweepers had been unable to operate. Indeed, the Turks' mine expert, a Lieutenant Colonel Geehl, having observed the area in which the Allied battleships were operating, laid mines in the area on the night of March 8. When the French battleship *Bouvet* suddenly sank with the loss of 700 sailors, horrified onlookers did not understand that it had struck a mine, but believed that a Turkish artillery shell had exploded in the vessel's powder magazine.

The attack pressed on. Two hours after *Bouvet* sank, the British battle cruiser *Inflexible* struck a mine, as did the battleships *Irresistible* and *Ocean.* The battle cruiser was badly damaged, but the two battleships sank. In addition, two more British ships were badly damaged by mines.

Chaos reigned among the Allied fleet, and de Robeck, confused and fearful of operating ships in mined waters, retreated with his remaining, crippled ships to his base on the island of Lemnos.

Words of War

A **minelayer** is a ship designed, modified, or simply used to lay explosive marine mines in patterns called "mine barrages."

From the Front

From the British perspective, after the loss and damage of major ships, the attack must have seemed an unmitigated disaster. Actually, it had succeeded quite well. The beleaguered de Robeck, however, had no way of knowing this when he ordered the retreat.

169

While it is true that de Robeck had suffered severe losses and had made few apparent gains, it is likely that, had he pressed the attack, the straits would indeed have fallen. Doubtless, however, such perseverance must have appeared to him suicidal at the time.

Hasty Muster

While de Robeck was leading his abortive all-navy assault, Kitchener had reconsidered the availability of troops for service against the Dardanelles, released a few divisions (including one French unit), and hastily began assembling them in Egypt and on Lemnos. The total strength of this group, dubbed the Mediterranean Force, was 78,000 men under the command of General Ian Hamilton, a hardened veteran of the Boer conflict.

Everything about this deployment was slapdash and haphazard. Before he left London for the Dardanelles on March 13, Hamilton was given a cursory briefing, in which he was instructed not to use his men until the navy had exhausted every effort on its own. When Hamilton arrived at the straits, however, it was just in time to see the collapse of the costly March 18 all-navy assault. The very next day, Hamilton contacted Kitchener to inform him that the navy could never force the straits on its own. Admiral de Robeck was actually inclined to try an all-navy assault one more time, but he was easily persuaded by Hamilton to conduct a joint army-navy operation. Churchill objected but then allowed the change in plan.

If the briefing given Hamilton had been sketchy, the preparations for the land portion of assault were even more haphazard. Incredibly, the first contingent of troops and their weapons had been loaded in separate ships, so the soldiers arrived on Lemnos without their equipment. Sorting out the problems of supply and getting Hamilton's force *combat-loaded* into the ships for an amphibious assault consumed an entire month.

For the Turks, the bumbling British delay came as a godsend. Under the able leadership of German General Liman von Sanders (who, in 1913, had been appointed head of the German military mission to Constantinople, charged with assisting in the modernization of the Turkish Army), some 60,000 Turks were advantageously deployed on the Gallipoli Peninsula in strongly defended positions. They were now well supplied, securely dug in, and totally prepared for the long-delayed Franco-British onslaught.

Words of War

An amphibious attack force is **combat-loaded** into ships—that is, loaded by unit and with all necessary equipment so that the force can be landed in good order and 100 percent ready to fight, without having to take the time to assemble.

Words of War

An **amphibious assault** is an attack in which ground forces are transported to the battlefield by ships and are deposited on shore by various landing craft. The land action of most amphibious assaults is supported by naval artillery bombardment from battleships or other warships.

First Landings

Amphibious assaults were not a novelty in 1915. Examples of armies landing on hostile shores are to be found throughout history. Historically, however, amphibious assaults were fairly uncomplicated. The main trick was to find a landing point where the enemy had not yet formed its ranks, and then to land there and form one's own battle ranks before the defenders could arrive and assemble in sufficient strength.

From the Front

One of the most important weapons of World War I was barbed wire. Although barbed wire was first patented in the United States in 1867, it wasn't until 1874 that Joseph Glidden of De Kalb, Illinois, invented a workable machine for its mass production. On the ranges of the American West, barbed wire made the cattle industry practical and profitable. On the various fronts of World War I, the wire greatly impeded the advance of attacking troops, slowing them up and making them highly vulnerable targets for machine gun fire as well as artillery bombardment.

In the past, combat was chiefly between opposing armies massed in compact bodies formed in ranks. But modern technology had changed this. Although amphibious assault was not new, the methods of defending against it were. The machine gun and barbed wire made it possible for very small forces of defenders to offer effective resistance all along a shore so that it was no longer necessary to resist a landing army with an entire army formed in ranks. Instead, relatively few machine gunners could delay and disorganize a landing force, buying plenty of time for the main body of defenders to arrive on the scene and stage a full counterattack that could push the invaders into the sea.

The plan called for a series of main landings as well as diversionary *feints and demonstrations*. While the French troops conducted a feint at Kum Kale, on the Asiatic mainland, and the Royal Naval Division sailed up to the base of the Gallipoli Peninsula for a demonstration against Bulair, the British 29th Infantry Division would make the

Words of War

Feints and demonstrations are diversionary attacks by relatively small forces intended to decoy defenders away from the main attacking force.

main attack at Cape Helles, at the very tip of the peninsula. The Australia-New Zealand Army Corps—called ANZAC—would land a dozen miles farther up to make a supporting attack.

Under Fire

The attack commenced on April 25, with the diversionary actions against the mainland and Bulair successfully drawing Turkish attention from the main attack. The ANZAC landed at "Anzac Cove," which was a mistake, being one mile north of its intended landing place. The steep cliffs, narrow beach, and general confusion as troops built up on this narrow strand made for a slow advance. Initially, the ANZAC met no resistance, but as it managed to move inland, it came under fire from a Turkish division commanded by General Mustapha Kemal—who, later known as Atatürk, would be celebrated as nothing less than the father of the modern Turkish state. Kemal's troops were outnumbered, but they held the high ground and beat back the ANZAC, pushing it to a narrow sliver of beachhead and holding it under fire there.

In the meantime, at Cape Helles, the British 29th Division also landed across five beaches, designated S, V, W, X, and Y. They encountered light resistance at S, X, and Y beaches, but at W beach, the invaders were met by a nightmare of heavy fire. The beach was well protected by barbed wire, the troops became entangled in it, and they were raked by merciless machine gun fire. The landing parties here suffered severe casualties, although survivors managed to gain a toehold on the beach.

Voices of Battle

"He is young. He has lion-hearted courage. No number of enemies can fight down his ability and force. His hour of triumph will come."

—J.L. Gavin, editor of the London *Observer,* in 1915, after Churchill's resignation as First Lord of the Admiralty

Blunders and Bloodshed

The situation was even more desperate on V beach, at Sedd-el-Bahr. This was the site of the principal landings of the main attack. For this purpose, an old collier (a coal transport), the *River Clyde,* had been hastily converted into an improvised infantry landing craft to supplement troop barges, which were being towed to the shore by motorboats. Two thousand troops were to disembark from the *Clyde* through doors cut into her bow. But the beach was so well defended by machine guns that 70 percent of the first thousand troops who tried to exit the ship were cut down before they even reached the beach. The second thousand troops remained huddled in the old collier, and the few troops who had managed to reach shore hugged the land under the heights. By mid-morning, it was apparent that the landings had collapsed.

Apparent, too, was the ongoing machine-gun slaughter. Yet General Ian Hamilton declined to intervene by ordering troops to be shifted to the less heavily defended beaches. He had delegated operational command to the 29th Division commander and decided to allow him to conduct the battle however he saw fit and at whatever cost. That commander, however, had been able to establish little communication with the beaches and could not exercise effective, coordinated control of the landing. Even given Hamilton's appalling indifference to the lives of his men, the situation might still have been saved by the individual initiative of on-scene, lower-level unit commanders. Such commanders would prove the keys to success during the great D-Day landings at Normandy during World War II. But this was not the case at Gallipoli. Even though the Allies outnumbered the defenders six to one, they were pinned down and were slaughtered.

By May 8, British mismanagement of the Gallipoli landings had created a set of beachheads now deeply scarred by the ubiquitous trenches of this war. Stalemate had replaced advance. As on the Western Front, maneuver was no longer an option. The miseries of these latest trenches were many: Sporadic machine gun fire from the heights took its toll, but so did continual exposure to the intense sun. Rapidly, disease spread by flies and fleas began killing more men than Turkish bullets claimed.

Combatants

Winston Churchill believed that his political career had been ended by the Gallipoli fiasco. In the immediate wake of this bitter experience, after resigning from the Admiralty, he took up painting, which became both a solace and a passion for the rest of his life.

He did not remain out of the war long, however. He accepted command of the 6th Royal Scots Fusiliers and fought with them in France until May 1916, when he returned to England. In July 1917, David Lloyd George, Churchill's friend and political ally, and the new prime minister, named him to the Cabinet post of Minister of Munitions. Churchill poured himself into the work of increasing munitions production and actually achieved a shell surplus before the war had ended.

But it was for his service during the *next* world war that Winston Churchill would be best remembered. He served as Britain's gallant, brilliant, and stalwart prime minister from 1940 to 1945, leading Europe's sole remaining wartime democracy to victory against the Nazis and their allies. He served as prime minister again from 1951 to 1955. In addition to his political career as one of the giants of the twentieth century, Churchill was a memoirist and historian of lofty, formidable, and prolific achievement. In 1963, the United States Congress conferred upon him honorary citizenship, an act unique in American history. Churchill died in 1965, at the age of 91.

Heads Roll

While British and ANZAC soldiers languished, a shudder of bitter recrimination shook the British government in London. The Cabinet fell, First Sea Lord Fisher resigned in protest over the weakening of the Grand Fleet to reinforce Gallipoli, David Lloyd George moved from Chancellor of the Exchequer to Minister of Munitions—and Churchill, the dynamic instigator of the entire operation, was removed as First Lord of the Admiralty and relegated to a minor Cabinet post. Infuriated, he resigned from the government and went to the Western Front as lieutenant colonel in command of the 6th Royal Scots Fusiliers.

Second Landing

The government architects of the Gallipoli operation suffered, at worst, blows to career and reputation—and perhaps to conscience. In the meantime, the troops on the beaches were bleeding and dying.

In operations on the Western Front, retreat was almost always an optional alternative to total disaster. But at the backs of the Allied troops on Gallipoli was the sea. Retreat could not be a simple matter of withdrawal, but would involve a complex, slow, and suicidally dangerous process of amphibious evacuation. As soldiers tried to clamber aboard boats, they would be fully exposed to enemy machine guns. For this reason, Lord Kitchener, originally a vehement opponent to the entire Dardanelles operation, now found himself its principal supporter. While others called for evacuation, Kitchener pointed out that such an operation would incur a 50 percent casualty rate.

The alternative? Kitchener now advocated reinforcement of Hamilton and a new attack. The Dardanelles campaign, originally an unwelcome sideshow to the war on the Western Front, now became a British obsession, and Gallipoli was redesignated as the principal theater of operations for the summer of 1915, five fresh British divisions were shipped off to Ian Hamilton's command, and that general was given top priority for receipt of ammunition and supplies.

Hamilton resolved to use his new resources to make a landing at Suvla Bay, a few miles north of where the ANZAC had landed in the first assault. The immediate objective was to outflank the Turkish defenders and draw them away from the beachhead tenuously established by the ANZAC. On this beachhead would follow the main British attack.

The renewed assault began on August 6. During the three months between it and the initial landings, fighting on the rocky slopes of the peninsula had been continuous, intense, bitter, and totally fruitless. Naval combat had taken place as well, but after German U-boats and Turkish destroyers sank three British battleships, the Allied capital craft withdrew to protected harbors. This meant that although Hamilton now had a far more substantial land force at his disposal, he lacked adequate support from naval gunfire. A new disaster, stemming from lack of coordination between naval and army elements, was in the offing.

The ANZAC was called on to advance, at night, through tangled gullies and ridges with the object of storming the heights of the Sari Bar range and driving the Turks off of it. The new British landings at Suvla Bay, to the north, would make a secondary, supporting attack. In the meantime, at Cape Helles, on the tip of the peninsula, a holding attack would pin down Turkish reserves and keep them out of the principal action. It was far too complicated a plan, and, to make matters worse, General Hamilton imposed such tight security that many of his senior commanders were left uninformed until the very last minute.

During August 6–8, the operation flashed with moments of hope and promise. The holding attack at Helles succeeded admirably, and the Suvla Bay landing, made without enemy opposition, put troops in a position for real gains.

Final Failure

But the ANZAC assault became entirely disoriented in the dark of a moonless night and was quickly bogged down. It was renewed in the morning but never attained its objective, the Sidhi Bahr Ridge, which dominated the Turkish forts and artillery emplacements controlling the narrows of the Dardanelles. Had this ridge been taken, the bitter campaign at last would have been crowned with success.

But the bravery and determination of the Turkish troops (something the British and ANZAC had entirely discounted) combined with poor planning to ensure that the ridge would not be conquered.

Just as the ANZAC assault failed, the Suvla Bay landings ultimately came to nothing. Lieutenant General Sir Frederick Stopford, who led that assault, lacked the drive and initiative to capitalize on the surprise he had achieved with the initial landing. Ordered to move inland to seize the high ground, he delayed, giving Sanders, the German commander of Turkish troops, sufficient time to summon reinforcements and effectively block further movement from Suvla Bay.

Evacuation

If there is a bright spot in the whole tragic and disgraceful Dardanelles campaign, it is the evacuation. On October 15, General Hamilton was relieved of command and was replaced by General Sir Charles Monro, a commander as skilled and adept as Hamilton had been stodgy and cloddish. Running counter to Lord Kitchener's recommendation, Monro reported that evacuation was now the only viable option. His careful evacuation plan was approved on November 23. After destroying what equipment they could not remove, the British and ANZAC withdrew from their trenches in groups, leaving firing parties to simulate the usual nighttime activities. Troop-filled barges and boats were quietly towed to waiting troopships. The highly disciplined soldiers kept perfect silence. By December 10, Monro had managed to remove major supplies and most of the surviving troops.

Monro left campfires and lights burning while he withdrew some 35,000 rear-guard troops. To screen this, Monro's men rigged rifles with improvised timed firing mechanisms and left these behind to give the impression that the trenches were manned. The rear guard was evacuated during January 8–9, 1916, under cover of darkness. Incredibly, not a single man of this remaining force was lost.

Russia, Hanging

The failure of the Dardanelles campaign was total. The eminent American military historians R. Ernest Dupuy and Trevor N. Dupuy have called it "the most poorly mounted and ineptly controlled operation in modern British military history" (with the "possible exception of the Crimean War"). More than a quarter-million Allied troops were killed or wounded.

Although the Turks lost nearly as many men—251,000 versus 252,000 for the Allies—they still controlled the Dardanelles, which meant that Russia was entirely and permanently cut off from France and Britain. Doubtless, this fact did not in and of itself doom Russia to the coming revolution and ignominious separate peace with Germany, but it surely helped seal the fate of the czar and his war effort.

For the Allies, especially the British, the failure was a grave blow to collective self-confidence and morale. The objective had been partly to boost morale by defeating a *lesser* enemy than the Germans. The Turkish army, which had performed so miserably in the Balkan Wars and, more recently, in the Caucasus, had defeated the British, even though it was almost always substantially outnumbered. Much of the credit must go to the brilliant German commander of the Turkish forces, Liman von Sanders, but it is also true that Mustafa Kemal, his chief subordinate, had performed with great skill and daring, as had the Turkish soldiers, whose gallantry verged on fanaticism.

As for conditions on the Western Front—if anything, they now promised to be grimmer than ever.

The Least You Need to Know

➤ Winston Churchill (and others) proposed seizing the Dardanelles and Constantinople as an indirect means of breaking the deadlock on the Western Front and reestablishing lines of communication and supply with Russia.

➤ An initial assault on the Dardanelles, using warships without support from land forces, failed after a number of Allied vessels were sunk by mines.

➤ Two amphibious assaults, combining army and navy elements, poorly planned and poorly executed, failed disastrously; the Allies finally withdrew, and Russia was left permanently isolated for the remainder of the war.

Chapter 15

The Other Fronts, 1915

In This Chapter

➤ Italy joins the Allied cause

➤ The frustrations of Isonzo

➤ New battles in the Caucasus

➤ The Turks practice genocide

➤ The Turks abortively attack the Suez Canal

➤ Misguided military ambition in Mesopotamia

Through 1914 and 1915, where Americans stood on what they called "the war in Europe" greatly varied. Most deplored such acts as the brutal German invasion of "little Belgium," and, to be sure, everyone was appalled by the ongoing loss of life on both sides, especially along the Western Front. The British intelligence service mounted a masterful propaganda campaign to manipulate the war news published in American papers. Consistently, the Germans were painted as brutal monsters bent on nothing less than the destruction of civilization.

It was unrestricted submarine warfare that did the most to turn American public opinion against Germany, but even so, the United States was home to a very large population of German immigrants and the descendants of such immigrants, many of whom continued to support the interests of the ancestral homeland during the war—not just with rhetoric, but also with financial aid contributed to various fund drives. Pacifists and committed isolationists—people who believed that the United States should not enter the war under any circumstances whatsoever—were in the minority in 1915, but so were those who advocated immediately pitching in against Germany.

The majority of Americans believed that Germany and the other Central Powers were wrong, but they were happy that President Woodrow Wilson had maintained U.S. neutrality. Wilson was carried to a second term in the White House in 1916 in large part on the slogan, "He kept us out of war."

It was undeniable. Americans could be thankful that their large and bountiful land was one of the few places in the world untouched by the great conflict. By 1915, the "European War" not only was being fought on the Western and Eastern fronts, but it had engulfed just about all of Europe—and many other places as well.

Enter Italy

As explained in Chapter 5, "Battle of the Frontiers," Italy was nominally part of the Triple Alliance with Germany and Austria, but it had refrained from joining them in the war. As Italy stood on the sidelines, the Allies practiced some shrewd, adroit, and highly secret diplomacy, promising Italy territorial gains at the expense of Austria-Hungary in exchange for an alliance.

End of the Triple Alliance

At last, on April 26, 1915, Italy signed the secret Treaty of London with Great Britain, France, and Russia, by which its obligations under the Triple Alliance were abrogated. The prize was the Italian-populated Trentino and Trieste (both under Austrian control) as well as the South Tirol, Gorizia, Istria, and northern Dalmatia. Less than a month later, on May 23, 1915, Italy formally declared war on Austria-Hungary.

The Italian Army

The Italian army was large, at 875,000 men, but was poorly equipped, with particularly severe deficiencies in artillery, ammunition reserves, and transport.

Another problem was at the command level. On July 1, 1914, the eve of war, General Alberto Pollio, chief of staff since 1908, died suddenly of a heart attack. He was hastily replaced by General Luigi Cadorna, a deeply flawed commander on the verge of retirement at the time of his appointment. Stubborn, pugnacious, crusty, and a mean-spirited martinet, Cadorna managed equally to alienate politicians (which resulted in chronic underfunding of the army), his subordinate commanders, and the rank-and-file troops. He was a harsh, even cruel, disciplinarian and an entirely uninspiring leader.

From the Front

In 1914, the Italian army had only 595 vehicles and depended on some 200,000 horses and other draft animals for transportation. In 1916, there were only 112,000 rifles to train 228,000 conscripts. When it joined the fighting, the army was allowed only 148 million of the 551 million–lire emergency funding it had requested.

Combatants

Luigi Cadorna (1850–1928) was a man obsessed by the Isonzo Front, into which he fed the Italian army as a butcher might feed beef into a meat grinder. The son of an important Italian military family, Cadorna devoted his life and career to the army, yet did not hold a combat command prior to World War I.

Named to the post of chief of staff on July 1, 1914, after the sudden death of General Alberto Pollio, Cadorna—assuming that Italy would join the other Central Powers in a war against the Allies—prepared the army to fight France. Cadorna did succeed in mobilizing a massive army, but never acquired the advanced equipment, especially artillery, needed to defeat the Austro-Hungarian forces. Additionally, he was unpopular with troops, with fellow officers, and with civilian politicians.

Once Italy entered the war, Cadorna focused on defeating the Austro-Hungarians in the mountainous border region. Here the terrain made attack difficult, and the Italian general doomed his forces to a dozen futile and extremely costly battles along the Isonzo River. Despite repeated failure, Cadorna refused to yield to the reality that attacks against the well-defended mountain positions were destined to fail.

In 1917, after the Austro-Hungarian army broke through Italian forces at Caporetto, Cadorna, thoroughly discredited, was relieved of command. A postwar investigation blamed him for Italy's many failures in World War I, but the dictator Benito Mussolini, in need of a popular hero, officially rehabilitated Cadorna by promoting him to field marshal in 1924.

A Dream of Vienna

Cadorna had no combat experience and was, at best, a mediocre military strategist. However, he did have a certain plan, and he shared with other Italian military men a certain dream.

The plan was simple and twofold. Despite the existence of the Triple Alliance, Austria-Hungary, long an enemy of Italy, had heavily fortified its Italian frontier. The risk of an Austrian attack from Trentino, which bordered Venetia to the northwest, was significant. Also vulnerable was the northern Italian region bordering the Carnic Alps. Cadorna adopted a primarily defensive posture in these areas—with some limited advances anticipated—and instead concentrated his main effort on an offensive that would proceed eastward from the province of Venetia across the lower valley of the Isonzo (Soca) River. His objective was to push a salient into Austro-Hungarian territory with the aim of taking the town Gorizia on the east bank of the Isonzo.

That was the *stated* aim of Cadorna's strategy. Like other Italian military men, however, he had bigger dreams of an objective much greater than Gorizia. He envisioned the Italian army—like a latter-day Roman legion—marching through Trieste and ultimately into Vienna, capital of the hated Dual Monarchy.

The First Battles of Isonzo

The gulf separating the dream from the reality would prove wide indeed—and initially muddy as well. Concentrating on men and arms, Cadorna ignored the weather. He began his advance eastward in May 1915, only to find his armies halted by seasonal flooding of the Isonzo.

The Allies greeted the entry of Italy into the war with great hopefulness because it opened up a whole new front against the enemy. This would mean more pressure on the Central Powers from a new direction and, therefore, reduced pressure on the Allies' other fronts. Moreover, they saw in this new front the possibility of movement in contrast to the stalemate of the Western Front. The flooding, which halted the advance, put an end to that possibility. With the halt of the Italian army, both sides dug in, and the Isonzo Front became yet another line of trenches.

Luigi Cadorna was unwilling to accept the permanence of trench warfare, however. Determined to renew his advance at any cost, he ordered what became a brutal series of offensives, known as the Battles of the Isonzo.

Cadorna enjoyed significant superiority of numbers over his opponents, Austrian Archduke Eugene, in overall command of the Italian Front, and General Svetozan Borojevic von Bojna, with 100,000 men, in command of the Isonzo sector of that front. Against this force, the Italian Second and Third Armies (under Pietro Frugoni and the Duke of Aosta, respectively) hurled some 200,000 troops and 200 guns. Despite their greater numbers, in the First Battle of Isonzo (June 23–July 7), the Italians battered in vain against the well-developed Austrian defenses.

From July 18 to August 3, Cadorna made a second attempt, this time backed by more artillery. The Austrians had also augmented the defenders, however, and held firm. Cadorna was forced to break off the attack when his artillery ammunition ran out.

Cadorna need have looked only to the trenches of France for a lesson in the invulnerability of highly

From the Front

The first two battles of Isonzo cost the Italians 60,000 casualties versus 45,000 for the Austro-Hungarian army. Absolutely nothing was gained by these sacrifices.

prepared positions to frontal assault. But, clearly, common sense and sound judgment were among the earliest of the hundreds of thousands of casualties that this war had already produced. Cadorna heedlessly mounted a third offensive at Isonzo from October 18 to November 4. This time, the Italian general had 1,200 guns at his disposal.

The result? Another costly repulse.

That seemed hardly to matter to the determined Italian. On November 10, Cadorna resumed the fight. He broke off the engagement on December 10, the two battles having cost 117,000 Italian dead and wounded. On the Austro-Hungarian side, almost 72,000 men had been lost. The front had not budged an inch.

Death in the Caucasus

Luigi Cadorna's dream of Vienna bled to death at Isonzo much as Enver Pasha's fantasy of dealing ruin to Russia had died in the Caucasus (see Chapter 10, "The Sick Man and Serbia"). Although the Turkish army would never fully recover from Enver's misbegotten invasion attempt, it was by no means finished as a combat force.

Voices of Battle

"I had seen nothing sacred, and the things that were glorious had no glory and the sacrifices were like the stockyards in Chicago if nothing was done with the meat except to bury it ... Abstract words such as glory, honor, courage, or hallow were obscene."

—Ernest Hemingway, in *A Farewell to Arms* (1929), a novel based on experiences on the Isonzo Front

Malazgirt

Under one of Enver Pasha's new subordinates, Abdul Kerim, a Turkish force attacked and defeated a Russian corps at the Battle of Malazgirt, north of Lake Van, not far from the Ottoman Empire's frontier with Persia.

Kara Killisse

A Turkish triumph was rare, and General Abdul Kerim pressed his eastward advance with great caution. Russian General Nikolai Yudenich dispatched General N.N. Baratov with a force of 22,000 Cossacks—warriors who had earned a legendary reputation for ferocity—to intercept the Turks.

The Battle of Kara Killisse resulted in heavy Turkish casualties and the withdrawal of the Turks.

Genocide

By the late 1880s, some 2.5 million Christian Armenians lived within the Ottoman Empire. Russia encouraged those in the eastern provinces to agitate for Armenian

181

territorial autonomy. By 1890, two Armenian revolutionary parties had been formed; in response to Turkish oppression, Armenian radicals rose in revolt. In 1894, when the Armenians in Sasun refused to pay the heavy taxes levied against them, Turkish troops and Kurdish tribesmen massacred thousands of them and burned their villages. Two years later, Armenian revolutionaries seized the Ottoman Bank in Istanbul, provoking an even bloodier response. At the instigation of government troops, mobs of Muslim Turks attacked and killed more than 50,000 Armenians.

As terrible as these acts of genocide were, even worse came as part of the world war.

Long-oppressed Armenians from the Caucasus eagerly formed volunteer battalions to work with the Russian army against the Turks. In 1915, when the battalions began recruiting Turkish Armenians from behind the Turkish lines, the Ottoman government ordered the mass deportation of some 1.75 million Armenians to Syria and Mesopotamia. Of this number, about 600,000 died of exposure and starvation en route through the desert. Doubtless, many of this number were simply murdered by Turkish soldiers and police.

Voices of Battle

"Who remembers a million Armenians?"

—Adolf Hitler, before ordering the invasion of Poland in 1939

Van Falls ...

While the general Turkish Armenian population was being persecuted, deported, and killed, Armenian rebels seized the important Turkish fortress of Van on April 20 and held it until the Russians arrived on May 19.

... And Is Retaken

Against a backdrop of oppression, misery, and murder, the fighting between the Russians and the Turks in the Armenian mountains seesawed erratically. On August 5, the Turks retook the Van fortress, and the Russians withdrew. In September, under the command of the Grand Duke Nicholas, newly appointed Viceroy of Caucasia, the planning began for a major new offensive (see Chapter 17, "Italy, the Eastern Front, and Elsewhere, 1916").

The Holy Land and Mesopotamia

By 1915, the world-engulfing conflict was just beginning to spread to Egypt and Palestine. The most valuable prize in the region was the Suez Canal. Completed in 1869, the canal runs north-south across the Isthmus of Suez in Egypt and joins the Mediterranean to the Red Sea. Its strategic importance lay in its status as the shortest maritime route between Europe and all the lands around the Indian and western Pacific oceans.

Thrust Against the Canal

On January 14, 1915, Djemal Pasha, the Turkish Minister of Marine, with German General Friedrich Kress von Kressenstein as his chief of staff, led 22,000 men in a secret march across the Sinai Peninsula from Beersheba. Their objective was the Suez Canal.

On February 2, advance elements of the expedition reached the canal and began an assault, but they were quickly beaten back. After losing 2,000 men, Djemal Pasha withdrew to Beersheba.

This abortive action would be the war's only Turkish attack against the canal. Although the canal remained under British control, fear of a renewed attack tied down large numbers of British troops that had been intended for service as reinforcements for the Dardanelles campaign (see Chapter 14, "The Gallipoli Disaster"). In this way, the Turkish attack, inconsiderable in itself, produced a lasting drain on British strength in the region and contributed to the miserable failure at Gallipoli.

Rocking the Cradle of Civilization

In the world of 1915, the most important fuel for war was coal, which fed the fires that heated the boilers of the great battleships. Oil was a distant second to coal in strategic importance, but it was important nevertheless as a fuel for land vehicles and as a lubricant. Accordingly, the British Cabinet had prevailed on the Indian colonial government to mount a modest expedition to protect the flow of oil from the great Anglo-Persian pipeline. At Qurna, this force easily brushed aside Turkish resistance (April 12–14), an achievement that prompted British military planners to order a further advance, with the ultimate object of capturing Baghdad.

The enterprise was yet another symptom of military frustration. At every front, progress was slow or nonexistent. Here, in this out-of-the-way corner of the war, a victory had been quickly and easily won. The temptation to achieve more victories proved irresistible, even though the strategic value of pressing on to Baghdad was dubious at best. Taking Baghdad would certainly result in no immediate advantage. In the long term, there were oil sources to be gained, as well as the political advantage of extending British imperial influence into territories held by the Ottoman Empire. Traditionally, too, the British had always been keen on defending the approaches to India.

Major General Charles V.F. Townshend led a reinforced division and naval flotilla up the Tigris River, took a Turkish outpost near Qurna on May 31, and then proceeded to Amara, which he occupied on June 3.

Coordinating his movements with those of Townshend, Major General George F. Gorringe led a small force up the Euphrates to protect Townshend's flank. At Nasiriya, beginning on July 24, he hammered away at strong Turkish defensive positions, which took a month of hard fighting to neutralize.

183

Townshend, who had been sent reinforcements, was now ordered to attack and capture Kut-el-Amara, a village at the confluence of the Tigris and Shatt-el-Hai rivers. His 11,000 men and 28 guns arrived just below Kut by September 16. Townshend saw that he was facing a very well-defended position manned by a force of 10,000 and well-furnished with 38 guns. The British general realized that his communications and supply lines were highly strained and vulnerable, and he decided to await supply before attacking.

While awaiting supplies, Townshend intensively studied the situation at Kut and concluded that, although it was very substantially fortified, the Turkish position had a key weakness. The Turkish forces were divided astride the Tigris River, with the only bridge five miles upstream. This meant that the Turks had severely limited their own lateral mobility. Townshend exploited this weakness by ordering two brigades to conduct a demonstration on the right bank of the Tigris to decoy the Turkish reserves. This accomplished, he then moved the two decoy brigades back north of the river under cover of darkness on the night of September 27. With his full forces, he attacked and enveloped the left flank of the divided Turkish army, driving two-thirds of the defenders out of their positions.

It was a textbook instance of effective maneuver, but combat in the desert made demands far beyond any textbook. Although Townshend had achieved a neat and efficient victory, his troops were too worn out by contending with bad weather and marching great distances to press their advantage. The defeated Turks withdrew, but they did so intact and in good order, taking up new positions farther up the Tigris at Ctesiphon.

After resting, reorganizing, and doing his best to resupply his spent troops, Townshend commenced an advance to Ctesiphon during November 11–22. The military wisdom of this move was highly questionable, but the emotional lure of Baghdad—the prospect of capturing a major city—proved overwhelming.

Words of War

Regulars are members of a nation's permanent, standing army, maintained in peace as well as war. They do not include reservists or auxiliary troops, who are called on exclusively in emergencies or time of war.

Unfortunately, once he arrived at Ctesiphon, Townshend found that the Turks had fortified their positions formidably and had been reinforced by tough Anatolian infantry to a total strength of 18,000 *regulars* in addition to various Arab auxiliaries. Townshend led a significantly smaller force of 10,000 infantry, mostly Indian colonial troops, in addition to a thousand cavalry and 30 guns. He also had a squadron of seven airplanes—the first time this weapon had appeared on the Mesopotamian Front. (The planes were used mainly for reconnaissance.)

Despite his disadvantage in numbers, Townshend attacked on November 22 with great ferocity—and with absolutely everything he had. Nothing was kept in reserve.

Initial results were highly encouraging, as the first Turkish line crumpled before the Anglo-Indian onslaught. But then came the Turkish counterattacks, which were unremitting. Over the next four days, Townshend held out against wave after enemy wave. At last, he decided that no choice remained but to withdraw, which he did only after evacuating his wounded.

Fortunately for Townshend, the Turks were too battered to pursue his retreat with any degree of enthusiasm. He fought a single substantial *rear-guard action* at Umm-at-Tubal on December 1 and then arrived back at Kut on December 3. Realizing that his infantry was too exhausted to retreat farther, Townshend sent his cavalry to the rear and holed up at Kut to await reinforcements. Beginning on December 7, the Turks returned to Kut to lay siege to this position. (The outcome of this action is discussed in Chapter 17.)

And Persia

Perhaps the most remote front in this world war was in Persia. Although that nation proclaimed its neutrality at the outset of the conflict, Russian troops quickly occupied most of northern Persia, and the British rushed in to occupy the northwestern Persian Gulf coast as soon as Turkey entered the war. The British purpose was to protect oil supplies and to create a base of operations for action in Mesopotamia. In the meantime, the Turks seized almost all of Persian Kurdistan.

As we saw in Chapter 10, the Battle of Sarikamish, in the Caucasus borderlands of Russia and Persia, resulted in initial Turkish gains at the expense of the Russians before the Turks were driven out with disastrous losses by January 30, 1915. After this, fighting continued sporadically in western Persia—mainly on the periphery of action in the Caucasus and Mesopotamia—throughout the rest of the year.

Words of War

A **rear-guard action** is combat conducted primarily to protect a retreat main force, which is always vulnerable at its rear.

From the Front

The Anglo-Indian forces suffered 4,600 casualties out of 11,000 men engaged at Ctesiphon. The Turks lost 6,200 killed and wounded.

Although the fighting in Mesopotamia was gallant and sometimes even brilliant—a dramatic contrast to the bloody monotony of the Western Front—it cost far more than it gained. The British War Office, remote in London, was out of touch with the realities of combat in Mesopotamia, where distances were great, water and other supplies were scarce, travel was difficult, and communications were nearly nonexistent.

The lure of "exotic" fronts in Mesopotamia and Persia, especially for the British, was precisely because they were remote from the Western Front. While that unspeakably grim battlefield was frozen in a perpetual death grip, it seemed that the peripheral

185

fronts still offered scope for action, for conquest, and for measurable results beyond the mere tally of corpses. Few planners paused to weigh the strategic worth of prosecuting the war in these regions. After all, what would have been gained by taking Baghdad? Little of any concrete value. Certainly, such a victory would have been welcome to the Allies, but it would not have shortened the war.

The Least You Need to Know

➤ Promised large territorial gains at the expense of Austria-Hungary, Italy abrogated the Triple Alliance and joined the Allied cause.

➤ The Italian army was large, but it was underfunded, poorly equipped, and poorly led; its commander-in-chief, Luigi Cadorna, committed the army to a long series of costly and fruitless offensives along the Isonzo sector of the Austro-Italian front.

➤ For hapless Turkish Armenians in the Caucasus region, World War I became an excuse for mass deportation and genocide at the hands of the Turks; the Armenian massacres were among the worst civilian atrocities of the war.

➤ The chief military target in the Middle East was the Suez Canal, which the British successfully defended against the Turks throughout the war.

➤ The British conducted gallant but costly campaigns in Mesopotamia with the ultimate goal of taking Baghdad, a military objective of dubious value.

Chapter 16

"They Shall Not Pass!"

> **In This Chapter**
>
> ➤ Falkenhayn's plan to "bleed France white"
>
> ➤ Verdun: the opening situation and initial assault
>
> ➤ Pétain's pledge: "They shall not pass!"
>
> ➤ German offensives, French responses
>
> ➤ The British take the initiative at the Somme

Throughout history, the world has known such little peace that the question is unavoidable: What makes war so appealing to so many so much of the time?

One answer is that fighting it out, showing down an enemy, and dealing with him "once and for all" seems to offer the most direct and definitive way of solving international problems. But World War I showed the lie behind this long-cherished belief. By the end of 1915, the war was many horrible things, but whatever it was, it was by no means direct and definitive. Instead, it loomed over Europe like some combination of ravenous beast and intractable puzzle. It ate men, machines, and money, and it defied all attempts to kill it. What was the solution to the puzzle of stalemate?

At the end of 1915, Germany's highest commander, Erich von Falkenhayn, had an idea.

Falkenhayn Writes to the Kaiser

On Christmas day, 1915, Falkenhayn sent a letter to Kaiser Wilhelm II outlining what he saw as the way to bring about a favorable conclusion to the war.

He first proposed that Britain, whose industrial might and maritime power was the foundation of the alliance against Germany, must be utterly demoralized. To demoralize Britain, two things needed to happen:

➤ Unrestricted submarine warfare, directed chiefly at British shipping, had to be renewed.

➤ Britain's continental allies had to be destroyed.

Falkenhayn then addressed priorities concerning these Allies:

➤ Italy was not sufficiently important to merit effort from Germany; Austria-Hungary should receive no German aid on the Italian Front at this time.

➤ Although it was true that short-term gains had been made against Russia on the Eastern Front and would doubtless continue to be made, victory here would not decisively determine the outcome of the war.

Falkenhayn explored this last point at length:

➤ Russia, he declared, was on the verge of revolution, but even if a full-blown revolution did not come soon, the nation's internal troubles were so great that it would soon be compelled to give up. So why tie down so many German troops on a foregone conclusion?

➤ Even if Russia collapsed, it did not offer strategic objectives. The capture of St. Petersburg would have symbolic significance only. The capture of Moscow would lead only to the vast, desolate interior of the Russian nation.

➤ The Ukraine was rich in grain and other raw resources, which Germany (like Britain and France) sorely needed. But the Ukraine was accessible only through Romania, a power whose neutrality Germany did not feel that it could afford to violate at this time.

Then Falkenhayn proceeded to a consideration of the peripheral fronts. He dismissed them with a figurative wave of his hand:

➤ Action in the colonies, in the Middle East, the Caucasus, and Mesopotamia, was simply irrelevant to the outcome of the war.

This left the Western Front. Falkenhayn believed that the British position here was presently too strong to attack directly. France, therefore, was the priority target of choice.

To Bleed France White

"The strain on France," Falkenhayn wrote to his kaiser, "has reached breaking point—though it is certainly borne with the most remarkable devotion. If we succeed in opening the eyes of her people to the fact that in a military sense they have nothing more to hope for, that breaking point would be reached and England's best sword knocked out of her hand."

But just how to reach that breaking point?

Falkenhayn proposed directing a limited offensive on a single point that the French perceived to be so vital that they would be compelled "to throw in every man they have." Falkenhayn concluded, "If they do so, the forces of France will bleed to death."

Later, the German commander-in-chief put this another way. He would conduct an operation that "would bleed France white."

Target: Verdun

Even as he wrote to the kaiser, Falkenhayn had his objective in mind: the fortress of Verdun.

Time out of mind, Verdun had been a fortress. Located in a loop of the Meuse River, it occupied a strategic blocking position in the Meuse River valley. It had figured as an important fortress at least since Roman times, again in the seventeenth century (when the renowned military architect Sebestien le Prestre de Vauban designed its defenses), yet again during the Napoleonic era, and during the Franco-Prussian War (1870–1871) had been the last of the French fortified cities to fall to the Germans. In 1885, the circle of detached forts surrounding the fort's central citadel and the small fortified town of Verdun was augmented by another circle of forts five miles beyond the center of town. These new forts were strengthened with concrete as well as armor plate, and they now not only guarded passage through the river valley region, but also dominated a key railroad junction leading to points south, southwest, west, and north in France.

Yet for all its historical and geographical importance, at the beginning of 1916, Verdun was occupied only by a small *garrison*, and its fortress guns had been dismantled and transported elsewhere on the Western Front for use as field artillery.

What had happened?

Voices of Battle

Henri Desagneaux, a lieutenant in the French Second Infantry Regiment, described the central citadel of Verdun as "a real underground town, with a narrow-gauge railway, dormitories, and rooms of every type; it's safe here, but very gloomy."

Words of War

A **garrison** is a body of troops stationed in and assigned to defend a fortress or a fortified town.

After the collapse of mighty Liège in Belgium during the opening days of the war (see Chapter 5, "Battle of the Frontiers"), the French, who had relied so heavily on fortified defenses, suddenly lost all faith in the efficacy of fortifications. Indeed, the Battle of the Frontiers in August 1914 had flowed around Verdun, as if it weren't even there. Ever since the Western Front had hardened into trenches, Verdun had been a *quiet sector.*

And there was even more to make Verdun a vulnerable target. It was isolated from the rest of the front, exposed to attack on three sides. Communications from Verdun to the French rear were poor, yet the fortress lay only a dozen miles from the nearest German railhead. Verdun's advance trenches—three miles from the fortress line— consisted of a single main trench line and one secondary trench.

Words of War

The phrase **quiet sector** was used during World War I to describe an area of the front in which, typically, little action occurred.

If Verdun had been downgraded in immediate military importance by the French, Falkenhayn understood that it was still of great symbolic significance. With the Western Front stalemated, the French would not willingly allow a German breakthrough at the ancient fortress. By pressing on this one point, the German commander guessed that he could force the French to keep feeding reinforcements into a front only eight miles wide. To Falkenhayn, it all seemed a brutally simple scenario promising victory: If the French gave up at Verdun, they would lose Verdun and allow a German breakthrough. If the French did not give up, they would be "bled white," their army eaten up. He called it Operation Judgment.

Preparation

Yet operations in this war rarely proceeded as simply as plans called for. The German Crown Prince was given the mission of assaulting Verdun with his Fifth Army. His plan was for an overwhelming assault on both sides of the Meuse River. Concerned that this would produce too many losses, the conservative Falkenhayn ordered the attack to be confined to the east bank of the river.

It was set to begin February 12, but bad weather intervened, and the operation was postponed to the 21st. In the meantime, the delay resulted in French detection of the German buildup. Papa Joffre, slow to realize that Verdun was in peril, finally began ordering reinforcements to be sent to the menaced sector. For his part, the commandant of Verdun, Lieutenant Colonel Emile Driant, wasted no time in digging in deeper and doing everything possible to prepare for an onslaught. Despite his efforts, however, most of his units failed to improve their trench systems.

Driant was a bold, impetuous, and even insubordinate officer. He was a member of Parliament, and he was a popular writer whose books were sensational speculations on the future of warfare. Now he would prove himself also to be a practical soldier of great courage. Driant posted himself with two battalions of elite *chasseurs* at the forefront of the coming battle, the very tip of the Verdun salient, on the east bank of the River Meuse.

At 7:15 on the morning of February 21, fire came from the sky. The Crown Prince had massed 1,400 guns along a tightly packed, eight-mile front. He now commenced the bombardment. Each hour, all morning and into the afternoon, the guns fired, pouring 100,000 shells each hour into that small front.

The German idea was that the heavy bombardment would leave very few Frenchman left to fight. But, again, reality turned out not to be so simple. After the first artillery assault, scouting parties were sent in to probe the defenses. What they found, to their surprise, was that the destruction had been far from complete. It seemed clear that surviving parties of French troops, about half the original fighting force, were prepared to put up a determined defense. The initial German probe was withdrawn, and another artillery bombardment was ordered. In retrospect, it is probable that a massed advance at this point might well have succeeded in taking Verdun, but, to the Germans, it continued to seem highly formidable.

From the Front

In the Bois des Caures, the forward position where Driant had his headquarters, 80,000 shells fell in an area of 500 by 1,000 yards.

By the end of the day, the Germans had succeeded in overrunning only the front-line trenches. Driant was killed, and his two battalions were virtually annihilated. Yet German assault troops were withdrawn to allow more artillery preparation, and the momentum of the attack was sacrificed. Because of this, French artillery was able to get into position to enfilade (fire laterally, through and across) the advancing German lines from across the river.

Failure at Fort Douaumont

The German attack faltered, in part, because the German objective had never been simply to overrun Verdun. Rather, it was to provoke the French into a series of counterattacks, which would be monumentally costly to them. That is, it was not so much the German offensive that would "bleed the French army white," but the stubborn determination of the French army itself. Falkenhayn hoped to provoke a kind of mass suicide.

To prevent unnecessary losses among his own infantry, Falkenhayn was determined to rely as much as possible on artillery bombardment. When it came time for the follow-up infantry attack, he launched it from only one side of the Meuse. Had he gone for broke and attacked from both sides, as the Crown Prince had wanted to do, the Germans would have certainly overrun the weakly held positions over the entire eight-mile front. Verdun would have fallen—a German triumph, to be sure, but not the one Falkenhayn most wanted. If the battle could be prolonged, more French would die.

Although Verdun, then, was still in French hands, the situation was desperate. On February 23, a lieutenant of the 72nd Division sent a message to headquarters: "The commanding officer and all company commanders have been killed. My battalion is reduced to approximately 180 men (from 600). I have neither ammunition nor food. What am I to do?"

How could headquarters make an answer? The next day, the second line of trenches was overrun, but two outer forts, Vaux and Douaumont, held out. On the 24th, a fresh French division was sent in piecemeal. It broke under German artillery fire.

At last, on the 25th, Douaumont fell. As popular lore had it, the fort was captured by a German sergeant who had been blown into the fort's moat by the force of an exploding shell. Dazed, he picked himself up and decided to explore the interior of the battered hulk of a fort. There he found a handful of French soldiers. He told them that he was accompanied by a large force of troops, and the Frenchmen, doubtless reeling from the incessant bombardment, took him at his word.

In reality, the feat was not quite so extraordinary—though almost so. That sergeant was part of several elements of the 24th Brandenburg Infantry Regiment, which had used infiltration tactics to probe toward the fort without losing a single man. The unit commander, Lieutenant Eugen Radtke, backed up his sergeant in the actual capture of the fort. The fall of Fort Douaumont sent a shiver of panic through the defenders of Verdun, including the fresh reinforcements who were just beginning to arrive. Many of the soldiers looted food stocks in anticipation of a siege.

"Ils Ne Passeront Pas!"

Thanks to the heedless unflappability of Papa Joffre at the top of the French high command—he promised to court-martial any commander who voluntarily gave up ground—and thanks also to the initiative of lower-level commanders, the panic was quelled. And when General Langle de Cary, in overall command of the Verdun defenses, decided on the evening of February 24 to evacuate the Wöevre plain and the east bank of the Meuse, Joffre fired him. Joffre's second in command, Edouard de Castelnau, an officer with a reputation as a "fighting general," nominated Henri Philippe Pétain as Langle de Cary's replacement.

Pétain had risen slowly in the prewar army because he refused to fall into line with the prevailing doctrine of "offensive to the utmost," which he thought a prescription for costly disaster. In consequence, while many of his contemporaries had achieved general-officer rank, Pétain started the war as a mere colonel of the 33rd Regiment (Charles de Gaulle was a lieutenant in that outfit). He soon proved himself as unflappable as Joffre—a man wholly undeterred by losses, no matter how severe. As a result, the promotions came rapidly, and when he was called on to defend Verdun, he was already in command of the entire Second Army.

Combatants

Henri Philippe Pétain (1856–1951) was the son of a peasant family who managed to gain entrance to the prestigious École de Saint-Cyr, the French military academy. Graduating near the top of his class, he was commissioned an officer of the elite *chasseurs alpins*, mountain troops, in 1876. However, he achieved promotion slowly because of his advocacy of defensive strategy and tactics, which ran counter to the prevailing French doctrine of offense at any cost.

At the outbreak of World War I, Pétain was no more than a colonel in command of the 33rd Regiment, but in this capacity he quickly distinguished himself. In February 1916, when the all-important fortress of Verdun was menaced, it was Pétain to whom France turned. He was credited with the phrase that made him a popular hero of the war: *"Ils ne passeront pas!"* ("They shall not pass!")

Pétain's tremendously costly but ultimately successful defense of Verdun earned him promotion to the command of Army Group Center, but put his subordinate, the hyperaggressive and brilliantly dashing Robert Nivelle, in command of the Verdun sector. From this position, Nivelle was then promoted ahead of Pétain. When Nivelle failed disastrously with his Chemin-des-Dames offensive in April 1917, however, Pétain was called in to relieve him and to assume supreme command of all the French armies. He stressed preparedness and reasonable objectives rather than enforcing the long-cherished but typically suicidal policy of all-out attack.

At war's end, Pétain was made Marshal of France and served in other military roles before becoming a civilian politican. With the military collapse of France early in World War II, French president Albert Lebrun asked this hero of Verdun to form a new government, and on June 22, 1940, Pétain negotiated surrender to the Germans. He would thus go down in history as the man who sold out his nation to the Nazis, creating the cowardly collaborationist Vichy government.

The critic of the doctrine of the offensive telephoned the commander of XX Corps at what was now the front line of Verdun's defenses: "I have taken command. Tell your troops. Hold fast." To his superiors, he pledged *"Ils ne passeront pas!"*—"They shall not pass!"—which instantly became the battle cry of Verdun and, indeed, the French motto for the conduct of the rest of the war.

Pétain's Courage

Pétain would now prove his courage and resolve. The defense of Verdun would make him France's first high-level hero of the war.

Yet whom did that courage serve?

Falkenhayn could not have asked the French to send a commander better suited to his own plan for Verdun. He had hoped for a commander willing to bleed his own army white, and Pétain was prepared to do just that. Had Joffre and Pétain given more thought to the tactics of Verdun than to its symbolism, they would have abandoned it as something that had ceased to be a fort and was now a death trap. Better to have withdrawn to the woods behind Verdun, where there was room for maneuver and terrain much more easily defended. Such a tactical move would have proved much more costly to the Germans and much less so to the French.

Falkenhayn must have been delighted that the French had taken his bait, that they suddenly deemed Verdun a kind of sanctified place and its defense a cross between a holy mission and a patriotic duty. What he had not counted on was just how determined the defense would be—and, under Pétain, just how effective.

From the Front

The phrase *"Ils ne passeront pas!"* usually attributed to Pétain, is sometimes credited to his subordinate, the mindlessly aggressive General Robert Nivelle.

The "Sacred Way"

Pétain was willing to spend lives, but he would do so in a way that would exact maximum casualties from the Germans. He threw himself into organizing two keys to the defense of the position. The first was artillery. Pétain assumed personal command of the French guns, and he used them mercilessly, determined to give the Germans what they had given the French. He would bombard them in the front lines and as they filed forward through the steep, narrow valleys east of the Meuse.

The second key was supply. Verdun would become the focus of a massive supply effort. Pétain designated the one road that led to a depot, Bar-le-Duc, 50 miles westward, as an artery for the exclusive use of supply trucks. Troop columns were ordered to march to the side, in the fields, to keep the road absolutely clear. An entire division of *Territorials* was assigned continually to repair the road by filling in shell craters as soon as they were made. The route was christened the *Voie Sacrée*—the Sacred Way.

Words of War

Territorials are reserve troops, typically past the usual age of eligibility for service, who are assigned such rear-echelon duties as supply, construction, and miscellaneous labor.

Wave Upon Wave

The Germans launched another major assault against Verdun on March 6. It made excellent headway at first, but then Pétain pushed the offensive back with a series of counterattacks driven by a single order: "to regain every piece of ground lost."

Over the course of the month, the Germans hurled wave after wave against the reinforced French. Falkenhayn reluctantly committed another entire army corps from his jealously hoarded reserves for an attack up the left bank of the river toward a small ridge with the sinister name of Le Morte-homme, the Dead Man. It would be the scene of see-saw fighting for the remainder of the campaign. During this fighting, Pétain insisted on rotating troops rapidly in and out of the front line. Casualties on both sides mounted horribly, but the French always seemed to find fresh troops—or, at least, rested troops—for the trenches.

On April 9, the Germans launched their third major offensive against both sides of a salient that had been thrust into their lines. Once again, Pétain checked the advance. Through the end of May, a terrible rhythm of attack and counterattack was played out until German energy flagged. In the meantime, Pétain, in large part on the strength of his performance at Verdun, was promoted to higher command and was replaced at Verdun by the dashing Robert Nivelle.

From the Front

About 3,500 trucks were mustered to transport 2,000 tons of stores daily to the Verdun garrison. Any truck that broke down en route was pushed off to the side so that the flow of goods would not be interrupted. Before the Battle of Verdun was concluded, 12,000 trucks traveled the *Voie Sacrée* (the Sacred Way).

Fall of Fort Vaux

Despite heavy casualties, the Germans did manage to push closer and closer to Verdun, and Fort Vaux, on the east bank of the Meuse, finally fell on June 9, having held out since February. By this time, its garrison was without water, and the fort had ceased to be a building at all, but was a heap of rubble. In a show of chivalry rare in this brutal, by-the-numbers conflict, the German Crown Prince offered his personal congratulations to the commandant of Fort Vaux, a major named Raynal.

The victory at Fort Vaux seemed to reinvigorate the Germans, who very nearly succeeded in breaking the French line in late June and early July. Indeed, on June 23, they advanced toward Fort Souville, almost in sight of Verdun itself. The Germans now unleashed their newest form of poison gas, phosgene, which worked by turning into hydrochloric acid in the lungs (see Chapter 12, "Deadlock"). Even Pétain, overriding Nivelle, recommended withdrawal from the western Meuse line, but Joffre refused.

The French Attack

Joffre was soon vindicated in his refusal. The Germans were once again losing steam. A Russian offensive in the East put a sudden demand on the forces hammering Verdun. Fifteen divisions had to be withdrawn for duty on the Eastern Front.

Erich von Falkenhayn had staged Verdun to bleed the French army white. In the process, he was doing the very same to his own army. As its casualties approached 400,000 men, Falkenhayn was relieved of command, on August 29, 1916, to be replaced by the team that had been so successful in the East: Erich Ludendorff and Paul von Hindenburg.

By fall, the French also had a new commander, Charles Mangin. In October, he took his army on the offensive, managing to retake Fort Douaumont on October 24 and Fort Vaux on November 2. Both sides rested for a time; then Mangin renewed the offensive, pushing his lines forward, very nearly to the position the French had held at the beginning of the battle in February. During December 15–18, Mangin took 11,000 German prisoners and acquired 115 big German guns. This was the last action of the Verdun campaign. The French had held their ground at the staggering cost of 542,000 killed and wounded. Hindenburg and Ludendorff did not have as much invested in Verdun as Falkenhayn had, and they decided to break off the ill-fated assault and, once again, assume the defensive all across the Western Front. German losses for the period totaled 434,000 killed and wounded.

Voices of Battle

"Cowardice, as distinguished from panic, is almost always simply a lack of ability to suspend the functioning of the imagination."

—Ernest Hemingway, *Men at War* (1942)

Words of War

A **holding attack** is designed to hold the enemy in its present position to prevent it from reinforcing elements opposing the main attack.

Offensive on the Somme

For their part, the French were gratified to be on the offensive at last. Joffre had long planned a big push along the Somme River in northwestern France, but he had had to delay it to defend Verdun. As it is, the First Battle of the Somme commenced on June 24, while Verdun still raged. Because of the demands of Verdun, the French were able to provide only 16 divisions instead of the 40 they had planned to commit to the attack. It was, then, the British, not the French, who took the lead, beginning with a monumentally destructive seven-day artillery preparation.

Following the long barrage, the British Fourth Army, under General Henry S. Rawlinson, made the principal thrust north of the Somme, while General Edmund Allenby led the Third Army in a supporting action to the north of Rawlinson. Simultaneously, south of the Somme, Ferdinand Foch's French Army Group of the North made a *holding attack.*

At last, on July 1, the British infantry, in coordination with a *rolling barrage,* was hurled against the strongly defended German Second Army. The Germans yielded an inconsequential amount of ground, purchased at the cost of 60,000 British casualties, including 19,000 dead.

Despite losses that should have stopped any army, the British pressed their meager gains with smaller, limited attacks. Falkenhayn was forced to transfer reinforcements from Verdun to counter the tenacious British—and, in this respect, Sir Douglas Haig did achieve an important objective: The Somme offensive relieved pressure on Verdun. (Yet Haig would go down in history as the commander who ordered more British soldiers to their deaths than any other.)

Action on the Somme continued to grind on for some two weeks until, on July 14, a British nighttime attack directed by Sir Henry Rawlinson broke through the German second line. The breakthrough bogged down and failed, however, because of poor communications. Rawlinson's cavalry were, for the most part, too far back to be brought up in time to exploit the breach. Nine hours elapsed before the cavalry joined the battle-weary 7th Infantry Division. By this time, the Germans had managed to rally their reserves. The German defenders mowed down horses and horsemen in a hail of heavy machine gun fire. Following this, massive German counterattacks engulfed the poorly coordinated British advance. British casualties were heavy, and the German second line was resealed.

Through the rest of the summer, the Somme degenerated into a series of smaller but still costly actions. At last, on September 15, Haig unleashed another major offensive, southwest of the village of Bapaume. The offensive employed for the first time the tank, the British innovation discussed in Chapter 12. The new weapon caused shock and panic where it was used, but there were hardly enough of these as-yet slow, underpowered, and unreliable (early models suffered from poorly designed gear systems) machines to make a significant

Words of War

In the context of a planned offensive, a **rolling barrage** is an artillery bombardment in which a "curtain" of artillery fire moves toward the enemy ahead of the advancing troops and at the same speed as the troops.

From the Front

British losses at the Somme on July 1—41,000 wounded, 19,000 dead—still stand as the heaviest in Britain's military history. Consider that, during the World War II "D-Day" landings at Normandy, the largest assault operation of that or any war, the combined Anglo-American armies fought 20 days before sustaining 60,000 casualties.

impact on the battle as a whole. Moreover, the British made the mistake of employing their new weapon as a machine gun carrier to support infantry rather than as a shock weapon to force a breakthrough.

The First Battle of the Somme spanned June 24 to November 13, 1916, and ultimately resulted in measurable gains of ground for the British and French. Substantially, however, the German lines held. Yet in this war of attrition, the Germans were being most thoroughly ground down. While the British lost 420,000 men killed and wounded and the French 195,000, German losses numbered about 650,000.

The Germans did remain on the defensive at the Somme and were forced into a constant series of desperate defensive actions to keep the British from forcing a breakthrough. It was a type of warfare in which both sides were "bled white." What caused heavy German casualties on the Somme was a determination not to give up ground. When Ludendorff visited the Somme Front, he reported that the German defenders "fought too doggedly, clinging too resolutely to the mere holding of ground, with the result that the losses were heavy." True, everything about trench warfare favored the defenders, and, likewise true, the Germans had made themselves masters of defensive tactics. Yet the desire to produce something more than merely defensive results drove the Germans at Verdun, even as it drove the French and the British.

German offensives cost the Germans far more than the Allied offensives did. Particularly hard hit were experienced junior officers, who fell in disproportionate numbers. The First Battle of the Somme, therefore, had a major impact not just on numbers in the German army, but on the command structure of that army. The loss of so many veteran officers would never be fully made up. As for the stalemate on the Western Front, it remained unbroken, the flood of Allied and German blood notwithstanding.

The Least You Need to Know

➤ Verdun was a complex of French fortresses targeted by the Germans in the belief that the French would defend them ultimately to the point of sacrificing much of their army.

➤ The defense of Verdun did prove inordinately costly—but to the Germans as well as the French.

➤ The British-led offensive in the First Battle of the Somme resulted in the heaviest losses in British military history, but it also exacted a crippling toll on the German army, which lost huge numbers of men and a significant proportion of its junior- and middle-level officer corps.

➤ The defense of Verdun and the First Battle of the Somme were Allied victories achieved at great cost and with negligible gains in territory.

Chapter 17

Italy, the Eastern Front, and Elsewhere, 1916

In This Chapter

➤ The failure of Austrian offensives against Italy

➤ The Brusilov Offensive almost knocks out Austria-Hungary

➤ Romania enters the war—and suffers disaster

➤ The Allies recruit Arab aid against the Turks

➤ British defeat at Kut-el-Amara

➤ Russo-Turkish battles in the Caucasus

Historians speak of the Allied effort versus the effort of the Central Powers, as if World War I had been a contest between two great opposing teams. Often, however, the conflict was also intramural, with the "teams" breaking down as different constituents pursued individual agendas.

As Verdun and the Somme raged on the Western Front, the Austrian high commander, Field Marshal Conrad von Hötzendorf, went his own way, consumed with what amounted to a vendetta against Italy, a nation that he personally hated. He also believed that a single massive blow might knock Italy out of the war, thereby eliminating the Austro-Italian Front and allowing Austria-Hungary to turn its attention exclusively to helping Germany defeat Russia. Conrad pressured Germany's commander-in-chief, Erich von Falkenhayn, to coordinate a joint German-Austrian assault against Italy.

Falkenhayn, heavily burdened on the Western and Eastern Fronts, refused, but Conrad, undeterred, decided to proceed on his own. He formulated an offensive in the Trentino, behind the main Italian armies on the Isonzo front. He believed that he could drive through Trentino's mountain passes, occupy the plain of northern Italy, and, by so doing, entrap the Italians who were on the Isonzo Front as well as those stationed in the Carnic Alps.

More Battles on the Isonzo

Field Marshal Conrad's plan would come to be known as the Asiago Offensive. It was set into motion after the Fifth Battle of the Isonzo (see Chapter 15, "The Other Fronts, 1915," for the first four) during March 11–29. Like the other Isonzo engagements before it, the battle consisted of a series of inconclusive and bloody assaults on well-defended Austro-Hungarian lines.

Like Conrad, Luigi Cadorna, Italy's overall commander, labored under an obsession: that the Austrian lines at Isonzo had to be breached and could be breached. Yet Cadorna was not so thoroughly obsessed that he failed to notice that Conrad was assembling no fewer than 15 divisions to menace the Trentino. Accordingly, Cadorna ordered General Roberto Brusati's First Army to prepare for an anticipated Austro-Hungarian offensive.

It was a prudent and highly astute move from a commander who previously had demonstrated precious little acuteness of judgment or prudence. Unfortunately, if allies were sometimes inclined to pursue their own agendas, so were generals. Brusati chose largely to ignore Cadorna's orders and instead conducted local operations to improve his local front. The result was that Brusati's men were unprepared for the onslaught of Austrian Archduke Eugene's Eleventh and Third armies.

From the Front

The Italians lost 147,000 men, including 40,000 taken prisoner. In addition, 300 valuable artillery pieces and other equipment were sacrificed. Austrian losses totaled 81,000, 26,000 of which were POWs.

At first, the Austrians made very substantial gains, although the rugged terrain introduced immediate problems with keeping the advance supplied. Then Cadorna surprisingly rose to the occasion. Fearing a massive invasion, the Italians panicked—and called on the Russians to mount an offensive that would draw the Austrians away from Italy—but Cadorna kept his head. Quickly and deftly, he broke off the Fifth Battle of Isonzo to transfer half a million men to the threatened front in the Trentino. By June 2, the Austrian advanced had been checked.

Before 1916 closed, four more Isonzo battles would take place. The Sixth Battle of the Isonzo was fought during August 6–17. Because the Austrian lines were now depleted by the Trentino Offensive and by transfers to the Eastern Front (see the next section, "An Italian Appeal"), the Italians managed to take Gorizia.

This did not represent a genuine breakthrough of strategic importance, but it did boost flagging Italian morale—at the cost of 51,000 Italian dead and wounded, versus 40,000 Austrian casualties.

The Seventh (September 14–26), Eighth (October 10–12), and Ninth (November 1–4) Battles of the Isonzo continued to wear away at the Austro-Hungarian army, but they took an even greater toll on the Italians, who lost 75,000 men versus 63,000 Austrians, killed, wounded, or taken prisoner.

An Italian Appeal

Russia, always eager to be a good ally, responded to a French request for an offensive drive in the Vilna-Naroch area of what today is Lithuania. The French needed all the help they could get to relieve the pressure against Verdun (see Chapter 16, "'They Shall Not Pass!'").

The March 18 Battle of Lake Naroch was preceded by a two-day artillery preparation—the heaviest yet on the Eastern Front—but the Russian infantry follow-up bogged down in the mud of a spring thaw. While the German defenders lost 20,000 men, the Russians suffered 70,000 casualties at Lake Naroch and another 30,000 in action farther north.

Despite this crushing failure, the Russians again responded to a call for aid, this time from the Italians, who feared imminent invasion by the Austrians through the Trentino. The results of this Russian offensive, however, would be quite different from Lake Naroch.

The Brusilov Offensive

General Aleksey A. Brusilov was a rarity among the czar's high commanders. He was not only a courageous commander, but he also was a highly skilled one. In contrast to his colleagues, he understood the value of surprise and had the imagination to devise ways by which to achieve it.

On June 4, he moved against the Austro-German line in two places. He did so in a series of well-planned and well-executed maneuvers that were not preceded by any of the usual preliminaries: the massing of troops or the use of artillery preparation. Thus, surprise was total, complete, and devastating. For once, the Russians had benefited from excellent intelligence work and aerial reconnaissance, which located weaknesses in the Austro-Hungarian trench systems and front lines.

Austrian Rout

Almost immediately, the entire Austrian Fourth Army was routed, and the Seventh Army soon followed it. Seventy thousand prisoners fell to Brusilov's offensive.

Combatants

Aleksey A. Brusilov (1853–1926) was the only Russian field commander of World War I who could be called brilliant. He was born in the Caucasus to a military family, graduated from the military academy, and quickly distinguished himself as a young officer in fighting against Turkey during 1877.

Brusilov became associated with the Cavalry School at St. Petersburg and was appointed its commandant from 1902 to 1906. By the outbreak of World War I, he was a full general and given command of the Eighth Army in Galicia. After initial defeats, he went on the offensive with great success against the Austro-Hungarian forces. Superiors recognized his ability and gave him command of the entire Southwestern Front in March 1916.

He planned and executed two extraordinary offensives against the Austro-Hungarians, which embodied advanced tactical thinking unknown throughout the rest of the Russian army. While the first offensive (1916) was highly successful, nearly knocking Austria-Hungary out of the war, the second (1917) was hampered by lack of supply and the effects of the Russian Revolution.

After Soviet Russia concluded a separate peace with Germany in the fall of 1917, Brusilov retired from active duty. Although he was an aristocrat, he embraced the new communist government and joined the Red Army in 1920, but never accepted a field command.

Had higher command or Brusilov's colleagues acted to coordinate with the offensive, Austria-Hungary might well have been knocked out of the war, thereby freeing Russian troops to concentrate exclusively on the Germans, and freeing Italian forces for direct aid to the effort on the Western Front.

But this was not to be. German General Alexander von Linsingen led his army group in a counterattack against Brusilov on June 16, which succeeded in checking the Russians' northern advance. Although Brusilov was able to renew the offensive on July 28, achieving further gains, he began to run short of ammunition and other supplies. In the meantime, German reinforcements were transferred from Verdun (see Chapter 16) and propped up the reeling Austro-Hungarians. Brusilov's offensive petered out in exhaustion on both sides.

Romania's Entry

Although it was not decisive, the Brusilov Offensive had major consequences. It significantly weakened the Central Powers' ability to maintain offensives in Italy and Verdun. Austria-Hungary continued to fight, but it had suffered such severe losses that it would never again figure as a major military power in this war.

Yet, despite its gains, the Brusilov Offensive had also cost Russia dearly. Russian casualties topped a million men, a figure so appalling that the nation was driven with increasing velocity to the precipice of a revolution that it had been approaching all along.

The Brusilov Offensive had at least one additional effect. Romania had declared itself neutral even as it allowed the Allies to court its entry into the war. Despite Allied promises of substantial territorial acquisition, Romania continued to hold itself aloof, largely unimpressed by Allied performance in the war until the early results of the Brusilov Offensive. On August 27, 1916, Romania at last declared war on Germany and Austria-Hungary.

The nation's first act of war was to invade Transylvania, an Austrian-controlled territory that it had long eyed jealously. Erich von Falkenhayn, relieved as chief of the Imperial German General Staff and now assigned to command of the Ninth Army, met and repelled the Romanian invaders. In the meantime, General August von Mackensen led the German-reinforced Bulgarian Danube Army across the Danube River on November 23 into the Dobrudja region.

> ### Voices of Battle
>
> "... the Brusilov offensive was, on the scale by which success was measured in the foot-by-foot fighting of the First World War, the greatest victory seen on any front since the trench lines had been dug on the Aisne two years before."
>
> —John Keegan, in *The First World War* (1999)

The Romanian commander, General Alexandru Averescu, now found himself trapped between the forces of the two Germans, Falkenhayn and Mackensen. Averescu's response was bold and desperately aggressive. He divided his forces in an attempt to envelop Mackensen's left flank while simultaneously blocking Falkenhayn's advance. His objective was to prevent the two enemy armies from linking up and thereby crushing him—and he might have succeeded in doing just this, had the Russian forces in the area properly coordinated action with him. But the Romanians had even greater supply and coordination problems than the Russians, and Falkenhayn and Mackensen were able to break through to each other. Together they hammered the Romanians at the Battle of the Arges River during December 1–4.

Defeat for the Romanian army was very nearly total and absolutely disastrous. What was left of the army fled north into Russia, clutching at the tiny portion of their own country that they still controlled. Although some 60,000 troops of the Central Powers had become casualties, 300,000 to 400,000 Romanians were killed or wounded—about half in combat and half as a result of disease. Of even greater importance, the rich grain and oil fields of Romania were now in German hands. This was a great gain in a war of attrition.

In the Bird Cage

As we saw in Chapter 10, "The Sick Man and Serbia," the French had placed the quarrelsome and politically unpalatable General Maurice P. Sarrail in command of Allied forces sent to aid Serbia against Bulgar-German forces. Sarrail and his troops arrived too late to be of any help to Serbia, whose army, badly crippled, was pushed back to Albania. In December 1915, the remnants of that army were shipped to the island of Corfu. In the meantime, the Allies had obtained control of the Greek port of Salonika, and it was to this city that the Serbian survivors were transported from Corfu.

By July, the Serbian army had been reconstituted at Salonika as a force of 118,000 men. Sarrail's troops were added to this to make an army of a quarter-million men. With this force, Sarrail decided to leave the fortified "Bird Cage," a ring of forts around Salonika, to conduct an offensive up the valley of the Vardar River (which flows through Serbia down into Greece and into the Gulf of Salonika).

Attack and Counterattack

By the time Sarrail got under way, the Bulgarians had taken the initiative and, in cooperation with German forces, attacked the Allies at the Battle of Florina (a Greek village a few miles south of the Serbian frontier) during August 17–27. The Allies were pushed southward until Sarrail mounted a counteroffensive from September 10 to November 19. This slowly drove the Bulgar-German forces northward, out of Greece and into Serbia. On November 19, the Allies took the southern Serbian town of Monastir.

At this point, however, the Allied offensive lost steam. Sarrail, a troublemaker in France, proved a troublemaker in the Balkans. He fell to disputing with his subordinates, and the campaign ended in disarray at the cost of 50,000 Allied lives. The Bulgar-German forces lost some 60,000 killed and wounded.

Operations in Albania

Beginning in July and lasting through November, a corps of Austrians dueled with an Italian corps in Albanian territory west of Greece. The Italians succeeded in pushing the Austrians north and then joined forces with Sarrail's army at Lake Ochrida.

Little came of these actions in Greece and Albania during 1916, and disease proved a far more formidable foe than bullets. Yet neither side wanted to pull out of this very peripheral front, lest such an action be interpreted as an admission of defeat. Pride and propaganda were fed with human lives.

Action on the Turkish Fronts

Action on the "Turkish Fronts," encompassing the region of Egypt, Palestine, and Arabia, as well Mesopotamia and the Caucasus, became more intense in 1916 than in the previous year.

Sinai Bridgehead

Early in 1916, General Sir Archibald Murray began work on extending the Suez Canal defenses eight miles into the Sinai Desert. The intention was to prevent Turkish forces from firing on the canal itself. The extension required a tremendous amount of work to create adequate entrenchments and fortifications, as well as to establish communications and a supply of water. In the midst of this activity, the Senussi tribes of western Egypt staged an anti-British insurrection, which required a diversion of Murray's forces to suppress. Work resumed on the canal defenses in March and was completed in July.

The Arab Revolt

In the autumn of 1915, British and French officials negotiated an agreement with Hussein, the *grand sherif* of Mecca, pledging (albeit vaguely) to help him gain territory and to support Arab independence from Turkey. In return, Hussein would cooperate with the Allies in operations against the Turks.

On June 5, 1916, Hussein attacked the Turkish garrison at Medina. Hussein then proclaimed independence for the Arabs and stormed the Turkish garrison at Mecca, which surrendered on June 10. Although Medina withstood the onslaught, Hussein's actions greatly hampered the Turkish war effort in the region.

Attached to General Murray's staff was a young captain named T.E. Lawrence. Assigned to observe the ultimately unsuccessful Arab operations at Medina, he concluded that the Arab cavalry could not reasonably challenge the well-defended Turkish positions. With the permission of his superiors, Lawrence persuaded Hussein's third son, Feisal, field commander of the Arab army, to break off

From the Front

Advanced technology enabled the British to rapidly construct a road through the desert. Instead of pavement, impossible to lay on the desert sand, engineers used prefabricated steel mesh to create a ribbon deck across the sand over which wheeled vehicles could easily travel. Such mesh substitutes for pavement would be widely used by U.S. forces in World War II, especially to construct airfields on captured Pacific islands.

Words of War

The **grand sherif** was the chief magistrate of Mecca when that place was controlled by the Ottoman Turks.

205

direct attack against Medina and instead to use his forces to disseminate propaganda among the Arabs and to raid the overextended Turkish lines of communications. These indirect battle tactics proved highly effective. The Turks had no choice but to halt their offensive operations south of Medina, and they also had to assign valuable troops to defend long stretches of the Hejaz railway.

Voices of Battle

"Our tactics were always tip and run, not pushes, but strokes. We never tried to maintain or improve an advantage, but to move off and strike somewhere else. We used the smallest force, in the quickest time, at the farthest place."

—T.E. Lawrence, on guerilla tactics, in "The Evolution of a Revolt," *Army Quarterly*, 1920

Lawrence's brilliant advice earned him an instant reputation among his British colleagues and, more important, obtained for him a position as Feisal's chief adviser. As we will see in Chapter 23, "The War Beyond the Trenches, 1917–1918," Lawrence—dubbed Lawrence of Arabia—became one of the few figures of truly heroic, even mythic, proportions to emerge from World War I. His early work with Feisal was the basis of this legendary reputation, as the tall, handsome, and enigmatic Englishman fought side by side with the Arabs, attired not in British khaki, but in the flowing robes of an Arab warrior.

Battle of Rumani

On August 3, 1916, German General Kress von Kressenstein led 15,000 Turkish troops with German machine gunners in an attack on the railhead that the British had built in Sinai. Although the attack came as a surprise, the British forces responded swiftly, repelling the attackers and inflicting more than 5,000 casualties on them. British losses amounted to no more than 1,100 men killed and wounded.

In Mesopotamia

In Chapter 15, we left British General Charles Townshend and some 8,000 troops besieged by Turkish forces at Kut-el-Amara, to which they had taken refuge after exhaustion and lack of supplies put an end to British dreams of capturing Baghdad. Riding to his rescue was General Fenton J. Aylmer leading two Indian divisions. Aylmer, checked by Turkish resistance in January, was replaced by General George F. Gorringe. His tactic was a March 7 surprise attack against the Turks on the south bank of the Tigris.

Turkish forces, repeatedly underestimated by the British, often proved highly effective under the skilled leadership of German officers. The aged Kolmar von der Goltz commanded the Turkish Sixth Army, which handily repulsed Gorringe's attack, successfully preventing his rescue of Townshend.

The British tried several more times to reach Kut but were foiled in every attempt. By April, Townshend's food supply failed. With starvation looming, the British general surrendered Kut and his force of 2,070 British and approximately 6,000 Indian troops. The cost to the British relief forces had been high—21,000 casualties—but General von der Goltz, aged 73, was not able to relish his victory. He succumbed to cholera just before Townshend surrendered.

Despite the brilliant and daring performance of Townshend and his men, the gains to be made on the Mesopotamian Front had never been worth the risks, and the entire campaign had been a foolish, tragic waste of resources.

In August, Sir Frederick S. Maude was appointed to the Mesopotamian command but was restricted to an entirely defensive role while the British War Office in London debated with the Indian Army command on whether to abandon the chaotic Mesopotamian Front altogether. On December 13, Maude was given permission to try a new offensive, and he embarked up both banks of the Tigris with an army of 166,000 men, most of them Indian troops. Where they went and what they did early in 1917 is covered in Chapter 23.

From the Front

India contributed mightily to the British war effort. Added to some £80 million in military supplies was a cash gift to the Empire of £100 million. About a million Indian troops served in the war, on the Western Front as well as in German East Africa, the Middle East, and Mesopotamia. Indian casualties numbered at least 100,000 killed and wounded.

The Caucasus: Russia's Winter Offensive

As we have seen, competence was a rare and precious commodity among Russian commanders. By luck of the draw or poor planning, the Russians deployed two of their very best commanders not on the major sectors of the Eastern Front against the Germans, but against the Austrians (with the Brusilov Offensive) and on the peripheral fronts. Like Brusilov, General Nikolai N. Yudenich was a highly competent commander who was used against lesser opponents. In January, he advanced from Kars in northeast Turkey to defeat the Turkish Third Army at the Battle of Köprukov on January 18. When the Turks retreated to the fortified town of Erzurum, Yudenich successfully stormed the defenses in a three-day battle spanning February 13 to 16. While fighting here, he also made an amphibious assault on the Black Sea port of Trebizond, which fell on April 18.

The Caucasus: Turkey Counterattacks

During the summer, the Turks staged counteroffensives against Yudenich. The Turkish Third Army, now under new command, attacked along the Black Sea *littoral plain,* while a new Turkish Second Army attacked Yudenich's left flank.

A lesser commander than Yudenich would have been caught between the two Turkish armies and might well have suffered defeat because of the flanking attack. Yudenich, however, moved adroitly and aggressively on July 2, splitting the Turkish Third Army at the Battle of Erzinjan and then routing it on July 25. The already battered Turkish force suffered 34,000 new casualties.

With the Third Army disposed of, Yudenich turned against the Second Army. He was less successful here—although he prevented envelopment of his own forces—and Mustafa Kemal, commanding a Turkish corps, captured two towns, Mus and Bitlis, on August 15. Yudenich soon retook both, however, on August 24. With this, both the Russians and Turks retired to winter quarters, exhausted.

Words of War

A **littoral plain** is the flat region adjacent to the sea; the coastal region.

On all of the peripheral fronts—the Italian, the Middle Eastern, the Balkan, and the so-called Turkish Fronts—action was costly (with disease typically claiming even more victims than bullets did) and almost always inconclusive. Nevertheless, military planners continued to cling to the belief that because these fronts offered at least some room for maneuver, they might well prove to be the source of measurable progress denied at the deadlocked Western Front. In fact, proportionate to the number of men engaged, they were no more productive and just as prodigal in waste of human life as was combat in the trenches of France.

The Least You Need to Know

➤ Austro-Hungarian commander Field Marshal Conrad von Hötzendorf pursued a costly and fruitless campaign against Italy in defiance of Austria's ally Germany, even as Italy's Luigi Cadorna continued to waste lives in battle after battle on the Isonzo River.

➤ The Brusilov Offensive against Austrian forces was not only one of Russia's few World War I successes, but, in terms of territory gained and casualties inflicted, it was perhaps the most successful offensive of the war.

➤ The Allies enticed Romania into the war with promises of territorial gains; that nation's army was all but completely destroyed, and most of Romania was overrun by Bulgar-German occupiers.

➤ The Allies successfully recruited Arab aid against the Turks in Egypt, but the Quixotic British expedition dispatched to capture Baghdad, held under siege and brought near starvation, surrendered at Kut-el-Amara.

➤ The peripheral fronts saw much action in 1916—a good deal of it very costly, and none of it decisive.

Part 4

Troubled Seas and Fiery Skies

World War I claimed as its battlefield not just the earth, but the sea and the sky as well. Much of the seaborne action took place underwater, when Germany unleashed the destructive force of U-boat torpedo attacks. However, the sea was also the scene of the biggest naval battle in history, at Jutland, where the great dreadnoughts and battle cruisers of the British Grand Fleet and the German High Seas Fleet clashed in a combat of unparalleled scope and violence.

World War I greatly accelerated the development of military aviation, and the warring parties struggled to claim the sky as a kind of ultimate high ground from which to observe the enemy's every move. "Winged knights" jousted in gossamer aircraft to win supremacy in the skies, their one-on-one combats capturing the imagination even of a war-weary world.

A Tale of Two Fleets

Chapter 11, "A *World* War," covered the action at sea early in the war. After the disaster suffered at the Battle of the Falklands in December 1914, German naval officials kept most of the surface fleet in home waters, for fear that the Imperial Navy would lose more capital ships. The Germans increasingly turned from the surface to the water below and conducted an intensified program of submarine warfare, chiefly targeting supply as well as passenger vessels, including many civilian ships. Few expected that 1916 would bring one last great battle between surface fleets, let alone bring the biggest naval battle in history.

The Enemy Below

Although the submarine was not an innovation of World War I—it had made its combat debut during the American Revolution as a one-man, human-powered submersible designed to wreak havoc on moored vessels—the Great War was the first conflict in which it was used extensively.

By 1900, three innovations had made the combat submarine practical: the development of the all-steel hull, efficient electric motors and batteries for underwater propulsion (on the surface, gas or diesel motors were used), and the self-propelled Whitehead torpedo.

On the eve of the war, most submarines were small, displacing only 100 to 750 tons, although some craft displaced more than 2,000 tons. Later in the war, some boats displaced as much as 2,650 tons. All carried torpedoes and, for combat on the surface, medium-caliber deck guns. Periscopes permitted a view of the surface while submerged. The maximum diving depth for the early World War I vessels was 300 to 500 feet, but the boats had to surface or at least come to periscope depth to fire torpedoes. Torpedo attacks could be made from as far as 10,000 yards away, although most submarine captains preferred coming in closer.

Words of War

A **Q-ship** was a warship disguised to look like a merchant vessel, with its guns and other weaponry hidden. Its primary purpose was to lure submarines into ambush.

Words of War

A **depth charge** is an explosive weapon launched or otherwise jettisoned from a surface ship and set to detonate at a given depth to rupture the hull of an enemy submarine.

The hazards of submarine service were many. Structural and mechanical failures were routine, breathable air was at a premium, and the presence of huge storage batteries was always dangerous. If seawater contaminated the sulfuric acid in the batteries, toxic gases would be released. In the cramped confinement of a submerged boat, asphyxiation of the crew—22 to 36 officers and men, typically—could occur in a matter of minutes.

A submarine sailing on the surface was vulnerable to artillery fire and to ramming. Larger, heavier surface vessels could easily run down and roll over the lighter, low-profile subs. The Allies also developed *Q-ships*, vessels disguised to look like civilian merchantmen, but covertly armed with medium-caliber artillery. Submarines that surfaced either to issue a warning of intended torpedo attack or to use their deck guns (to conserve valuable torpedoes) were vulnerable to ambush by a Q-ship.

Early in the war, submerged submarines were essentially safe from attack or retaliation by surface ships. This changed in 1916, when the hydrophone, an underwater listening device, was developed by the British and installed on Royal Navy vessels. Also at this time, *depth charges* were made available. Equipped with hydrostatic timers, which could be set to explode at a certain depth, these devices were highly effective at destroying submerged boats. Even deadlier to the U-boats were mines, which, late in the war, the British and Americans laid across the exits from the Baltic into the North Sea.

World War II submarines often worked in formations called by the Germans "wolf-packs." This enabled a high degree of coordination when preying on enemy shipping. In World War I, however, submarines typically sailed solo, cruising for targets of opportunity and attacking when and as they could. As more merchant vessels were equipped with radios, it became easier to track the whereabouts of submarines and to warn other ships of their presence. Early in 1917, the Allies also adopted the *convoy system,* in which merchantmen traveled in groups escorted by several warships, equipped with hydrophones and depth charges. With this, submarine attack became far riskier for the hunter.

A German Proclamation

At the outbreak of hostilities, the British Royal Navy held the lead in building and stockpiling submarines: 74 were operational in August 1914, and a total of 203 would be in service by 1918. France had 75 boats by the end of the war, and Russia had completed construction of 59 at the time of its separate peace with Germany. Italy operated a handful of small submarines. When the United States entered the war, it did so with 47 submarines and added another 20 by the time of the Armistice.

Although submarines were widely used by the Allies, it was Germany that would become most closely—and infamously—identified with what Germans called the Unterseeboot, or "U-boat." Germany entered the war with only 29 craft ready for action, but with its surface fleet threatened, the nation threw itself into a submarine building frenzy, launching no fewer than 372 new boats before the armistice. Another 162 were under construction—but never completed—at the time of Germany's capitulation.

The German navy's reliance on submarines had not been planned before the war. The original intention had been to use U-boats chiefly for reconnaissance to aid and protect the surface fleet. But, as we saw in Chapter 11, on September 22, 1914, a single U-boat, the obsolescent U-9, sank three British cruisers, the *Hogue, Aboukir,* and *Cressy,* off

Words of War

The **convoy system** is a method of grouping together supply, passenger, or merchant ships in formations that may be readily defended by warship escorts.

Voices of Battle

"All the waters surrounding Great Britain and Ireland, including the whole of the English Channel, are hereby declared to be a war zone. From February 18 onwards, every enemy merchant vessel found within this war zone will be destroyed without it always being possible to avoid danger to the crews and passengers.

"Neutral ships will also be exposed to danger in the war zone ...."

—German Admiralty Declaration, February 4, 1915

the Dutch coast. After this extraordinary demonstration of the weapon's effectiveness, the Germans put their major naval effort into submarine warfare.

Within six months after the declaration of war, U-boats began attacking merchant shipping and soon turned their attention almost entirely away from warships to concentrate on commerce vessels. On February 4, 1915, Berlin declared a "war zone" around the British Isles, and official warnings were published in newspapers across the world. Within the war zone, U-boats were authorized to attack merchant ships— if possible, giving warning first, but, if necessary, attacking without warning while submerged.

A Pledge and Secret Orders

As discussed in Chapter 11, the policy of "unrestricted submarine warfare" created worldwide outrage, especially among neutral nations, including the United States. American anger rose to a crisis with the sinking of the British liner *Lusitania*. Of the 1,959 on board, 1,198 lost their lives, including 128 United States citizens.

In response to President Woodrow Wilson's diplomatic protest, Kaiser Wilhelm II issued secret orders not to sink any more passenger ships. In addition, on May 10, three months after the British liner *Sussex* was sunk (also with loss of American lives), Germany issued the "Sussex Pledge," promising to sink no passenger vessel without warning. But on August 15, 1915—entirely without warning—a U-boat sank another British passenger steamer, the *Arabic*. Yet again, Americans died. Wilson issued another protest, and the kaiser, fearing U.S. entry into the war, secretly ordered a halt to all U-boat activity around the British Isles.

From the Front

German U-boats sank 5,554 Allied and neutral merchant ships during World War I, a terrible toll. Yet this also was only a small portion of the thousands of Allied sailings throughout the war. The Germans lost 178 U-boats in combat.

The Germans were still free to sink passenger and merchant ships after surfacing and giving fair warning, but the threat of retaliation from Q-ships led to a call for the resumption of unrestricted submarine warfare. German politicians, fearing that such a resumption would bring America into the war, blocked it until the beginning of 1917. At that point, feeling that America's eventual entry into the war was inevitable in any case, on January 9, 1917, the kaiser ordered unrestricted submarine warfare to resume effective February 1. On February 3, President Wilson severed diplomatic relations with Germany.

The Jutland Opportunity

Despite the success of the U-boats, Vice-Admiral Reinhard Scheer wanted to make productive use of Germany's High Seas Fleet of great surface ships, whose commander he had been appointed in January 1916. His plan was to provoke an encounter on the open sea between the entire High Seas Fleet and some smaller portion of the British fleet. If Scheer could contrive the confrontation so that the entire British fleet could not assemble, he would enjoy a temporary superiority of numbers that would surely bring victory.

As Scheer wanted to lure out elements of the British fleet, so the British admirals wanted to lure the Germans into fatal action. In February 1916, German cruisers swept past the Dogger Bank, and three weeks later a combined zeppelin and High Seas raid attempted to draw the British Harwich Force out to sea. The British replied with a series of similar raids, including a seaplane attack on supposed zeppelin sheds at Hoyer. These operations failed, and Scheer resolved to ambush Admiral David Beatty's battle cruiser squadron at Rosyth, halfway up Britain's eastern coast, and attack and destroy it before reinforcements from the Grand Fleet's main base at Scapa Flow, on the northern tip of Scotland, could arrive. To bait the trap, Scheer ordered five battle cruisers (designated the 1st Scouting Group), together with four light cruisers (the 2nd Scouting Group, under Rear Admiral Friedrich Bodicker, who was screened by two flotillas of destroyers), to sail north under the command of Vice Admiral Franz von Hipper from Wilhelmshaven, Germany, to a position off the southwestern coast of Norway. Scheer, commanding the battle squadrons of the main High Seas Fleet, would follow 50 miles behind and would entrap Beatty's ships between the High Seas Fleet and Hipper's and Bodicker's squadrons.

From the Front

The Battle of Jutland is also called the Battle of the Skagerrak because it was fought in the Skagerrak, an arm of the North Sea, about 60 miles off the coast of Jutland, Denmark.

It was a daring and risky plan that depended entirely on secrecy; however, the radio message initiating the operation was intercepted by British naval intelligence. On May 30, the *entire* British Grand Fleet set off for Norway's southwestern coast.

The Stakes

For both sides, the stakes were the highest possible. Admiral Scheer saw an opportunity to reduce the British Grand Fleet, thereby evening the odds of the naval war and putting Germany in position to dominate the high seas. Moreover, if the British fleet was sufficiently damaged, the British blockade of Germany might well be broken. Sir John R. Jellicoe, the British admiral, understood that he had an opportunity to surprise the German High Seas Fleet and to overawe or destroy it with superior British numbers. He was also well aware, as Winston Churchill would later put it in a history of the war, that "he was the only man on either side who could lose the war in an afternoon."

Combatants

John Rushworth Jellicoe (1859–1935) was a journeyman admiral called on to conduct the biggest naval battle in history. The son of a merchant ship's master, he entered the navy as a cadet in 1872 and soon built a career as an expert in naval gunnery. In 1897, Jellicoe served as a member of an important ordnance committee and then was made commander of H.M.S. *Centurion* the following year, serving as flag captain to Admiral Edward Seymour on the China Station. During the Boxer Rebellion, Jellicoe sailed in the First Peking Relief Expedition (June 10–26, 1900) and was severely wounded in one exchange.

In 1905, Jellicoe was appointed director of naval ordnance at the Admiralty and then was promoted to rear admiral (August 1907) in the Atlantic Fleet. In 1908, he returned to the Admiralty as third sea lord and then was made acting vice admiral in command of the Atlantic Fleet in December 1910. He transferred to the Home Fleet as commander of the 2nd Division and was confirmed as Vice Admiral in November 1911. The following year, he supervised gunnery experiments and was responsible for introducing important innovations.

Promoted to Second Sea Lord, Jellicoe was second in command of the Home Fleet under Admiral Sir George Callahan, whom he replaced as commander-in-chief of the Home Fleet at the outbreak of World War I on August 4, 1914.

In the Battle of Jutland (May 31–June 1, 1916), Jellicoe generally exhibited less aggressiveness and less tactical skill than his German counterpart, Reinhard Scheer, but he did avoid potential disaster and, at great cost, achieved a strategic victory by effectively neutralizing the German High Seas Fleet.

Jellicoe was elevated to First Sea Lord (November 28, 1916–December 1917) and was made Viscount Jellicoe of Scapa in December 1919. That same year he was made Admiral of the Fleet, and from 1920 to 1924 he served as Governor-General of New Zealand. He was made earl in 1925.

Substantial losses would be very bad for the Germans, but such losses would be totally catastrophic for the British. Naval superiority was the chief advantage the Allies enjoyed. It kept them supplied, and it prevented the Germans from cutting them off entirely. If the British lost many ships, that advantage would collapse. With it would collapse the Allied war effort.

German High Seas Fleet

Admiral Scheer led 99 vessels into battle, many of them of the most advanced new design. These included the following:

16 dreadnought-class battleships
6 pre-dreadnought-class battleships
5 battle cruisers
11 light cruisers
61 destroyers (standard, light destroyers)

British Grand Fleet

Admirals Jellicoe and Beatty had 151 ships, but a number of them were of older design than the German vessels. They included these:

28 dreadnought-class battleships
9 battle cruisers
8 armored cruisers

26 light cruisers
5 destroyer leaders (heavy destroyers)
73 destroyers (standard, light destroyers)
1 minelayer
1 seaplane

From the Front

Both the British and the German fleets had about 45 submarines available, but these were never called upon in the Battle of Jutland.

"Engage the Enemy Closer"

At 2:20 in the afternoon of May 31, Beatty's advance guard of light cruisers spotted Bodicker's scouting ships, light cruisers, and opened fire. Both English and Germans were surprised, but Hipper had spotted Beatty first and, after making visual contact with the British battle cruisers, turned, then began to steam back toward the German main fleet. At 3:31 P.M., Beatty turned on a course parallel to Hipper's squadron. This is precisely what Hipper had hoped for; however, he was unaware that Beatty had signaled Admiral Hugh Evan-Thomas, in command of a squadron of four new super dreadnoughts, to follow.

Now the two battle cruiser forces opened fire on one another at a range of 16,500 yards. The German guns were bigger and their gunnery more accurate than the British, and the German ammunition was superior. By the cold mathematics of war, this gave Hipper all the cards. Within 50 minutes, Beatty's flagship, the *Lion*—and *Princess Royal* and *Tiger* as well—had been severely damaged, and the lightly armored British battle cruisers began to fall. The *Indefatigable* exploded and capsized, and the *Queen Mary* was sunk 20 minutes afterward. The *Seydlitz*, *Derfflinger*, and *Lutzow* had also taken heavy hits.

Beatty was left with four ships against Hipper's five, although Evan-Thomas was steaming behind him with the great battleships. Recognizing that the Germans had a gunnery advantage at long range, Beatty refused to turn tail but instead boldly ordered his ships to "engage the enemy closer."

Flagships Fall

A lesser man than Beatty would have panicked. After all, in the opening minutes of the engagement, the German guns had proved more powerful and more accurate than the British, and the German ships themselves stronger, capable of taking multiple hits and still remaining serviceable. But Beatty kept his head, and he kept his focus on the objective at hand. In the meantime, Hipper had sighted the super dreadnoughts of Evan-Thomas's 5th Battle Squadron. A running fight ensued, in which ships on both sides took substantial damage. H.M.S. *Queen Mary* exploded and sank at 4:26 P.M. At this time, Beatty was still to the west of the German squadron, a position that silhouetted his ships against the evening sun. Throughout the engagement, while the great ships raced southward, the light cruisers and destroyers fought their own grim duels between the lines of battling leviathans.

Voices of Battle

"There seems to be something wrong with our bloody ships today."

—Sir David Beatty, to his flag captain, on British losses sustained in the opening hour of the Battle of Jutland

At about 4:30, Commodore Goodenough's 2nd Light Cruiser Squadron, which had steamed ahead of Beatty, sighted the masts and black coal smoke of Scheer's battleships. He sent a radio signal to Jellico: "Have sighted enemy battle fleet, bearing SE. Enemy's course North." Jellicoe's main force was now approaching in great parallel columns from the northwest.

Beatty, now warned that the German fleet was about 12 miles ahead, immediately ordered a turn back toward Jellicoe and the fleet. As the British battle cruisers headed north, Beatty attempted to signal Evan-Thomas, but poor visibility delayed the order until the super dreadnoughts were dangerously close to the Germans. These battleships were severely mauled as they turned away. Meanwhile, Beatty, still paralleled by Hipper, turned his ships to the northeast across the front of Jellicoe's advancing fleet.

At the head of the fleet and in advance of it was the 3rd Battle Squadron, consisting of three battle cruisers and two light cruisers led by Rear Admiral Sir Horace Hood. Hood raced to the southeast to support Beatty, believing that Beatty was still ahead. Seeing gunfire to the west, however, he now turned and headed toward the action. He was quickly engaged in a swirling battle with Hipper's cruisers and destroyers.

Then Hood's luck ran out. He found himself under fire from both Scheer and Hipper. As usual, the British ship proved less survivable than its German counterpart. Hit at 6:34, Hood's flagship exploded, breaking in two before it plunged to the bottom, carrying with it the admiral and all hands. Two British cruisers, *Defence* and *Warrior*, were also sunk. Despite these losses, the British Grand Fleet had now maneuvered across the front of the German High Seas Fleet. This maneuver, a classic naval battle tactic, is called *crossing the T*. Scheer's fleet was positioned like the vertical stroke of the letter *T*, while the British fleet was perpendicular to it, like the *T*'s horizontal stroke, blocking the progress of the Germans. Moreover, in this position, more of the British ships could bring to bear more fire than the German ships could return. The British vessels were arrayed so that they had clear fields of fire, whereas the German ships were stacked up, one behind the other.

Jellicoe took every advantage of his excellent position. Yet, despite their intense peril, the German ships survived. They were built superbly, and their crews were courageous and thoroughly disciplined under withering fire.

In a display of brilliant seamanship, Scheer generated a *smoke screen* and dispatched his destroyers to attack whatever they could—all in an effort to mask a perfectly executed 180° "battle turn" by his entire fleet. It was a supremely difficult maneuver that required that all of the ships turn simultaneously, but it was a maneuver the Germans had practiced constantly. This sent the German fleet westward and took Scheer's ships out of the range of most of the British fleet. Jellicoe had been taken totally by surprise.

But now it was Scheer's turn to be fooled.

He had no intention of running away from the British. At 6:55, he executed another 180° turn to steam back toward Jellicoe's fleet. Presumably, he believed that the British admiral had divided his forces, which would give him a new opportunity to take advantage of his own temporarily superior numbers. This proved a terrible mistake because Scheer was now once again under the guns of the *entire* British force. Jellicoe had—yet again—crossed Scheer's *T*. The outcome of the battle suddenly seemed a foregone conclusion. Scheer looked to be doomed.

Words of War

Crossing the T is a classic naval battle maneuver in which a fleet is maneuvered so that it is perpendicular and broadside to the enemy. In this way, more guns can be trained on the enemy, which, in turn, cannot bring as many of its guns to bear.

Words of War

A **smoke screen** consists of heavy smoke, purposely produced by ships (usually destroyers) to obscure the enemy's view of ship movements.

The "Death Ride"

But Scheer did not give up. While four German battle cruisers charged suicidally in what contemporaries called a "death ride" toward the British line, Scheer turned the rest of his fleet away from Jellicoe.

The "death ride" battle cruisers were hammered and severely damaged—two of them, the *Seydlitz* and the *Derfflinger,* were consumed in flames—yet they remained in action. Under cover of a smoke screen, fast German destroyers now closed in on Jellicoe's battleships to fire torpedoes.

Historians of the Battle of Jutland refer to this moment as "the crisis." If Jellicoe had boldly ordered the Grand Fleet to advance through the confused and disorganized array of German battle cruisers, Scheer would almost surely have been defeated. Instead, however, the British commander was overcome by fear of torpedo attacks from the destroyers. In a fit of prudence, he ordered his fleet to turn away—precisely when boldness would have meant victory. By the time the British admiral decided to re-engage the enemy, Scheer had disappeared over the horizon.

Most astoundingly of all, the four German battle cruisers, though badly battered, had come through the death ride, having both accomplished—and survived!—a suicide mission.

Jutland: Darkness Falls

Scheer knew all too well that he had not escaped. After all, Jellicoe had achieved the principal objective of his own maneuvering: He had positioned the Grand Fleet between the German High Seas Fleet and the German ports. But Scheer had decided that the High Seas Fleet could not survive another all-out slugfest.

Short of options, Sheer turned to the southeast under cover of darkness, heading directly into the formation of light cruisers that brought up the rear of Jellicoe's fleet. From about 9:30 until 3:00 in the morning, the battle degenerated into a bloody chaos of intensive gunfire and ship-to-ship collisions, some accidental and some deliberate. Screened by the mayhem, Scheer limped away, having eluded Jellicoe's blocking action in the hellish night.

Keeping Score

Some historians call Jutland an indecisive or drawn battle. In truth, the outcome was quite definite, if paradoxical. That the British lost more than the Germans in ships and men makes the Battle of Jutland a tactical victory for the Germans. Three battle cruisers, 3 cruisers, 8 destroyers, and 6,274 officers and men were sacrificed on the British side. The Germans lost a battleship and a battle cruiser, in addition to 4 light cruisers, 5 destroyers, and 2,545 officers and men.

A tactical victory is measured in raw numbers such as these. Whoever loses the most loses, and whoever loses the least wins. Yet, while grave, the British losses were not sufficient to reduce the numerical superiority of the British fleet over the Germans. And, as a result of the Battle of Jutland, the German High Seas Fleet would never again seriously venture out from the security of its home ports. Although still intact, the High Seas Fleet had been neutralized as an instrument of war. This was a result that affected the war's big picture. For the British, it was a strategic victory—albeit achieved at shocking cost.

End of an Era

In the history of naval warfare, the Battle of Jutland stands as a kind of grand finale. Never again would so many great ships fight it out within eyesight of one another. In terms of maneuver, it was an old-fashioned naval battle, the kind that Admiral Horatio Nelson and his ilk had fought against Napoleon's navy at the start of the nineteenth century. But in terms of firepower, Jutland was unmistakably modern. It was the first and last time these two discordant elements—classic combat maneuver and modern firepower—would be combined.

High Seas Coda

After Jutland, surface action on the high seas was all anticlimactic. On August 18, the German High Seas Fleet briefly sortied out of its home waters to meet the British Grand Fleet. But both Admiral Scheer and Admiral Jellicoe withdrew without even making contact with one another. From the Battle of Jutland onward, German surface naval activity was limited to two hit-and-run light-cruiser raids on the British coast (see Chapter 11) and some surface action against merchant vessels. Otherwise, the German navy remained submerged, dealing death from underwater until the day of Armistice. And in pursuing this course of unrestricted submarine warfare, Germany brought on its own ultimate defeat by provoking neutral America to enter the war against it.

The Least You Need to Know

➤ The submarine was not a World War I invention, but it came to rapid maturity as a highly destructive weapon in that war.

➤ Germany's policy of unrestricted submarine warfare was destructive to Allied shipping, albeit not decisively so; ultimately, the policy sealed Germany's doom by provoking the United States to shed its neutrality and join the Allied cause.

➤ Admiral Reinhard Scheer provoked the Battle of Jutland in an effort to reduce the British fleet and thereby end British control of the seas and the British blockade of German shipping.

➤ Although the British Grand Fleet enjoyed numerical superiority over the German High Seas Fleet, the Germans possessed stronger (more "survivable") ships, better guns, and better ammunition than their British counterparts.

➤ The Battle of Jutland ended in a tactical victory for the Germans, who inflicted more damage than the British did, but it was a strategic victory for the British, who maintained control of the seas and effectively bottled up the High Seas Fleet in German home waters.

Winged Knights

For most soldiers in World War I, injury or death came in a curiously impersonal manner: a stream of machine gun fire, indifferent as spray from a hose; the directionless explosion of an artillery shell; a chance whiff of poison gas; an attack of disease, dysentery, cholera, or influenza—whatever the filth of the trenches might spawn.

The defense against injury or death was equally impersonal. Rarely was there any individual opponent to outwit, outrun, or outthink. Instead, a soldier kept his head down and groveled in the mud of a trench. Men who had recently embraced loving wives and adoring children now hugged the indifferent earth.

Perhaps worst of all, never before had war been both so costly and simultaneously so futile. On the Western Front especially, there was nowhere to move—not forward, not back, not side to side.

But a man could still look up.

The sky, clean and clear and pure, still offered room for maneuver and, it seemed, an opportunity to fight an enemy one to one in a contest that, while still deadly, at least seemed to make sense—and even seemed gallant, heroic, and chivalric. This chapter looks at the air war.

The Air War: First Phase

In 1903, inventors Wilbur and Orville Wright fitted a 170-pound, 12-horsepower motor to the craft they christened *Flyer I*. They took the 750-pound gossamer contraption of fabric and wood to Kill Devil Hill, Kitty Hawk, on the morning of December 17. They flipped a coin. It came up heads, and Orville assumed his position at the controls, lying on his belly across the bottom wing of the craft. The engine erupted into life. The aircraft raced down a rail track laid on the beach for it. Then it took to the air. For 12 seconds, it flew over a distance of some 120 feet.

The Wrights made three more flights that first day, Wilbur managing to keep *Flyer I* aloft for almost a minute, over a distance of 852 feet. By 1908, the brothers had developed and improved the airplane sufficiently to secure a contract with the U.S. Department of War for the first military aircraft.

But the United States military soon lost interest in flying weapons, and America quickly fell behind England, France, and Germany in the development of aircraft, especially for the purposes of war.

Reconnaissance

In Europe, progress in aircraft development and design had come a long way by the outbreak of war in 1914, but engines light enough to be borne aloft still had to be quite small and therefore were feeble. This meant that aircraft could carry nothing more than a pilot and perhaps an observer. So, in World War I, airplanes were at first limited chiefly to reconnaissance duties.

Before the outbreak of war, most military planners continued to put emphasis on tethered balloons or, in the case of Germany, airships. Indeed, aerial observation was still viewed as a rather novel adjunct to traditional cavalry reconnaissance, and most armies gave no thought to interdicting—attacking—the enemy's aerial observers. Nevertheless, armies had recognized some value to airborne reconnaissance almost a half-century before the Wrights' *Flyer*.

During the Civil War, intrepid observers were lofted in baskets suspended below balloons filled with highly buoyant but highly combustible hydrogen gas. In World War I, balloons and airships were also used for observation, but the far more maneuverable airplane was even better suited to the observation role, especially if equipped with a radio for real-time communication with the ground. Unfortunately, few aircraft could carry the bulky and heavy radio equipment of the day, so most aerial observers had to land to make their report, or drop a message canister. Observers did have cameras, and photos they took were quickly processed and analyzed.

At the First Battle of the Marne (see Chapter 6, "The Marne: Massacre and Miracle"), for example, aviator reconnaissance was invaluable to the counterattack of the Anglo-French armies, which prevented the German capture of Paris.

As both sides became increasingly aware of the value of airborne reconnaissance, they began innovating ways of shooting down the planes. Given the fragility of the fabric-covered wood-framed craft, ground rifle or machine-gun fire was often enough to bring down a plane. But very soon, specially designed antiaircraft guns were developed, as was antiaircraft ammunition.

Another development occurred as well. As reconnaissance craft flew over an enemy base, the enemy began sending up its own aircraft to give chase. Early on, air-to-air combat consisted of airmen exchanging potshots with small arms. In a single-person craft, only a pistol was practical. If an observer was on board, rifle or even shotgun fire was a possibility.

Very soon, as we will see, the belligerents began experimenting with ways of arming airplanes with specially mounted machine guns—and the reconnaissance aircraft evolved into the fighter.

From the Front

The most effective antiaircraft ammunition used a time fuse, which detonated the shell at a certain altitude, blasting out thousands of shrapnel fragments. It was difficult to hit a fast airplane with a direct shot, but the fragile craft and its pilot, seated in an open cockpit, were highly vulnerable to exploding shrapnel fragments.

Strategic Bombing

Airplanes are heavier-than-air craft. Their ability to fly—their lift—depends on a stream of air flowing over an aerodynamically shaped wing. With the technology available during World War I, that airflow was produced by the propulsion of a piston engine–driven propeller or propellers. As we saw in Chapter 5, "Battle of the Frontiers," Count Ferdinand Zeppelin developed his first airship, or zeppelin, in 1900. Although it was also propelled forward by a motor-driven propeller, lift was provided not by wings, but by highly buoyant hydrogen gas, which inflated rubberized cloth "balloonets" inside the cloth-covered, aluminum-framed hull of the zeppelin. Thus, the airship, or zeppelin, was a lighter-than-air craft.

Zeppelins were big, slow, and difficult to maneuver. The hydrogen gas that gave them their lift was highly combustible. All in all, they made easy and inviting targets. However, the zeppelin was capable of carrying much more weight aloft than any aircraft available in 1914, and it had greater range and could achieve higher altitudes. German military planners therefore were quick to seize upon the zeppelin as a platform for aerial bombardment—and not just for the occasional explosive device tossed overboard, but even for large-scale *strategic bombardment*.

225

In contrast to *tactical bombardment*, which is directed at military targets on the battle-field, strategic bombardment is undertaken against civilian targets, typically with the intention of destroying the enemy's war industries and thereby shortening the war. Strategic bombing requires aircraft capable of carrying large numbers of bombs over great distances. The zeppelins, German planners hoped, could do just this. In the end, however, they proved ineffective at true strategic bombing and could do little more than carry out harassing raids over Great Britain and France. Flying at high altitude to avoid being shot down, the zeppelins were incapable of dropping bombs accurately.

At the outbreak of the war, however, the German army used some of the 10 military zeppelins then available not to attack major enemy cities, but to bombard garrison outposts and fortifications and for reconnaissance. After losing three zeppelins in daylight raids over fortified positions, however, the German army quickly abandoned the lighter-than-air craft as a weapon.

Yet the German navy remained enthusiastic. As discussed in Chapter 13, "A New Year and No Hope," zeppelins under navy command bombarded London in 1915. Although the second zeppelin raid on the British capital, carried out on September 8, 1915, caused considerable damage, no nation (including Germany) possessed enough airships or sufficient aerial aiming technology to carry out a truly effective program of strategic bombing. Moreover, it was quite easy to defend against zeppelin raids. The British shot down the airships with antiaircraft guns as well as with fighter airplanes firing special incendiary bullets, which caused the zeppelins' hydrogen to ignite and explode. Aside from enemy defenses, the zeppelins also had to contend with the weather. High winds, lightning storms, and the like were at least as deadly as bullets. Of the 73 zeppelins the German navy had, 53 were lost by 1918. Half the German army's fleet of 52 also came to bad ends.

Words of War

Strategic bombardment is aerial bombardment on a large scale, typically directed at civilian targets, especially those involved in the production of war-related materiel. This program of bombardment is "strategic" because it is intended as a direct means of shortening a war.

Words of War

Tactical bombardment is aerial bombardment of military targets at the front. Typically, tactical bombardment is on a relatively small or concentrated scale and is in direct support of ground operations.

With its great range and lifting capacity, the zeppelin seemed a ready-made platform for strategic bombing, but both sides soon moved to develop airplanes specifically designed for bombing missions. The first of these to see action was the French Voisin, a single-engine craft capable of achieving 85 miles per hour and carrying as much as 661 pounds of bombs. On August 14, 1914, barely two weeks into the war, the Voisin was used to bomb the zeppelin hangars at Metz-Frascaty.

Surprisingly, the perpetually backward Russian military was quick to develop a specialized force of bombers. Designed by Igor Sikorsky (who would later gain fame as the inventor of the first truly practical helicopter), the Ilya Muromets was an improvement on the inventor's earlier design, the Russky Vityaz, the world's first four-engine airplane. Built in 1913, the Ilya Muromets boasted a 100-foot biplane wingspan, accommodated a crew of five, and even included sleeping compartments for crew members. With a ceiling of 9,000 feet and a top speed of 85 miles per hour, it could remain aloft for five hours and could carry a bomb load of about 1,500 pounds. The airplane was defended by three or four machine guns.

The Ilya Muromets craft were among the most successful bombers of the war. They carried out some 400 missions over Germany and the Baltic states, yet suffered very few casualties.

Italy was next to build a bomber, the trimotor Caproni of 1915, capable of a swift 94.4 miles per hour and able to carry an almost 1,200-pounds bomb payload. Although lightly defended by only two machine guns, the bomber was successful enough to see service throughout the war.

From the Front

The ultimate in World War I zeppelin development was the LZ-70. Measuring 740 feet long, it could top 16,000 feet and had a spectacular range of 7,500 miles. Late in the war, it was shot down in flames.

Great Britain introduced more bomber types than any other combatant nation. The first two-engine Handley Page bomber appeared at the end of 1916 and could carry almost 1,800 pounds of bombs at 90 miles per hour. Early the next year, another Handley Page model carried the same capacity, but at a significantly improved 97.5 miles per hour.

By the end of the war, the Handley Page company introduced the mammoth V/1500 four-engine bomber capable of carrying a 7,500-pound payload in the form of thirty 250-pound bombs. Because it was introduced so late, however, this large craft saw no combat service in the war. In the meantime, though, the De Havilland firm produced two bombers, De Havilland 4 and 5, each high-speed (up to 120 miles per hour) craft with a four-bomb capacity. Other single-engine planes, the Bristol F.2A/B, the S.E. 5a, and the Sopwith Camel, were capable of fighter as well as bomber roles, although they were not suited to heavy strategic bombing.

From the Front

The Germans also built a small number of highly advanced four-engine, all-metal bombers called *Riesenflugzeug*, or R-planes. Carrying a crew of seven, they could deliver a bomb payload of 4,000 pounds. Too heavy and ungainly to be very practical, few saw service.

Germany introduced two strategic bombers in 1916, the Freidrichshafen and the Gotha. Both were twin-engine planes capable of carrying 1,000 to 1,100 pounds of bombs and able to hit 87 miles per hour. The Gotha was the most widely used of the German strategic bombers, doing considerable damage to enemy supply depots and railheads behind the lines.

Despite the array of bombers that the belligerents built, the craft were never produced in sufficient quantity to have a significant effect on the course and conduct of the war. While the Germans directed most of their attacks against the towns of southeastern England, ultimately inflicting only minor damage, the British concentrated with better effect on industrial targets, zeppelin facilities, and U-boat bases.

Dogfight!

When the topic of World War I aerial warfare is mentioned, it is not likely that the subject of reconnaissance, zeppelins, or strategic bombing will come up—rather, attention turns to air-to-air combat between fighter planes, the so-called *dogfight*. From the ranks of the fighter pilots—a tiny, elite corps of men, each with a pitifully short life expectancy—came many of the war's few truly popular heroes: René Fonck of France, Edward "Mick" Mannock of Great Britain, William Bishop of Canada, Eddie Rickenbacker of the United States, and Manfred von Richthofen of Germany. All of these became household names.

Words of War

A **dogfight** is the term generally used for air-to-air combat between fighter aircraft.

In a war whose every day produced casualties by the thousands, one-on-one aerial combat seems out of place and anachronistic, harking back to the days when one knight jousted against another on a "field of honor." But while it is true that World War I aerial combat quickly acquired romantic associations, this fighting was born of practical necessity. With each passing week of stalemate on the Western Front, accurate artillery bombardment was seen as ever more important. Increasingly, aerial reconnaissance figured as a key to the precise placement, distribution, and aiming of artillery; therefore, the side that controlled the sky above the battlefield had a very significant advantage.

From Revolver to Machine Gun

At first, reconnaissance pilots took random shots at each other with pistols. In more sophisticated two-man aircraft, the observer might arm himself with a rifle or, better yet, a shotgun.

Words of War

In a **pusher configuration,** the aircraft's propeller is behind the engine and creates a thrust that pushes the airplane forward.

In 1913, the year before the war, the British Vickers company introduced a *pusher configuration* aircraft, with its propeller behind the engine and equipped experimentally with a mounted machine gun operated by the observer, who sat in front of the pilot. This design was improved in 1915 as the Vickers F.B.5.

Gunbus—it was the first production aircraft specifically designed with air-to-air armament.

But the Vickers pusher design—as well as a subsequent French Voison pusher—was inherently inferior in performance, speed, and maneuverability to aircraft with a more conventional *tractor configuration*, with the propeller at the nose in front of the engine. Yet, if the propeller was at the nose, how could one devise a way to prevent the machine gun, firing through the rotation of the propeller, from hitting and damaging the props with catastrophic results?

In 1913, German designer Franz Schneider had patented an interrupter mechanism, a device that synchronized the firing of the machine gun with the rotation of the prop, so that the bullets always passed safely between the turning blades. The German military showed no interest in the device, however. Also before the war, the French engineer, Raymond Saulnier experimented with an interrupter mechanism, but was unable to keep it from malfunctioning. He then turned instead to simply attaching triangular steel plates to the props, which would deflect bullets. In December 1914, French pilot Roland Garros approached Saulnier to install the deflector plates to his Morane-Saulnier monoplane. Garros's plane crashed and was captured by the Germans, who turned his prop over to Dutch aircraft designer Anthony Fokker.

Words of War

In a **tractor configuration,** the propeller is mounted in front of the engine, at the nose. It creates thrust and lift by directly accelerating the air that passes over the plane's wings, in effect pulling the craft forward as a tractor pulls a trailor.

Words of War

A **monoplane** has a single set of wings, in contrast to the double-decker biplane.

The brilliant Fokker thought the deflectors crude and, by May 20, 1915, developed instead the first practical synchronized machine gun, which he fitted to his "Eindecker," the Fokker E-III monoplane. Combined with the Eindecker's high degree of maneuverability, Fokker's interrupter gear gave the Germans a substantial period of air superiority in 1915.

Because the machine gun itself had to be rigidly mounted on the airplane's fuselage to ensure the accuracy of the synchronization, it was aimed by pointing the entire plane in the desired direction and altitude. This meant that the pilot, the man in direct control of the aircraft, not an observer, had to operate the machine gun. The single-man fighter plane was born.

Coffins with Wings and Props

The two earliest planes specifically designed as fighters were the British Bristol Scout D (introduced in 1914) and the French Morane Type N (introduced in 1915). These planes were quickly outclassed by Germany's Fokker E III or Eindecker, a highly maneuverable monoplane featuring two synchronized machine guns. From July until October 1915—a period dubbed by Allied pilots the "Fokker Scourge"—the Eindecker reigned supreme over the Western Front. Its presence accelerated development of the French Nieuport and the British De Havilland 2, which brought improvements in speed and maneuverability that matched the Eindecker.

From this point on, the air war largely became a race to produce planes with higher performance and maneuverability. Typically, improvements came first in engine design, with the object being the production of lighter, more efficient, and more powerful power plants. In turn, this spurred revisions of the airframe—the aircraft itself.

Although aircraft speeds did not improve dramatically during the war, progressing from the 80-mile-per-hour range in 1914 to the 120-plus-mile-per-hour range by the end of the war, great strides were made in reliability and maneuverability. And a victorious dogfight depended almost entirely on the ability to outmaneuver the adversary.

Despite advances in design and technology, World War I aircraft ended the war the way they had entered it: as flying coffins. Most World War I fighter airplanes were built primarily of fabric stretched over a frame of light but reasonably sturdy wood. The fabric was treated with a kind of volatile varnish or shellac called dope, which stretched and smoothed the surface of wings and fuselage—and which also made the fabric and wood that much more flammable. Wherever possible, flight surfaces—wings and tail assemblies—were reinforced with wire cable.

Under the best of conditions, the structural and mechanical reliability of the planes was limited, especially when flying at high speeds and in tight maneuvers while being shot at. Mortality among pilots was high, and if the impact of a crash didn't prove fatal, the fire that surely followed would.

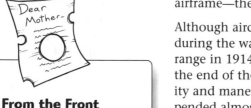

From the Front

By 1917, the average life expectancy of a pilot on the Western Front was three weeks. Late in the war, the Germans began issuing parachutes to their pilots, but British and French leaders persisted in refusing to issue them because they believed they would diminish the aggressive spirit of their pilots. To some extent, parachutes were also viewed as unreliable; although the parachutes themselves functioned well, harnesses and opening mechanisms left much to be desired.

Fighter Tactics

Air-to-air combat occurred on several of the war's fronts but was most intense on the Western Front. In contrast to the way in which the air forces of World War II would be deployed, there was little unified strategic purpose motivating the air corps of the Great War other than to gain air superiority, which ensured a platform for accurate reconnaissance. Instead, they settled into a routine of launching a squadron from the base, or aerodrome, to patrol a given sector in search of enemy reconnaissance or fighter aircraft. When a recon airplane was sighted, it was shot down. When the patrol encountered an enemy fighter patrol, a dogfight would ensue, and ground troops would be treated to a display of spectacular maneuvering, bursts of gunfire, and flaming death.

In the summer of 1916, the German High Command ordered air ace Oswald Boelcke to form the first *Jagdstaffel*, a squadron specializing in hunting and shooting down enemy aircraft. It was Boelcke who first articulated the eight basic principles of aerial combat:

Voices of Battle

"With one sentence, one can settle the topic: 'Aerial Combat Tactics,' namely: 'I get within 50 meters of the enemy from behind, aim neatly, then the opponent falls.'"

—Manfred von Richthofen, the "Red Baron," German ace and top ace of the war

1. Always try to secure advantages before attacking; keep the sun behind you—and in the enemy's eyes.

2. Always carry through an attack when you have started it.

3. Fire only at close range and only when your opponent is properly in your sights.

4. Always keep your eye on your opponent, and never let yourself be deceived by ruses.

5. In any form of attack, it is essential to fight your opponent from behind.

6. If your opponent dives on you, do not try to evade his onslaught, but fly to meet it.

7. When over the enemy's lines, never forget your own line of retreat.

8. Attack on principle in groups of four to six. When the fight breaks up into a series of single combats, take care that several pilots do not go for one opponent.

The Allies quickly developed similar tactics, and British squadron commander and ace "Mick" Mannock added the following:

From the Front

The most famous defensive maneuver was the "Immelmann turn," a half-loop with a half-roll on top. Another common life-saving maneuver was the chandelle, a quick dive to gain speed followed by a very steep climbing turn.

➤ Hide in clouds or the sun.

➤ Attack with superior numbers.

➤ Shoot first, ask questions later. It is better to shoot at a friendly plane by accident than to be caught off guard by an enemy patrol.

Patrols usually flew in one of five formation patterns designed to facilitate attack while defending against surprise. Most attacks began with a dive on the enemy, typically from out of the sun. Cold steel nerves were indispensable because success depended on holding fire until the enemy was at very close range. If the pilot fired too soon, not only would the attack almost certainly miss, but, by alerting the prey, the hunter also might well find himself the hunted.

A fast dive always carried the attacker below the target, but using the momentum of the dive, a skilled pilot would quickly regain altitude for a renewed attack.

The spectacle of a dozen or so aircraft of opposing patrols climbing, turning, and diving to attack and avoid attack appeared to ground observers like a spectacular aerial ballet. The unit led by the most celebrated German ace, Manfred von Richthofen, was so adept at combat maneuvers—performed in planes that were not camouflaged, but defiantly painted in bright colors—that Allied pilots dubbed it the "Flying Circus."

The fact is that pilots whose skills even approached that of a Richthofen or any of the other aces were rare. Mortality was so high that recruits were typically given their wings after little training and then rushed to the front to replace their fallen predecessors. They rarely had the opportunity to gain valuable experience by building up flying time in quiet sectors. This created a vicious cycle because new pilots were often shot down on their first or second patrol.

The Aces

If the killing of thousands day after day along an immobile trench line ceased to have meaning, the death of a few individuals in aerial combat duels somehow seemed more comprehensible. Of course, it was still death, but it was death in a contest between individuals rather than among masses. As if to underscore this, the French introduced a system of recognition of *aces*. A pilot achieved ace status after downing five enemy aircraft. Almost immediately, the Germans and the British also began programs of ace recognition.

Words of War

In World War I, an **ace** was a pilot who scored five confirmed victories (that is, kills).

Among the French aces, the most celebrated—indeed, worshiped and adored—was Georges Guynemer, who scored 54 victories before disappearing into a cloud bank on September 11, 1917, never to be seen again. Two other French aces, Charles Nungesser (45 victories) and René Fonck (75 victories), were chiefly responsible for creating the romantic, swashbuckling popular image of the air ace. An ex-prizefighter, Nungesser lived it up during his off-duty hours in the nightclubs of Paris, and he decorated each of his planes with a trademark black heart enclosing a skull, crossbones, a coffin, and candlesticks. Remarkably, the dashing Nungesser survived the war but was killed in

1927 when, shortly before the flight of Charles Lindbergh, he attempted a solo flight across the Atlantic.

Fonck, with 75 victories to his credit, was hailed as the Allied "Ace of Aces." He made combat a personal matter when he set out to shoot down Kurt Wisseman, the German pilot who claimed credit for having downed Guynemer. A pilot of matchless daring and skill—twice, on May 9 and September 26, 1918, he downed a half-dozen planes in a day of flying—Fonck also survived the war. He died peacefully in Paris in 1953.

Unlike France and Germany, the British Royal Flying Corps officially played down the exploits of aces as showy and bad for general morale. British pilots were actively discouraged from personalizing their planes with distinctive insignia—though many did just this—and individual exploits were not generally reported to the press as they were in France and Germany. Nevertheless, Britain's Royal Flying Corps also produced a crop of aces, the most prolific of whom were Edward "Mick" Mannock (73 victories) and William Bishop (72 victories), a Canadian. Mannock met his death in June 1918 when he fell victim to ground fire. Bishop survived the war and, after the Armistice, helped found the Royal Canadian Air Force.

The greatest of all aces was Germany's Manfred von Richthofen, who scored 80 victories before he was shot down on April 21, 1918. Nicknamed the "Red Baron," he painted his Albatross D-III biplane bright scarlet in 1917, then did the same for his later, better-known, Fokker triplane. Richthofen was adored throughout Germany and both feared and respected as an adversary by Allied pilots.

Canadian pilot Roy Brown claimed credit for downing the Red Baron, but it is also possible that Australian ground gunners fired the fatal shots. The latter possibility was vehemently denied both by Richthofen's German compatriots and by Allied fliers, who could not accept on behalf of Richthofen anything less "honorable" than death at the hands of another pilot. In any case, the Australian unit that recovered Richthofen's body buried him with full military honors in Bertangles, France. The body was later reburied in Wiesbaden, Germany.

The United States produced one ace of signal fame, Edward Vernon "Eddie" Rickenbacker. Born in Columbus, Ohio, in 1890, Rickenbacker developed an early passion for automobiles, which grew into a career as a pioneering professional race car driver. He participated in the first Indianapolis 500 and set an early speed record at Daytona Beach, Florida: 134 miles per hour. By 1916, he had earned national fame as the third-ranked American racer.

Voices of Battle

"One does not need to be a crack pilot or marksman, but only to have the courage to fly within the closest proximity of the opponent."

—Manfred von Richthofen, on becoming an ace

Combatants

Manfred Albrecht von Richthofen (1892–1918) was born of a noble family in Breslau. Enrolled in cadet school by his father, who wanted him to become an army officer, Richthofen was a poor student who showed little interest in anything other than gymnastics and horsemanship. At the outbreak of war, he was a cavalry lieutenant on the Eastern Front. When his regiment was posted to infantry duties in the trenches—a life Richthofen found intolerable—the young man obtained a transfer to the air service.

In the early months of German aerial warfare, two-man observation crews consisted of an enlisted pilot and an officer observer, rather like a working-class chauffeur and his upper-crust passenger. Richthofen, an officer, began his flying career as an observer but soon trained as a pilot. He received his license on December 25, 1915.

Richthofen joined air ace Oswald Boelcke's fighter squadron in September 1916 and rapidly racked up one victory after another. In January 1917, Richthofen was given command of his own squadron and, on July 1, after receiving the coveted "Blue Max," Germany's highest valor award, he was put in command of the first large fighter formation—a unit of 40 planes. Just six days later, however, Richthofen was wounded in the head and was sent on an extended convalescent leave. German military authorities were in no hurry to return him to active duty because they saw him as a highly valuable morale-boosting instrument of propaganda.

Nevertheless, he did ultimately return to combat, leading his infamous "Flying Circus." He was killed on April 21, 1918.

When America entered the war, Rickenbacker lobbied for the creation of a U.S. flying corps consisting of auto racers and mechanics. Although his idea was not seriously considered, he enlisted on May 25, 1917, and went to France as a sergeant driver in General John J. Pershing's Motor Car Staff. A frequent passenger was Colonel William "Billy" Mitchell, pioneering proponent of American air power, who helped Rickenbacker get an assignment to flight school in France.

After joining the 94th Squadron—called the "Hat-in-the-Ring Squadron," for its soon-to-be-famous insignia—Rickenbacker was promoted to officer status and proceeded to rack up the 26 victories, including many scored against Richthofen's Flying Circus, that made him a multiple ace.

From the Front

Rickenbacker survived the war, returning to the United States as a popular hero. He worked first as an executive in the automobile industry and then in the airline industry. In 1938, he became president, general manager, and director of Eastern Airline. During World War II, he was a special adviser to Secretary of War Henry Stimson. On an inspection mission, his plane was forced down in the Pacific, and Rickenbacker led seven other survivors through a heroic 23-day ordeal on rafts. He died in 1973.

Lafayette Escadrille

Although Rickenbacker was a pioneer of American military aviation, the Hat-in-the-Ring Squadron was not the first U.S. air combat presence in France. On April 20, 1916, well before the United States ended its neutrality to enter the war, the American Volunteer Squadron of the French Air Service—better known as the Lafayette Escadrille—went into operation and flew until February 18, 1918, when it was absorbed into the U.S. Air Service as the 103d Pursuit Squadron.

Thirty-eight American volunteers (and four Frenchmen) flew more than 3,000 missions over every sector of the Western Front, suffering a 30 percent casualty rate and scoring 39 confirmed victories and perhaps a hundred unconfirmed ones. In all, these figures are not impressive. Nevertheless, the symbolic impact of the Lafayette Escadrille was great. It demonstrated that, U.S. advocates of neutrality notwithstanding, truly "honorable" Americans were prepared to lay their lives on the line to defend democratic civilization against the dreaded "Hun."

From the Front

The American Volunteer Squadron, the Lafayette Escadrille, was named after the Marquis de Lafayette, the young French nobleman who rendered General George Washington and the Continental Army invaluable service during the American Revolution.

Ground Attack

Air-to-air combat—the dogfight—was deadly, but it was perceived as inherently noble, something bright and clean and heroic in a dirty, brutal war. The fact is, however, that late in the war the airplane had begun to evolve into yet another engine of anonymous killing on a larger scale.

By 1917, both sides began producing planes specially modified for *ground attack,* the killing of troops at the front in the trenches. For example, the Sopwith Salamander, a modification of the famed Sopwith Camel air-to-air fighter, had an armored cockpit and two machine guns that fired downward, through the aircraft floor, at a fixed angle designed to rake enemy trenches while flying over them at low altitude. Very late in the war, the Germans produced such two-seater aircraft as the Hannover CL.III, armed with a forward-firing machine gun operated by the pilot, and a flexible machine gun that could be pointed downward, operated by an observer who also controlled racks of fragmentation grenades designed to be dropped on the trenches.

The Germans used ground-attack aircraft at the Battle of Cambrai in November and December 1917 (see Chapter 21, "Allies Imperiled"), with very destructive results. At the end of the war, the German Junkers CL-I, made entirely of metal and well armored, proved to be the deadliest and most advanced ground-attack aircraft. However, it was introduced too late to see much combat or have any effect on the war's outcome.

Still, the direction that air combat was taking had become clear to anyone willing to see it. The next war would not feature latter-day knights dueling in the clouds for the honor of their nations. The next war would use airplanes as yet another vehicle of instant, extensive, technologically sophisticated, and anonymous devastation.

Words of War

Ground attack describes the use of aircraft against military personnel and other targets on the ground. Used in coordination with assault by ground troops, it is also called "close air support."

The Least You Need to Know

➤ The first use of aircraft in World War I was as bombers and, even more important, as platforms for reconnaissance.

➤ The fighter plane developed first as a means of shooting down reconnaissance aircraft and then as a means of attacking other fighter aircraft.

➤ Air-to-air combat, the dogfight, was widely seen as a noble contest between gallant adversaries, the best of whom earned legendary reputations as aces.

➤ By the end of the war, both sides had begun developing a ground attack role for aircraft, transforming this instrument of "noble" combat into yet another means of delivering death on a large and indifferently brutal scale.

Part 5

Doughboys

At the low point of Allied fortunes, in spring 1917, the United States declared war against Germany after having struggled for almost three years to remain neutral. These chapters tell how the United States mobilized for war and how General John J. Pershing fought both France and Britain to maintain the independence of the U.S. fighting force so that it would not be frittered away in fruitless defensive combat. Here are the first triumphs of the American doughboy and the emergence of such American heroes as Sergeant Alvin York and Captain Eddie Rickenbacker.

Part 5 takes the war through Armistice Day, November 11, 1918.

Chapter 20

"He Kept Us Out of War"

In This Chapter

➤ Wilson's neutrality policy

➤ The United States war trade

➤ U.S. efforts to mediate peace

➤ The United States prepares for war

➤ The Zimmermann Telegram

➤ Wilson declares war

Woodrow Wilson, elected 28th president of the United States in 1912, was a new kind of American leader: an avowed intellectual and idealist. The son of a stern Presbyterian minister, he studied at Davidson College in North Carolina, at Princeton, and at Johns Hopkins, from which he received a Ph.D. in government and history. Wilson wrote political science texts and became a professor at Wesleyan University and then at Princeton, of which he was ultimately named president. Later, the corrupt New Jersey political machine tapped Wilson as a "pliable" gubernatorial prospect, only to end up with a thoroughly incorruptible, zealously reform-minded governor who would not tolerate machine politics.

Before completing his term as governor, Wilson was sent to the White House on a platform of progressive reform. During his first presidential term, the income tax was introduced, protectionist tariffs were lowered, the Federal Reserve Act (1913) reformed currency and banking law, and antitrust legislation was strengthened in 1914 by the Federal Trade Commission Act and the Clayton Anti-Trust Act. In 1915, Wilson supported legislation that federally regulated working conditions of sailors, and in 1916 he signed into law the Federal Farm Loan Act, providing low-interest credit to farmers.

Labor reform came with the Adamson Act, granting an eight-hour day to interstate railroad workers, and the Child Labor Act, curtailing children's working hours.

The accomplishments of his first term prompted many to deem Wilson a great president and might well have been sufficient to earn him another four years; however, Wilson was propelled to his second term in large part on the slogan, "He kept us out of war." Of all the president's accomplishments, most Americans were most gratified by Wilson's having managed to maintain U.S. neutrality.

But with each passing day, month, and year, the pressure to fight in the "European War" mounted.

Staying Neutral

From the moment war broke out in the summer of 1914, Woodrow Wilson committed the United States to a policy of absolute neutrality, showing no favoritism to any side. This was not easy. The United States in 1914 was riding the crest of an unprecedented wave of immigration and was populated by first- and second-generation immigrants from all the warring nations. Nevertheless, most Americans believed that what happened in Europe, clear across the Atlantic, should be of no concern to the United States.

Strict neutrality did not prevent Americans from participating indirectly in the war. All of the belligerents turned to America for war materiel and other goods. As a neutral nation, under international law and custom, the United States had a right to trade with any and all of the warring parties, and it did just that, to the profit of many industrialists and financiers.

Yet the actions of the Central Powers, particularly Germany, made it increasingly difficult to avoid taking sides. Germany's unprovoked declarations of war on France and Russia were impossible to justify. Its violation of Belgian neutrality, a brutal invasion terrible enough as it was, was magnified by Allied propaganda into an atrocity of barbaric proportions. Germans were no longer portrayed as the people who had given the world Beethoven, Goethe, and good beer, but as mindless, butchering "Huns."

Inexorably, the flow of trade between the United States and the European belligerents turned increasingly away from the Central Powers and more toward the Allies. In part, this was the result of America's growing moral revulsion from the Central Powers, but it also happened to make good business sense: High demand, an ample supply of gold, favorable shipping, and the realities of geography made dealing with the Allies far more reliable and profitable than doing business with Germany and the other Central Powers.

And Germany did nothing to ameliorate this situation. On the contrary, each of its actions seemed to violate some rule of "civilized" warfare. It bombed civilian London and other British towns, it used poison gas at Ypres, and, most shocking of all, it unleashed a stealthy and devastating program of unrestricted submarine warfare against commercial shipping.

240

The Lusitania *Strain*

From the American point of view, the bedrock foundation of its rights as a neutral nation was freedom of the seas. This was a matter of philosophical principle, as President Wilson understood, but it was also much more.

By 1917, American firms had done some $2 billion in business with the Allies, and U.S. banks had made $2.5 billion in loans. The fact was that, Wilson's strict policy of nonfavoritism notwithstanding, American industry and American banks were betting on an Allied victory. Without it, in the wake of German demands for war reparations from the defeated Allies, they would stand to lose untold fortunes. Like it or not, the fate of the American economy was becoming wedded to that of the Allied cause. Prosperity or depression hung on an Allied victory or defeat.

From the Front

Contrast the $2.5 billion in bank loans made to the Allies by 1917 with the mere $45 million U.S. banks had loaned to Germany.

To do business with the Allies, American business needed freedom of the seas. The War of 1812 had been fought (ostensibly, at least) over this very issue. Unrestricted submarine warfare—the German policy of using U-boats to attack merchant and passenger vessels without even surfacing to give fair warning—was a direct assault on freedom of the seas. And this policy was not restricted to the merchant shipping of the Allies. Neutral nations, including the United States, whose ships ventured into the "war zone" declared by Germany on February 4, 1915, around the British Isles (see Chapter 11, "A *World* War") were also liable to attack.

As we saw in Chapter 11, the May 7, 1915, sinking of the British liner *Lusitania,* in which 124 of the 1,198 lives lost were American, brought anti-German sentiment in the United States to a fever pitch. President Wilson issued a stern yet measured note of diplomatic protest to the Germans, which prompted Secretary of State Williams Jennings Bryan, a firm neutralist, to resign for fear that the note would inevitably push the nation into the war.

The note, we saw, did not bring an immediate end to unrestricted submarine warfare. In August, another passenger ship, the *Arabic,* was sunk with loss of American lives. But after this came the kaiser's orders restricting submarine operations to avoid drawing the United States into the conflict.

Early United States Mediation Efforts

If Bryan had resigned because he actually thought Wilson wanted war, he was mistaken. The president made repeated efforts to avoid American entry into the war by bringing the war itself to an early end.

Colonel Edward M. House was a Texas politician who became a trusted intimate of Wilson, a friend, adviser, and confidant, as well as a quasiofficial personal envoy. When World War I broke out in Europe, House made himself the administration's expert on the conflict. Accordingly, early in 1916, Wilson sent him to London and Paris to sound out Allied leaders on the possibility of U.S. mediation between the belligerents.

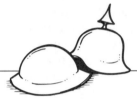

Combatants

Theobald von Bethmann-Hollweg (1856–1921), born into a Frankfurt banking family, became a civil servant and was appointed Prussian minister of the interior in 1905 and state secretary in the Imperial Office of the Interior in 1907. He became chancellor of Germany on July 14, 1909, and introduced moderately liberal policies, which he often failed to defend against more forceful conservatives, especially the militarists. His attempt to negotiate reduction of naval armaments with the British in March 1909 and February 1912, for example, failed because of the intervention of Admiral Alfred von Tirpitz. Bethmann-Hollweg did work successfully with Sir Edward Grey, the British foreign secretary, to forestall the expansion of the Balkan Wars into an all-out conflict between Austria-Hungary and Russia. But this foreign affairs success was rare. Ultimately, Bethmann-Hollweg's political coalition was one of conservatives and centerists. He did advocate and assist in the expansion of the German military and was in favor of breaking the Allied "encirclement of Germany."

In 1914, Bethmann-Hollweg did not believe that war was in Germany's best interest, but his issuance of a so-called blank check to Austria-Hungary, granting it Germany's blessing for whatever steps it thought necessary against Serbia, was a fatal step toward war and rendered useless Bethmann-Hollweg's subsequent warnings to Austria-Hungary to practice restraint.

Bethmann-Hollweg typifies the weak-willed nature of all too many civilian politicians during the era of the Great War, who instantly capitulated to military desires to provoke conflict. Only when the war was under way did Bethmann-Hollweg stand up to Tirpitz and the other militarists in resisting—for some time—the fatally provocative policy of unrestricted submarine warfare. His advocacy of electoral reforms turned conservative militarists as well as civilian politicians against him, and he resigned on July 13, 1917.

House was earnest and not unskilled, but his efforts were also naive, and Wilson would have been better advised to make a more official and concerted effort at mediation. In any event, House's talks with British Foreign Secretary Sir Edward Grey produced the House-Grey Memorandum of February 22, 1916, which declared that the United States might enter the war if Germany rejected Wilson's mediation, but that the right to initiate U.S. mediation rested with Great Britain.

The memorandum was ambiguous. On one level, it was a genuine effort at initiating binding mediation. On another, it could be interpreted as the first diplomatic step toward U.S. entry into the war. In any case, with the approach of the presidential elections of 1916, Wilson decided to suspend his peace initiative, lest its veiled threat to enter the war provoke controversy that might conflict with his "he kept us out of war" platform. Besides, at this point, German politicians, led by Chancellor Theobald von Bethmann-Hollweg, had managed to argue their nation's military into postponing renewal of a declaration of unrestricted submarine warfare. This Wilson read as victory in his effort to keep the country out of the war.

Renewed Mediation Attempts

Yet even after he had achieved re-election, Wilson held off from taking any direct action toward peace. The Bulgar-German victory over Romania in the meantime emboldened Germany to propose peace on its own terms. Bethmann-Hollweg, fatigued by keeping the militarists at bay, agreed that if the German proposals were rejected, unrestricted submarine warfare should be resumed.

On December 12, 1916, Bethmann-Hollweg proposed outrageous peace terms that included *annexation* of Liège and a border strip of Belgium as well as the occupied portion of northeastern France. Clearly, this was unacceptable to the Allies, and Wilson finally stepped in on December 18, 1916, inviting both the Allies and the Central Powers to clear the air by stating their "war aims." In the meantime, however, Robert Lansing, who had replaced William Jennings Bryan as secretary of state, secretly encouraged the Allies to offer terms that, like those proposed by Germany, were too sweeping to gain acceptance. With some justification, therefore, the Germans entertained the suspicion of collusion between Wilson and the Allies. They agreed to the opening of negotiations, but they defiantly left their own statement of December 12 virtually unchanged. By mid-January 1917, the December peace overtures collapsed.

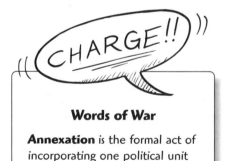

Words of War

Annexation is the formal act of incorporating one political unit or nation into another.

Peace Without Victory

On January 22, 1917, Wilson took a new tack with an appeal for international concil-iation based on achieving "peace without victory." In response, Britain confidentially communicated its willingness to accept Wilson's mediation. Austria-Hungary likewise was ready to listen to peace proposals. In Germany, however, the militarists had won their victory over diplomats like Bethmann-Hollweg. Not only had the decision been made to exclude Wilson from any peace initiative, but also to declare the resumption of unrestricted submarine warfare. With unabashed duplicity, on January 31, 1917, Bethmann-Hollweg restated Germany's peace terms, invited President Wilson to per-severe in his mediation efforts, but also announced that unrestricted submarine war-fare would begin the next day.

Words of War

Armed neutrality was the United States policy, initiated on February 26, 1917, of arming merchant vessels and taking other military steps—short of war itself—to protect American commerce.

Words of War

Jingoism is extreme nationalism characterized by a chauvinist and belligerent foreign policy.

America Drifts Toward War

In response to the German declaration of unrestricted submarine warfare, Woodrow Wilson severed diplo-matic relations between the United States and Ger-many on February 3, 1917, after a U.S. warship, the *Housatonic,* was torpedoed and sunk.

Preparedness Movement

On February 26, the president asked Congress for the authority to arm United States-flagged merchant ves-sels and to take all other military measures to protect American commerce. He called this new policy *armed neutrality,* and it was the first official step in an ongo-ing preparedness movement.

Until the German declaration of unrestricted subma-rine warfare, Wilson had met calls for instituting a formal program of military preparedness with the re-sponse that America was and would remain the "champion of peace."

Despite Wilson's official position, the United States began in various ways preparing for war as early as August 1914. The so-called "preparedness movement" was urged by such Republican "interventionists" as former President Theodore Roosevelt, financier J.P. Morgan, chief Wilson rival Senator Henry Cabot Lodge, and a number of interventionist organizations.

In some respects, the preparedness movement was a realistic response to the world situation. However, it also thrived on and, in turn, fed war fever, *jingoism,* intolerant and bigoted feelings of "100 percent Americanism," and anti-German hatred.

After the sinking of the *Lusitania,* the army's chief of staff, General Leonard Wood, opened up the first of the so-called "businessmen's military training camps," at Plattsburg, New York. By the summer of 1916, well before the Selective Draft Act was signed in May of 1917, 40,000 men had been put through basic training in these camps on an "unofficial" basis, albeit by officers and noncommissioned officers of the regular United States Army. Although unofficial, the "Plattsburg movement" was given support by a government-funded propaganda machine under the direction of a prominent advertising executive named George Creel (see Chapter 22, "Over Here and Over There").

Voices of Battle

"I am not now preparing or contemplating war or any steps that need lead to it."

—President Woodrow Wilson, speech, February 1917

Wilson also encouraged American industry and commerce to assume a war footing, which they were quite willing to do, given the profitability of supplying materiel to the Allies. Whether here or abroad, there was a lively market for military goods. To facilitate and coordinate this transition to a war economy, Wilson created a number of emergency federal agencies, including the Council of National Defense, the Civilian Advisory Committee, and the Shipping Board. Even so, America was woefully unprepared to fight when it entered World War I. War production approaching a sufficient scale did not get under way until 1918.

While the nation anxiously eyed transatlantic Europe, relations with the United States' southern neighbor, Mexico, deteriorated as that nation fell into the throes of a civil war. Francisco "Pancho" Villa, a Mexican bandit who had evolved into a popular revolutionary leader, broke with another revolutionary, Venustiano Carranza, in 1914. After Wilson officially recognized Carranza as president of Mexico in October 1915, Villa embarked on a course of guerrilla raids that included several sorties into New Mexico and the killing of 17 U.S. citizens in the town of Columbus. In response, Wilson dispatched a "Punitive Expedition" against Villa in 1916, under the command of General John J. Pershing.

The Punitive Expedition failed to apprehend Villa, but it did prompt Congress to strengthen the American military by passing the sweeping National Defense Act of 1916. The legislation appropriated funds for the enlargement of the regular army, the creation of federal oversight of the National Guard (hitherto, this force had been strictly organized on the state level, like a militia), and a massive expansion of the navy. The foundation had been laid for a full national mobilization.

The Zimmermann Telegram

If the pursuit of Pancho Villa had momentarily diverted American attention from Europe to Mexican border region in 1916, another development in March 1917 dramatically and unexpectedly linked that southern neighbor with the war overseas.

The German High Command as well as Germany's political leaders understood that the resumption of unrestricted submarine warfare would inevitably bring the United States into the war, but they decided to take a desperate gamble, betting that it would require at least a year before American troops would reach Europe in sufficient numbers to have an effect on the Western Front. In that time, the Germans believed, U-boats would wreak such havoc on Allied shipping that peace would come on German terms.

As we will see in Chapter 22, the Germans grossly underestimated the American will and, even more important, the nation's mighty industrial and economic capacity. However, Germany felt that it had another option available for keeping America out of the war. Foreign Minister Alfred Zimmermann believed that, through his deft diplomacy, he could drag the United States into armed conflict with Mexico and Japan. This would give the Americans plenty to occupy themselves with.

It was a delusional plan based on the slightest of historical precedents. Back in 1906, Kaiser Wilhelm II, propelled by his own anti-Asian prejudices, sought to enlist the United States as an ally in his crusade against what he called the "Yellow Peril." He trumped up stories about Japanese imperialist activity in Mexico—stories that did catch on with the sensationalist American press but that did not impress President Theodore Roosevelt. In the United States, this German agitation came to nothing and was soon forgotten. But now, in the desperate year of 1917, after three unimaginably long years of bloody stalemate, Zimmermann and other German policymakers saw in this episode the possibility of a joint Japanese-Mexican war against the United States.

Indeed, Germany had a recent history of covert involvement in Mexican politics. When civil war broke out in that nation in 1910, Germany attempted to trade arms in exchange for the establishment of a German naval base in Mexico. Subsequent military intervention by a newly elected President Wilson cut these plans short. Next, at the outbreak of World War I, Germany covertly supported the Mexican coup d'état of General Victoriano Huerta, rival to Venustiano Carranza, the leader supported by the Wilson administration. The idea was to create a situation in Mexico that would occupy the United States military and divert American arms from the Allies. Again, however, the Wilson government foiled German efforts by arresting and imprisoning Huerta in Texas.

With Huerta neutralized, Germany began covertly supporting no less a figure than Pancho Villa. After Villa's raids into New Mexico, Wilson dispatched the Punitive Expedition into Mexico under General Pershing to apprehend the bandit-revolutionary. This action had been taken with the consent of President Carranza, but, before long, in response to popular pressure, Carranza angrily demanded the withdrawal of American troops from Mexican soil. Observing this, Zimmermann felt confident that he could exploit a growing breach between Mexico and the United States.

On January 16, 1917, Zimmermann sent a secret, coded telegram, via the German ambassador in Washington, D.C., to the German minister in Mexico. It authorized him to propose a German-Mexican alliance to President Carranza. In return for a declaration of war against the United States, Mexico would receive Germany's support in the reconquest of its "lost territory in Texas, New Mexico, and Arizona." Carranza was also to be asked to invite Japan to adhere to the anti-American alliance.

Unfortunately for Zimmermann, President Wilson, in compliance with Carranza's demand, had ordered the withdrawal of U.S. troops from Mexico on January 25, and the pull-out was completed on February 5—before the German minister in Mexico had even delivered the proposal to Carranza. In view of Wilson's compliance, Carranza was in no mood to start a war with the United States.

And for Germany, there was worse to come. Not only did the Zimmermann Telegram fall flat, but it fell into the hands of British Admiralty intelligence, which intercepted it, decoded it, and made it available to President Wilson. Enraged, Wilson published it to the American people and the world on March 1, 1917.

Voices of Battle

The Zimmermann Telegram read:

"We intend to begin on the first of February unrestricted submarine warfare. We shall endeavor in spite of this to keep the United States of America neutral. In the event of this not succeeding, we make Mexico a proposal of alliance on the following basis: make war together, make peace together, generous financial support and an understanding on our part that Mexico is to reconquer the lost territory in Texas, New Mexico, and Arizona. The settlement in detail is left to you. You will inform the [Mexican] President of the above most secretly as soon as the outbreak of war with the United States of America is certain and add the suggestion that he should, on his own initiative, invite Japan to immediate adherence and at the same time mediate between Japan and ourselves. Please call the [Mexican] President's attention to the fact that the ruthless employment of our submarines now offers the prospect of compelling England in a few months to make peace." Signed, ZIMMERMANN.

"Safe for Democracy"

The combination of Germany's refusal to respect U.S. rights as a neutral nation and the evidence of the Zimmermann Telegram, with its attempt to incite two nations to war against the United States, made it virtually impossible for Woodrow Wilson to avoid war. On April 2, 1917, he went before Congress to ask for a declaration of war. It was voted up on April 6.

247

Wilson had this to say:

> "We have no quarrel with the German people. We have no feeling towards them but one of sympathy and friendship. It was not upon their impulse that their government acted in entering this war. It was not with their previous knowledge or approval. It was a war determined upon as wars used to be determined upon in the old, unhappy days when peoples were nowhere consulted by their rulers and wars were provoked and waged in the interest of dynasties or of little groups of ambitious men who were accustomed to use their fellow men as pawns and tools."

Thus the president acutely and succinctly analyzed the almost mindless mechanism that had propelled Europe into war. He continued:

> "Self-governed nations do not fill their neighbor states with spies or set the course of intrigue to bring about some critical posture of affairs which will give them an opportunity to strike and make conquest. Such designs can be successfully worked out only under cover and where no one has the right to ask questions. Cunningly contrived plans of deception or aggression, carried, it may be, from generation to generation, can be worked out and kept from the light only within the privacy of courts or behind the carefully guarded confidences of a narrow and privileged class. They are happily impossible where public opinion commands and insists upon full information concerning all the nation's affairs."

Wilson then articulated the leading idealistic principle that had moved him to ask for the declaration and that would guide him through the war. It would be "a partnership of democratic nations" against a "natural foe to liberty." It would be a "fight ... for the ultimate peace of the world and for the liberation of its peoples, the German peoples included: for the rights of nations great and small and the privilege of men everywhere to choose their way of life and of obedience."

Then Wilson declared in a phrase that would ring through the remaining history of the century, "The world must be made safe for democracy." And the president disavowed all the motives that had operated in the summer of 1914. "We have no selfish ends to serve," he said. "We desire no conquest, no dominion. We seek no indemnities for ourselves, no material compensation for the sacrifices we shall freely make. We are but one of the champions of the rights of mankind. We shall be satisfied when those rights have been made as secure as the faith and the freedom of nations can make them."

Applause for a Message of Death

President Woodrow Wilson had made a stirring speech. In going to war, he began by claiming for America the moral high ground, although the minority who still advocated neutrality pointed out that the nation's motives were not as lofty and disinterested as the president would have them seem. Considering how much money U.S. industrial and financial firms had invested in the Allies, a lot of very rich Americans would lose a lot of cash if a defeated France and Britain were crushed by war reparations that caused them to default on their massive debts.

Wilson himself had his doubts and was keenly, painfully aware of what he was asking of his fellow citizens. His eloquent war message was greeted with deafening applause by the members of the House and the Senate assembled in special joint session.

"Think what they were applauding!" Wilson remarked to his personal secretary, Joseph P. Tumulty, shortly after delivering the speech. "My message today was a message of death to our young men."

The Least You Need to Know

➤ From the very start of war, President Woodrow Wilson attempted to maintain a strict policy of neutrality for the United States, showing favoritism to no side.

➤ American industrial and banking firms freely did business with the Allies as well as the Central Powers, but they favored the Allies because trade with them was more reliable and more profitable. In lending vast sums of money to the Allies, American financiers were, in effect, banking on an Allied victory.

➤ In the face of repeated German provocations to war, President Wilson attempted unsuccessfully to mediate peace; the Germans perceived his efforts as a prelude to U.S. entry on the Allied side.

➤ The resumption of unrestricted submarine warfare coupled with the revelation of German attempts to incite Mexico and Japan to declare war on the United States (the Zimmermann Telegram) moved Wilson to ask Congress for a declaration of war against Germany in April 1917.

Chapter 21

Allies Imperiled

In This Chapter

➤ Changes in Allied leadership

➤ The Nivelle Offensive is born—and dies

➤ Mutiny on the Western Front

➤ A British offensive in Flanders

➤ Revolution takes Russia out of the war

"I am in blood/Stepp'd in so far," Shakespeare's murderous Macbeth says some two-thirds of the way through his great grim drama, "that, should I wade no more,/ Returning were as tedious as go o'er." And so the belligerents must have felt at the start of 1917, the third full year of the great grim war. They were past the point of no return.

The Central Powers had put a sweeping peace proposal on the table, hinged on annexation of large portions of the territory that they presently occupied. The Allies rejected it out of hand, without leaving open the possibility of further negotiation. It seemed that too much had been sacrificed on either side to stop the sacrifice now. On both sides, politicians and soldiers had come to an agreement: No resolution was acceptable except by defeating the enemy on the field.

Despair on the Western Front

The Americans were about to enter the Great War at a low point for the Allies. Every major Allied offensive had failed. The Central Powers, especially Germany, were in possession of huge tracts of Allied territory. On the Western Front, the armies continued to grind against one another. Men died, and nothing was gained by their deaths.

Yet the Allies were hardly giving up. Thanks to conscription, the fighting strength of the British Army on the Western Front had multiplied to some 1.2 million men and was increasing yet more. France had summoned most of its colonial troops to Europe, so it now fielded 2.6 million men. Add the ever-gallant Belgians, and the Allies had 3.9 million men broadcast across the Western Front opposing 2.5 million Germans.

Shake-Up in British Government

That Britain, which had begun the war by losing most of its small professional army, was committed to the brutal mathematics of attrition was made evident by the New Year's Day promotion to field marshal of Sir Douglas Haig, under whose command more British lives were lost than under any other commander in British military history.

If Brits retained faith in their military leadership, they turned their collective doubt against the civilian government. Prime Minister H.H. Asquith was forced to create a coalition government in May 1915, which was then replaced altogether in December 1916 by a new coalition under David Lloyd George.

Papa Joffre Loses Command

In France, the people lost confidence in their civilian as well as their military leaders. In December 1915, the Cabinet had been shaken up, and Aristide Briand, a long-time critic of the Western Front strategy and a political enemy of Joseph Joffre, was named premier. Nevertheless, it was Briand who named Joffre commander-in-chief in December 1915, encouraging him to defend Verdun at all costs. A year later, however, Briand, disgusted by the lack of progress under Joffre, replaced him with Robert Nivelle, persuaded that the dynamic hero of Verdun could break the Western Front deadlock. Briand did not have the opportunity to test his faith in Nivelle, however. In March 1917, the month before Nivelle launched his promised offensive, Briand's government was ousted for the same reason that Briand had removed Joffre: lack of positive results in the war. Briand was replaced as premier by Alexandre Ribot, who, as we are about to see, did not favor the great offensive that Nivelle proposed.

At 61, Robert Nivelle was just four years younger than Papa Joffre, but, he was slender, suave, energetic, and dashing—he looked positively youthful compared to the rotund, slow, deliberate, and even doddering Joffre. The British liked him because (in the words of one British general) he was "good-looking, smart, plausible, and cool"— and he spoke fluent English as well.

The Verdun Formula

Best of all, Nivelle had an alternative to the static policy of defense and attrition. He had been appointed precisely because of what he had achieved with his counterattacks at Verdun (see Chapter 16, "'They Shall Not Pass!'"). The success of these had depended on what Nivelle now called the "Verdun formula." This formula consisted of using relatively small groups to attack specific objectives. The attacks were always preceded by what Nivelle called a "deception" bombardment: He would bombard the German lines and then halt the barrage, which prompted the Germans to reveal their own artillery positions by returning fire. When the artillery had revealed itself, Nivelle would commence a rolling barrage, sending his infantry in small units directly behind a curtain of concentrated fire that crept forward into the German lines, just ahead of the advancing French infantry.

Nivelle's self-assurance and total confidence in the Verdun Formula combined with his incurable optimism and his espousal of national glory to make a potent package. Most of the Allied commanders were eager to believe that the plan he presented in January for a series of early spring offensives was the answer, the "formula" for dissolving the Western Front deadlock. Surprisingly few questioned the feasibility of applying tactics that had worked with small groups and along the very narrow front at Verdun to the vastly larger and broader scale of huge sectors of the Western Front.

Voices of Battle

"We have the formula!"

—General Robert Nivelle, regarding his counterattack tactics at Verdun, 1916

Nevertheless, there *were* important dissenting voices. General Henri Philippe Pétain, Nivelle's commander at Verdun, was unchanging in his advocacy of a sustained defensive strategy, and the new premier, Alexandre Ribot, agreed with Pétain. Besides, with the United States about to join the war, a risky French offensive now seemed wasteful. Ribot's minister of war, Paul Painlevé, also objected to the Nivelle Offensive, and he even revealed that General Alfred Micheler, the field commander whose army group had been tapped to lead the assault, was pessimistic about its chances for success.

Nivelle didn't debate such objections. Instead, he responded to them with an indignant threat to resign. The brand new government felt (as Nivelle knew it would) that it could hardly afford to goad France's most popular and aggressive general into quitting. Thus blackmailed, Ribot and Painlevé reluctantly signed on to the Nivelle Offensive.

General Nivelle believed it possible "to break the enemy's front in such a manner that the rupture can be immediately exploited; to overcome all the reserves with which our adversary can oppose us; to exploit with all our resources the result of this decisive battle."

More specifically, Nivelle proposed that the British would make preparatory attacks north and south of the old Somme battlefield, at Arras and Bapaume with Cambrai as the objective, to draw out the German reserves. In the meantime, French forces would launch the major offensive in Champagne, north of the Aisne. This main attack would combine, as Nivelle put it, "great violence with great mass"—that is, intense artillery bombardments (the violence) followed by massive frontal attacks (the mass). Nivelle proposed merely to multiply the intensity of small-unit tactics, which had worked on the concentrated Verdun front, to cover a much larger area.

Ludendorff's Move

Although Nivelle's blind faith in the feasibility of magnifying small-unit tactics to the scale of a major offensive was at best questionable, one shortcoming was absolutely certain. He had failed to consider that his adversary, Erich Ludendorff, was nobody's fool. The German commander had watched developments at the front and had astutely grasped the significance of Nivelle's having replaced Joffre. It was obvious to him: The advocate of defense was out, and the champion of offense was in; therefore, an offensive was in the offing, and the only place it could come was on the Somme.

Crystallizing a Defensive Strategy

Acting on this insight, Ludendorff embarked on moves not only intended to frustrate Nivelle's plans, but also to strengthen the German front.

Nivelle's plan depended on the existence of shallow German defenses in Champagne. The less there was to break through, the easier the break would be. Ludendorff quickly deepened his defenses by establishing a third line of troops, well out of range of the French artillery. Next, he resolved purposely to withdraw to this new, intensively fortified line of defense.

The Hindenburg Line

It was called the *Siegfriedstellung,* the Siegfried Zone, or, by the Allies, the Hindenburg Line. The German lines between the towns of Arras and Reims formed a large salient bulging into French-held territory. Instead of beefing up forces along this salient, the Hindenburg Line formed the base of the salient, as much as 20 miles behind the original German front line. From the German position east of Arras, the line ran to the southeast and the south. It passed west of Cambrai and Saint-Quentin, rejoining the original German line at Anizy, between Soissons and Laon. The Allies remained unaware of this line of fortifications because of the German air superiority during the winter of 1916–1917 kept Allied reconnaissance aircraft out of the area.

Words of War

Booby traps are typically explosive devices triggered by some form of human contact and hidden in apparently innocuous places, such as houses.

On February 23, before the Nivelle Offensive commenced, Ludendorff made a preliminary feint back from the front of the salient. Then came a full-scale withdrawal to what was a much shorter, and therefore much more readily defended, line sited on ground the Germans strongly held and could readily defend. This move was completed on March 16. The towns that lay within the territory evacuated by the Germans, including Bapaume, Péronne, Roye, Noyon, Chauny, and Coucy, were simply left to the Allies—after having been rendered quite inhospitable. The Germans mined the roads, destroyed the trees, poisoned the wells, and blew up houses and other buildings. For good measure, they sowed the ruins with an array of *booby traps.*

The Hindenburg Line itself was ingeniously fortified. At the front was a lightly held outpost line that traversed ground thoroughly swept by machine gun fire. Behind this were two heavily fortified defensive lines, one behind the other. Behind these lines were the German reserves protected by elaborate fortified underground barracks. Ludendorff's tactic was to hold the shortened, more heavily fortified Hindenburg Line with relatively few troops. When an attack came at a particular sector or point, the reserves, flexibly positioned in the rear, could be quickly moved up to mass against the attackers.

Battle of Arras and the Nivelle Offensive

The Western Front had changed so little month after month that this massive German withdrawal came as a bewildering shock to Robert Nivelle. Certainly, it was not what he had planned for—and yet, the eternal optimist, he refused to reconsider or alter his plan.

On April 9, he ordered the commencement of the British preliminary attack at Arras. At first, all went remarkably well. The initial bombardment benefited from greatly improved artillery technique and a new poison gas shell that the British had developed. The gas soon silenced the German artillery, and snow grounded German air operations.

At the northern end of the 15-mile battlefront, Vimy Ridge was taken by the Canadian Corps. Unfortunately, the British reserves were unable to exploit this breach because of congested conditions in the rear lines and the shell-torn ground that they had to traverse to pass through the front. British Cavalry could not get up. The small numbers of MK I and II tanks were employed in "penny packets" and quickly broke down or fell prey to German artillery and armor-piercing machine gun rounds. Congestion had not been a problem for Nivelle's small units during the Verdun counterattacks. On an enlarged scale, however, exploiting initial gains in a timely fashion became far more difficult because large masses of troops could not move with sufficient speed and flexibility. Although the British gamely sustained the attack until May 5, by that time German resistance had been augmented sufficiently to repulse all assaults against the line. At Monchy-le-Preux, British cavalry broke through only to be mowed down by concentrated German machine gun fire. An attack by British tanks and Australian infantry at Bullecourt, which was not preceded by an artillery bombardment, failed because of poor coordination and strong German resistance. The advances made in the first five days of the British offensive would be the sum total of the British advance for the entire battle.

After repeated postponements, which gave the Germans time to shift reserves, Nivelle finally launched his own offensive—the principal attack—in Champagne on April 16, buoyed by confidence in the initial stage of the British attack. Nivelle moved along the Aisne River front from Vailly east to Craonne and Reims. His strength was indeed massive at 1.2 million men and 7,000 guns.

The outcome of this great enterprise, however, was a disaster.

To begin with, the element of surprise, which had demonstrated its value time and time again, had neither been achieved nor even sought. The irrepressible Nivelle had been highly vocal in his boasts of certain victory. Second, the Germans were quick to shoot down French observation craft over Champagne. This allowed German artillery to function with impunity and to destroy virtually all French tanks while they still were being driven up in columns, before they could be deployed against the trenches.

Voices of Battle

"German machine guns, scattered in shell holes, concentrated in nests, or appearing suddenly at the mouths of deep dugouts or caves, took fearful toll of the troops now labouring up the rugged slopes of the hills."

—General E.L. Spears, British liaison officer observing the Nivelle Offensive

As for the French artillery, the tactic of the rolling barrage can be devastating to a defender, but it is difficult to coordinate successfully with the advance of the attackers. The barrage moved ahead much too rapidly for the infantry, which became trapped in a blanket of machine-gun fire. The slaughter was horrific. as the French infantry struggled for the Chemin des Dames Ridge, a geographical feature that dominated most of their sector.

No one could deny the determination and gallantry of the individual French poilu. Despite all that went wrong, the troops managed to take the first German line before they were stopped. However, this represented an advance of perhaps 600 yards, whereas Nivelle had called for an initial thrust of six miles.

In five days, Robert Nivelle had lost 120,000 French soldiers, killed and wounded. He captured 21,000 or more German prisoners, but other German casualties were relatively light.

The French Mutinies

If the Nivelle Offensive seemed a wasteful fiasco to the government leaders who had both disapproved and allowed it, to many front-line French soldiers it came as nothing less than senseless mass murder and the proverbial last straw.

Words of War

A **mutiny** is any rebellion against constituted authority. In the case of the French on the Western Front, "mutiny" was a kind of collective strike or work stoppage rather than a violent rebellion.

On April 29, French veteran troops who had flung themselves to slaughter against barbed wire, entrenched machine guns, and carefully presighted artillery, began to rebel. There was no violence against their commanders, just mass refusals to move up front or to attack. Soldiers shouted, "We'll defend the trenches, but we won't attack." During the first three weeks of May, word of the rebellion traveled swiftly through the long trench line, and the French Western Front was paralyzed by mass *mutiny*.

The utter senselessness of the slaughter produced by the Nivelle Offensive was only one in a long series of soldiers' grievances. Others included their terrible and wholly inadequate rations, poor medical care, and a command policy of refusing to grant even a few days of leave from time to time.

Mutiny or not, failure of the offensive or not, Nivelle ordered yet more attacks. On May 15, however, War Minister Painlevé had had enough. He relieved Nivelle and replaced him with Pétain. Nevertheless, the mutiny had now become the gravest imaginable of crises, as reserve troops refused to go into the line. By June, 54 French divisions were hit by mutinies, and only two reliable divisions stood between the Germans and Paris.

Fortunately for the Allies, the forces of French censorship were among the most effective aspects of wartime government. French counterintelligence agents successfully blocked all news of the mutiny, keeping not only the French people, but also General Ludendorff in the dark for weeks. By the time Ludendorff caught wind of dissent in the French ranks, the British under Haig had renewed attacks to distract him and his army. Indeed, so total were the effects of French censorship and propaganda that the full extent of the mutiny would not be known for more than a decade.

For his part, Pétain moved swiftly to suppress the mutiny. Instead of cracking down on the soldiers, he ascribed their rebellion to what he termed "collective indiscipline," not gross insubordination or a premeditated conspiracy to rebel. He aggressively addressed the soldiers' grievances and introduced steps to improve rations and medical care. Most of all, he instituted a regular program of rotating leaves, which sent more soldiers home more often. To the disgust of the British command, Pétain also promised to limit his operations to an "aggressive defense," calling for local attacks of limited duration.

Doubtless, the troops were also heartened by the new strategic policy that Pétain rapidly instituted, in which the overall posture would be defensive, punctuated by numerous offensive moves of limited, more realistic scope. Finally, of course, there was the hopeful prospect of relief offered by the impending arrival of the Americans.

Flanders Fields

Sir Douglas Haig, commanding the British forces on the Western Front, briefly renewed the offensive at the Battle of Arras in an effort to draw off some of the pressure on Nivelle's offensive. Relations between the British and the French—and between

From the Front

After being replaced by Pétain, Nivelle was offered command of an army group, which he declined. Instead, seeking to clear his name and reputation, he voluntarily submitted to review by a military commission, apparently with the tacit understanding that he would be whitewashed. He was. He then left the European theater of war altogether in 1918 to command French troops in Algeria. After the war, he was appointed to the Supreme War Council.

From the Front

While Pétain put down the French mutiny mainly through positive measures, the crisis also occasioned 3,427 courts-martial, by which 554 soldiers were sentenced to death before firing squads. Forty-nine were actually shot. With so many troops involved in the mutiny, punishment was chiefly by example: Those sent for trial were selected by their own officers and non-commissioned officers.

Haig and Nivelle, in particular—had been strained. Nivelle demanded very direct control over British forces on the Western Front, which the British civilian government, over Haig's objections, in large measure gave the French commander. Haig valiantly fought to preserve the autonomy of the British forces (they were, he declared, to "be regarded by General Nivelle as Allies and not as subordinates") even as he faithfully carried out Nivelle's instructions during the great failed offensive.

With 54 French divisions torn by mutiny, Haig was now compelled to assume the burden of action on the Western Front. In fact, the British general embraced the task enthusiastically. While the French army healed itself, adopting a posture of what Pétain called "limited liability" pending the arrival of the Americans, Haig had virtually unlimited authority.

He determined to carry out long-cherished plans for a major offensive in the northern sector of the Western Front, in Flanders. Haig's Third Ypres Campaign was motivated by the following objectives, of great concern to the British, but of only minor interest to the French:

➤ Germany's U-boat campaign was exacting a heavy toll on British shipping. It was believed that the U-boat pens were located in Belgium, at Ostend and Zeebrugge. With an advance into occupied Belgium, these bases could be destroyed. The U-boats were chipping away at Britain's mastery of the seas. If the British lost control here, not only would the island nation be immediately imperiled, but the blockade of Germany also would fail, and even the ability to transport American troops to Europe would be severely compromised.

➤ Pétain might be willing to wait for the Americans, but it would be 6 to 12 months before U.S. forces would appear in sufficient numbers to make a significant impact. Haig felt that the Allies could not afford to suspend offensive activity for so long a period.

➤ The government of Prime Minister David Lloyd George, discouraged by the Western Front deadlock, had turned increasingly to the Italian Front and the Middle East for a breakthrough. Haig felt that placing faith in these peripheral fronts was a dangerous delusion that threatened to draw off needed strength from the Western Front—there, and nowhere else, Haig believed, the war would be won or lost. If he failed to use his forces now, the British general worried, they might be taken from him and frittered away on a secondary front.

➤ Finally, there was the reason that Britain had declared war in the first place: to restore Belgium as a sovereign and neutral state.

Battle of Messines

Ypres was a British salient, an area of strength projecting into the German lines. Before a full-scale offensive could be launched from this salient, however, it was necessary to secure the high ground dominating the area, the Messines-Wytschaete ridge. Haig chose General Sir Herbert Plumer and his Second Army to assault this position.

Haig was renowned for careful, thorough preparation, and the Battle of Messines was certainly among the most thoroughly planned and prepared battles of the war. For 18 months prior to *zero hour,* British engineers had excavated a half-dozen *mine shafts* under the German front lines. Each of these tunnels ended in a chamber that was packed with high explosives, carefully fused so that it could be detonated at will. The British also massed 2,400 guns of all types—one gun for each yard of front— and the Royal Flying Corps also finally established air superiority over the Messines sector.

Words of War

Zero hour, now a familiar term for the precise time scheduled for a project to be launched, originated during World War I to describe the hour appointed for the commencement of a battle.

As usual, artillery preparation was also employed. All too often, as we have seen, artillery preparation—sustained artillery bombardment preceding infantry action— wasted time and effort; worse, the cratered landscape that resulted from it was a hindrance to any subsequent advance. In this case, however, the 17 days of intensive bombardment were well thought out. To begin with, the bombardment was directed chiefly at enemy artillery emplacements, not at entrenched troops. Haig did not plan to exploit the bombarded area with his infantry, so their progress was not impeded here. The main objective of the artillery preparation attack was to knock out opposing guns.

Zero hour, at dawn on June 7, began with the detonation of the mine shafts. Five hundred tons of buried high explosive produced a blast so tremendous that it was heard as far away as London. It blew off the crest of the Messines-Wytschaete ridge and caused untold German casualties, many, doubtless, either blown to bits or buried alive.

For the British attackers, the blast served as a signal to intensify the artillery barrage and to unleash a mixture of smoke and poison gas. By the time the British troops went over the top, the German defenders had not only been greatly reduced by

Words of War

In a military context, **mine shafts** are tunnels ending in a "gallery" under an enemy position. Often these galleries shafts are packed with explosives, designed to detonate directly under the enemy.

casualties, but they also were thoroughly demoralized. The advancing British increased the level of demoralization by rolling over trench lines with tanks and by deploying more poison gas using the brand-new Levens projector, which was designed to hurl poison gas canisters squarely into the enemy trenches. It proved the most effective gas weapon of the war.

From the Front

German losses at Messines were 25,000, of which 7,500 were taken prisoners. British casualties were 17,000 killed and wounded.

From the Allied point of view, the Battle of Messines must be considered the most satisfying local success of World War I combat. British victory was complete: The Germans not only vacated the ridge, but they also were too dazed and depleted to mount an effective counterattack. In contrast to the usual pattern in which an Allied attacker seized a German position only to be forced to relinquish it again, the Messines-Wytschaete ridge was taken and then remained in British hands.

Passchendaele

Victory at Messines emboldened the government of David Lloyd George to authorize the rest of the Third Ypres Campaign, provided that the French participated. What the British government didn't know was the full extent of the French mutinies; French high command had kept them almost as secret from the British as from the Germans. As for Haig, he was pleased to be acting independently.

But the success of Messines was not to be repeated. To begin with, British high command was inflexible in its thinking and declined to "reinforce success," which would have required making Messines Ridge the point of the main attack. Because Messines had begun as a diversion, the rigid decision was that it must remain a diversion. Another problem was that organizing the main assault took more time than anticipated, creating a lag between the initial inroads made at the Battle of Messines and the principal assault. When Haig finally commenced the operation, he did so with the biggest artillery preparation of the entire war, beginning on July 18 by lobbing 65,000 artillery shells from 3,091 guns. This time, however, the shells fell directly on the territory staked out for the British advance. They cratered the poorly drained ground, and the heaviest rains the region had seen in 30 years transformed no man's land into a virtually impassible morass.

Nevertheless, the infantry assault, led by the young and aggressive General Hubert Gough, slogged into it—only to encounter extremely well-prepared German defenses. The British forces had been buoyed by wildly optimistic intelligence reports to the effect that German resources were so depleted that Germany could not maintain its armies in the field for more than four to six months and that reinforcements from the Eastern Front could not be rapidly transferred to the Western Front. Both assumptions were false. Delays caused by the bad weather and the prolonged artillery preparation had permitted the Germans, who were quite adequately supplied, to reinforce Flanders with many troops released from the east.

British troops became bogged down in the mud and were slaughtered by machine-gun fire, including *strafing* fire from German air attacks. They were also subjected to attacks with the newly developed mustard gas, which caused intense chemical burns on contact with skin, eyes, or lining of the human lung.

Against all odds, the British infantry took Passchendaele Ridge as well as Passchendaele village by November 6. Once there, however, the troops found themselves in a dangerous salient, completely bogged down in the mud. Even so, the net gain in territory was slight in terms of the ultimate goal of reclaiming Belgium: a mere five miles. The cost had been 300,000 British dead and wounded, plus 8,528 French casualties. German losses were also high, however, at 260,000.

Words of War

Strafing is attacking ground troops by machine guns fired from low-flying aircraft.

Voices of Battle

One of the most famous poems to emerge from World War I, "In Flanders Fields," was written by Britisher John McCrae during the Second Battle of Ypres, in 1915. It applies to the Third Battle as well:

"In Flanders fields the poppies blow
Between the crosses, row on row,
That mark our place; and in the sky
The larks, still bravely singing, fly
Scarce heard amid the guns below.

"We are the Dead. Short days ago
We lived, felt dawn, saw sunset glow,
Loved, and were loved, and now we lie
In Flanders fields.

"Take up our quarrel with the foe:
To you from failing hands we throw
The torch; be yours to hold it high.
If ye break faith with us who die
We shall not sleep, though poppies grow
In Flanders fields."

➤ *Cambrai*

Undeterred by the terrible costs of Passchendaele, Haig ordered General J.H.G. Byng's Third Army to attack at Cambrai, France, some 50 miles south of the site of the Belgian battle. This time, terrain conditions were highly favorable for the attackers, and Byng did not precede the assault with an artillery preparation, so both the element of surprise and the excellent ground were preserved. For the first time in the war, large numbers of tanks—200 of them—were employed in the advance.

Initially, the attack went very well for the British. A five-mile breach was punched into the Hindenburg Line, which Byng was ready to exploit with cavalry as well as infantry. Unfortunately, the tanks, which had made a spectacular first impression on the German defenders, began to break down in large numbers after they had penetrated the enemy. This gave time for German reinforcements to plug the gap, which the British cavalry and infantry follow-up now proved too weak to breach. On December 3, Haig ordered a partial withdrawal.

In some respects, the Battle of Cambrai was all too typical of Western Front action. Both sides suffered approximately equal casualties, about 45,000 each (including 11,000 Germans and 9,000 British taken as POWs), and no territory was permanently gained by either side. In another respect, however, the battle was something of a breakthrough, at least from the perspective of tactics. Cambrai demonstrated that an advance can succeed without artillery preparation—indeed, that it was often folly to sacrifice surprise and favorable terrain to bombardment. It also suggested that the tank, if used in sufficient numbers, could be a valuable tool against entrenched positions. (Of course, this assumed the eventual mechanical improvement of the vehicles.)

A Separate Peace

Like Cambrai, the entire western campaign of 1917 had hard lessons to teach, particularly to the Allies. Whether the generals and politicians chose to heed them was another matter.

The most important lesson concerned the necessity of unified command, of very close cooperation among the Allies. Combined, the Allied armies substantially outnumbered the forces of the Central Powers and, for the most part, were better equipped and supplied. Yet, between them, Nivelle and Haig had spent the lives of half a million men without gaining anything tangible. The problem? In large part, the English, French, and Italians failed to coordinate action effectively. Offensives were either French, or British, or Italian. Although British soldiers participated in supporting such operations as the Nivelle Offensive, they did so in ancillary, subordinate, and often grudging ways. Only after Nivelle was out of the picture did Haig unleash his own separate—and ultimately unproductive—offensive in Flanders.

Of all the lapses in unity of command, however, the greatest came with the advent of revolution in Russia. By the end of 1917, it would altogether remove the great Eastern Ally from the war.

The Revolution of 1917

The Russian Revolution of 1917 was actually two revolutions. The first took place in March (according to the outmoded Julian calendar then used in Russia, it was still February), and the second occurred in November (or, by the old Russian calendar, October).

Ever since August 1914, the war had been an almost endless string of disasters for Russia. As Czar Nicholas II poured more resources into the hopeless struggle, the Russian economy, never good, fell apart entirely. In Petrograd (St. Petersburg, recently renamed because it sounded too German), food riots broke out in March 1917, the Petrograd garrison joined the revolt, and Czar Nicholas II abdicated the throne.

The Russian parliament, or Duma, appointed a "Provisional Government," which immediately found itself challenged by the rival Petrograd *Soviet* of Workers' and Soldiers' Deputies, 2,500 delegates who had been chosen from factories and military units in and about Petrograd. When the "official" Provisional Government voted to continue Russia's participation in the war, the Soviet issued Order No. 1, directing the military to obey the Soviet Government, not the Provisional Government.

Words of War

A **soviet** was any popularly elected legislative assembly. Soviets existed on local, regional, and national levels.

Between March and October 1917, the Provisional Government and the Soviet Government vied for control of the nation, which, during this period, continued to starve. The revolutionary leader Aleksandr F. Kerensky briefly seized the reins of government and attempted to establish a coalition of the Provisional Government and the soviets, but the issue of whether to go on prosecuting the war continued to divide the suffering nation deeply.

During the spring and summer of 1917, the radical forces opposed to the Provisional Government coalesced around a single intellectually forceful leader, Vladimir Ilyich Lenin, who, since 1903, had been the leader of a radical wing within the Russian Social Democratic Labor Party. He called his faction the Bolsheviks—the "majority"—while those who didn't share his radical beliefs he dubbed the Mensheviks, the minority. Never mind that the group Lenin labeled the "minority" far outnumbered the group he called the "majority."

A Second Brusilov Offensive

While the Bolsheviks and Mensheviks wrestled over control of the Provisional Government, General Aleksei Brusilov, whose offensive against Austrian forces had been one of the few Russian triumphs of the war (see Chapter 17, "Italy, the Eastern Front, and Elsewhere, 1916"), led the Eleventh and Seventh Armies—two of the nation's few remaining viable military units—against combined German, Austro-Hungarian, and Turkish forces under German general Felix von Bothmer at Lvov (Lemberg), near the Polish frontier. The skillful Brusilov pierced the enemy lines for some 30 miles along a 100-mile front, and his subordinate commanders on either of his flanks made substantial inroads against the Austrian Second and Third Armies.

Combatants

Nicholas II (1868–1917) was the most hapless of monarchs in an era of hapless monarchs. He became czar after the death of his father in 1894, but he was intellectually and temperamentally unprepared for the role. Personally charming, he was nevertheless shy and even timid. He had no interest in politics, and although he was fond of uniforms, his was far from a military mind.

Devoted to his wife, Alexandra, he deferred to her in matters both personal and political. Their son and heir apparent, Alexis, was a hemophiliac, whose suffering seemed to find relief in the faith-healing ministrations of a rustic Orthodox monk, Grigory Yefimovich Novykh (1872?–1916), better known as Rasputin—a name that means "the debauched one." An illiterate peasant, Rasputin acquired a reputation as a mystic and a healer. He was introduced to the royal court in 1905 and, by 1908, began to exercise an inordinate influence, first over Alexandra and then the czar. In the meantime, his sexual debauchery created a scandal throughout St. Petersburg. Worse, he insinuated himself in the administration of the state. When Nicholas left court to take personal command of the army in September 1915, Rasputin, through Alexandra, ran the country for all intents and purposes.

As a military commander, Nicholas proved disastrous. As a head of state, Rasputin, popularly called "the Mad Monk," was even worse. At last, a cabal of nobles, led by Prince Yusupov, succeeded in murdering Rasputin on the night of December 29–30, 1916. As for the czar, he responded to the riots that broke out in Petrograd in March 1917 by abdicating the throne in favor of his brother, Michael—who, quite prudently, declined the honor. Nicholas and the entire royal family were imprisoned by revolutionary forces and finally were executed, in secret, by firing squad, on the night of July 16–17, 1918. For years, rumors persisted that his daughter Anastasia had miraculously survived the night of carnage, and a woman purporting to be her later appeared in Paris; however, DNA testing performed on the exhumed remains of the family members in 1994 put these rumors to rest.

But with his nation dissolving beneath him, even Brusilov was unable to sustain the offensive. Morale and supplies were both reduced to a trickle. On July 19, General Max Hoffmann led a German counterattack, which made short work of the hungry and thoroughly demoralized Russian armies south of the Pripet Marshes in Galicia. All that prevented Hoffmann from pushing deeper into Russian territory was his own lack of supplies and an insufficiency of reserve troops.

Offensive at Riga

With the southern end of the Russian front destroyed, German General Oscar von Hutier led his Eighth Army against the northern end of that front at the important Baltic Sea port of Riga (in modern Latvia) and its associated fortress on September 1.

Hutier's innovative tactics were rapid and intense. He, at least, had heeded the lessons of the Western Front. Instead of the customary long artillery preparation, he began with a brief, albeit violent, bombardment followed without delay by an infantry advance. The artillery fire was directed almost exclusively at the enemy's rear rather than his front lines; this was to prevent those front lines from being reinforced from the rear. The advance and the positions from which the advance came were heavily masked by smoke and the concentrated use of poison gas. This mask preserved the element of surprise until the last possible moment.

Hutier put special emphasis on the use of light, rapid infantry units—shock troops called *Sturmbattaillon* (Storm Battalions)—to penetrate the enemy lines at various weak points and to ensure that the ability to maneuver would be retained. The shock troops would rapidly build up local superiority at various places along the front, while, in the meantime, artillery support was nimbly shifted from fire directed against enemy artillery positions to fire directed in support of the infantry advance. The Germans called this flexible use of artillery the *Feuerwalz,* or fire waltz.

Stunned by the rapid German success at Riga, the awestruck Allies dubbed the enemy general's technique "Hutier tactics." The Russian Twelfth Army crumbled and ran from the field in utter panic.

The Bolshevik Revolution

The panic at Riga reflected the chaos that prevailed in the rest of Russia. In October 1917, Lenin and his chief lieutenant, Leon Trotsky, led the Bolsheviks in the second revolution of the year, a virtually bloodless coup that toppled the Provisional Government and transformed Russia into a communist state.

The Treaties of Brest-Litovsk

Among the very first acts of the new government was the conclusion of a "separate peace" with Berlin, which resulted in an immediate armistice on December 15, 1917, formalized the following year by the two Treaties of Brest-Litovsk. The Ukrainian

Voices of Battle

"The war of 1914–1918 was imperialist (that is, an annexationist, predatory, war of plunder) on the part of both sides; it was a war for the division of the world, for the partition and repartition of colonies and spheres of influence of finance capital, etc."

—Vladimir I. Lenin, speech, 1920

Republic signed first, on February 9, 1918, but Soviet Russia delayed until ruthless German advances against undefended territory finally moved Lenin's hand. He signed on March 3.

The treaties not only took Russia out of the war, thereby freeing tens of thousands of German troops for service on the Western Front, but they also delivered either to German occupation or into the hands of newly created German puppet governments Poland, Lithuania, the Baltic Provinces, Finland, and the Ukraine.

For Russia, Brest-Litovsk was total defeat. As Baron von Kühlmann, one of the German treaty negotiators, wryly remarked, "The only choice they have is as to what sort of sauce they shall be eaten with." For Germany, it was the first major breakthrough of the war. And for the Western Allies, Brest-Litovsk meant facing a reinvigorated enemy who no longer had to watch his back.

The Least You Need to Know

➤ By 1917, despair over the course of the war caused major shake-ups in the Allied leadership.

➤ The disastrous failure of Robert Nivelle's offensive on the Western Front drove a large portion of the French army to mutiny.

➤ After the failure of the Nivelle Offensive, Henri Philippe Pétain replaced Nivelle as French general in chief and adopted a defensive posture as Britain's General Douglas Haig led a costly, fruitless offensive in Flanders.

➤ After the Bolshevik Revolution, the new communist government made a "separate peace" with the Central Powers, yielding much territory to Germany and taking Russia out of the war.

Sauerkraut
Liberty
Cabbage

Chapter 22

Over Here and Over There

> ## In This Chapter
>
> ➤ The struggle to mobilize for war
>
> ➤ Financing the war: the Liberty Loans
>
> ➤ General Pershing takes command of the AEF
>
> ➤ The U.S. Navy goes to war
>
> ➤ The first Americans arrive

Since 1914, United States factories had been producing at higher than normal rates in response to demand from the belligerents overseas, but President Wilson, wanting to maintain the appearance of complete neutrality, did not order much in the way of contingency planning to put industry on a full war footing. More shocking was the almost complete absence of planning on the part of the U.S. Army. The army had sent observers to Europe, and they had faithfully filed reports from the front lines, narrating in vivid detail the scope and scale of the daily devastation. Just as faithfully, however, instead of passing the reports on to higher command, military bureaucrats filed them in the archives of the War College—at the time, the body responsible for U.S. military intelligence—as they were received.

Nevertheless, once war was declared, industry and the nation generally scrambled quickly to achieve the levels of production necessary for war.

American Resources

In the spring of 1917, the beleaguered Allies looked to America for troops, but, even more immediately, they hungered for munitions and other war materiel. Military missions from England, France, and Italy came calling, orders in hand. They regarded America's legendary industrial capacity much as they had regarded, at the start of the war, Russia's reputation as a great strategic "steamroller." Here was the answer to the crisis of the Western Front! Just turn on the tap, and arms, ammo, and other supplies would come flooding out.

But the representatives of the Allies found themselves facing yet another disappointment. American industry was tooling up, to be sure, but American government had yet to create most of the necessary sweeping and complex legislation to shift industry into high gear. In fact, Americans would not be exporting planes, machine guns, tanks, and artillery to Europe, but would be going to war with much of their equipment bought and borrowed from France and England.

From the Front

The American soldier's distinctive wash basin–style helmet was not even American, but was imported from England. The British persuaded the Americans that troops could not survive in the trenches wearing the felt campaign hats (which look to us today like something Smokey the Bear wears) that had served them in such theaters as the American West and Spanish Cuba.

An Arsenal of Democracy

Among all of America's industries, the factories producing explosives came into the war with a running start. Since 1914, this industry had been growing to supply the belligerents (mostly the Allies) with gunpowder and high explosives. Yet now a crisis loomed. Every bit of powder was being exported, and, with United States entry into the war, the European Allies ordered even more powder. Where, then, were *American* troops to turn for gunpowder and high explosives?

Belatedly, the U.S. War Department drew up agreements with Du Pont and other manufacturers to build new plants. These factories were rapidly made operational; nevertheless, by Armistice Day 1918, U.S. explosives manufacturing capacity had reached barely one-third of what had been projected.

From the Front

In comparison with the armies of Europe, the United States Army was almost insignificant. In April 1917, on the eve of U.S. entry into the war, the Army consisted of 127,588 officers and men, with an additional 80,446 in the National Guard. (By the end of the war, the U.S. Army numbered 3,685,458.) U.S. naval strength around 1914 was more impressive, although well below that of any of the major European powers: 10 dreadnoughts, no battle cruisers, 26 pre–dreadnoughts, 21 heavy cruisers, 11 light cruisers, 50 destroyers, and 39 submarines.

Delays were also experienced in putting into production the one weapon that U.S. observers had concluded was absolutely indispensable to trench warfare: the machine gun. As early as 1916, the War Department had started looking for a standard gun to adopt for the U.S. Army. When the British Lewis gun proved inadequate—too light, and with limited magazine capacity—the army sponsored competitive trials of various guns after a year's delay, ultimately settling on the simple, high-performance, domestically manufactured weapon offered by John M. Browning. This decision was made on May 1, 1917, but it wasn't until October that production could get under way, and it was May 1918 before significant shipments of the new weapon began to arrive at the front.

Faced with production problems such as those that plagued the explosives and arms industries, the Wilson administration created the War Industries Board in the summer of 1917. This agency was charged with determining what munitions and supply items needed to be produced, what quantities were required, what firms should be producing them, and even what prices were fair. Members of the board, patriotic captains of American industry who volunteered to serve for the nominal compensation of a dollar a year (and who were therefore called *dollar-a-year men*) not only had to determine and allocate output, but they also had to procure and regulate the input of raw materials. Finally, the board worked with other agencies to ration certain civilian goods.

Later, in 1918, a National War Labor Board was also formed to manage the nation's strained labor force, ensuring that, with four million men having traded their tools for rifles, a supply of labor remained available at a cost that industry could bear. That labor also had to be allocated among the various industries, and labor relations had to be handled efficiently, fairly, and firmly to avoid potentially disastrous strikes.

Citizens to Soldiers

In April 1916, Newton D. Baker became U.S. secretary of war. The former mayor of Cleveland, Ohio, he had no military experience whatsoever. That same year, the National Defense Act was passed, authorizing the expansion of the United States Army to 175,000—286,000 in the event of war.

Words of War

Dollar-a-year men were prominent citizens, typically industrialists and financiers, who volunteered their services to the war effort for the nominal salary of $1 a year.

From the Front

During April 1917, the month the United States entered the war, the French army lost approximately as many men in the Nivelle Offensive (see Chapter 21, "Allies Imperiled") as the United States Army had on active duty.

In 1916, the regular army numbered 133,000, a force so small that General Peyton C. Marsh remarked that it was "scarcely enough to form a police force for emergencies within the territorial United States," let alone fight a war in Europe, where nations fielded armies numbering in the millions.

By Armistice Day, 1918, the United States had mobilized an army of more than 4.5 million. In contrast to the government agencies responsible for war production, those charged with assembling the army worked with extraordinary speed and efficiency. Although the concept of *conscription,* the draft, created controversy in many quarters as un-American, and although some two million men— and women—would patriotically volunteer for service during the course of the war, a military draft seemed the only way to raise a sufficiently large army quickly.

Ordered to draw up legislation for a Selective Service Act, General Enoch H. Crowder, although personally opposed to conscription on principle, presented Secretary of War Baker a completed document within 24 hours of the order. On May 18, the Selective Service Act of 1917 was signed into law. Over the next two years, 23.9 million men were registered for the draft, and 2.8 million, most between the ages of 21 and 30, were actually drafted.

Words of War

Conscription is the concept and process of inducting personnel into the armed forces on a compulsory basis.

Patriots and Slackers

It was one thing to draft men—register them, weigh any requests for deferment or exclusion, pass the men through rudimentary medical examination, and give them a date to report for duty—and quite another thing to transform these civilians into soldiers.

To begin with, there was the monumental task of housing the influx of new recruits. Immediately, 16 *cantonments* were built for National Guard units. Because these men were already part-time soldiers, having received training as National Guardsmen, they were expected to be among the first to ship out for France. Therefore, most of them would be housed in temporary tent cantonments erected in the south, where winters were mild. Most raw, civilian recruits would require longer periods of training and so were housed mainly in the north, in 16 newly constructed wooden barracks.

To build the barracks as fast as possible, the usual practice of competitive bidding among contractors was bypassed, and Colonel I.W. Littell, commander of the Division of the Quartermaster Corps, responsible for housing the soldiers, used new legislation that allowed him to grant contracts on a "cost-plus" basis. The

Words of War

A **cantonment** is a group of temporary billets for troops.

contractor was paid 6 to 10 percent more than the actual cost of completing the project on time. Littell managed to build his cantonments on time.

Not that they were comfortable or attractive. Whether built of canvas or wood, barracks were spartan—for most men, a stark contrast to the comforts of the homes that they had left.

Clothing the new *doughboys* was also a monumental task, and stocks of uniforms always ran somewhat behind demand. Yet, by December 1917, more than 1.6 million men had been issued the drab, utilitarian uniform of the U.S. Army. When the peaked felt campaign hat was exchanged for the British-style "wash basin" helmet, the uniform would become one of the most practical for the rigors of war in the trenches.

Once housed and clothed, the recruits had to be trained. In 1917, "basic training" was truly basic, consisting of as much as six months of drill—learning how to march in obedience to orders—and acquiring the rudiments of marksmanship and hand-to-hand fighting. Based on demonstrated aptitude—or the luck of the draw—some soldiers were singled out for specialist training in the weaponry of modern warfare, especially machine guns, chemical warfare, artillery, vehicle maintenance and repair, and radio communication.

An army of 4 million would require more than 200,000 officers. In 1917, however, there were but 6,000 officers in the regular army and another 14,000 in the National Guard. The rest were hurriedly commissioned from the enlisted ranks, from civilian occupations, and from the Officer Training Corps (OTC). Half the officer corps of the wartime army were so-called 90-day wonders, products of three months' training in the OTC. A third of the officers were commissioned directly from civilian life and entered the army as officers, and the remainder of new officers were recruited from the ranks. Despite the best efforts stateside, most soldiers and officers required extensive additional training after they arrived in France.

Words of War

Doughboy was the familiar name for American infantrymen in World War I. The origin of the term is obscure, but most authorities believe that it was coined before World War I, in the 1860s, when the large buttons on army uniforms were thought to resemble "doughboys," bread dough that has been rolled thin and deep-fried.

From the Front

The United States Army of World War I refused to accept women for military service, except as nurses. The U.S. Army Nurse Corps had been created in 1901; by December 1917, 424 regular nurses and 3,600 reserve nurses were serving. At the time of the Armistice, this number had grown to 3,500 regular nurses and 18,000 reservists. The U.S. Navy accepted some 11,000 women to serve as clerks and typists as well as nurses.

In contrast to what would be the case in World War II, a substantial vocal minority continued to oppose American entry into the war and also protested the draft. Officials feared a repetition of the bloody Draft Riots that had erupted in New York and spread to other Northern cities during the Civil War. Nothing of the kind occurred, but the Supreme Court upheld the constitutionality of the draft, and militant draft protests were limited to a few isolated rural areas as well as to sporadic clashes between police officers and individual resisters.

Absence of organized protest didn't mean that draft evasion was unusual. It was estimated that as many as 3 million young men successfully avoided draft registration; most were never found out. Of those registered and called up, 338,000 (12 percent of draftees) failed to report for induction or deserted shortly after arrival at training facilities.

Those who avoided, evaded, or otherwise defied the draft were popularly labeled *slackers* and were rounded up in "slacker raids" of highly dubious constitutionality. Military and civilian law enforcement officials would regularly and randomly stop men in major cities and demand to see their draft registration cards. About half of the 338,000 delinquents were apprehended in this fashion.

A number of those opposed to the war claimed *conscientious objector* (CO) status, requesting exemption from service on religious or even political grounds. Of 64,693 draft registrants who called themselves conscientious objectors, 20,000 were drafted, and 80 percent of these were persuaded to serve as regular combat soldiers. Of the 4,000 or so who persisted in refusing to bear arms, 1,300 accepted unarmed service in the medical corps or in other noncombatant roles. Of the rest, most were furloughed as agricultural laborers. Finally, 540 others were court martialed and imprisoned.

Words of War

Slackers were those who failed to volunteer for military service, who evaded the draft, who did not purchase Liberty Bonds or Liberty Stamps, or who otherwise shirked what was perceived as their wartime patriotic duty.

Words of War

A **conscientious objector** is an individual who declines compulsory military service on the grounds of religious, moral, or political belief.

The army into which America's young men were drafted was entirely segregated. (At the time, only the U.S. Navy integrated white and black servicemen—and only to a very limited degree, with African-Americans relegated to service as cooks and "mess boys.") Nevertheless, the nation's all-white draft boards inducted disproportionate numbers of African-Americans, and two all-black infantry divisions were raised during the war; one of these, the 95th, served under French command. The boards were much more liberal in granting deferments to whites than to blacks.

Wilson Hires an Ad Man

Woodrow Wilson did not rely on the law alone to mobilize his nation for war. Recognizing that Americans cherished a tradition of avoiding what George Washington himself had warned his countrymen against—"foreign entanglements"—the Wilson administration embarked on a furious campaign to sell the war to the American people.

The Propaganda War

One week after securing the declaration of war, Wilson created the Committee for Public Information and named the prominent journalist George Creel to serve as its director: the war effort's chief ad man.

To fight the propaganda war, Creel commanded his own army of more than 150,000 men and women, who wrote, published, and distributed patriotic pamphlets and also designed, printed, and distributed a myriad of dramatic and stirring posters. Materials included artist James Montgomery Flagg's famed image of Uncle Sam pointing his finger at the viewer and declaring, "I Want You"—an adaptation of an earlier British recruiting poster featuring a stern Lord Kitchener making just such a gesture and uttering the words "your country needs you." The Committee for Public Information—popularly called the Creel Committee—also produced propaganda films exhibited as short subjects accompanying the features shown in the nation's movie theaters. The committee managed a corps of public speakers, dubbed "Four-Minute Men" because each delivered a slickly prepared four-minute speech "on a subject of national importance." The name, of course, was a take-off on the Minutemen of the American Revolution.

The Liberty Loans

Fighting World War I would cost the United States $30 billion. Part of the cost was financed with the graduated federal income tax, enacted by the Sixteenth Amendment in 1913, but fully two-thirds of

Voices of Battle

There was no part of the great war machinery we did not touch, no medium of appeal we did not employ. The printed word, the spoken word, the motion picture, the telegraph, the cable, the wireless, the poster, the sign board—all these were used in our campaign to make our own people and all the other people understand the causes that compelled America to take arms.

—George Creel, *How We Advertised America*, Creel's postwar memoir of the propaganda effort he directed

Voices of Battle

"Over there, over there,
Send the word, send the word, over there,
That the Yanks are coming, the Yanks are coming ...
And we won't be back till it's over, over there."

—George M. Cohan, "Over There," song of 1917

the price tag was met through citizens' voluntary purchase of war bonds in a program of so-called Liberty Loans. Each Liberty Loan—there would be four, in addition to a Victory Loan and a more modest Liberty Stamp program—was a major fund drive, and each set lofty goals, which were always substantially exceeded.

America's favorite celebrities, including such Hollywood movie stars as Douglas Fairbanks and Mary Pickford, donated their time and talents to Liberty Bond rallies aimed at selling the bonds as quickly as possible. The purchase of bonds was considered a patriotic duty, and those who failed to buy their fair share risked being branded as slackers.

From Sauerkraut to Liberty Cabbage

Arm-twisting to buy Liberty Bonds was not the only social pressure on Americans to support the war. Federal and local law enforcement officials often made life miserable for pacifists, sundry intellectuals, socialist workingmen, and avowed communists—anyone who expressed dissatisfaction with the war.

In many places, especially the rural Midwest, German-Americans were subject to various forms of persecution, including acts of vandalism against their houses and businesses and, most insidiously, efforts to discourage or even legally ban the public use of the German language. Iowa's wartime governor, for example, championed legislation to ban the use of the German language *everywhere,* in circumstances ranging from German-language newspapers to telephone conversations. Over the years, America's large German immigrant population had bequeathed to the landscape any number of German place names, and now towns that had been founded as Berlin or New Hamburg were rechristened Liberty or New Liberty. Even the German condiment that graced the "all-American" hot dog, sauerkraut, was given the new appellation of "liberty cabbage."

The Yanks Are Coming!

By late 1917, the United States Navy and the British Royal Navy were enjoying success in dealing with much of the German U-boat threat along the great 3,000-mile Atlantic convoy routs. The problem now, however, was that too few ships were available to transport the American troops when they were ready to go to France. A special Shipping Board was created to oversee the acquisition and building of ships, and the United States shipbuilding industry quickly developed methods of prefabrication that slashed shipbuilding times so that, by the end of the war, America was the world's leading builder of ships. In the meantime, 444 civilian vessels were commandeered and 91 German ships were seized in American ports, including the enormous passenger liner *Vaterland* (*Fatherland*), which was rechristened *Leviathan* and operated as one of the fastest and most efficient troop carriers for the American Expeditionary Force.

Combatants

John Joseph Pershing (1860–1948) was raised on a Missouri farm and taught school from 1878 to 1882, when he obtained an appointment to West Point. After graduating in 1886, he was commissioned a second lieutenant in the Sixth Cavalry and served in the West during the late phase of the Indian Wars. From 1891 to 1895, he taught at the University of Nebraska as commandant of cadets. He was promoted to first lieutenant in 1892 but took time out to earn a law degree (awarded June 1898). He then saw service with the Tenth Cavalry—a black regiment of "Buffalo Soldiers" commanded by white officers. It was from this assignment that Pershing earned his nickname, "Black Jack." He served with the Tenth Cavalry from October 1895 to October 1896, was appointed aide to General Nelson A. Miles, and then returned to West Point as an instructor in tactics.

During the Spanish-American War, Pershing fought at El Caney–San Juan Hill (July 1–3, 1898), but he was felled by malaria. He served stateside in several administrative roles. Then, from 1899 to 1903, he engaged in the pacification of the Moros, who resisted American authority in the Philippines.

In 1905–1906, Pershing was stationed in Japan as a military attaché and observer in the Russo-Japanese War. The assignment turned out to be Pershing's great opportunity, for it brought him into contact with President Theodore Roosevelt, who, greatly impressed with Captain Pershing, prompted his promotion—in one step—to brigadier general on September 20, 1906. From December 1906 to June 1908, Pershing commanded a brigade at Fort McKinley, near Manila, and then accepted an appointment as military commander of Moro Province in the Philippines in November 1909. He served in this post until early 1914, continually conducting small-scale operations against recalcitrant Moro rebels.

In April 1914, Pershing was assigned command of the Eighth Brigade in San Francisco but was almost immediately dispatched to the Mexican-American border during the civil war in Mexico. On August 27, 1915, while Pershing was on the border, a fire swept through his family's quarters in the Presidio at San Francisco. Pershing was devastated to learn that his wife and three of their daughters had perished in the fire. Francisco "Pancho" Villa, whom Pershing would soon be assigned to capture, was among the many military and political leaders who wrote or wired their condolences to the general.

On May 12, 1917, Pershing was named commander of the American Expeditionary Force (AEF). The action of this force would, of course, turn the tide of the war, and Pershing returned to the United States after the armistice in triumph. He was promoted to general of the armies—the U.S. Army's first (and, to date, only) *six*-star general. He retired in 1924 as the army chief of staff.

Black Jack Pershing and the AEF

Shortly after the declaration of war on Germany, President Wilson and Secretary of War Newton Baker reviewed a roster of U.S. Army generals in search of one to lead a symbolic division to Europe, which would be known as the American Expeditionary Force (AEF). They settled on John Joseph Pershing, the commander who had led the Punitive Expedition against Pancho Villa in 1916 (see Chapter 20, "He Kept Us Out of War") and who had served with distinction in the Spanish-American War of 1898, as well as in the American West. There, as a young lieutenant, he had commanded the African-American "Buffalo Soldiers" of the Tenth Cavalry and earned the nickname "Black Jack," of which he was quite proud.

Pershing was an officer of great ability and courage, and he was also a fine administrator and logistician. Almost immediately, his assignment burgeoned from commander of a symbolic division to commander of an AEF that was now defined as a vast army—all of the land forces of the United States in Europe.

President Wilson decided to take a hands-off approach to the day-to-day conduct of the war. He placed his full confidence in Newton D. Baker, who, in turn, gave Pershing virtual carte blanche to deploy and command the AEF as he saw fit. Baker instructed the general to proceed to France at once to establish a logistical base to support U.S. participation in the war. He further instructed him to cooperate with the Allies, but Baker was clear that Pershing alone was personally authorized to decide when and how the AEF would fight. Above all, American forces were to remain under Pershing's separate and independent command. In essence, General Pershing was sent into the field with more authority and more responsibility than any other Allied commander.

Sims and the Navy

With 300 ships manned by 67,000 officers and men, the U.S. Navy in 1917 was much better prepared for war than the army. The chief of naval operations, Rear Admiral William S. Benson, was the navy's senior admiral, but Secretary of the Navy Josephus Daniels nominated Rear Admiral William S. Sims, head of the U.S. Naval War College, to serve in London as naval attaché and liaison with the British and French. He was then appointed to command U.S. naval forces operating in European waters.

In contrast to British and French army commanders, who jealously guarded their authority and thereby compromised the effective collaboration of their forces, Sims enjoyed a very close working relationship with the French and, even more, with the British. This greatly contributed to the efficiency of Allied antisubmarine warfare, but it also created continual friction between Sims and his boss, Benson, who accused Sims of putting the interests of Britain ahead of those of the United States.

In fact, under Sims, the United States Navy was deployed quickly and performed admirably. His single greatest contribution to the war at sea was his advocacy of convoys, the grouping together of transport and cargo vessels so that they could be more effectively escorted by warships and thereby defended against U-boat attack. At the time, the convoy was an entirely novel and highly controversial concept. Sims succeeded in persuading both a reluctant Royal Navy and an even more skeptical Josephus Daniels and Admiral Benson to test the convoy idea. The results were nothing short of spectacular. In April 1917, 870,000 tons of Allied shipping were lost to U-boat attack. In May, when two experimental convoys were attempted, losses dropped to 600,000 tons. As convoys became standard, the losses leveled off at 350,000 tons per month.

Like the army's Pershing, the navy's Sims was a strong and strong-minded individual whose grasp of tactics and purpose outweighed any desire for personal advancement or the gratification of ambition and ego. Both Pershing and Sims were more than willing to defy the political status quo, to endure harsh criticism, and to accept the heaviest possible burden of responsibility to accomplish what each saw as his mission. The United States and its new allies were fortunate indeed to have the services of these two principal commanders.

The British and the French got along with Admiral Sims from the very beginning. However, it would take more time for them—especially the French—to appreciate the leadership savvy of General Pershing.

"Lafayette, We Are Here"

Pershing and his small staff, hand-picked by the general, arrived in France on June 14, 1917. It has often been reported that Pershing, stepping off the boat, proclaimed, "Lafayette, we are here!" This wonderful phrase suggested that the United States was now repaying the debt incurred when the Marquis de Lafayette not only contributed personally and gallantly to the success of the American Revolution, but also worked to bring about a full Franco-American alliance.

A wonderful phrase, indeed—but wholly out of character for the stern, cool, and remote Pershing. It was actually spoken by Major Charles E. Stanton, paymaster of the AEF, in an address at Lafayette's tomb in Picpus Cemetery, Paris. As for Pershing, he was eager to get to work, and he brushed aside most of the tumultuous welcoming ceremonies—except for one brilliant gesture. At Napoleon's tomb, Marshal Joseph Joffre (no longer commander-in-chief of French forces, but still the nation's senior solider) symbolically presented the Napoleon's saber to Pershing. Acting on instinct, the American general kissed it. Widely reported, this act electrified and inspired all France.

"Lafayette, we are here!" But just who and what had arrived?

From the Front

Pershing was uncompromisingly honest in his repeated denials that he had proclaimed "Lafayette, we are here!" In his 1931 memoir, *My Experiences in the World War*, he set down once and for all that he had never "said anything so splendid."

In June, it was Pershing and a skeleton staff. When would the bulk of the troops arrive? How many would be sent? How would they get to France? What would be done with them when they got there? Pershing himself later wrote that "the War Department was face to face with the question of sending an army to Europe and found that the General Staff had never considered such a thing. No one in authority had any definite idea how many men might be needed, how they should be organized and equipped, or where the tonnage to transport and supply for them was to come from." As the general observed, when he went to look for contingency plans, "the pigeon hole was empty."

With characteristic energy and penetration, Pershing quickly assessed the Allied situation firsthand and drew up the first real plan for American forces in Europe. Dated July 10, 1917, it was titled "General Organization Project" and called for a balanced force of combat and support troops in France totaling a staggering 3 million men within two years.

Pershing's First Fight

As if roused from a stupor, the War Department responded to Pershing's report that no more than 420,000 men could be supplied within a year. Pershing, always the realist, was forced to estimate that a sizable, effective U.S. force could not be sent into battle before February 1918. With this, the Allied rapture that greeted the general's arrival in France quickly faded.

The desperate impatience of France and England is not difficult to understand. By the end of 1917, the armies of the two nations had suffered combined casualties of 5.8 million killed and wounded, whereas the Germans had incurred 3,349,000 casualties.

Pershing appreciated this. He also understood that, in addition to having suffered so many losses, the Allies had ample reason for feeling desperate in the wake of the failed Nivelle Offensive. This defeat made it quite likely that the Germans would, sooner or later, break the stalemate on the Western Front. But Pershing also saw the folly of desperation. Yes, the Allies were running short of men. Yes, Americans could fill their thinning ranks. But then Americans would become what so many British and French soldiers were already: cannon fodder.

Putting Americans under British and French command, integrating U.S. troops into the Allied forces as soon as they arrived, would probably stave off Allied defeat in 1918. But it was no way to *win* the war.

Pershing's first fight, then, was not against the Germans, but with his French and British allies, both of whom wanted American troops immediately as replacements—period. Pershing's plan was to build an army of 1 million men *before* sending a single American soldier off to fight. This meant getting the force into

Words of War

Unity of command is the concept of the Allied armies operating under the direction of a single final authority rather than wholly independently of one another.

France, training it for combat (for Pershing perceived that the basic training troops had received stateside was hardly sufficient preparation for the realities of trench warfare waged by hardened veterans), and commanding it as a distinct American unit rather than diluting it by integration with the Allied armies.

Whatever else Pershing would achieve in Europe, his victory in this first—and very bitter—battle was key. Courageously backed by President Wilson and Secretary Baker, Pershing successfully resisted the Franco-British push to bring the doughboys into the war piecemeal. Although the American general would wisely yield his uncompromising position during moments of extreme crisis, sending American divisions to help French and British forces early in 1918, he kept the American army from being frittered away in the all too familiar tragic pattern of this war. Yet, while protecting the autonomy and integrity of the American forces, Pershing simultaneously worked with his British and French counterparts to bring about what they alone had failed to achieve: *unity of command.*

Pershing saw what Generals Nivelle, Pétain, French, and Haig had consistently failed to see—that if each commander cared only for the operations of his own nation's army, the great leverage offered by effective coordination among the Allies was lost. Paradoxically, the American general who outraged his Allied colleagues by insisting that the U.S. Army remain a "separate and distinct" force provided some of the insight and energy that, in November 1917, prompted the Allies to create the Supreme War Council. Its aim was forging the fighting men of three nations into a single great, coordinated instrument of combat. The tide would at last begin to turn.

The Least You Need to Know

➤ Despite awareness since 1914 of the possibility for eventual American involvement in the war, the United States government and military took remarkably few steps to prepare and, therefore, had to scramble furiously to mobilize after war was declared on Germany.

➤ The Wilson administration created effective programs of pro-war propaganda and instituted Liberty Loans to provide much of the financing required by the war.

➤ The American Expeditionary Force (AEF) was sent to Europe under the command of the extremely capable General John J. Pershing; the U.S. Navy in European waters was also ably commanded by the strong-willed Admiral William S. Sims.

➤ On arrival in France, Pershing was welcomed as a savior, but he soon found himself embroiled in a struggle with the French and British to preserve the essential independence of the AEF and to keep it from being destroyed piecemeal by premature integration with Allied forces.

Chapter 23

The War Beyond the Trenches, 1917–1918

In This Chapter

➤ The Isonzo bloodbath continues on the Italian Front

➤ The Battle of Caporetto nearly finishes the Italians

➤ The tables are turned on Austria-Hungary

➤ A new French commander on the Balkan Front

➤ The triumphs of Allenby and Lawrence in the Middle East

On December 7, 1916, David Lloyd George was promoted from the British cabinet's munitions minister to prime minister. He was known as a man passionately devoted to winning the war, but he believed that the best strategy was "indirect," a concentration of operations on the peripheral fronts, and he endeavored to take some of the emphasis off the Western Front. His advocacy of a full Allied push on the Italian Front proved unsuccessful, however, when the entry of the United States into the war and the withdrawal of Russia from it refocused the attention of all belligerents on the Western Front. Nevertheless, during the last two years of the war, the peripheral fronts—the Italian, Balkan, and Turkish Fronts—remained highly active.

The Italian Front

By early 1917, it was becoming clear to Italian General Luigi Cadorna that the Isonzo campaign was in trouble and that his forces were especially vulnerable if the Germans decided to send troops to aid the Austro-Hungarians on this front. General Robert Nivelle, at this time still in overall command of French forces, dispatched General Ferdinand Foch to meet with Cadorna to discuss Franco-British assistance to Italy. Had Britain's Prime Minister, David Lloyd George, had his way, Allied strength would have been diverted from the Western Front to collaborate with the Italians on a push from the south, as Lloyd George said, to "knock the props out" from under the Central Powers. Both the French and the British commanders opposed siphoning off manpower from the Western Front, however, and it was decided to aid Cadorna only in the event of an extreme emergency. Staff officers worked out a contingency plan for Franco-British forces to be transported to the Italian Front in case of need.

Isonzo Continues

For his part, Cadorna promised the other Allies that he would not give up at Isonzo. During the Western Front battles of early 1917, French and British commanders, although unwilling to commit their troops to the Italian Front, insisted that the Italians keep up the pressure on the Austrians as part of a universal Allied offensive.

From May 12, 1917, to June 8, Cadorna once again mounted an offensive on the Isonzo front. His army made minuscule gains of territory through the course of 17 days of fighting. Although Austrian casualties reached 75,000 killed and wounded, Italian losses were more than twice that number at 157,000.

Incredibly, Cadorna focused on his slight territorial gains rather than on his horrendous human losses. He resolved to make an all-out effort, pouring in 52 Italian divisions supported by 5,000 guns.

The Eleventh Battle of the Isonzo opened on August 18 with the Italian Second Army, under General Luigi Capello, attacking the Austrian line north of Gorizia and the Italian Third, commanded by the Duke of Aosta, pushing south of this into the hills between Gorizia and Trieste. This advance was quickly checked by the Austrian Fifth Army, but Capello, to the north, advanced rapidly and captured the high ground at Bainsizza Plateau.

It was a moment of combined triumph and folly. The Austrians were so badly battered that they were on the verge of collapse. Capello, however, advanced so quickly and so far that he soon outran both his supply lines and his artillery. It is suicidal to leave one's infantry thus exposed, so Capello reluctantly had to halt his advance. This gave the all-but-defeated Austrians an opportunity to call on the Germans for help.

"Hutier Tactics"

Now it was the Italians' turn to suffer a shock. Cadorna was in the midst of preparing for continued offensive operations and was completely unaware of the combined Austrian and German concentration (seven divisions and most of the artillery of the newly formed Austrian Fourteenth Army were German) at the small town of Caporetto. Cadorna also took little note of the growing crisis within his own army. Despite General Capello's success, the otherwise unremitting series of Italian offensives had yielded little progress at tremendous cost in casualties. Morale was plummeting and discipline dissolving. Within the ranks, a strong communist and pacifist element was agitating, encouraging mutiny and desertion. Cadorna had also thoroughly undermined his own officer corps. In the 19 months before the Caporetto battle, through the fruitless series of Isonzo battles leading up to it, Cadorna dismissed 217 general officers, 255 colonels, and 335 battalion commanders for having failed to achieve the impossible objectives set for them.

By October, Cadorna began to suspect that the Austrians were building up in preparation for an offensive. He started to shift from offensive preparations to defensive; however, the one place he believed an attack would *not* come was in the sector around Caporetto. Rocky and mountainous, it seemed a most unlikely choice for any major offensive thrust. This misjudgment was compounded by the behavior of General Capello. Loath to lose the momentum of a successful offensive, Capello chose to ignore Cadorna's order to prepare defenses.

If the Austrians had borrowed some German troops and artillery, they also borrowed a German commander, General Otto von Below, and German savvy—the so-called "Hutier tactics" that had proven so effective against the Russians at Riga (see Chapter 21, "Allies Imperiled"). These tactics were based on surprise and rapid movement intended to penetrate, disrupt, and disorganize enemy defenses.

Italian Disaster

The Battle of Caporetto—also called the Twelfth Battle of the Isonzo—commenced at 2 A.M. on October 24, 1917, with a massive artillery barrage of high explosives, gas, and smoke. Just six hours later, the infantry assault began. Following Hutier tactics, the first wave studiously avoided any Italian strong points and instead concentrated on penetrating the line. Subsequent Austro-German waves of attackers would exploit these early breaches and roll up the strong points, making use of grenades and *flame-throwers* to do the job.

The violence of the Austro-German assault was devastating to the already demoralized Italian troops. Those in the front lines either surrendered or fled. Cadorna had located his reserves too far to the south to be brought into place rapidly, and his subordinate commanders had not planned with one another for mutual support in case of need.

By nightfall, the attackers had penetrated a dozen miles, routing and capturing the defenders. Cadorna ordered a retreat to the defensive line of the Tagliamento River, a withdrawal completed by the end of October.

Words of War

The **flame-thrower** is a weapon of early origin, dating back at least to the eighth century. By World War I, the weapon had been augmented by the use of compressed air to propel the burning fuel, which could be projected quite far. Because the flame-thrower was dangerous to use—it was prone to explode—it was generally less effective as a military weapon than as an instrument of terror intended to demoralize the enemy.

Battle of the Piave

The one stroke of good fortune accorded the Italians was the very speed with which Below's forces had moved. They had penetrated so far and so fast that they were out-running their lines of supply. Because the Austro-German forces had to slow down, they lost the possibility of further surprise and instead attacked the Italian line at Cornino on November 2. Once again, Cadorna was forced to order a withdrawal, taking up positions north of Venice, on the Piave River, which he had previously fortified. Cadorna had 300,000 troops left under his command. More 600,000 had died, had been wounded, had been taken prisoner, or had deserted.

From the Front

A look at the Italian casualty figures from Caporetto testifies to the army's desolated morale. Ten thousand were killed in action, 30,000 were wounded, 293,000 were taken prisoner, and 400,000 simply fled and deserted the ranks.

Words of War

A **diversionary attack** is an action intended to divert and distract the enemy, draining off his resources, while a principal attack or other action is launched elsewhere.

This withdrawal proved to be Cadorna's last action. He was subjected to an investigation and then relieved of command, to be replaced by General Armando Diaz. By November 10, French troops began arriving on the Italian front to aid and reinforce Diaz. Soon they were joined by the British as well. Thus bolstered—and aware, too, that they were now fighting to save their homeland—the Italians held the Piave line with renewed vigor and endurance. The front hardened into the familiar entrenched stalemate.

By late spring 1918, the Germans pulled their troops off the Italian Front, again leaving the Austro-Hungarian forces to fight alone. At this point, the two Austro-Hungarian commanders, Count Conrad and General Svetozar Borojevic von Bojna, fell to arguing over who should have the honor of delivering the coup de grace to Italy. A waffling Archduke Joseph settled the dispute by allowing both to attack simultaneously. It was hardly a decision worthy of King Solomon, for the mountainous terrain in this region would prevent communication between the divided forces, which meant that they had to act independently. Because neither alone was sufficient to achieve victory, the Austrians marched into battle with a self-imposed disadvantage.

The Battle of Piave began with a *diversionary attack* at the Tonale Pass. The Italians repulsed it on June 13, and then the two Austrian commanders commenced their main attacks. Conrad targeted the city of Verona, while Borojevic had Padua as his objective. The Italian general, Diaz, had intercepted some Austrian deserters, who betrayed the offensive. Diaz quickly prepared his positions, and when Conrad's Eleventh Army struck the Italian Fifth and Sixth armies, it was soon thrown back by vigorous counterattacks. This action effectively put Conrad's forces out of the action.

That left Borojevic, who attacked along the lower reaches of the River Piave. At first, he seemed to enjoy great success, penetrating the Italian lines for 3 miles. But then Diaz went after the Austrian supply lines with bombers, and he shifted into position an entire army, the Ninth, which he had held in reserve. This fresh force compelled Borojevic, completely cut off from the possibility of reinforcement, to withdraw. His troops stole away during the night of June 22–23.

Italy's Counteroffensive

To the chagrin of the other allies, especially Ferdinand Foch, the French liaison commander with the Italians, General Diaz failed to press his advantage. He did not order an immediate counterattack. Instead, he waited for conditions on the Western Front to turn favorable for the French and British, who could then release troops to make a combined offensive.

By October, Diaz, whose army had been supplemented by British and French divisions, was at last ready to begin. He targeted Vittorio Veneto, across the Piave. Diaz anticipated a victory because he surmised that the Austrian troops were heavily demoralized in light of their government's recent request for an armistice.

Diaz was shocked by the tenacity and determination of the Austrians, who fought fiercely and pushed back the Italian Fourth Army, inflicting heavy losses in the process, in the October 23 Battle of Monte Grappo.

Beginning on the next day, the Austrian Sixth Army arrested the advance of the Italian Eighth on the Piave line. As the two armies tangled, French and British reinforcements managed to gain positions to the left and the right of the Austrians. A single American regiment, the 332nd Infantry, also joined the fray; together, the Allied forces split the Austrian Front. They exploited the gap and reached Sacile on October 30. From this point on, the breach in the Austrian line widened, more Italian forces poured in, and the Austrian defense collapsed.

The Italian forces marched on Belluno on November 1 and the Tagliamento River the next day. In the meantime, the British and French advanced against and took Trent on November 3. In the combined action, 300,000 Austrians surrendered. On this same day, Trieste fell to the Allies—and

From the Front

The aged Austro-Hungarian Emperor Franz Josef had died on November 21, 1916, and was succeeded by Karl I, who stepped down as head of the government on November 11, 1918, after the general armistice was signed with Germany. He refused officially to abdicate, however, and unsuccessfully attempted to regain his throne as king of Hungary in 1921. He died, in exile on Portuguese Madeira, on April 1, 1922.

Austria-Hungary signed an armistice. The Dual Empire was out of the war as of November 4, 1918.

Balkan Stalemate

In Chapter 17, "Italy, the Eastern Front, and Elsewhere, 1916," we left Allied forces under the quarrelsome French general Maurice Sarrail stalemated in the Balkans. On the books, he carried almost 600,000 men in his command, although he never had an effective force of more than a quarter-million. Now, however, he had fewer than 100,000 fit for duty. Along the stalemated battlefront, disease—principally malaria—had idled many of his troops.

Allies at Cross Purposes

Plagued by disease among his ranks, Sarrail also disputed with his subordinate commanders, and he operated in a highly unstable political climate in which Greece, behind his lines, was torn between a pro-Allied faction and the official government of King Constantine, which ostensibly preserved neutrality but clearly favored the Central Powers.

In this atmosphere, Sarrail made several thrusts against the Bulgar-German forces. Both the Battle of Lake Prespa (also called the Battle of Djoran), March 11–17, 1917, and the Battle of the Vardar, May 5–19, ended inconclusively. Sarrail's failure of leadership was total, and any hope of coordinated effort among the demoralized Allied forces was lost.

The only bright spot for the Allies was the abdication of King Constantine on June 12, 1917, thanks to a combination of Allied political pressure and the continuing influence of Eleutherios Venizelos, who had earlier been forced to resign as premier under Constantine. With the ascension to the throne of the pro-Allied King Alexander, Venizelos was reappointed premier; on June 27, Greece entered the war on the side of the Allies. Although this significantly augmented Allied strength, the armies here were in such disarray that no new offensive was developed.

Breakthrough

Back in France, in November, the government of Premier Paul Painlevé collapsed under pressing fears that France was losing and would indeed lose the war. The nation's president, Raymond Poincaré, now had to make one of the most critical decisions of the entire war. He could appoint as premier Joseph Caillaux, who favored immediate negotiation of peace with Germany. This would amount to defeat for France but an end to the bloodletting. Or, he could name Georges Clemenceau, a relentless critic of what he called defeatism and a man who would settle for nothing less than the unconditional surrender of Germany. There was no love between Poincaré and Clemenceau, who often directed his fiery barbs at the French president. But, in the end, Poincaré could not abide a dishonorable end to the war. On November 16, 1917, he appointed Georges Clemenceau premier of France.

Among the first acts of the new premier was to order the relief of Maurice Sarrail, who was replaced in the Balkans by the vigorous General M.L.A. Guillaumat on December 10. The new commander immediately set about the task of reorganizing the tattered Allied forces on this front and of training the Greek army. He commanded that force in a successful action against Bulgar-German forces holding Skra Di Legen Ridge before he was recalled to France to command troops defending Paris.

Guillaumat's replacement was Franchet d'Esperey, one of the finest tacticians of the French army. He prevailed upon the Supreme War Council to allow him to mount a major offensive using his polyglot and malaria-ridden command of 600,000 Serbian, Czech, Italian, French, and British troops, of which perhaps 200,000 were now fit for duty. With these he would oppose some 200,000 Bulgarians, whose German allies (save for some senior officers) had been withdrawn for service on the Western Front.

Voices of Battle

"War is much too serious a matter to be entrusted to generals."

—Georges Clemenceau

Under d'Esperey, the multinational offensive was superbly coordinated—a vivid contrast to the muddled failures of Maurice Sarrail. Covered by heavy artillery support, the Serb contingent was deployed on September 15 between elements of the so-called French Orient Army. This enabled the Serbs to penetrate the Bulgar defenders and push northward while the French, on either side of the resulting gap, attacked both Bulgar flanks.

On September 18, the British contingent leaped into the fray with a diversionary attack on the Bulgars' far right. This diversion gained unanticipated momentum, which propelled the Brits all the way to the Vardar River by September 25. At this point, the Bulgarian forces had been split in two.

From the Vardar, the British drove on to Stumitsa, which they reached on September 26, while the French cavalry charged through the principal battle area to take Skoplje on September 29.

In earlier Balkan action, when the Germans were present, the Central Powers ruled the sky, terrorizing Allied troops with air attacks. Now that the Germans were gone, the Allied air forces quickly attained supremacy and threw the retreating Bulgars into a panic, transforming what might have been an orderly withdrawal into a rout.

Crossing the Danube

Franchet d'Esperey led his Serbian and French troops northward, compelling Bulgaria to agree to an armistice on September 29. With the war in the Balkans over, d'Esperey marched across the Danube to attack Budapest and then Dresden, Germany. The crossing was effected on November 10–11, just at the point that the German armistice put an end to the Great War.

287

On the Turkish Fronts

On the far-flung Turkish fronts, activity intensified during 1917–1918, especially in the Middle East and Mesopotamia.

Caucasus

The first of the two Russian revolutions of 1917 immediately withdrew the czar's forces from the Caucasus region. By March, Turkish troops in the mountains were free to bolster other fronts.

Palestine and Syria

At the beginning of 1917, the Battle of Magruntein (January 8–9) resulted in the ouster of all Turkish forces from the Sinai Peninsula. This put the British commander, Sir Archibald Murray, in position to make an assault into Palestine. His first task would be to dislodge the Turks from their strong positions along ridges between Gaza and Beersheba, which formed a natural portal into Palestine.

On March 26, the First Battle of Gaza commenced with an attack led by Sir Charles M. Dobell. The action was beset by error and ill fortune, mainly due to a total breakdown in communications between mounted forces and infantry. After losing almost 4,000 men out of a force of 16,000, Dobell withdrew.

Murray managed to contrive a report to higher headquarters that portrayed the battle, which was at best a draw, as an unequivocal British victory. This prompted an order to advance immediately on Jerusalem. Accordingly, Dobell was ordered to make a second assault on the Turkish positions at Gaza. This Second Battle of Gaza (April 17–19) began with a reckless frontal assault against thoroughly prepared Turkish defenses.

Predictably, it was a slaughter. The British, thrown back, suffered 6,444 dead and wounded, while the Turkish defenders lost perhaps a third of that number. Murray, whose report had triggered the suicidal attack, relieved Dobell, but the War Office, in turn, removed Murray, replacing him with General Edmund Allenby.

It was an excellent choice. A cavalryman, Allenby had energy and tactical skill well suited to this particular theater of the war. He was, to boot, a charismatic leader.

Armed with simple marching orders from the War Office—"Jerusalem before Christmas"—Allenby swung into action, beginning by boldly moving British headquarters from a first-class Cairo hotel to the fighting front. But Allenby did not confuse bold action with rash action. He insisted on building up reinforcements before making his assault. He assembled seven infantry divisions and a cavalry unit, consisting of horses and camels and dubbed the Desert Mounted Corps, a total of 88,000 men. He proposed to do battle against the Turkish Eighth Army, commanded by the German general Kress von Kressenstein, and elements of the Turkish Seventh—a total of perhaps 35,000 men. Despite their superior numbers, the British labored under the handicap of all desert fighters: a limited and tenuous water supply. For their part, however, the Turks, though well established defensively, had a long and vulnerable supply line stretching all the way to Constantinople.

The Third Battle of Gaza, also called the Battle of Beersheba, began early in the morning of October 31, 1917. Unlike Dobell, Allenby avoided a clumsy frontal attack. Deploying three of his divisions in front of Gaza to deceive the Turks into anticipating a frontal assault, he sent the bulk of his forces in a surprise assault on Beersheba. The key objective was the town's water supply, its wells. An attacker who seized and controlled these would take the city. An attacker who failed to capture the water supply would certainly fail in an assault against the well-established defenses.

Allenby sent his infantry against the Turkish defenders from the front while the Desert Mounted Corps pounded far to the east, and then came around against Beersheba from that direction. It was an Australian cavalry unit that, after an all-day battle, penetrated the defenses and captured the wells.

In a panic, the defenders began to evacuate, in the process leaving the flank of the Turkish Seventh Army exposed. Recognizing an opportunity when he saw one, Allenby struck north on November 6. He was able to split the Seventh from the Eighth Army. Although Allenby dispatched the Desert Mounted Corps toward Gaza to trap the Eighth Army there, the Turks moved faster and retreated farther up the coast. In the meantime, what was left of the Turkish Seventh Army fell back on Jerusalem.

Allenby's main force pursued the retreating Turks. The British general threw caution to the wind in outrunning his supplies, especially water. When General Erich von Falkenhayn appeared with a Turkish reserve force (the "Yilderim Force"), the Battle of Junction Station was fought from November 11 to November 14. Following this fierce fight, Allenby resumed his assault on Jerusalem itself, attacking Turkish positions there on December 8 and occupying the city on the 9th. The British general had fulfilled his orders— "Jerusalem by Christmas"—and on December 26 successfully fended off a Turkish counterattack.

From the Front

The entire Jerusalem campaign had cost Allenby's 88,000-man force 18,000 casualties, a 20 percent casualty rate that would have been high by any standard other that which prevailed in World War I. The Turks lost 25,000 (including 12,000 taken as POWs)—a devastating casualty rate of 71 percent.

Lawrence of Arabia

Having taken Jerusalem, Allenby now found his army besieged not by Turks, but by his own War Office, which repeatedly drained his forces, looking for hardened veterans to transfer back to the Western Front. Thus, the general was limited to conducting small operations in the vicinity of the city.

Combatants

Thomas Edward Lawrence (1888–1935) was the illegitimate son of Sir Robert Chapman by his daughters' governess, Sara Maden. A brilliant student at Oxford, he traveled to the Middle East as a scholar in 1909 to study the Crusader castles of the Holy Land. During 1911–1914, he was awarded a traveling endowment from Magdalen College, which enabled him to join the expedition excavating Carchemish (Barak) on the Euphrates. Lawrence's archaeological interests gave him a pretext for exploring northern Sinai early in 1914, ostensibly for scientific reasons, but actually at the behest of the British military, to reconnoiter the situation in Turkish Palestine as the world hovered near war.

Just before the outbreak of war, Lawrence returned to Britain and was commissioned in the British army. At the outbreak of hostilities, he was assigned to the War Office's map department but was soon dispatched to Cairo as an intelligence officer attached to the Arab section. Sent to accompany another officer, Ronald Storrs, on a mission to Shaerif Husein in the Hejaz during October 1916, Lawrence remained to visit the army of Husein's son Faisal outside Medina. On his return to Cairo in November, he was assigned to Faisal's army as a political and liaison officer. Lawrence worked with Faisal to mold the ongoing Arab revolt into a force that would aid the British cause in the Middle East. He became an organizer of irregulars, whipping up the flagging insurrection and resupplying the army. He also assumed strategic leadership of Faisal's forces. Lawrence soon gathered about himself a private army of devoted followers. He himself adopted Arab dress and became the scourge of Turkish desert garrisons.

After the war, Lawrence was chosen as a member of the British delegation to the Versailles peace conference, at which he struggled in vain to save Arab independence. During 1921–1922, he was an adviser on Arab affairs to the Middle Eastern Division of the Colonial Office, but he was soon disillusioned with colonial government policy and left government service in 1922. He found himself hounded by the near-legendary status that his wartime exploits had earned for him, and he enlisted in the Royal Air Force under a pseudonym in August 1922. When a newspaper revealed his secret in January 1923, he resigned and enlisted in the Royal Tank Corps in March, calling himself T.E. Shaw. (In 1927, he made the change legal.)

Lawrence transferred back to the RAF in 1925. The following year he published his wartime memoirs, a massive literary masterpiece titled *The Seven Pillars of Wisdom*. The first edition was strictly limited to a mere 150 copies and was by his own direction the only edition of the book published while he was alive. However, in 1927, he published to a wider audience a shorter version of the memoir, *Revolt in the Desert*.

Lawrence left the RAF in 1935 and was fatally injured in a motorcycle accident near his home, Cloud Hill, in Dorset.

With Britain's conventional forces all but idled, T.E. Lawrence, the remarkable British liaison with Emir Faisal's Arab army, whom we met in Chapter 15, "The Other Fronts, 1915," came into prominence. As a result of operations earlier in the war, he had already concluded that Faisal's small force of tribal warriors—about 6,000 men—could not be used effectively to augment a conventional, European-style military force. Their strength was as a highly mobile, extremely stealthy guerrilla band. Shedding his British khaki for Arab dress, Lawrence joined the ranks of Faisal's warriors and assisted Faisal in leading them in a series of raids all along the Hejaz Railway, the principal supply line for the Turks. This indirect action kept some 25,000 Turks confined to their blockhouses and other outposts, effectively neutralizing them.

In August 1917, Lawrence led a small camel force to disrupt Turkish rail communications and, ultimately, to capture the port of Aqaba with a surprise strike from the rear. With this achievement under his belt, Lawrence approached Allenby in the early fall of 1918 with a plan for the Arabs' participation in the offensive that Allenby planned as the decisive campaign of the war in the Middle East. Lawrence proposed that the Arabs form the British right flank in the army's advance through Palestine to Damascus, Syria.

Allenby concurred—without knowledge of Lawrence's ulterior motive. An archaeologist by training, Lawrence had first come to the Middle East in 1909 and had spent much time working and living among the Arabs, whom he had come to love and respect. With the advent of war, he saw their value to the British as allies, but he also saw that the British could—and should—in turn help the Arabs achieve genuine and enduring independence from the Ottoman Empire. He understood, however, that British promises of support for independence had been made in bad faith and that, at the end of the war, neither the British nor the French were likely to honor the commitments they had made to the Arabs. Therefore, Lawrence secretly proposed to lead the Arab contingent in advance of Allenby and to capture Damascus before the main body of British troops arrived. This would give Faisal a claim on the city as the new capital of an independent Arabia.

As Allenby's main column advanced on Damascus (see the section "Holy Land Ending," later in this chapter), Lawrence, who had obtained 2,000 camels from the British army's grandiosely named Imperial Camel Brigade, rode with the Arabs to attack Deraa, which drew Turkish attention from Allenby's principal objectives. Perceiving Lawrence's intentions at this point, Allenby ordered him not to close on Damascus. The British general insisted that this would be a British, not an Arab, victory. Lawrence violated his orders and moved on Damascus.

By September 30, 1918, the Turks evacuated Damascus. Lawrence, at the head of 3,000 Arabs, entered the city some three hours in advance of Allenby. In view of the fact that Lawrence had greatly aided Allenby's campaign, using his 3,000 men to tie down more than 15,000 Turks, the errant Britisher was not court-martialed. Instead, he was promoted from major to colonel. Characteristically, Colonel T.E. Lawrence resigned his commission at the very moment of his greatest triumph and recognition.

He did not relish having attained personal glory as an officer in an army that, as he had predicted, was now turning its back on its Arab allies.

Lawrence returned to Britain on the very day of the armistice, November 11, 1918, and attempted unsuccessfully to intercede at the highest levels of government in England and France to save Arab independence.

Voices of Battle

"Nine-tenths of tactics were certain enough to be teachable in schools; but the irrational tenth was like the kingfisher flashing across the pool, and in it lay the test of generals. It could be ensued only by instinct (sharpened by thought practicing the stroke) until at the crisis it came naturally, a reflex."

—T.E. Lawrence, on military genius, in *The Seven Pillars of Wisdom* (1926)

Holy Land Ending

The activities of T.E. Lawrence were so sensational and of such mythic proportions—reported to the world press by the young American correspondent Lowell Thomas, and celebrated in two monumental works of genius, Lawrence's own great memoir, *The Seven Pillars of Wisdom* (published privately in 1926, commercially in 1935), and the magnificent film directed by David Lean, *Lawrence of Arabia* (1962)—that they tend to overshadow the victory that Allenby had achieved with his final offensive.

By early autumn of 1918, the Turks were now under the command of the highly capable German general Liman von Sanders (who replaced Falkenhayn). He deployed some 36,000 men of the Turkish Fourth, Seventh, and Eighth armies in exceedingly well-developed defensive works from the Mediterranean Sea north of Jaffa all the way to the Jordan Valley. Allenby decided to oppose these defenders with a force that he had managed to build up despite demands for men to be sent to the Western Front. He had 57,000 infantry and 12,000 cavalry, in addition to 540 guns.

Allenby knew that even a significantly superior force could be annihilated by well-entrenched, skillfully led defenders. Therefore, he decided to concentrate on the Mediterranean seashore, pry open a gap in the Turkish line there, and breach it with his fast-moving cavalry while his infantry swept through the Jordan Valley, pivoting north and east like a great gate. The complex plan called for precise coordination between cavalry and infantry components. Most of all, it demanded secrecy to preserve the element of surprise.

Allenby dispatched British planes to sweep the skies clear of German observers. He set up elaborate decoy camps—unmanned dummy installations—and paraded his cavalry near Jerusalem to deceive the Turks into thinking that the British concentration lay near that city. Allenby even placed ads in the local newspapers announcing a great horse race to be held on the very day secretly set for the launch of the offensive! (For who would schedule a battle on the day of the big race?)

The opening action, the Battle of Megiddo, commenced at 4:30 A.M. with a brief and intense artillery barrage followed by the advance of the entire British line. Surprise was total—as Allenby had planned, his XXI Corps ripped a wide gap through the Turkish line along the seacoast. Through this the British Desert Mounted Corps rode while British fliers bombed rail junctions and all the Turks' headquarters, thereby knocking out communications.

As the British cavalry pushed through the Turkish Eighth Army, which seemed to dissolve before its advance, the infantry maneuvered in its great wheeling pattern, sweeping all before it. By September 20, the Turkish Eighth Army had been crushed, and the Seventh, routed, fell back in disarray.

From September 22 to October 30, Allenby pursued the fleeing remnants of the Turkish army. Damascus fell on October 1—entered first by T.E. Lawrence leading Faisal's Arabs—and Beirut followed on October 2. While elements of Allenby's infantry occupied these key cities, his Desert Mounted Corps led a farther advance to the Syrian city of Homs (occupied October 16) and to Aleppo (occupied October 25), on Syria's border with Turkey.

With the British at their doorstep, the Turks, thoroughly defeated, agreed to an armistice on October 30, 1918, and were now out of the war.

From the Front

Megiddo was clearly the most brilliant British action of World War I—possibly of any of England's wars. Three enemy armies were annihilated and 76,000 prisoners were taken. The cost to Allenby was 853 killed, 4,482 wounded, and 385 missing. Megiddo, the fortress-city gateway to Mesopotamia, was the site of the first military battle recorded in history, about 1469 B.C.E., that pitted Egypt's King Thutmose III against forces led by the Mitanni King of Kadesh.

Mesopotamian Campaign

British operations in Mesopotamia had been costly throughout the war, but they had at least accomplished the objective of protecting the oil fields in the region. In October, a British force was hurriedly marched north out of Baghdad to secure the oil fields of Mosul and to attack the Turkish Tigris Group, which surrendered to British General A.S. Cobbe on October 29. The Turkish armistice was concluded the very next day, but Cobbe was ordered to take and occupy Mosul in any case. This was contrary to the provisions of the armistice, but Cobbe prevailed, and the Turkish garrison of Halil Pasha withdrew without a fight.

The Caspian stronghold of Baku also fell to the British—after the Turkish armistice—and the entire Allied fleet steamed through the Dardanelles, scene of Allied fiasco in 1916 (see Chapter 14, "The Gallipoli Disaster"), on November 12, the day after the general armistice, anchoring in Constantinople on November 13. With this quiet coda to the spectacular achievements of Allenby—and T.E. Lawrence—in the Middle East, the war on the Turkish fronts had come to an end.

The Least You Need to Know

➤ The Isonzo sector of the Italian Front remained the scene of repeated battles, which almost finished off Italy. With Allied aid, the Italians were able to mount an effective counterattack that ultimately spelled the end for Austria-Hungary.

➤ On the Balkan Front, the brilliant General Franchet d'Esperey replaced the ineffective Maurice Sarrail and succeeded in forcing the Bulgarians to conclude an armistice.

➤ Two of the most brilliant commanders of the war were the British General Edmund Allenby and the British guerilla-style leader T.E. Lawrence. Their victories in the Middle East did the most to drive Turkey out of the war.

New Blood

Using elementary physics, we are told, just about any situation involving objects in motion can be reduced to a set of straightforward mathematical expressions. For the sake of creating these expressions, physicists invent ideal conditions, states of perfect nonfriction, total vacuums, absolute temperatures, and points in space without physical dimension. The reason? For each real-world factor tossed into the equation, the mathematics becomes increasingly complex and confusing. Admit enough of the real world, and the behavior of the simplest objects moving in the simplest ways becomes nearly impossible to account for and predict.

Thus, the European Allies, wearing away in a war of attrition, looked to the Americans as a beginning physics student looks to a problem of an object in motion: A few deft calculations, and the object is moved from here to there. But, from the very beginning, this war had shown how rudely the real world treats calculations, theories, and plans. By 1917, three years of war had reduced the thinking of the European Allies to starkly simple arithmetic: so many hundreds of thousands of men sent to the trenches, so many hundreds of thousands lost, so many hundreds of thousands needed to replace them. As France, Britain, and Italy saw it, the Americans were just more numbers waiting to be fed into the equation. American General John J. Pershing had not yet learned to think of men as numbers, though; as he saw it, simply plugging them into the Great War equation was neither possible nor desirable.

This chapter takes the American Expeditionary Force into action.

The Buildup

General Pershing and his small staff of 40 regular army officers, 2 marine officers, 17 reserve officers, 5 civilian interpreters, and 123 enlisted men and clerks were welcomed in Paris on June 14, 1917. After the tumult of greeting and ceremony died down—and it did so quickly—Pershing learned just how desperate the Allied situation was. He learned of mutiny in the French ranks (see Chapter 21, "Allies Imperiled"), of demoralization, of dwindling reserves, and of an enemy willing and able to remain on the defensive, it seemed, indefinitely.

Having arrived in France with fewer than 200 other American soldiers, John J. Pershing was well aware that, at just this moment, he had nothing to offer the Allies. There was a paper creation called the American Expeditionary Force (AEF), but right now, it consisted of a general and his small staff, along with a hastily thrown-together First Division on its way.

Voices of Battle

"Gee! I often think of the time when I was at home. Mama, you know I believe that one day I will come back to you and the loved ones I left behind. Wouldn't you be glad to have your soldier boy with you again? My prayer to God is that we will have peace with all the nations and we boys get back home with our dear ones."

—George W. Lee, AEF, to his mother in Greensboro, North Carolina, from France, 1917

Pershing set to work to make the AEF a reality.

As we saw in Chapter 22, "Over Here and Over There," Pershing's first fight was not with the Germans, but with the English and the French, against their desperate demand that he feed them troops just as soon as they arrived from America. At length, Pershing obtained Allied consent to allow him instead to concentrate the incoming army into viable units that would not simply be frittered away. He secured French approval to concentrate the AEF in Lorraine, which put the Americans quite close to the German border and, in particular, near the so-called St.-Mihiel salient, the pocket of German strength that the Allies had been unsuccessfully attacking since 1915.

Besides the tremendous task of raising an army and transforming citizens into soldiers, there was the problem of transporting the men and their equipment. Troops were carried in convoys typically consisting of four sections of 14 troop ships each. Each of the four sections was escorted by one cruiser and four to five destroyers. Submarine attack was an ever-present danger, of course, but the greatest obstacle to be overcome was a shortage of shipping. The 56 troop transports of the first convoy, for example, carried about 14,500 men total. The target strength for the AEF in Europe was four million men—one million by May 1918!

When the men disembarked in French ports, they had to be transported to the Lorraine sector via railroad. Pershing commissioned the vice president of the Pennsylvania Railroad, William W. Atterbury, to come to France to manage the AEF rail system. Working with French officials, he laid down a thousand miles of new track and imported 1,500 locomotives and 18,000 railway cars from the United States. The equipment was shipped in parts and was assembled on-site.

Supply was a problem of gargantuan proportions: 18 million tons of supplies and equipment would be required. The principal supply facility, the Gievres Storage Depot, was staffed by 25,000 men who handled 2,300 railway cars daily. The warehouse facilities, built expressly for the AEF in France, offered 4 million square feet of storage, including the largest refrigeration plant in the world. Within this single depot were 43 miles of railroad track.

Pershing was not only concerned that his troops should be consolidated rather than fed to the front like so much cannon fodder, and he was not only determined to see that they were adequately supplied—he also wanted them fully combat-trained before service at the front. The men he received were hardly raw recruits—they had undergone basic training before shipping out from the United States—but Pershing instituted in France additional training to bring the soldiers up to what he deemed combat level. Nor was Pershing content with the training methods of the veteran British and French. He believed that they emphasized trench warfare tactics to the exclusion of the offensive tactics of attack. The result, he concluded, was defeatism, a loss of confidence in the ability to attack. Against the common wisdom of European Allies, Pershing believed that the war was about to enter a more fluid phase in which offensives would play a key role.

Pershing ordered for his troops a month of training in individual weapons, field craft, and *small-unit offense*. This was to be followed by a month in the trenches of a quiet sector. A final month was to be devoted to additional advanced training.

From the Front

Pershing's 90-day training program was criticized by the Allies as too elaborate and a waste of time. Although Pershing persisted in maintaining the program, few soldiers actually completed each phase before going into combat.

Words of War

Small-unit offense encompasses the skills and tactics required to enable soldiers to fight as a team on the level, typically, of the company (in World War I, 256 men) and the platoon (128 men).

Despite every effort, only 175,000 Americans were in France by the end of 1917. Except for a month that the First Division spent in the trenches during October-November, no Americans had even seen the front after eight months of U.S. involvement.

Voices of Battle

"This war, like the next war, is a war to end war."

—Attributed to Prime Minister David Lloyd George, 1918

Wilson Makes Fourteen Points

If General Pershing was determined not to waste American lives, so was President Wilson. He knew that he was sending young men off to die in a "foreign war," and he resolved that these sacrifices would not be made in vain. He told the American people that the "Great War" would be a "war to end all wars," and he meant it.

On January 8, 1918, President Wilson announced to Congress "Fourteen Points," which he called "the only possible program" for peace:

> "Gentleman of the Congress .... The day of conquest and aggrandizement is gone by; so is also the day of secret covenants .... We entered this war because violations of right had occurred which touched us to the quick and made the life of our own people impossible .... What we demand in this war, therefore, is nothing peculiar to ourselves. It is that the world be made fit and safe to live in; and particularly that it be made safe for every peace-loving nation which, like our own, wishes to live its own life, determine its own institutions, be assured of justice and fair dealing by the other peoples of the world as against force and selfish aggression. All the peoples of the world are in effect partners in this interest, and for our own part we see very clearly that unless justice be done to others, it will not be done to us. The program of the world's peace, therefore, is our program; and that program, the only possible program, as we see it, is this:

> I. Open covenants of peace, openly arrived at ....

> II. Absolute freedom of navigation upon the seas ... alike in peace and in war ....

> III. The removal, so far as possible, of all [international] economic barriers ....

> IV. Adequate guarantees given and taken that national armaments will be reduced to the lowest point consistent with domestic safety.

> V. A free, open-minded, and absolutely impartial adjustment of all colonial claims ....

> VI. The evacuation of all Russian territory and such a settlement of all questions, affecting Russia as will secure the best and freest cooperation of the

other nations of the world in obtaining for her an unhampered and un-embarrassed opportunity for the independent determination of her own political development ....

VII. Belgium, the whole world will agree, must be evacuated and restored, without any attempt to limit the sovereignty which she enjoys in common with all other free nations. No other single act will serve as this will serve to restore confidence among the nations in the laws which they have themselves set and determined for the government of their relations with one another. Without this healing act, the whole structure and validity of international law is forever impaired.

VIII. All French territory should be freed and the invaded portions restored, and the wrong done to France by Prussia in 1871 in the matter of [seizing the] Alsace-Lorraine [region], which has unsettled the peace of the world for nearly 50 years, should be righted, in order that peace may once more be made secure in the interest of all.

IX. A readjustment of the frontiers of Italy should be effected along clearly recognizable lines of nationality.

X. The peoples of Austria-Hungary, whose place among the nations we wish to see safeguarded and assured, should be accorded the freest opportunity of autonomous development.

XI. Rumania, Serbia, and Montenegro should be evacuated; occupied territories restored ....

XII. The Turkish portions of the present Ottoman Empire should be assured a secure sovereignty, but the other nationalities which are now under Turkish rule should be assured an undoubted security of life ....

XIII. An independent Polish state should be erected ....

XIV. A general association [league] of nations must be formed under specific covenants for the purpose of affording mutual guarantees of political independence and territorial integrity to great and small states alike."

Whatever else the war might have meant to American bankers and industrialists, Wilson was determined that it would ultimately serve the highest possible purpose: to bring to the world a reign of productive, peaceful, and just civilization.

The German Offensives

Since the compromise and failure of the Schlieffen Plan at the end of the war's first month in 1914 (see Chapters 5, "Battle of the Frontiers," and 6, "The Marne: Massacre and Miracle"), Germany had come to rely increasingly on a defensive approach to the war, at least on the Western Front. The idea was to let the Allies wear down their armies in fruitless attacks on the German trenches. Few generals naturally favor defense-based strategies. History and instinct both teach that wars are won by vigorous, aggressive offense, not by hunkering down defensively. Yet World War I had proven to be different from anything that had come before. Reluctantly perhaps, the Germans had come to the decision that it was more effective to let the Allies destroy themselves than it was to attempt to destroy the Allies.

By the winter of 1917–1918, however, Erich Ludendorff realized that the picture was changing dramatically. With the impending approach of massive American manpower on the Western Front, he decided that it was necessary to push for a decisive victory *before* the new troops began pouring in. With Russia now out of the war, Ludendorff believed that a massive concentration of a series of offensives on the Western Front could bring victory.

Ludendorff shifted large numbers of troops from the east, and he instituted a rigorous training program designed to convert soldiers who had been accustomed to defensive warfare to troops capable of aggressive offense. The best of his trainees he assigned as shock troops to head up the assaults.

In contrast to any number of British and French all-or-nothing offensive pushes, Ludendorff developed a plan founded on careful analysis of the Allied situation. He understood that the British and French were often at cross-purposes—the British always were concerned to maintain lines of communication with the English Channel ports, and the French focused on the protection of Paris. Ludendorff decided to exploit this inherent divergence of purpose by driving a wedge between the two Allies and then turning on the British to destroy its army. With the British out of the war, the French would surely negotiate a favorable peace.

Somme Offensive

The first of the Ludendorff offensives, on the Somme, code named "St. Michael," began on March 21, 1918. From north to south, the German Seventeenth, Second, and Eighteenth armies attacked the British on their right flank along a 60-mile front from Arras to La Fère. Intensive artillery bombardment was combined with "Hutier tactics" (see Chapter 23, "The War Beyond the Trenches, 1917–1918") to achieve a penetration of the British lines, which drove back Rawlinson's Fifth Army.

As Ludendorff had correctly surmised, Marshal Pétain was indeed more concerned with protecting Paris than he was with reinforcing the line of his British colleagues. Although French reinforcements arrived to help the British, Pétain made little attempt to coordinate this support. General Sir Henry Wilson, British chief of staff, sent up a wail of protest, calling for the appointment of "Foch or some other French general who will fight" to take over supreme command from Pétain.

The Supreme War Council responded. Although it did not remove Pétain from overall command of the French army, it appointed Ferdinand Foch as commander-in-chief of the Allied forces in France. Pershing not only approved of the appointment, but he also offered eight American divisions to Foch on an emergency basis.

Combatants

Ferdinand Foch (1851–1929), born in the Pyrenees as the son of a civil servant, joined the infantry as a private at the start of the Franco-Prussian War. In 1885, he was sent to the École Supériere de la Guerre, the French war college, at which he later taught, lecturing eloquently on such issues as flexibility, the massing of firepower, and on what he called the "mystique of the attack."

Georges Clemenceau, at the time a commissioner in charge of military affairs, made Foch director of the École Supériere, and he was subsequently promoted to general of brigade (1907). In 1913, he assumed command of XX Corps at Nancy and occupied this post at the outbreak of World War I. His sector fell under heavy attack, and he counterattacked with great vigor during August 14–18, 1914. However, his unit was surprised by the counterattack of Crown Prince Rupprecht's Sixth Army at Morhange. Foch fell back with heavy losses during August 20–21. Where lesser commanders would have allowed defeat to turn into a rout, Foch kept his command intact and organized an orderly withdrawal accompanied by damaging counterthrusts that were costly to the Germans. Similarly, at the First Battle of the Marne, during September 5–10, 1914, Foch sent a message to General Joseph Joffre: "My center is giving way, my right is falling back, situation excellent, I attack."

After General Philippe Pétain replaced Robert Nivelle on May 11, 1917, he appointed Foch chief of the General Staff. In this new post, Foch moved with great speed on the Italian front and enjoyed significant success. He was appointed to the Allied Supreme War Council, charged with coordinating Allied offensive efforts in November 1917. He then became Allied supreme commander for the Western Front on March 26, 1918. In this capacity, Foch coordinated the successful Allied response to General Erich Ludendorff's five major offensive pushes.

On August 6, 1918, Foch was promoted to marshal of France and two days later launched the major Allied counteroffensive that would bring the war to its conclusion on November 11. It was Foch who dictated the terms of the Armistice, and he served as president of the Allied military committee at the Versailles Treaty conference in January 1920. Foch was also charged with overseeing and enforcing the terms of the Armistice and the subsequent peace.

Following his death in 1929, Foch was laid to rest in a place of supreme honor, under the dome of Les Invalides, in company with Napoleon. Foch was the best of the French commanders of the Great War.

By April 5, 1918, after creating a 40-mile salient, the German advance ran out of steam. Foch had shifted French reserves to check the advance at Montdidier. The Somme Offensive had inflicted some 240,000 Allied casualties, including the taking of 70,000 POWs; however, it had been just as costly to the Germans, whose heaviest losses were among the elite shock troops.

Like a number of World War I campaigns, the Somme Offensive was a tactical success—a 40-mile breakthrough is highly significant—but a strategic failure. The offensive prompted the Allies to institute a truly unified command for the first time in the war. Aimed at splitting the British and the French, the offensive ended up uniting them, along with the Americans.

The Bombing of Paris

To stoke French fears for their capital, the Germans deployed a new "wonder weapon," the so-called Paris gun, with a huge barrel, 117 feet long, and the capability of firing shells of 15-inch caliber more than 70 miles. At least seven of these giant barrels were manufactured, although they were mounted and used one at a time. The great range of the weapon meant that Paris could be bombarded from well behind the German front lines. The Paris guns inflicted 876 casualties among Parisians and were certainly demoralizing, but they had no significant effect on the outcome of the war.

Lys Offensive

At the time, of course, Ludendorff did not recognize the adverse strategic effect of his Somme Offensive. Single-mindedly determined to inflict the maximum possible damage before the Americans entered the war in force, he launched an attack on the British at the Lys River (the "Georgette" Offensive), forming part of the Belgian-French border. The attack directly threatened the English Channel ports. The initial impact of the assault was devastating. A Portuguese division fighting under British control in the sector was all but completely annihilated, creating a gap that threatened the British flanks.

Within three hours of the initial onslaught, the German Sixth Army reached the open country behind the British rear lines. The defenders were caving in everywhere.

"Backs to the Wall"

By April 12, the British had been pushed far back, and British General Douglas Haig pleaded with Ferdinand Foch for reinforcements. The Frenchman replied that he had none to give but that he had complete confidence in the tenacity of the British fighting man. With no alternative, Haig penned "General Order of the Day, April 11, 1918," which became famous as the "Backs to the Wall" order. The general simply instructed his men to stand their ground—to the death.

Surprisingly, perhaps, the order actually succeeded in inspiring the defenders. They stood their ground and also began to push back so that, by April 29, Ludendorff was compelled to break off this second German offensive. Not only was British resistance unyielding, but Ludendorff's troops were suffering from extreme exhaustion and were tethered to ever-lengthening and increasingly unreliable lines of supply and communication.

American forces played a small role in assisting the British on the Lys. For the most part, AEF units trained with British as well as French forces in the area, both in special training areas and in quiet sectors along the front. American medical, engineering, and aviation units were actively engaged to a limited degree.

The first major U.S. action occurred on April 20, when two companies of the 26th Division came under heavy attack near Seicheprey along the St.-Mihiel salient. About 2,800 regular German troops spearheaded by 600 elite shock troops overran the American positions. A large number of Americans were taken prisoner, and 669 others were either killed or wounded. German losses were slight.

From the Front

British losses in the Lys Offensive were 239,000, among whom were 28,000 dead. The Germans, who had come so close to a major victory with this offensive, lost 348,300, including some 50,000 dead. The British were still in a position to replace their losses. The Germans, however, were suffering from acute shortages of manpower. For the most part, their losses were irreplaceable.

Aisne Offensive

Faced with the failure of offensives against the British, Ludendorff was plagued by second thoughts and came to believe that he might have been mistaken in concentrating against the British. He now decided to shift his operations against the French.

The third German offensive, "Operation Blücher," on the Aisne River, began spectacularly well for the attackers. It commenced on May 27 against lightly held French positions on the Chemin des Dames ridge. This was supposed to be a diversionary attack only, but it was so successful that it became the major effort of the offensive. In 24 hours, the Germans advanced 20 miles; by May 30, they reached the Marne, just 50 miles outside Paris.

Americans in Action

Militarily, the battle near Seicheprey, in the Lys Offensive, had not been a particularly significant encounter, but neither had it been an auspicious maiden engagement for the Americans. The German propaganda machine churned out accounts of the raid that portrayed Americans as incapable of fighting. What would they do now in the crisis on the Marne?

Saving Cantigny

Pershing rushed the U.S. Second and Third divisions to reinforce the French along the Marne. In the meantime, Major General Robert Lee Bullard launched the first U.S. offensive of the war, at the village of Cantigny, some 50 miles northwest of the action at Chemin des Dames and about 60 miles north of Paris.

Cantigny was the site of a German advance observation point and was very strongly fortified. On May 28, the U.S. First Division attacked the village and drove out the Germans. Later in the day and on the next day, the Americans successfully repulsed German counterattacks.

Cantigny was a spearhead German position, and the American victory here must be accounted nothing more than a local success. But it *was* a success—moreover, it was a victory against some of Germany's best troops, hardened veterans of Hutier's Eighteenth Army. The engagement erased the shock and shame of Seicheprey.

Château-Thierry

Château-Thierry, on the Marne, was the very nose of the German offensive. From here, it was less than 50 miles southwest into Paris. The U.S. Second and Third Divisions rushed to block the Germans from crossing the Marne at this point. As the Americans moved to the front, they passed troops of the French Sixth Army, limping back from it.

Voices of Battle

"I am very happy in my work .... Let me tell you this, we can beat the Boche [Germans] to a frazzle if we go into this with heart and soul .... We can beat the Boche only by fighting, and we are better fighters and better killers than the Boche .... Our killing spirit must be aroused but it is rising and Lord! I hope I am in the drive when it comes—when the Americans bloody their bayonets!"

—Lieutenant Lambert Wood, AEF, letter to his parents from France, December 7, 1917

The Third Division defended the Marne bridges, successfully holding them against the Germans and then counterattacking. The French Tenth Colonial Division, inspirited by the Americans, joined the fray and pushed the German onslaught back across the Marne at Jauglonne.

Most impressive was the Americans' sheer eagerness to fight. This was of immediate material aid to the Allies, of course, but its spiritual boost to flagging Allied morale was perhaps of greatest value.

Belleau Wood

After a shaky start at Seicheprey, the United States Army had acquitted itself admirably at Cantigny and Château-Thierry. Now it was the Marine Corps' turn.

Acting as the spearhead of the Army's Second Division, the Fourth Brigade of marines, under the command of James Guthrie Harbord, was ordered to capture Belleau Wood. This required a deadly advance across a wheat field, which was swept by machine gun fire. The casualties incurred on June 6, 1918, were the heaviest single-day losses in Marine Corps history—a record that would endure until November 1943, during World War II, when the Marines took the Japanese-held island of Tarawa.

During June 9 through June 26, the Marines and the Army's Second Division took, lost, and retook Belleau Wood and the nearby villages of Vaux and Bouresche no fewer than half a dozen times before the Germans were ejected for good.

The French name for Belleau Wood was Bois Belleau. Following the fierce battle, the French renamed it Bois de la Brigade de Marine.

Voices of Battle

"Come on, you sons of bitches! Do you want to live forever?"

—Sergeant Dan Daly, to his Marine platoon in the Battle of Belleau Wood

From the Front

Only 20 marines in the battalion that initially attacked Belleau Wood emerged unwounded. Total cost to the Marine Corps and the Army was 9,500 killed and wounded, with 1,600 lost as POWs.

Two More German Offensives

The late spring and early summer of 1918 brought two more major German offensives, as General Ludendorff adhered to his belief that the Allies had to be hit hard before the Americans could be fully deployed.

The German Deserters

General Erich Ludendorff may have been determined to push his forces to the maximum effort, but this demanded a sacrifice of extraordinary proportions from men who had endured almost four years of war. For most of those years, the German Western Front strategy had been defensive: a grim, exhausting, demoralizing hunkering down in the trenches. Now, at the eleventh hour, Ludendorff was ordering his men to take the offensive. For the Americans, especially as led by General Pershing, an offensive posture came naturally. The troops were fresh to the battle, and they were filled with optimism. For most of the grizzled German veterans, however, hope had died long ago, and the desertion rate increased alarmingly.

Noyon-Montdidier: The Franco-American Response

It was German deserters who, captured by the French, outlined the upcoming fourth and fifth German offensives. The next assault, they said, would come at Noyon and Montdidier. This was just southeast of Cantigny and northwest of Château-Thierry. The French commanders, Foch and Pétain, prepared accordingly. On June 9, when the attack commenced, the French were ready to defend against the preparatory artillery barrage with massed and highly effective *counterbattery fire,* which rapidly blunted the onslaught of the German Eighteenth Army.

The Germans made some inroads into the Allied lines, but a combined Franco-American counterattack checked the advance of the German Eighteenth Army by June 11. The next day, the Allies repulsed an attack by the German Seventh.

Ludendorff was becoming aware that, costly as his offensives were to the Allies, he was losing men even faster than they were. By this time, too, more than 250,000 Americans were arriving in France each month. By June 1918, 7 of the 25 U.S. divisions in France were in action at the front. This represented a compromise on the part of Pershing, who still resisted repeated French and British demands to release more troops to the front. The European Allies pushed and prodded in an effort to incorporate U.S. troops permanently into their commands. Pershing successfully—and tirelessly—resisted.

> **Words of War**
>
> **Counterbattery fire** is an artillery assault directed specifically against the enemy's artillery with the object of knocking it out.

Even as the American commander continued to husband his forces, he joined Ferdinand Foch in sending a message to the U.S. War Department asking for 80 U.S. divisions by April 1919 and 100 by July. The War Department considered these demands impossible to meet—but, in the meantime, the Americans kept coming.

Champagne-Marne

Increasingly desperate, Ludendorff was determined to end the war with the fifth German offensive in five months. Clearly, the Americans had joined the war at its most intense point.

Ludendorff's principal objective remained the destruction of the British army in Flanders; however, his strategy, as earlier, was to precede the main thrust with a preliminary offensive against the French (and now the Americans as well) in the Champagne region.

The focal point of the attack was the fortified city of Reims, well to the east of Château-Thierry. Once again, however, Foch had been informed by German deserters of the impending attack. (Intelligence garnered from POWs as well as aerial reconnaissance confirmed the information.) The initial advance by German shock troops was arrested by pre-emptive Allied artillery fire during the night of July 14–15, and, east of Reims, General Henri Gouraud's Fourth Army arrested the German attack within a matter of hours.

West of Reims, the Germans reached the Marne and crossed it with 14 divisions. Fighting was fierce, and American troops became heavily engaged. Colonel Ulysses G. McAlexander's 38th Infantry Regiment succeeded in blunting the onslaught. He successfully held his position by fighting in three directions simultaneously. Indeed, the U.S. Third Division, of which McAlexander's regiment was a part, earned the nickname "Rock of the Marne" for its determined and highly successful defense of the region west of Reims.

Americans—and the European Allies—were thrilled by the latest victories, which had come not only at the low point of Allied fortunes, but also in the midst of the most determined German offensives since the opening moves of 1914. Yet Americans were also learning the price of war. Four companies of the U.S. 28th Division, serving with a French division, became stranded and were left behind during the initial retreat from positions along the Marne. Overtaken and surrounded by the enemy, most of the Americans were killed or captured.

Nevertheless, the experience of the German offensives had vindicated General Pershing's strategy of preparation for a new, more fluid phase of the Great War, as men finally rose up from the stagnant trenches and engaged in great offensives in the open.

From the Front

The Allied response to the fifth of Ludendorff's offensives was particularly complex. It can be looked at as a successful defense, as it is here, or as the trigger of a successful Allied counteroffensive, as it is examined in the next chapter.

The Least You Need to Know

➤ With logistical genius, General John J. Pershing and his staff built up the American Expeditionary Force in France, continually resisting Allied efforts to rush green troops into doomed combat.

➤ In January 1918, President Wilson enunciated his sweepingly idealistic war aims in "Fourteen Points," which would become the basis for peace.

➤ With the entry of the United States into the war, and with Russia out of the war, German General Erich Ludendorff shifted his overall strategy from defensive to offensive in an effort to end the war with a decisive blow before American troops arrived in significant numbers.

➤ After a shaky start during the Lys Offensive, U.S. troops quickly proved their fighting will and ability.

Second Marne

The failure of the Champagne-Marne Offensive, the fifth of Erich Ludendorff's great offensives, severely demoralized the German army. German losses were indeed staggering, but for the Allies they were actually even heavier. That they had managed to inflict more casualties than they received brought no encouragement to the Germans. Ludendorff had promised his troops and his government that total victory would result from a powerful offensive. In light of the promise, the failure of *five* offensives seemed that much greater. Worse, the offensives had cost Germany its best soldiers—those trained as shock troops—and they were now being replaced by men from the rear, reservists, and even former prisoners of war returned from Russia. None of these had much fight in them.

Also taking its toll by mid-1918 was the merciless British naval blockade. Ersatz goods could make up for only so many needs. Shortages were now critical. Food supplies for soldiers were meager, and for civilians even worse. When equipment wore out or was destroyed, it became increasingly difficult to replace.

Despite recent losses, with a quarter-million to 300,000 American troops arriving in Europe every month, the Allies were reinvigorated. Defeatism was dissolving into a hunger for victory. Yet four years of war had made the Allies wary of acting too quickly. The leaders who had once advocated such doctrines as "attack to the uttermost" were now willing to put off final victory for another year or more.

Turning Point: The Second Battle of the Marne

On the eve of the German offensives, the European Allies had clamored for the immediate piecemeal deployment of American troops. Pershing resisted. Now that the offensives had been crushed, Allied feelings of urgency gave way to a belief that Pershing had been right. The French and British, somewhat encouraged but overwhelmingly battle-weary, resolved to hold off the final push until the Americans had arrived in their millions. For their part, the British had been sufficiently impressed by the potential of the tank as a weapon capable of overcoming the trench that they also wanted to delay a final push until tanks had been produced in sufficient quantity to make a real impact.

Historical hindsight is always clearer than the vision of those who live the moment. Nowhere is this more true than in the case of war. It seems clear to us, looking back, that the Germans were clearly headed for defeat by July 1918. To most of the French people and government, however, worn down by so much bloodletting and unwilling hosts to a German invasion of four years' duration, the five recent German offensives felt like fresh French defeats. Ludendorff had thrust toward Paris to divert resources from the north, where his intended principal target was the British army. As the French saw it, though, Paris was in real danger of falling. As they had done in August 1914, the government began to make plans for evacuation.

General Ferdinand Foch saw the situation more clearly. He had been holding out, waiting for a maximum American buildup, but now he saw an opportunity he could not afford to miss. He resolved to turn the fifth German offensive into an occasion of Allied counterattack.

> ## CHARGE!!
>
> ### Words of War
>
> A **counteroffensive** is aggressive action in response to an attack, as opposed to merely protective or defensive action.

The Rock of the Marne

The successful defense against the fifth of Ludendorff's offensives, the Champagne-Marne Offensive, also called the Peace Offensive, may be seen as the first phase of the Second Battle of the Marne.

One of the key elements that allowed this Allied defense to be converted into a *counteroffensive* was the action of the U.S. Third Division, in particular the 38th Infantry of that division, which we met briefly in Chapter 24, "New Blood," as the "Rock of the Marne." That this regiment was able to defend a large loop of the river enabled the Third Division to beat back every German thrust. Where the Third Division defended, no German unit made it across the Marne, and this continual repulse ultimately moved General Ludendorff to break off the offensive along the river.

Foch Versus Pétain

The majority of Ferdinand Foch's colleagues did not interpret Ludendorff's withdrawal from the Marne as a German defeat. They interpreted it as a tactical withdrawal, temporary in nature. Foch, however, saw it for what it was: the desperate action of a battered, demoralized enemy. Moreover, on July 17, 1918, Foch further divined that Ludendorff was pulling troops away from the Marne sector, which had threatened Paris, to send them north against the British positions.

In this great transfer of resources, Foch saw an opportunity. He decided that the time was now ripe for an Allied counteroffensive in earnest, and he understood that it must be launched before the Germans could commence their offensive against the British. This was no time to wait for tanks or for more Americans.

Foch rolled the dice. He concentrated his forces around the Marne salient, the bulge of German penetration, and decided to leave the British armies of Douglas Haig exposed before the growing German concentration to the north. The trick was to allow Ludendorff to weaken the Marne sector while Foch built it up, and then to attack before Ludendorff had concentrated enough troops in the north to overwhelm Haig.

Marshal Henri Philippe Pétain strenuously disagreed with his colleague over just how the counterattack should be mounted. The two commanders puzzled over their maps. A salient is a bulge, an outcropping of enemy strength. Expressed in geometric terms, it is a rough arc. Pétain advocated an attack across the chord, or base, of the arc. This would require the transfer and massing of large numbers of Allied troops along the west face of the German salient. Given sufficient time, it was a very sound tactic that could entrap the Germans as in a big sack that was pinched and tied by closing it up along its chord. Driven by what he himself had called in one of his famous military textbooks the "spirit of the offensive," Foch believed that there was no time for movement of troops and that instead the counteroffensive should come not at the chord, but all along the great arc of the salient.

It would be the kind of brute-force frontal assault that the French had tried so often earlier in the war and that had been so disastrously unsuccessful. Pétain was understandably worried.

From the Front

By July 1918, Ludendorff estimated that 200,000 replacements were required each month. By drawing on those about to turn 18 years old, a total of 300,000 recruits were available for the entire current year. German hospitals were returning 70,000 convalescents to the ranks each month.

Voices of Battle

"The will to conquer is the first condition of victory."

—Ferdinand Foch, in *Foch Speaks*, 1929

Combatants

Douglas Haig (1861–1926) was born in Edinburgh to the wealthy family of a distiller. After an Oxford education, he enrolled at Sandhurst, the British army's military academy, from which he graduated at the top of his class in 1885. He served with distinction in India and Egypt, then in the Second (Great) Anglo-Boer War, in which he commanded the 17th Lancers, known as the "Death or Glory Boys."

At the outbreak of World War I, Haig commanded I Corps of the BEF under his former commander, Sir John French. He fought at Mons (August 23, 1914) and the Marne (September 5–9), as well as in Picardy and Artois during the Race to the Sea (October–November). In February 1915, Haig was appointed commander of First Army, and directed a moderately successful major attack at Neuve-Chapelle during March 10–13. During May 9–26, he launched another offensive, in Artois, but was stopped at Festubert. Hitting German positions at Loos during September 26–October 14 resulted in negligible gains and severe losses.

Blame for the disappointing performance of the BEF during the opening months of the war fell not on Haig, but on French. Haig replaced him on December 17, 1915, and immediately set about planning a massive British offensive at the Somme in an effort to relieve pressure on the French at Verdun. The result was punishing both to the Germans and to the BEF, which incurred heavy losses during June 24–November 13, 1916. Nevertheless, Haig was promoted to field marshal at the end of 1916.

Placed under command of French General Robert Georges Nivelle, Haig launched a moderately successful attack at Arras during April 9–15, 1917. Expecting major German offensives in Flanders early in 1918, Haig called for 600,000 reinforcements. He received a mere 100,000 troops, and the German Somme offensive nearly destroyed the British Fifth Army. When German General Erich Ludendorff pressed his second offensive around the Lys River during April 9–17, the British lines nearly dissolved again. Haig rallied his troops, who ultimately halted the German advance, and directed a counterattack at Amiens during August 8–11, which was a breakthrough. Haig directed the last Allied attacks in Flanders from September until the armistice. After the war, he worked tirelessly for the welfare and relief of veterans.

To the north, the British commander, Sir Douglas Haig, was also deeply concerned. The decision to mass against the Germans in the south precisely when it was clear that they were preparing to attack in the north was a gamble of desperate proportions. At stake was nothing less than all the British troops under Haig's command, now vulnerable to a massive attack.

The Allies Strike Back

In the midst of the shifting of German troops from the Marne salient, the major thrust of the Allied counteroffensive began. It was 4:35 on the morning of July 18—one of the war's many predawn sallies "over the top." In the past, such ventures, begun with a mixture of hope and terror, typically ended in death and the tragic fruitlessness of continued stalemate.

This time it would be different.

The French Tenth, Sixth, and Fifth armies, from left to right along the front, made the assault, while the French Ninth Army waited in reserve. The Tenth was commanded by General Charles Marie Emmanuel Mangin. He had been born in 1866 in the village of Sarrebourg, in Lorraine, territory lost to the Germans in the Franco-Prussian War of 1870–1871. He was spoiling for revenge, and he was the kind of soldier equipped to exact it. Boundlessly aggressive and courageous, he had fought before World War I primarily in the colonial service, against rebellious natives. Always leading from the very front of the front, he had been seriously wounded three times during colonial service.

On the Western Front, he was as unsparing of his men as he was of himself. Those outside his command called him "butcher" and "eater of men." Yet his own troops, many of them Africans from his former colonial command, loved him and willingly laid down their lives for him. Mangin himself displayed no fear. He was precisely the kind of general that Foch needed for his brute-force gamble.

Mangin's main attack was preceded by the advance of General Jean M.J. Degoutte's Sixth Army. Degoutte's advance and that of Mangin were coordinated with a rolling artillery barrage. In the past, this tactic, which called for a very brief artillery preparation followed by artillery firing just ahead of the advancing troops, had frequently failed. It was always very difficult to synchronize the rate of the artillery fire with the rate of the infantry's advance. Fire too far ahead of the infantry, and the effect of the barrage would be minimal. Fire too close to the advancing troops, and they would become victims of *friendly fire*.

Words of War

Friendly fire refers to shells or other missiles that inadvertently fall on one's own position or troops.

This time the rolling barrage technique worked perfectly. Moreover, by limiting artillery preparation, Foch had achieved total surprise. In following his gut instinct, he had also timed the attack exquisitely. The German commanders were indeed focused on shifting troops to the north. This had left the salient relatively weakly defended by second-line troops—yet, at the same time, there were hardly sufficient numbers of Germans on their way north to menace the British. Foch had found his moment, and he seized it.

From the Front

A U.S. Army division at this time consisted of 28,000 men and was divided into 2 brigades of 2 infantry regiments and 1 machine-gun battalion each; 1 field artillery brigade of 3 regiments; 1 engineer regiment; and 1 signal battalion.

There was more wrong with the German response. Advancing Allied troops noted that defensive structures—trenches and barbed wire—were poorly constructed or entirely absent. Within the German trench lines, sanitation had broken down: Latrines had not been built, and bodies remained unburied. Clearly, German discipline and morale were disintegrating.

The Yanks Weigh In

The main attack, by Mangin's Tenth Army, was spearheaded not by Frenchmen, but by Americans of the U.S. First and Second divisions. The First Division encountered no fewer than seven German divisions, defeating all of them and taking some 3,800 prisoners as well as 70 guns. The Second Division took 3,000 German prisoners, together with 75 guns.

Other U.S. outfits also fought valiantly, six other divisions in all.

Ludendorff Withdraws

While the French and Americans waded into the German line, Ludendorff, headquartered at Mons, was preparing his final instructions for the assault on the British positions to the north. He was interrupted by the first reports of the Allied counterattack. He reluctantly ordered two of his reserve divisions to respond and then had to order an additional two.

But the news only got worse for Ludendorff. He was forced to order indefinite postponement of the assault on the British; with his rail lines and roads now under attack, Ludendorff had no choice but to order a complete withdrawal from the Marne salient.

Ludendorff began the withdrawal across the Marne on the night of July 18. The French units to the east of the salient were impeded by difficult terrain and could not keep up with the units on the west face of the salient. This allowed the withdrawal of the bulk of the German troops that had occupied the salient. Although German casualties were heavy—including the loss of 30,000 prisoners and some 800 guns—the German armies were intact on August 6, when Marshal Pétain prevailed in his decision to call off the counteroffensive.

It was an understandable decision; despite the success of the counteroffensive, Allied losses had been high. Moreover, the Germans had retreated to their most thoroughly prepared defensive positions. Long and bitter experience had proven the futility of making a frontal assault on these.

Amiens Offensive

Whether Pétain's caution was wise is open to debate; however, Ludendorff interpreted the reluctance to press the counteroffensive as a sign that the action had been an isolated incident. He concluded, hopefully, that there would be no further attacks. Armed with nothing more than his own conclusion, Ludendorff resolved to mount a new offensive.

Ludendorff's rival, the German Crown Prince, known derisively as "Little Willie," responded to the idea of a new offensive by sending a letter to his father, Kaiser Wilhelm II. The war is lost, the letter declared. Let us accept whatever peace terms are dictated. Paul von Hindenburg attempted to mediate the extremes of Ludendorff's and Little Willie's positions. There would be no new German offensive, but the war would go on.

Just before initiating the counteroffensive on the Marne, General Foch had proposed to British General Haig that his armies coordinate an offensive on the southern flank of the German's Lys River salient. Flanders, Haig responded, was awash in mud during August and the early autumn. Mounting an effective offensive under such conditions was suicidal. He proposed instead Anglo-French collaboration in an attack east of Amiens in northwestern France, along the Somme River. The objective was to free up the rail network in the area.

Foch agreed and, in a demonstration of the new spirit of unity of command, placed the French First Army under Haig's direction. Haig, in turn, chose the British Fourth Army, under General Henry Rawlinson, to operate in conjunction with the French First.

Voices of Battle

"Monotonously, the lorries sway, monotonously come the calls, monotonously falls the rain. It falls on our heads and on the heads of the dead up the line, on the body of the little recruit with the wound that is so much too big for his hip; it falls on Kemmerich's grave; it falls in our hearts."

—Erich Maria Remarque, *All Quiet on the Western Front,* 1929

From the Front

The authorized strength of a German infantry division was 9,000 men. At Amiens, German divisions consisted of a mere 3,000 men each. War had taken its toll. U.S. divisions consisted of 28,000 men each.

315

Rawlinson preserved absolute secrecy in concentrating 15 infantry and 3 cavalry divisions along a 14-mile front weakly held by 6 under-strength German divisions. Two thousand guns were massed, together with 17 air squadrons, and almost the entire British tank corps, 604 tanks of all types; however, no artillery preparation preceded the assault. Rawlinson had learned the value of surprise.

A "Black Day" for the German Army

The British advance on August 8 was led by Canadian and *ANZAC* (*Australian-New Zealand Army Corps*) infantry, preceded by tanks, and protected by a thick blanket of fog. On their right, the French assault was preceded by a brief artillery preparation.

Words of War

ANZAC was the acronym for the **Australian–New Zealand Army Corps** and was also used to refer to a member of that corps. More familiarly, ANZAC troops were called "diggers."

The Allies rolled over the Germans, taking more than 15,000 prisoners and capturing 400 guns.

In his memoirs, written after the Armistice, Erich Ludendorff would call August 8 the "Black Day" of the German army. It was to this day that he traced the beginning of his nation's defeat.

Yet still the Germans refused to give up. They re-established a position 10 miles behind what had been the nose of the salient. On August 10, however, the French Third Army, under General Georges Humbert, pushed the Germans out of Montdidier. Yet on the next day, Douglas Haig, in the past all too eager to press the attack almost heedless of cost, now exercised caution. Against Foch's wish that he maintain unremitting pressure on the Germans, Haig paused to regroup his forces.

"The War Must Be Ended"

For Winston Churchill, who had participated in the Amiens Offensive, the sure sign that the German army was falling apart could be read on the faces of the POWs. The captured officers were stoically grim, but the enlisted prisoners smiled with barely contained expressions of relief and even jubilation. For them, the war was over. The concepts of victory and defeat had ceased to have meaning. The only thing that mattered to them was that the war had ended.

The offensive picked up again on August 21, when the British Third Army, on the left, and the French armies, on the right, resumed the attack. On the 22nd, the British Fourth came racing up the center, followed by the British First on the far left. Under this enormous pressure, the German positions crumbled. Ludendorff ordered a withdrawal not only from the Lys salient up in Flanders, but also from Amiens, to the south, in France.

Then the ANZACs struck, advancing across the Somme during August 30–31. They took the German-held village of Péronne and menaced St.-Quentin. Next, a Canadian corps forced its way through the German lines near Quéant on September 2. What had started as an orderly strategic withdrawal for the Germans turned into a full-out retirement, a withdrawal all the way to their last-ditch position: the Hindenburg Line.

As a result of the Amiens Offensive, the Germans suffered casualties numbering in excess of 100,000 killed, wounded, or taken prisoner. Some 22,000 British soldiers and 20,000 French were killed or wounded. It was an unalloyed Allied victory. Great advances had been made—the long Western Front stalemate had been irrevocably ended.

Perhaps even greater was the psychological victory, a source of elation to the Allies and utter misery to the Germans. Even the supremely tenacious Erich Ludendorff now declared, "The war must be ended!"

The Least You Need to Know

➤ Ferdinand Foch, in overall command of Allied troops on the Western Front, turned the bloody but successful defense against Ludendorff's fifth offensive into an Allied counteroffensive, which drove the Germans back from the Marne salient.

➤ Reluctantly, General Pershing had committed some American troops to the defense against Ludendorff; now they spearheaded the counteroffensive at the Second Battle of the Marne.

➤ When Pétain ordered a halt to the counteroffensive, Ludendorff mistakenly assumed that the Allies would break off offensive action. The result of this miscalculation was a stunning defeat at Amiens, after which the Germans retired to their last-ditch defensive works, the Hindenburg Line.

➤ Together, the Second Battle of the Marne and the Amiens Offensive constituted the definitive turning point of the war. Ludendorff would mount no more offensives.

A Million Men and More

America's General John J. Pershing wholeheartedly embraced his government's instructions that the United States Army was to remain a "distinct and independent force" and was not to be put under foreign control. This was not merely a matter of national pride. Pershing, as well as President Woodrow Wilson and Secretary of War Newton Baker, understood that American soldiers would not function well under the command of foreign officers. They were Americans, and they would serve as such.

Furthermore, the mass of the American public had only recently accepted the war and were now, in fact, enthusiastic about it—provided that *American* officers delivered *American* victories. Out of pressing necessity, Pershing had yielded to the extent of allowing certain U.S. regiments and divisions to serve within the British and French armies. The results, especially at the Second Battle of the Marne, were brilliant. By this time, however, Pershing had a force that was ready to take the field as an independent command. On July 27, 1918, he persuaded Marshal Ferdinand Foch to assign the Americans their own sector of the Western Front. Pershing's mission was to reduce the St.-Mihiel salient, which had been thrust into the Allied lines, jutting out to the Meuse River southeast of Verdun, since 1914.

From the Front

"At exactly 1 A.M., the artillery cut loose. It seemed as if all the artillery in France had suddenly opened up. The sky was red with big flashes, the air seemed full of Empire State Expresses, and the explosion of the heavier shells made the ground tremble. It was a wonderful and awe-inspiring sight."

—Lt. Phelps Harding, 306th Infantry Regiment, 77th Division, AEF, describing the opening of the St.-Mihiel offensive, letter to his wife, September 22, 1918

From the Front

Portugal entered the war in March 1916. The Allies requested only labor battalions from the Portuguese government, which insisted on sending combat troops in the form of a 54,000-man expeditionary force to Europe and another 50,000 to colonial Africa.

Against the St.-Mihiel Salient

Reducing the St.-Mihiel salient was an ideal assignment for the still comparatively green American Expeditionary Force. Although it was of great strategic and symbolic importance (as a long-standing German penetration into sacred French soil), the salient had been relatively quiet since the Allies had given up on taking it back in 1915.

The U.S. First Army, with the French II Colonial Corps attached to it, formally took over the sector on August 30. Just as Pershing was about to order the assault to begin, Foch suddenly reneged. From the north, British General Douglas Haig was reporting details of his assessment that the German army was at long last crumbling. Foch now wanted Pershing to divide a large part of the American forces between the French Second and Fourth armies in a grand offensive against the Meuse-Argonne sector. Once again, Pershing stood his ground—albeit with one compromise. The U.S. Army would *first* reduce the St.-Mihiel salient as planned and agreed, and *then,* immediately afterward, would be shifted to attack with the French in the Argonne Forest.

In the meantime, reeling from the Allied counteroffensives on the Marne and east of Amiens (see Chapter 25, "Second Marne"), German General Erich Ludendorff ordered a withdrawal on September 8 from the St.-Mihiel salient. It began on September 11.

Ludendorff's plan was to withdraw to the Hindenburg Line, the highly fortified defensive position that the Germans had designed as a last-ditch, do-or-die insurance against defeat. To withdraw in this way was to yield long-held territory, but it was a move that would also preserve the German army. Pershing was determined to prevent Ludendorff from withdrawing without a fight.

Early on the morning of the 12th, 16 U.S. divisions attacked, supported by French artillery and French tanks, as well as a mixed force of American, French, Italian, and Portuguese pilots flying some 600 planes (out of 1,400 deployed) under the command of U.S. military air pioneer Colonel William "Billy" Mitchell.

The U.S. I and IV corps smashed into the south face of the salient, while the French II Colonial Corps jabbed at the salient's nose and the U.S. V Corps closed in from the west.

Combatants

The only U.S. tank brigade to see action in World War I was led into battle during the St.-Mihiel Offensive by a young temporary lieutenant colonel named George S. Patton, a leader destined to become one of the most famous American commanders of World War II.

Born in California in 1885, Patton graduated from West Point and served with General Pershing during the Punitive Expedition against Pancho Villa in 1916 (see Chapter 20, "'He Kept Us Out of War'"). Pershing chose Patton to accompany him to France as his adjutant and headquarters commandant; however, Patton soon grew restless with this staff job and volunteered for a combat assignment with the fledgling U.S. tank corps. After completing tank training himself, Patton was assigned to create a light-tank training school in France for Americans. Patton created a training program and then recruited and trained two battalions of tank crews.

Patton led his tanks into battle against the St.-Mihiel salient in the fall of 1918, supporting the infantry attack. Although he was enthusiastically praised by the commanders of the units he supported, Patton was reprimanded by his superior, Samuel D. Rockenbach, because he had not taken time to send him sufficient progress reports.

Rockenbach ordered Patton to remain in headquarters henceforth and to direct his operations from there. The instructions failed to sink in. During the Meuse-Argonne Offensive, Patton went over the top with the other doughboys in an infantry assault. Shortly before noon on September 26, he was wounded by machine gun fire, which sidelined him from combat for the remainder of the war. Instead of another reprimand, Patton received the Distinguished Service Cross.

Patton went on to develop the U.S. Army's armored (tank) operations during the early months of World War II and commanded an important desert combat training center in California. He led victorious forces in North Africa and Sicily, and then in the spectacular breakout of the Third Army from the beaches of Normandy; through France, Belgium, and Luxembourg; and into Germany. Patton was fatally injured on December 9, 1945, in a freak automobile accident near Mannheim, Germany. He died on December 21.

The battle raged for 36 hours, but the outcome was never in serious doubt. The Germans had been taken totally by surprise. More than 15,000 surrendered, also delivering to the Americans some 250 guns. U.S. casualties numbered about 7,000 killed and wounded.

The salient was now completely cleared of the enemy. Not only was this a great morale boost for the French, but it also eliminated a long-standing threat to an Allied movement in the Champagne region. Moreover, it demonstrated the complete competence of the American army—a lesson lost on neither friend nor foe. With nearly half a million men involved, it was the largest United States military operation since the Civil War.

American Eagles

On April 6, 1917, the day President Wilson asked Congress to declare war on Germany, the air arm of the United States military consisted of about 200 obsolete planes and 1,200 officers and men. Of these personnel, no more than 60 were fliers—either pilots, observers, or aerial gunners. In 1917, the nation in which the airplane had been born at Kitty Hawk, North Carolina, back in 1903 was virtually a nonstarter in the race to control the skies.

With entry into the war, many Americans entertained romantic fantasies about what they called a "cavalry of the clouds." Even before April 1917, a group of intrepid American fliers had joined the French air corps as the Lafayette Escadrille (see Chapter 19, "Winged Knights"), and their exploits, while of little military significance, thrilled those on the U.S. homefront.

Soon a frenzy for aerial warfare gripped the American popular imagination as ferociously as the rising fever for the war itself. Congress responded. On July 21, 1917, it voted—after less than an hour of debate—$640 million dollars for aviation. At the time, it was the largest appropriation in United States history. With this money, American industry was to build 22,625 airplanes and 44,000 engines (the engines wore out more rapidly than the planes)—all by the end of 1918. As for the American air arm, it was to be expanded from its present virtual nonexistence to 345 combat formations, a force of thousands of men and machines.

Of course, it was delusion on a mass scale. How were all these planes to be produced? Where would all the new pilots come from? There were no answers to these impossible questions. By the end of 1917, United States factories had produced only 529 planes, licensed

From the Front

U.S. aircraft companies managed to produce 7,000 planes during World War I—a stunning achievement given the fact that, in the spring of 1917, there hardly was any American aircraft industry at all—but it fell far short of the 22,625 aircraft called for. Of the 7,000 produced, fewer than 1,200 saw service in Europe—and most of these were used strictly for training purposes.

copies of the ungainly British De Havilland DH-4. The record was better for production of a brand-new American-designed "Liberty engine," 2,390 of which had been turned out by the end of 1917.

Despite the wildly unrealistic expectations and the inevitable bitter disappointments, volunteers poured in for U.S. Army flight training. Eight Schools of Aeronautics were established to teach flight theory to the volunteers. Successful cadets were then assigned to a primary flying field for basic flight training. After this, advanced flight training was carried out, sometimes at U.S. bases but more often overseas in aviation schools staffed by British, Canadian, French, and Italian pilot instructors. The first unit to become operational was the 103rd Aero Squadron, which commenced operations on February 18, 1918, having absorbed fliers from the Lafayette Escadrille and its English equivalent, the British Flying Corps.

The U.S. Air Service gradually built up in Europe, spending most of 1917 through the late spring of 1918 in relatively quiet sectors, gaining valuable flying experience. By July of 1918, the Air Service had reached a high level of competence.

From the Front

On March 11, 1918, Lieutenant Paul F. Baer of the 103rd Aero Squadron scored the nation's first air combat kill of World War I. Baer not only survived the war, but he also became an ace with eight confirmed victories.

Billy Mitchell

Just before the St.-Mihiel offensive, the U.S. Air Service entered the period of its most intensive expansion. William "Billy" Mitchell, son of a United States senator from Wisconsin, got a college education and then enlisted in the First Wisconsin Infantry at the outbreak of the Spanish-American War in 1898. By 1912, he had obtained a coveted assignment to the Army's General Staff, but he relinquished this post in 1915 to transfer to the aviation section of the Signal Corps, which controlled the Army's infant aviation program. After flight school at Newport News, Virginia, Mitchell got his wings in 1916 and, later that year, was sent to Europe to observe air combat in World War I. Thus, Mitchell was already on-site when the United States entered the war in April 1917. He was appointed air officer of the American Expeditionary Force and was promoted to lieutenant colonel in June. In May 1918, he became air officer of I Corps with the rank of colonel and was the first senior U.S. officer to fly over enemy lines.

Mitchell combined great technical, tactical, and organizational skills with a vivid flair for leadership. He commanded a mixed force of Allied pilots and aircraft during the St.-Mihiel offensive, combining ground attack, bombing, and air-to-air combat missions with a force of 1,400 aircraft. It was the largest single concentration of air power in World War I, and it demonstrated just what air support of ground action could do. Following St.-Mihiel, the role of air power in the last six weeks of the war assumed major proportions, with American fliers taking a significant part in the action.

Combatants

After his success during the St.-Mihiel Offensive, William Mitchell (1879–1936) emerged as one of the leading commanders of World War I. Promoted to brigadier general, he was appointed to command the combined air services for the Meuse-Argonne Offensive and led a massive formation of bombers against targets behind enemy lines on October 9.

After the war, in 1919, Mitchell was named Assistant Chief of the Air Service and embarked on a controversial campaign to create a United States Air Force separate and independent from the Army. He went beyond this to advocate unified control of military air power rather than a division of control between the Army and the Navy. Both proposals were stoutly resisted by the military establishment.

The outspoken Mitchell had a volatile temperament, which frequently created friction with those in higher command. In particular, he outraged Navy officials with a boast that the airplane had made the battleship obsolete. To demonstrate this point, in 1921, he bombed the captured German dreadnought *Ostfriesland*, which his planes sank in an astounding 21.5 minutes. As a result of this demonstration, the Navy began development of the aircraft carrier as an offensive weapon—a fact that would prove the salvation of the American cause in the Pacific during World War II.

Mitchell relentlessly campaigned for enlargement of the present Army Air Corps and creation of an independent Air Force. Frustrated superiors caused his demotion to colonel and reduced his command authority. Undaunted, Mitchell took his campaign public, issuing on his own authority many statements to the press, not a few of which were provocative and inflammatory. When the Navy dirigible *Shenandoah* crashed in a thunderstorm on September 3, 1925, Mitchell went to the papers with accusations of War and Navy Department "incompetency, criminal negligence, and almost treasonable administration of the National Defense." In response to these accusations, Mitchell was court-martialed for and convicted of insubordination in December 1925. Sentenced to five years' suspension from duty without pay, he resigned his commission on February 1, 1926, continuing to speak out as a civilian from his Middleburg, Virginia, home until his death a decade later.

Among the visionary Mitchell's predictions was his early, and entirely unheeded, assessment of the Japanese threat to Pearl Harbor. He is considered the founding father of the U.S. Air Force.

Eddie Rickenbacker

Although the 103rd Aero Squadron was the first American air unit to become operational, and although the First Aero Squadron had been the first U.S. unit to arrive in France, it was the 94th Aero Squadron, called the "Hat-in-the-Ring" Squadron, after its distinctive insignia, that would become the most famous of U.S. air units. Its first enemy kill was achieved on March 29, 1918, by the most celebrated member of the Hat-in-the-Ring Squadron, Edward Vernon "Eddie" Rickenbacker, whom we met in Chapter 19.

Rickenbacker was soon put in command of *Flight* One of the 94th Aero Squadron, which found itself pitted against the so-called Flying Circus formed by Manfred von Richthofen, Germany's celebrated Red Baron and the most prolific ace of the war. Richthofen notched 80 confirmed kills before he himself was shot down and killed on April 21, 1918. His crack unit continued to fight on, however, and in encounters with them, Eddie Rickenbacker became an ace after he downed his fifth plane on May 30.

Words of War

A **flight** was the basic tactical unit in the Army Air Service, consisting of at least four aircraft.

Already a national hero as a result of his early success, Rickenbacker scored his most spectacular victory on September 25 when he single-handedly attacked seven enemy planes, shooting down two. For this action, he was awarded the Medal of Honor. Before the war was over, Rickenbacker would become America's top ace, with 26 victories to his credit.

The exploits of the Richthofens and Rickenbackers made headlines and captured the public imagination. Indeed, it was important to dominate the skies over the Western Front battlefields, for the air was the new "high ground" of combat, the perspective from which troop movements were most visible. And so, pilots contested one on one for control of the sky in the aerial duels known as dogfights. Nevertheless, of greater military importance than the duels between aces were ground attack and bombing missions, which could wreak havoc on supposedly "safe" rear-area positions, including headquarters, rail lines, and roads.

Meuse–Argonne Offensive

The St.-Mihiel Offensive was completed in 36 hours, after which Pershing immediately marched the entire U.S. First Army, without rest, 60 miles to the Verdun area to participate in Foch's great Meuse-Argonne Offensive.

Foch had a simple plan. The French and American armies would drive forward from the Verdun region toward Mézières, a key German rail junction and supply depot. While this was underway, the British would attack between Péronne and Lens, with the objective of controlling the rail junction at Aulnoye. Foch was determined not merely to hammer away at enemy troops, but to destroy or control their lifelines along the Western Front. Neutralize the two rail junctions at Mézières and Aulnoye, he reasoned, and the Germans would be cut off from the rear.

Pershing's first achievement was the efficient shifting of the half-million men of the First Army by night, complete with tanks and guns, over poor railroads and even worse roads, to maneuver his troops into position for the attack that would initiate the offensive. This was in a region that straddled the Meuse Valley, taking in the Argonne Forest on the left and the Aire Valley, as well as the heights, on either side of the Meuse River.

Arranging his First Army three corps abreast, Pershing commenced the attack at 5:25 on the morning of September 26. To Pershing's left was the French Fourth Army, which joined in the attack. Opposing the Franco-American force was a German army group under Max von Gallwitz and another commanded by the Crown Prince. In contrast to the sloppy defenses encountered at the Second Battle of the Marne, the German Meuse positions were extremely well-prepared. Three heavily fortified lines were contoured to rugged and heavily wooded terrain, which alone would be sufficient to slow any attacker.

The initial advance was very rapid, but it slowed greatly within the Argonne Forest and before the village of Mountfaucon, to which the Germans had rushed reinforcements. After penetrating the first two German lines, the American drive flagged along the line between Apremont and Brieulles by October 3.

From the Front

The phrase "Lost Battalion" was coined by a magazine journalist, and it caught on. Actually, more than a single battalion was involved in the incident—a machine gun battalion plus other units of the 77th Division—and these units were not "lost," but cut off from the main part of the division. Nevertheless, the episode is extraordinary.

The Lost Battalion

World War I was a war with many heroics but few individually celebrated heroes. One episode the press did seize on, however, was the ordeal of the so-called Lost Battalion.

During the assault on the Argonne Forest, the 77th Division had fought for seven days without rest until, on October 2, it came to a standstill before the heavily defended Ravine de Charlevaux. With great difficulty, the First and Second Battalions of the 308th Infantry and elements of the 306th Machine Gun Battalion advanced into the ravine and, under heavy machine-gun fire, made it across the ravine floor and partway up the slope. The troops established a position about 300 yards long and 60 yards deep on a steep, rocky hillside encumbered with thick undergrowth. Runners communicated with the American rear, but this line of communication was soon severed.

As night fell in the thick woods, German voices were heard on the left, and glimpses of German soldiers were seen. Cut off from the main body of the 77th Division, Major Charles W. Whittlesey, commanding this advance force, deployed his 550 men in a square, with his nine machine guns on the flanks, where they could sweep the valley.

Throughout the night, the enemy voices grew louder. Suddenly, the Americans were subjected to a rain of hand grenades. After this fierce assault there was a pause, during which Whittlesey ordered a counterattack. This fended off another grenade attack, but soon, the Germans opened up with their machine guns.

Whittlesey and his 550 men were besieged. Whittlesey sent out small patrols to probe for weak spots, and he dispatched runners to try to renew communications with the rear. It was to no avail, and these forays served only to reduce the already small number of defenders.

The troops had carried few rations with them, anticipating no problems with supply. Now the food was running low. None of the men had overcoats or blankets. Ammunition was also dwindling. There was no doctor to treat the wounded, and first aid supplies were so scarce that the medics removed bandages from the dead to reuse them on the wounded. When the water ran out, men began to venture down to the bottom of the ravine to fill their canteens at the stream. But the Germans had trained their machine guns on this area and opened fire against the thirsty. Whittlesey issued orders forbidding anyone to venture to the stream.

Continually under German fire, the "Lost Battalion" experienced a new horror on October 4 as a barrage of friendly artillery fire came down on the men.

Words of War

A **carrier pigeon** is a bird trained to carry messages in a small capsule fastened to the bird's foot.

World War I combined the latest developments in technology—tanks, aircraft, and radio—with some of the most primitive techniques of war: the trench and the horse-drawn wagon. Now, in desperation, Whittlesey turned to the primitive. For centuries, armies had used trained *carrier pigeons* to send messages from point to point. The major released the last carrier pigeon his unit had, a bird named Cher Ami, with a message giving their position and telling the artillery to cease firing.

Incredibly, Cher Ami made it through the barrage. The shelling stopped—then was resumed, this time falling where it was supposed to: on the Germans.

The ordeal of the Lost Battalion stretched into six days. Allied planes attempted to drop supplies, but these always fell too far beyond the American position and went straight into enemy hands. As the days and nights crawled by, the Germans shouted phony commands in English in an effort to deceive the defenders into showing themselves. These attempts failed, and the shouting back and forth soon degenerated into curses and insults punctuated by machine gun and rifle fire.

From the Front

Of the original 550 men of the "Lost Battalion," 194 walked out with their major. Another 199 had been wounded, and 111 had been killed. The unit had endured 104 hours under fire, without food or medical attention.

On October 7, the Germans abruptly ceased fire. Through an afternoon gone suddenly silent, an American private bearing a white flag stumbled toward the Lost Battalion's position. He told his commanding officer that he had been captured when he went out to retrieve one of the food baskets dropped by an airplane. The private delivered a message from the German commander to Whittlesey, appealing in "the name of humanity" for his surrender. Later, the press circulated a story that Whittlesey indignantly replied with a three-word sentence: "Go to hell." In fact, he made no reply—nor did he send back the message bearer, who was thus saved from incarceration in a POW camp.

With nightfall, the German assault resumed, but by 7 P.M. elements of other American units began to arrive. Soon the position was generally reinforced, the Germans were forced out, and Whittlesey was allowed to withdraw.

An American Hero: Sergeant York

American action in the Argonne Forest produced another remarkable story, that of Alvin C. York. York was a Tennessee backwoodsman who had been a hard-drinking hell-raiser in his early youth, but he had then allowed himself to be converted to the Church of Christ in Christian Union, a conservative congregation fundamentally opposed to drinking—and to war. York petitioned his draft board for deferment on religious grounds as a conscientious objector, but he was refused.

Inducted, York demonstrated extraordinary skill as a marksman during basic training. It was no surprise because York had long hunted wild turkey in the Tennessee hills. Officers in the 82nd Division were eager for the talented York to serve wholeheartedly, and they succeeded in persuading him that the United States was engaged in nothing less than a holy war.

At the height of the confused fighting in the thick Argonne Forest, York and his patrol, like the Lost Battalion, found themselves cut off and under fire behind the enemy lines. York's company had been ordered to take a position called Hill 240, one of three hills dominating a valley. From the ridge of these hills, German machine gunners raked the American troops.

"I could see my pals getting picked off until it almost looked like there was none left," York later recounted.

York was sent with a detachment of 16 men and a sergeant to outflank the machine gunners. This they did, barging into the small headquarters of the German machine gun battalion. The Germans, surprised while at breakfast, instantly surrendered. But then the machine gunners on another hill shouted something, the prisoners instantly dropped to the ground, and a burst of machine gun fire killed a half-dozen men of York's detachment.

York himself was left out in the open.

"There wasn't any tree for me, so I just sat in the mud and used my rifle, shooting at the machine gunners," he said.

To the former pacifist York, it was much like a familiar backwoods turkey shoot: "Every time one of them raised his head, I just tetched him off."

A squad of a half-dozen Germans charged York's position, but the Tennessean calmly "tetched" each of them off before any had run 30 feet. Drawing on instinct, he fired on the line of troops from rear to front so that they wouldn't run for cover at the sight of a man falling in front of them.

York had killed perhaps 20 Germans, while all the time shouting for them to surrender. At last, an English-speaking major offered to do just that if York would stop killing his men.

York and the seven other surviving members of his detachment marched out with 132 prisoners. For this, the backwoodsman received the Medal of Honor, the French Croix de Guerre, and a one-step promotion from private first class to sergeant.

Argonne Under Control

By October 4, no room was available for maneuver through the dense Argonne. Pershing now had no choice but to pour men into a costly series of dead-on frontal assaults. It took until the end of October for Pershing to penetrate through most of the third—and final—German line of defense. During this time, French Premier Georges Clemenceau grew so impatient that he moved to have Pershing relieved of command. Marshal Foch, however, was

Voices of Battle

"What you did was the greatest thing accomplished by any private soldier of all the armies of Europe."

—Marshal Ferdinand Foch to Alvin C. York, as he personally decorated him with the Croix de Guerre

From the Front

Alvin York became a national hero and, on his return to the United States in 1919, was given a tumultuous welcome. New Yorkers even renamed the uptown stretch of Avenue A as York Avenue in his honor. Lucrative offers poured down on him from all quarters. The unassuming York turned most of these down, except for a few propositions that raised money for education and other public services in the Tennessee hills to which he returned.

at the front, and he understood what Pershing was up against in the Argonne. He also saw clearly that the Germans were throwing everything they had against him, rapidly exhausting all their reserves. In terms of geography, Pershing may have been moving slowly, but he was using up the German army in the process. Foch refused to support Clemenceau's bid to remove the American general.

The first 11 days in November culminating in the Armistice saw the U.S. Army racing, now in the open, through the last German positions in the Meuse Valley. The U.S. First Division was about to take Sedan on November 6 when higher command ordered a halt. The honor of conquering that city, it was decreed, must be French. Only this would blot out the stain that had endured since the humiliating defeat at this place during the Franco-Prussian War in 1870.

On November 10, the U.S. Second Army, under General Robert Lee Bullard, launched an attack in its drive toward the village of Montmédy, only to break off the next day at 11 A.M. sharp—the hour of Armistice, the end of the Great War.

The Least You Need to Know

➤ General Pershing persuaded Marshal Foch to assign independent control of the St.-Mihiel sector to the U.S. Army.

➤ American forces cleared out the St.-Mihiel salient, which had endured since 1914, in 36 hours.

➤ In support of the St.-Mihiel Offensive, U.S. Colonel Billy Mitchell commanded the greatest air operation of the war, using a force of some 1,400 planes.

➤ American forces played a key role in the highly successful Meuse-Argonne Offensive, aimed at severing German rail and supply lines.

➤ Combat in the Argonne Forest produced two American legends—the "Lost Battalion" and Sergeant Alvin C. York.

Chapter 27

Eleventh Hour, Eleventh Day, Eleventh Month

> ## In This Chapter
>
> ➤ The assault on the Hindenburg Line
>
> ➤ Germany calls for an armistice
>
> ➤ President Wilson's hard line
>
> ➤ Ludendorff resigns, the kaiser abdicates
>
> ➤ Amid defeat and revolution, Germany surrenders
>
> ➤ The price of war

The level of Allied elation had been high at the start of the Meuse-Argonne Offensive. This was largely thanks to the actions of the Americans. Immediately after reducing the St.-Mihiel salient, they moved against the Argonne area. The Germans, exhausted both by recent events and by four years of mostly stalemated war, were dumbfounded. The five weak trench divisions manning the forward positions were overwhelmed on the very first day of the offensive by an American force four to eight times their number.

But the initial Allied jubilation soon faded as the American advance became bogged down in the Argonne Forest as Pershing's troops faced relentless German resistance, difficult terrain, and a lack of proper rail lines and roads to bring up supplies. American military engineers labored under heavy enemy fire to cut divisional roadways. Georges Clemenceau saw the slowdown as a failure of American command and called for Pershing's dismissal, but Marshal Foch understood that, although forward momentum had been stalled, the German army was suffering nonetheless.

Perhaps the more serious problem during that hellish October in what had once been a beautiful French forest was disillusion. Everything had gone so well at first that the

Allies suddenly saw visions of early victory. It was like a mirage of oasis to long benighted desert wanderers. And when that mirage dimmed and faded away, the first reaction was heartbreak followed by anger.

While most eyes were concentrated on the Americans and French in the bloody Argonne, the British began their offensive to the north, in Flanders.

Storming the Hindenburg Line

At the beginning of the war, the French battle doctrine of "offense to the uttermost" left little provision for defense. The result was that the Germans came within 30 miles of Paris in the first month of combat. From the beginning, however, German battle doctrine included a major defensive component, the most elaborate manifestation of which was the Hindenburg Line, discussed in Chapter 21, "Allies Imperiled." Unspeakably bitter experience had proved to the Allies that a relatively small number of troops could hold a well-entrenched, well-fortified position against vastly superior numbers. Battered and beaten as the Germans were in the autumn of 1918, they still had more than enough troops to inflict terrible casualties on any who dared to assault the Hindenburg Line. But unless that line was breached, the war would not end—at least, not anytime soon.

The Flanders Offensive

One of the greatest dividends of the Allies' Amiens Offensive (see Chapter 25, "Second Marne") was the capture of a complete and detailed plan of the Hindenburg Line. With this document, General Douglas Haig had precise knowledge of the locations of all defensive positions along the German Fourth Army front.

Voices of Battle

"They fought with terror, running blindly in the gas cloud .... Hundreds of them fell and died; others lay helpless, froth upon their agonized lips and their racked bodies powerfully sick."

—An unidentified British officer describing death by poison gas

Haig eagerly anticipated making a decisive, war-ending break through the Hindenburg Line. On the evening of September 26, 1918, he ordered a massive artillery barrage, which, thanks to the captured plans, was precisely pinpointed on such key targets as headquarters, artillery positions, and troop shelters. The British had developed a new, more concentrated form of mustard gas—the weapon the Germans had first unleashed in July 1917—which killed by burning out the lining of the throat and lungs. In heavy barrages, they laid down tons upon tons of the new agent.

On September 27, the British infantry of the First and Third armies went over the top and quickly captured the area around Cambrai, including Bourlon Woods, long a concentration of German strength. On the 28th, a combined force of British, French, and Belgian troops advanced through Flanders, taking the area in front of battered Ypres. On the 29th, the British Fourth Army, with French units in support, breached the Hindenburg Line.

The Hindenburg Line had achieved an almost legendary status during the late phase of the war. There was a feeling—entirely irrational—that finally to breach the line would be to break an evil spell and suddenly end the war.

No such thing happened. Haig was dismayed to see that his costly victory did not force the Germans out into the open. By October 5, the British attacks had succeeded in driving through the last of the Hindenburg Line positions, yet the Germans kept finding new positions to which to withdraw. Try as he might, Haig could not achieve a definite breakthrough. Just as Pershing's advance slowed in the Argonne Forest, so Haig's momentum now flagged in Flanders.

Advance to the Sambre and the Scheldt

If the Allies were discouraged, it was only because victory had not come miraculously and suddenly. For his part, Erich Ludendorff understood that Germany was defeated. Yet he found reason to fight on. His hope was to establish a new defensive line, still west of the German border, and carry out a grimly determined defense through the winter, which would compel the war-weary Allies to grant generous peace terms.

But the Allies were in no mood to grant terms. Discouragement at the failure of a miracle was only temporary. They realized now that they would win. Although Foch, Haig, and Pershing had often disagreed, they were now in agreement on one unshakable principle: They would maintain unremitting pressure on all sectors of the receding Western Front. Although geographical progress in the Argonne Forest was painfully slow, it was clear by mid October that Ludendorff was retreating because of American pressure there.

The Allies pursued. On October 17, General Sir Henry Rawlinson led his British Fourth Army against German defenses at the Selle River and broke through them. On October 20, General Julian Byng's British Third Army crossed that river at a point farther south. The German army group commanded by General Max von Boehn fell back toward the Sambre River, some 50 miles east of his original position, while Crown Prince Rupprecht's army group was pushed toward the Schelde River, about 40 miles east of the line held before the offensive. Boehn lost 20,000 men as prisoners of war, and still the British and Belgians kept coming, giving the Germans no time to reform new lines of defense.

The Germans Fold

With the advances through the Argonne Forest and in Flanders slowing, the Allies did not realize just how close victory was.

Even as the German armies grimly fought on, Erich Ludendorff advised Kaiser Wilhelm II on September 29 to seek an immediate armistice. He was reacting not only to

Words of War

In the imperial German government, the **chancellor** was appointed directly by the kaiser and was, in effect, prime minister, the highest civilian official in the government.

the situation on the Western Front, but also to the collapse of Bulgaria (see Chapter 23, "The War Beyond the Trenches, 1917–1918").

The kaiser agreed and appointed as *chancellor* of Germany Prince Max of Baden, a man with an international reputation for liberal moderation and general decency. The kaiser hoped that Max's appointment would encourage the Allies to negotiate in good faith and grant Germany generous terms.

Prince Max accepted the appointment, but he advised the kaiser to move more slowly to provide time for negotiation. Wilhelm II—this time with the backing of the military high command—directed Max to proceed immediately.

A Message from Prince Max

It is revelatory that, of the three major Allied leaders, Prince Max chose to communicate not with Lloyd George of Britain or Clemenceau of France, but with Wilson of the United States. On October 6, he cabled President Wilson asking for an armistice on the basis of Wilson's own Fourteen Points (see Chapter 24, "New Blood").

In the past, Wilson had shown himself to be the most reasonable and conciliatory of the Allied leaders, but if Max had expected a quick and easy affirmative reply to his request for an armistice, he was sorely mistaken. The prince and the president exchanged notes over the next two weeks. Wilson's final note was received in Berlin on October 23. Essentially, it proposed nothing short of Germany's complete and unconditional surrender as the only possible basis for an armistice; moreover, Wilson declared that neither the United States nor the other Allies would negotiate with what he called the present German military dictatorship.

End of a Dictator

Since 1917, Erich Ludendorff had been virtual dictator of Germany. It was he who had pushed through and endorsed the navy's demands for unrestricted submarine warfare, and it was he who had engineered the dismissal of Chancellor Theobald von Bethmann Hollweg, who had made overtures of peace to Woodrow Wilson. In one of his most brilliant diplomatic moves of 1917, Ludendorff had approved a plan to give Lenin safe passage from Swiss exile so that he might lead the Bolsheviks in a revolution that would bring about in Russia sufficient chaos to take that nation out of the war.

Ludendorff always presented himself as the epitome of the stern and aloof Prussian officer. In fact, he was a highly emotional, even mercurial man, given to extremes of optimism and pessimism bordering on deep depression. Depressed after the fall of

Bulgaria, he had rushed to urge the kaiser to seek an armistice. When Wilson replied with terms that amounted to a demand for unconditional surrender—and the end of military dictatorship—Ludendorff swiftly reversed himself. He now counseled the kaiser to reject any armistice based on unconditional surrender. Wilhelm rejected this counsel, and Ludendorff offered to resign. The kaiser accepted his resignation on October 26, effective on the 27th. One of Wilson's key conditions had now been met.

Combatants

With Paul von Hindenburg, Erich Ludendorff (1865–1937) was the architect of German victory on the Eastern Front. Educated in the Cadet Corps and commissioned as an infantry officer in 1883, Ludendorff focused his entire being on the military, to the exclusion of all else, including diplomacy. He joined the German General Staff in 1895 and played key roles in planning for war and mobilization. His incessant calls for dramatic increases in military spending irritated superiors in the military as well as in the civilian government, and he was dismissed from his staff post to command of a regiment and, later, a brigade.

As seen in Chapter 5, "Battle of the Frontiers," Ludendorff rose to greatness in the capture of Liège in 1914 and then served as Hindenburg's chief of staff on the Eastern Front. Based on his success there, Kaiser Wilhelm II appointed Hindenburg and Ludendorff to replace Erich von Falkenhayn in August 1916, after the failure of the Verdun Offensive (see Chapter 16, "'They Shall Not Pass!'"). Officially, Ludendorff was second in command to Hindenburg, but he became the de facto generalissimo of the German forces and the virtual dictator of the German government.

After his resignation on October 26–27, 1918, Ludendorff fled to Sweden to avoid the dangers of revolution-torn postwar Germany. He returned to Germany in 1919 and threw himself into radical right-wing politics driven by a fanatical belief in the destiny of the "Nordic race." He supported Adolf Hitler's 1923 bid for power—the Beer Hall Putsch—and in 1925 ran unsuccessfully against his former comrade-in-arms, Paul von Hindenburg, for the office of German president.

Toward the end of his life, during the mid-1930s, Ludendorff turned against Hitler and Nazism. Shortly before his death, he issued public warnings to his countrymen against the tyranny of Der Führer. These were, of course, too little too late.

A German Revolution

The kaiser's appointment of Prince Max of Baden was intended not only to impress the Allies with the sincerity of his desire to negotiate peace in good faith, but also to quell the growing discontent with the military dictatorship at home. But the fact was that Kaiser Wilhelm II was not willing to do what the Allies most wanted: abdicate the throne in favor of one of his grandsons. The kaiser's refusal to step down tied Prince Max's hands, and Germany found itself in the worst of all possible worlds. The kaiser wanted an armistice but refused to make the sacrifice necessary to obtain it. At the same time, the very fact that he wanted the armistice sapped the fight out of the German soldiers at the front. Nobody wanted to die in a lost cause. Finally, the combination of stubborn resistance and defeatism destabilized the German government. The nation, like Russia before it, drifted toward revolution.

The first stirrings of revolt had come as early as August 2, 1917, with a mutiny on board the battleship *Prinzregent Luitpold*. This was the first in a series of mutinies among sailors of the German surface fleet. Because it was bottled up in its home ports, the surface fleet received few supplies, and its sailors had almost nothing to do. Discontent festered amid fantastic rumors that the kaiser was planning personally to lead the navy in a final desperate offensive. The mutinies sparked a revolutionary movement onshore. At the end of October 1918, sailors stationed at Kiel mutinied rather than obey orders to put to sea. This act inspired the formation of revolutionary councils on the model of the Russian communist soviets, and by early November, more port towns saw mutinies. The rebellion spread inland among the civilian population.

From the Front

The Dutch government refused to extradite Wilhelm II, whom the Allies wanted to try as a war criminal. He remained in Dutch exile until his death at the threshold of World War II, on June 4, 1941. From a distance, he was cheered by the rebirth of German nationalism and might under Adolf Hitler.

On November 7, after Austria-Hungary capitulated to the Allies, Bavarian revolutionaries followed the Independent Socialist Party leader Kurt Eisner in declaring the overthrow of the monarchy and the creation of the Bavarian People's Republic. In response to this, Friedrich Ebert, leader of Germany's majority Social Democrat Party, prevailed on Prince Max to persuade the kaiser to abdicate, lest Germany become a communist state.

Wilhelm II continued to resist. But matters were entirely out of his hands now. Without consulting the kaiser further, Prince Max simply announced his abdication on November 9. When Wilhelm turned to Paul von Hindenburg for help, the general replied that the army would no longer support him. At this, Wilhelm II fled to the Netherlands (November 10), which had managed to remain neutral throughout the war.

With the kaiser deposed, Prince Max of Baden handed the government over to Friedrich Ebert, who delayed a decision on creating a German republic. Fearing that the communists would exploit any hesitation, Ebert's colleague, Philip Scheidemann, seized the moment. At two o'clock on the afternoon of November 9, he stepped out onto a balcony of the *Reichstag* and proclaimed to the crowd that had gathered below the creation of a German republic. In the blink of an eye, Germany had undergone a revolution.

A Railway Coach at Compiègne

With the resignation of Ludendorff, President Wilson approached the other Allies with a proposal that an armistice be concluded and peace negotiations begin. The Allies agreed in principle, but with two reservations. They would not agree to the second of the Fourteen Points, concerning freedom of the seas, and they would not renounce war *reparations*. Instead, they demanded "compensation … for damage done to the civilian population … and their property by the aggression of Germany." On November 5, Wilson dutifully informed Prince Max of these reservations. He went on to inform Max that Marshal Foch would communicate armistice terms to Germany's accredited representatives.

On November 8, the representatives, a delegation led by Matthias Erzberger, a civilian politician, arrived at Rethondes, in the Forest of Compiègne. There they boarded the railway carriage that served Foch as his traveling headquarters.

Words of War

The **Reichstag** is the German parliament.

Words of War

Reparations means compensation (usually monetary) required from a defeated nation as a condition of peace.

The Long Talk

Face to face with the enemy, Foch unflinchingly presented the Allies' terms for an armistice:

➤ Germany would immediately evacuate Belgium, France, and Alsace-Lorraine.

➤ Additionally, Germany would evacuate the west bank of the Rhine.

➤ Germany would demilitarize and neutralize the east bank of the Rhine between the Netherlands and Switzerland.

➤ German troops in East Africa—still fighting under the remarkable General Lettow-Vorbeck (see Chapter 11, "A *World* War")—were to surrender immediately.

337

➤ German armies in eastern Europe would withdraw to the prewar German frontier.

➤ The treaties of Brest-Litovsk and Bucharest, by which Russia and Romania ceded large territories to Germany, would be annulled.

➤ Germany would repatriate all prisoners of war.

➤ Germany would hand over to the Allies a large quantity of war materiel, including 5,000 pieces of artillery, 25,000 machine guns, 1,700 aircraft, 5,000 locomotives, and 150,000 railroad cars.

➤ Germany would acknowledge the right of the Allies to maintain its stranglehold naval blockade until a definitive treaty of peace was concluded.

Over the next few days within the confines of the sidetracked railway carriage, the parties debated, argued, and negotiated.

The German delegation pointed out that they and the Allies had a common enemy in the Bolsheviks. With Germany on the verge of collapse, there was a very real danger that communism would swallow it up, as it had Russia. This argument was sufficiently persuasive to move the Allies to agree to the following:

➤ The blockade might be relaxed to some degree.

➤ The quantity of armaments to be relinquished would be somewhat reduced in the interest of preserving the integrity of the new republic.

➤ German forces in Eastern Europe could remain in place for the time being—again to forestall an aggressive move from Russia.

Given the Allies' fear of a worldwide Bolshevik revolution, it is quite probable that the German negotiators could have obtained additional mitigation of the harshly punitive armistice terms. But they felt that time was against them. The revolution at home created a volatile situation—besides, Foch, Pershing, and Haig refused to let up on their offensive operations. Erzberger and the others feared a new massive blow on the Western Front, which not only would kill more German soldiers but also would open Germany to an out-and-out invasion. If Germany were frankly invaded, conquered, and humiliated, there would be room for no concessions at all.

Darkness Before Dawn

The fact was that although the Allied advance was relentless, it had not succeeded in destroying the German army, which continued in orderly retreat ahead of the Allied forces. Moreover, German troops had destroyed the roads and railways they left behind, which greatly impeded the progress of the advancing Allies.

Grimly, the Allied commanders began to plan a massive offensive set for November 14. It was intended to be the death blow of Germany. Foch would wield a combined

Franco-American force of 28 divisions with 600 tanks, poised to advance through Metz into north-eastern Lorraine. The ongoing offensive had eaten up all of the German army's reserves, which meant that a new offensive directed against the army's exposed left flank would very likely roll up the new German defenses running from Antwerp to the line of the Meuse River and would also cut off any possibility of retreat. Truly, this time, the German army would be destroyed.

And there was more. Waiting in the wings were additional American forces, with more arriving continually. Forty-two U.S. divisions, each 28,000 men strong, were now in France. The British were preparing a massive formation of heavy bombers to attack Berlin—hitherto untouched by the war, save for the dire shortages caused by the British blockade.

Pressed, then, the German delegation took what it could and, at five o'clock on the morning of November 11, 1918, wearily signed the Armistice.

All Quiet

The ceasefire was set for 11 A.M.—the eleventh hour of the eleventh day of the eleventh month—and the Allied generals saw to it that the fighting continued right up to the minute. After that, all was quiet on the Western Front.

Butcher's Bill

During the worst of the great plague that swept Europe in the Dark Ages—the Black Death—officials in London posted a list of each day's dead. Londoners called this list the "Butcher's Bill."

The following is the "Butcher's Bill" for World War I.

Voices of Battle

"We got the good news that hostilities had ceased. It was too good to believe. During the afternoon, Percy Boyce and me had a walk across to the Belgium border on the Mons Road. Went into the cathedral. Coming back we helped a couple of civilians back with their load."

—Private Charles Bottomley, Heavy Artillery, Canadian Corps, diary entry for November 11, 1918

From the Front

The war cost the neutral nations at least $1.75 billion in defense expenditures, property losses, and merchant shipping losses. However, many of the neutrals also profited from trade with Allies and the Central Powers.

The Allies

Nation	Mobilized Strength	Battle Deaths	Wounded	Cost in Millions of Dollars
France	8,410,000	1,357,800	4,266,000	49,877
British Empire	8,904,467	908,371	2,090,212	51,975
Russia	12,000,000	1,700,000	4,950,000	25,600
Italy	5,615,000	462,391	953,886	18,143
United States	4,355,000	50,585	205,690	32,320
Belgium	267,000	13,715	44,686	10,195
Serbia	707,343	45,000	133,148	2,400
Montenegro	50,000	3,000	10,000	NA
Romania	750,000	335,706	120,000	2,601
Greece	230,000	5,000	21,000	556
Portugal	100,000	7,222	13,751	NA
Japan	800,000	300	907	NA
Totals	**42,188,810**	**4,888,891**	**12,809,280**	**193,899**

The Central Powers

Nation	Mobilized Strength	Battle Deaths	Wounded	Cost in Millions of Dollars
Germany	11,000,000	1,808,546	4,247,143	58,072
Austria-Hungary	7,800,000	922,500	3,620,000	23,706
Turkey	2,850,000	325,000	400,000	3,445
Bulgaria	1,200,000	75,844	152,390	1,015
Totals	**22,850,000**	**3,131,889**	**8,419,533**	**86,238**
Grand totals	**65,038,810**	**8,020,780**	**21,228,813**	**280,137**

The war claimed many civilian casualties as well. Figures are available for the following Allies:

Nation	War-Related Civilian Deaths
France	40,000
British Empire	30,633
Russia	2,000,000
Belgium	30,000
Serbia	650,000

Nation	War-Related Civilian Deaths
Romania	275,000
Greece	132,000
Total	**3,157,633**

Civilian losses for the Central Powers have been estimated as follows:

Nation	War-Related Civilian Deaths
Germany	760,000
Austria-Hungary	300,000
Turkey	2,150,000 (includes Armenian victims of massacre)
Bulgaria	275,000
Total	**3,485,000**

Reduced to tables, the numbers defy comprehension. In reading these figures, we must struggle to bear in mind and heart that behind each digit was a human being, someone's child, someone's lover, someone's husband or wife, someone's father or mother.

The Least You Need to Know

➤ A massive, grueling assault on the Hindenburg Line, the German army's planned last-ditch defensive position, was the culmination of Allied military operations.

➤ The combination of military defeat and a swelling revolution at home drove the German government to call for an armistice.

➤ Effectively as preconditions of armistice, Erich Ludendorff, generalissimo and virtual dictator of Germany, was forced to resign, and Kaiser Wilhelm II was forced to abdicate.

➤ The Allies dictated harsh armistice terms, which Germany managed to mitigate somewhat by playing on fears of worldwide Bolshevik revolution.

➤ World War I ended at 11 A.M. on November 11, 1918.

Part 6

Lost Generations

After the Armistice, the Allies gathered in Paris to hammer out the document that became the Treaty of Versailles. The intensely idealistic Woodrow Wilson spearheaded the creation of a League of Nations, an international forum intended to render future wars unnecessary, if not illegal. However, the other Allied leaders were bent solely on punishing Germany and avenging all that it had done. The result was a tragic document so punitive that it virtually ensured a renewal of war in the future.

We conclude with a chapter on the social and cultural impact of America's experience of the war, the nation's simultaneous retreat into isolationism and emergence as a world power, its venture into social upheaval and renewal, and its withdrawal into a nearly mindless political conservatism.

Treaty of Versailles

Terms:
Germany
gets
Screwed.

Chapter 28

The Tragedy of Versailles

In This Chapter

➤ The last of the fighting stops

➤ Demobilization and the creation of the *Freikorps*

➤ The Allies hammer out the punitive Treaty of Versailles

➤ Wilson orchestrates the League of Nations

➤ The U.S. Senate repudiates both the Treaty and the League

With the scratching of pens in a railway car on an obscure siding in France, the Great War ended. At least, the shooting stopped.

Within this very railway car were sown the seeds of a new war, even more terrible. The German military and the Germans who favored the military would never forget that Matthias Erzberger, their nation's chief negotiator of the Armistice, was a civilian. Soon, right-wing German leaders and would-be leaders (Erich Ludendorff and Adolf Hitler among them) began to call the Armistice a "stab in the back" (in German, *Dolchstoss im Rücken*). They claimed that the German army, "undefeated in the field," had been betrayed in the hour of its greatest need. Much as French militarists had looked on World War I at its outbreak as an opportunity to avenge the humiliating defeats of the Franco-Prussian War, so German militarists would drag their people and the peoples of the world into a second great war to avenge this perceived betrayal.

In this chapter, we will see that, harsh as the Armistice was, the Treaty of Versailles that followed it punished Germany even more severely, creating the general German sense of humiliation and hopelessness that ensured a following for those who proposed the all-consuming program of conquest and vengeance that was the *second* world war.

After the Armistice

On the Western Front, hostilities continued to within minutes of the 11 A.M. Armistice deadline. In remote areas of the front, scattered fighting continued past the eleventh hour, until word of the Armistice reached all corners.

From the Front

Scattered fighting also persisted after the official hour of Armistice as individual officers and men vied for the "honor" of firing the last shot of the war.

Word of the Armistice was slow to reach Germany's East African colonies, where General Paul von Lettow-Vorbeck continued to skirmish with British troops in northern Rhodesia until November 13, when British General Louis van Deventer sent Lettow-Vorbeck a message informing him of the Armistice. The British commander's message announced that he had ordered a ceasefire and that he expected Lettow-Vorbeck to do the same. General Deventer did not bother to say which side had won the war. Lettow-Vorbeck complied immediately and then formally surrendered in a ceremony on November 25. His was the last German force to lay down its arms in World War I. The British officers present rushed to congratulate Lettow-Vorbeck on the brilliant campaign that he had waged against them since 1914.

German Evacuation

In Europe, 17 German armies, about 3 million men, immediately began the retreat specified in the final Armistice document: Belgium, France, Alsace-Lorraine, and Luxembourg were evacuated, and the troops withdrew to points 20 miles east of the Rhine.

German arms were not merely laid down, but turned over to the Allies. All the U-boats, 5,000 trucks, 2,000 planes, 150,000 rail cars, and rail lines in the formerly occupied areas were surrendered. On what had been the Eastern Front, all troops and German agents were withdrawn from Russia, Austria-Hungary, Romania, and Turkey. The Baltic was thrown open to Allied shipping, and the Black Sea ports were evacuated. The Russian fleet, which Germany had seized pursuant to the Treaty of Brest-Litovsk, was turned over to the Allies.

Words of War

Demobilization is the process by which a nation disbands a military force, typically after the end of a war.

Still maintaining the discipline of an army, the soldiers of Germany returned to their home soil—then *demobilized*, shedding uniforms and weapons.

This did not mean that all Germans were now unarmed. Although the official Imperial Army had largely ceased to exist, many of its discharged officers and veterans banded together in "irregular" forces. These groups were known by many names, but collectively they were called the *Freikorps,* the Free Corps. Their purpose was to fight the Bolshevism that rolled over Germany like a great red wave in the aftermath of the war. Through the 1920s, the *Freikorps* succeeded in this task by waging a brutal series of street battles and thereby secured the grudging support of the fledgling German Republic, while forming the nucleus of what, under Adolf Hitler, would become a new German army to enforce a new German ideology.

The End of the High Seas Fleet

On November 21, 1918, the once proud German High Seas Fleet of 74 vessels surrendered and was interned at Scapa Flow, the remote British anchorage at the tip of Scotland. Skeleton crews were interned along with their ships, living under tedious and difficult conditions with short rations and coal supplies often insufficient even to heat the crews' living quarters.

The sailors and officers waited through the long process of the negotiation of the Treaty of Versailles, the war's definitive peace treaty. On May 7, 1919, they learned the terms of the treaty: The German navy was to be reduced to 15,000 men, 6 small battleships, 6 light cruisers, 12 destroyers, and 12 torpedo boats. All other vessels were to be irrevocably turned over to the Allies. Moreover, the German navy would be permitted no U-boats, and German naval aviation was also banned. Two days after these terms were announced, Admiral Adolf von Trotha, naval chief since December 27, 1918, radioed Rear Admiral Ludwig von Reuter, commander of the interned High Seas Fleet. Trotha informed Reuter that the surrender of the fleet was "out of the question."

As the German naval command stalled for time, the Allied governments issued an ultimatum: Sign the Treaty of Versailles by June 21 (later changed to June 23) or hostilities would be resumed.

At 11:20 A.M. on June 21, 1919, Admiral Reuter's flagship signaled the fleet to *scuttle.* Quickly and efficiently, the crews aboard each ship opened

Voices of Battle

"In a fortnight we shall have no Empire and no Emperor left, you will see."

—Erich Ludendorff, to his wife, after resigning from command, October 26, 1918

Words of War

Freikorps was the collective name of German paramilitary groups, privately organized and without government sanction, formed by veterans after the war chiefly to fight the incursion of communist forces in Germany.

valves to let in the sea. They lowered lifeboats, mounting upon them white flags to signify their new status as prisoners of war. Before British vessels could react, 52 of the ships had sunk: 10 battleships, 5 battle cruisers, 5 light cruisers, and 32 destroyers. The British managed to save 22 other ships.

Later justifying his action, Reuter claimed that he thought Germany intended to refuse to sign the Treaty of Versailles. Nevertheless, Reuter did not implicate his government in his action, but took sole responsibility himself—even though Trotha, his superior officer, had ordered him not to surrender the ships.

Words of War

To **scuttle** a ship is to purposely sink it in a deliberate act of self-destruction, typically to prevent capture by the enemy.

Sabers rattled as a result of the scuttling of the High Seas Fleet, and there was talk of renewing hostilities. But, in 1919, no one wanted to go back to war. The fact was that the Allies would probably have scuttled most of the fleet in any case. In the end, Britain actually profited from Reuter's action because most of the vessels were subsequently raised and sold as scrap, the proceeds of which went directly to the English rather than being divvied up among the Allies. Worse, the scuttling losses were added to the monumental reparations bill handed Germany, which was forced to relinquish to the Allies even more ships and port equipment than had been specified originally by the Treaty of Versailles.

Voices of Battle

"There was historic irony in the Kaiser's naval officers choosing a watery grave for his magnificent battleships in a British harbour. Had he not embarked on a strategically unnecessary attempt to match Britain's maritime strength, fatal hostility between the two countries would have been avoided; so, too, in all possibility, might have been the neurotic climate of suspicion and insecurity from which the First World War was born. The unmarked graveyard of his squadrons inside the remotest islands of the British archipelago ... remains as a memorial to selfish and ultimately pointless military ambition."

—John Keegan, *The First World War*, 1999

Allies in the Rhineland

After the Armistice, American, French, and British forces advanced into the Rhineland and into Germany as armies of occupation. A force of 240,000 U.S. troops occupied Rhine positions and established a *bridgehead* 18 miles into Germany at Coblenz. The British established a similar bridgehead at Cologne, and the French did the same at Mainz. These troops were to be ready to resume the war—on German soil—if the Armistice were violated or if the Germans ultimately rejected the final treaty.

Hall of Mirrors

At Paris, on January 18, 1919, the Allies convened a peace conference among themselves, a conference wholly excluding Germany, Austria-Hungary, Bulgaria, and Turkey. The terms of peace were to be dictated, not negotiated. Twenty-seven Allied nations participated in the conference, which had as its object the creation of a definitive peace treaty. Of the participants, the four major Allied powers—Britain, France, the United States, and (to a lesser degree) Italy—dominated.

Words of War

A **bridgehead** is a forward position seized and held by troops advancing into enemy territory as a foothold for further advance.

Woodrow Wilson in Europe

The American delegation to the Paris Peace Conference was headed personally by President Woodrow Wilson. As vigorously as he had worked to mobilize his nation for war, Wilson now struggled to bring about a peace that he intended would mean the end of war itself.

Wilson's intense idealism, his determination that the sacrifice of so much life and treasure would not be in vain, blinded him to domestic political realities. He made no attempt to generate bipartisan support for his treaty plans, the centerpiece of which, pursuant to his Fourteen Points (see Chapter 24, "New Blood"), was to be the creation of a League of Nations, an international deliberative and arbitrative body that would settle disputes between nations without resorting to war. Correctly fearing that Republican isolationists would be opposed to the League, Wilson appointed no Republicans to the peace delegation. As if this omission did not sufficiently alienate Republicans, Wilson made peace and the League of Nations a political issue by appealing to voters to re-elect a Democratic Congress in 1918. That the 1918 contest went to the Republicans, who won majorities in both houses, should have signaled Wilson that he was getting out of touch with the sentiments of his own countrymen.

The Big Four

On his arrival in Europe, Wilson was given a tumultuous welcome and his leadership was greeted with nothing but expressions of absolute confidence. It soon became apparent, however, that Wilson's idealism, out of touch with the attitude of the American people, was also worlds apart from what the other three *Big Four* leaders wanted.

Each in their own way, Georges Clemenceau of France, David Lloyd George of Great Britain, and Vittorio Orlando of Italy wanted to conclude a settlement that did little more than simply and severely punish Germany. In contrast, Wilson championed a much more conciliatory settlement based on his Fourteen Points, especially points one through five:

➤ An insistence on "open covenants, openly arrived at"—that is, an end to the kind of secret treaties and alliances that had dragged Europe into war

➤ Freedom of the seas

➤ Removal of economic barriers to international trade

➤ Radical reduction of armaments to the lowest point consistent with domestic security

➤ Modification of all colonial claims on the basis of the self-determination of peoples

Eight additional points addressed specific postwar territorial settlements, and the 14th point called for the creation of the League of Nations.

Words of War

The **Big Four** leaders at the Paris Peace Conference were Woodrow Wilson, president of the United States; Georges Clemenceau, premier of France; David Lloyd George, prime minister of Great Britain; and Vittorio Orlando, premier of Italy.

Of the three European Allied leaders, it was French premier Georges Clemenceau who was most at odds with Wilson's conciliatory idealism. Except for Russia—which played no part in the peace conference—France had suffered most in the war, and Clemenceau not only wanted to secure his nation against future German attack by totally destroying Germany's ability to make war, but he also meant to exact a generous measure of vengeance. He favored a thoroughly punitive treaty.

British Prime Minister David Lloyd George and Italy's Premier Vittorio Orlando also had their own peace agendas. Personally, Lloyd George, like Wilson, favored moderation in the treatment of Germany; however, he had been elected on his promise that Germany would be punished. Moreover, he was also concerned that Wilson's Fourteen Points would interfere with British colonial policy. As for Orlando, his concern focused almost exclusively on ensuring that Italy would receive the territories that it had been promised in 1915 as inducement to join the Allied cause.

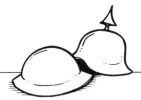

Combatants

Georges Clemenceau (1841–1929) was second only to Woodrow Wilson as the major force in the peace conference that drew up the Treaty of Versailles in 1919. Born in the Vendee, he originally studied medicine, but entered politics instead in 1876 as a member of the Chamber of Deputies (French legislature). He was sporadically in and out of office, but in 1906, as a senator, it was Clemenceau who developed the Entente Cordiale with Great Britain, which was the basis of the alliance in World War I.

Clemenceau declined office at the outbreak of the war, preferring the outsider's role of criticizing the government's conduct, policy, and strategy. He became an outspoken public advocate of total victory, although he also expressed his opinion that "Papa" Joffre's doctrine of massed offensive was insane. By mid 1917, calls for him to form a new cabinet grew increasingly intense, and, in November 1917, he was named premier and wielded nearly dictatorial power, asserting dominance not only over other politicians, but, for the first time in the war, over the military as well.

His conduct at the peace table was as aggressive as it had been during the war. He pushed to secure the borders of France and to reclaim territory lost to Germany in the Franco-Prussian War of 1870–1871. Most of all he sought to dismember Germany politically, cripple it economically, and emasculate it militarily. Despite some concessions to President Woodrow Wilson, he largely succeeded in achieving these goals, thereby unwittingly creating the desperate conditions that would propel Germany to new conquests and ignite World War II.

Compromises

For six months, Wilson hammered away at the others. He persuaded Clemenceau to abandon one of his chief demands, that the left bank of the Rhine be detached from Germany and put under permanent French military control, in exchange for British and American promises of future alliance and support. Ultimately, Wilson saw most of the content of his Fourteen Points embodied in the Treaty of Versailles. However, to achieve his purposes, he had had to agree to the punitive terms the other Allies imposed on Germany. This galled Wilson, who nevertheless soothed himself by reasoning that the inclusion of the League of Nations as part of the treaty was worth practically any compromise. In presenting the Treaty of Versailles to his fellow Americans, he called it the best compromise obtainable, for he believed that the

League of Nations itself would eventually rectify some of the injustices presently imposed upon Germany.

War to End All War

The Treaty of Versailles was a complex document, the size of a hefty book, consisting of 440 articles. Befitting its status as the document that would formally end the greatest war that the world had fought up to that time and that (some believed) would end all war, the document was taken to the great Hall of Mirrors of the Palace of Versailles—the very room in which Otto von Bismarck, following the French defeat in the Franco-Prussian War, had proclaimed the German Empire in 1871.

In the great hall, on the afternoon of June 28, 1919, the fifth anniversary of the assassination of Archduke Franz Ferdinand and his wife Sophie in Sarajevo, the completed treaty was opened for signature. The Allied powers signed, as did Germany and the other Central Powers. Germany's signature, however, was made under protest against the continuation of the "inhuman blockade" of its ports.

Fatal Terms

The chief provisions of the treaty included German territorial cessions, German admission of guilt for the war, German disarmament, and an assessment against Germany (and other Central Powers) of harsh monetary reparations. More sweepingly, the treaty put an end to the German empire and dismembered the empire of Austria-Hungary as well. Here were the key provisions:

➤ The population and territorial extent of Germany was reduced by about 10 percent.

➤ Alsace and Lorraine were returned to France.

➤ The Saarland (region of the Saar River) was placed under the supervision of the League of Nations until 1935.

➤ Three small northern German areas were given to Belgium.

➤ In accordance with a *plebiscite* in Schleswig, northern Schleswig was taken from Germany and returned to Denmark.

➤ The boundaries of Poland were redrawn. Poland was given part of what had been German West Prussia and Poznań (Posen), and a corridor of territory to the Baltic Sea was also carved out for Poland. (In the late 1930s, German recovery

Words of War

A **plebiscite** is a direct vote by the entire electorate, which is invited to decide an issue by a "yes" or "no" vote.

of this so-called Polish Corridor would serve as one of Adolf Hitler's most passionate causes.) Pursuant to a plebiscite, Poland also gained part of Upper Silesia.

➤ Austria-Hungary was dismantled, some of its constituents were given independence, and the Balkan states were re-formed as the Kingdom of Serbs, Croats, and Slovenes (renamed Yugoslavia in 1929). Austria and Hungary proper were set up as separate nations.

➤ The port city of Danzig (present-day Gdansk, Poland) was declared a free city, independent of any nation.

➤ Germany's overseas colonies in China, the Pacific, and Africa were taken over by Britain, France, Japan, and other Allied nations.

➤ Germany was compelled to sign and acknowledge a humiliating "war guilt clause," deeming itself the principal aggressor in the war. This was not only spiritually debilitating, but it also made Germany liable for all reparations to the Allied nations.

➤ Part VII of the treaty accused Kaiser Wilhelm II of having committed war crimes. He was guaranteed a fair trial, and the Allies reserved the right to bring unspecified others before war crimes tribunals. (Neither the kaiser nor anyone else was tried for war crimes following World War I. Wilhelm had fled to Holland after the war, and the Dutch government declined to extradite him to the jurisdiction of the Allies.)

➤ Reparations were called for; however, these had not been computed by the time the treaty was signed. In 1921, they were fixed at $33 billion, a truly staggering sum in those days. All of the Allied signatories understood that payment of such reparations would destroy the German economy forever, which would also have serious consequences for international finances. Nevertheless, bent on revenge, the Allies demanded that Germany pay, and the treaty allowed for punitive actions if Germany failed to make the payments according to a specified schedule.

➤ The German army was limited to 100,000 men, and the general staff was abolished.

➤ The production of armored cars, tanks, submarines, airplanes, and poison gas was prohibited, and other munitions production was drastically curtailed.

➤ Germany west of the Rhine and up to 30 miles east of that river was declared a *demilitarized zone.*

➤ Allied occupation of the Rhineland was set to continue for at least 15 years—and possibly longer.

Words of War

A **demilitarized zone** is a region declared neutral and in which no troops or armaments are permitted.

The Promise of the League

Woodrow Wilson understood that a coercive, punitive peace was no peace at all. He saw what the other Allied leaders refused to see: If you drive a nation and a people to desperation, they will do desperate things. Yet Wilson forced himself to believe that the inclusion of the Covenant of the League of Nations as part of the Treaty of Versailles would ultimately lift this peace out of the realm of vengeance and coercion and would bring about in the world a reign of international justice.

The 26 articles of the Covenant of the League of Nations set out three principal approaches to preventing war:

1. Arbitration to resolve international disputes
2. A program of general worldwide disarmament
3. The establishment of collective security through guarantees of rights and sovereignty

Sixty-three nations ultimately subscribed to the Covenant and became members of the League. They were represented in an assembly, which held regular sessions annually and additional emergency sessions as necessary. In a grand gesture of international democracy, the Covenant gave each member one vote; however, unanimity was required for all decisions—a stipulation that doomed the League to paralysis.

The League of Nations was a noble experiment that was at first received with hope and praise. Soon its fatal flaws became all too apparent:

➤ Including the Covenant as an inseparable part of the Treaty of Versailles compromised the League's impartiality, making it appear to be an instrument of the victorious Allies.

➤ The requirement of unanimity often prevented the League from taking meaningful action.

American Betrayal

The most crippling blow to the League of Nations was the refusal of the Republican-controlled United States Senate to join it.

While Wilson was away in Europe for six months, intensively concentrating on the treaty and the League, he lost touch with the changing mood of America. The people had put both the House of Representatives and the Senate into Republican hands, and the Republicans steered the nation rapidly away from involvement in the affairs of the world and back toward an *isolationism* that smacked more of the nineteenth century than the twentieth century.

The jubilation that had accompanied victory was now tempered by terror of a worldwide communist revolution. A so-called Red Scare swept Western Europe and, even more intensely, the United States. At the beginning of 1919, U.S. Attorney General Mitchell Palmer ordered a series of raids on the headquarters of radical organizations in a dozen cities, indiscriminately rounding up 6,000 U.S. citizens *believed* to be "sympathetic to Communism."

But it was not only the fear of Communism that chipped away at Wilson's dream for world peace and rational unity. Wilson's lapse in political savvy—his exclusion of all Republicans from the peace process—prompted Senator Henry Cabot Lodge (1850–1924) to lead Republican opposition to the League of Nations. Persuaded that the League was above politics, Wilson refused to negotiate with Lodge and the others, and he decided instead to bring popular pressure on the Senate by taking his case directly to the people.

Wilson embarked on a grueling 9,500-mile transcontinental whistle-stop speaking tour. On September 25, 1919, exhausted by war, the heartbreaking labors of making peace, and his battle on behalf of the League of Nations, Woodrow Wilson collapsed following a speech in Pueblo, Colorado. He was rushed back to Washington, but his condition deteriorated. A week later, he suffered a devastating stroke that left him partially paralyzed.

Wilson's Forlorn Hope

Ill and bitter, Wilson defiantly instructed his followers to accept no compromise on the League. Without the possibility of compromise, the Senate rejected the Treaty of Versailles and the League of Nations. Wilson served out the rest of his term, broken in spirit and health, while his wife, Edith Bolling Wilson, actually attended to the day-to-day business of government.

"Not for Us"

Warren G. Harding (1865–1923), the man who succeeded Wilson as president, was the conservative product of the Republican political machine. Unlike Wilson, he was neither an intellectual nor an idealist. He had ridden to the White House on a campaign promise to bring about a "return to normalcy." In his first speech to Congress, he declared, "We seek no part in directing the destinies of the world … [the League of Nations] is not for us."

Words of War

Isolationism is a national policy of refraining from involvement in political affairs beyond the nation's borders.

From the Front

Rejecting the Treaty of Versailles, the United States concluded separate, simple peace treaties with Germany, Hungary, and Austria in 1921.

Finale—or Act I?

The League of Nations did not immediately collapse without the support of the United States. From time to time, it even managed to resolve a few minor international disputes. However, it failed to meet its first major challenge. When the Japanese invaded Manchuria in September 1931, the League responded by sending a commission of inquiry in 1932, and Japan simply turned on its heel and walked out of the League the following year. The League of Nations was powerless to do anything to compel Japan to return the territory it had seized. Throughout the 1930s, the League failed to act effectively against the aggression of Nazi Germany and Fascist Italy. Ultimately, these aggressor nations made the League irrelevant by withdrawing from it.

The document to which the Covenant of the League of Nations was attached, the Treaty of Versailles, stands as one of history's great tragic tracts. Designed to prevent Germany from ever rocking the world again, it did nothing less than create the desperate political, economic, and emotional climate that made possible the rise of Adolf Hitler and Nazism. Seeking to end war, it made a second world war all but inevitable.

The Least You Need to Know

➤ In accordance with the Armistice, Germany evacuated occupied territories and rapidly demobilized, while the Allies occupied bridgeheads within Germany to enforce the Armistice and compel agreement to a definitive treaty.

➤ Despite Wilson's efforts at conciliation, the Treaty of Versailles had as its main objective the punishment and permanent crippling of Germany.

➤ The refusal of the Senate to ratify the Treaty of Versailles and the Covenant of the League of Nations sealed the doom of the inherently weak League.

➤ The harshly punitive nature of the Treaty of Versailles created a political desperation in Germany that provided fertile ground for the growth of the Nazi regime and thereby made World War II all but inevitable.

Chapter 29

Disease, Disillusion, and All That Jazz

In This Chapter

➤ The great postwar influenza pandemic

➤ Postwar conservatism and isolationism

➤ Postwar social changes

➤ The world of the Roaring Twenties

➤ The postwar "lost generation"

Americans had much to be proud of after World War I. Almost certainly, the Allies would have been defeated without the intervention of the United States. As many Americans saw it, their nation had indeed made the world safe for democracy.

Unfortunately, before the century was half over, it would become all too apparent that the world had been made safe by no means. In fact, it had been made an even more dangerous place than it had been in 1914. Nevertheless, it is beyond dispute that the United States emerged from World War I a great world power. Paradoxically, however, most Americans emerged from the war and the war years with a desire to have very little to do with the rest of the world.

The experience of war, with four million men in an army and two million sent to Europe, broadened the intellectual and cultural horizons of many. A new sophistication dawned in America. As a popular song of the era asked, "How ya gonna keep 'em down on the farm after they've seen Paree?" Yet as many American minds opened, others closed, and an unthinking, cynical, and thoroughly corrupt political conservatism also descended upon the nation.

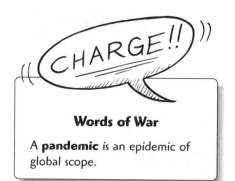

There were other mass emotions as well, most notably a combination of desperate energy, frenetic amorality, deep despair, and empty-headed hedonism known as the Roaring Twenties.

Social critics spoke of the postwar era's moral devastation and emotional burnout as a "malaise." More immediately, another sickness attacked the United States and the rest of the world. Popularly called the Spanish Flu, it would kill more people than the war that had just ended.

The Plague of War

In the ancient world, war frequently brought in its wake plagues of epidemic disease. The mass movement, filth, and deprivation of World War I created the conditions in which an influenza *pandemic*—called the Spanish Flu—swept the world.

First Cases

As far as anyone can tell, the term "Spanish Flu" is a misnomer. It is likely that the disease began not in Spain, but in a U.S. Army training facility at Fort Funston, Kansas. After taking hold here, it spread with alarming speed to assume pandemic proportions worldwide.

From the Front

In the dozen major American cities for which the U.S. Public Health Service kept records, 22 percent of the population caught the flu. A total of 20 million Americans contracted the disease, of whom 668,000 died, not including the 50,000 soldiers who had died of flu during the war. (U.S. combat deaths from enemy fire numbered 50,585.)

The first troops to fall ill at Fort Funston did not get terribly sick—fever, chills, upper respiratory symptoms characterized the illness, nothing more. But as it spread from North America to Europe and from west to east across Asia and the Pacific, the disease underwent a deadly mutation, beginning much like the original flu but then bringing on a virulent form of pneumonia that seemed to single out young adults for attack.

Pandemic!

By the fall of 1918, the flu reappeared simultaneously in Boston, in Brest, France, and in Freetown, Sierra Leone. All were important ports of embarkation for Allied troops. This time, the disease was accompanied by an alarming rate of mortality. In October and November 1918, one fifth of those infected died of pneumonia within hours of initially falling ill.

To avert public panic as well as to avoid betraying weakness to the enemy, wartime censors purposely underreported the incidence of the disease. United States and French authorities each claimed 10,000 deaths in 1918, and British authorities claimed a mere 3,500. Actually, in Great Britain alone, 4,000 were dying *each week* at the height of the pandemic, and some 668,000 Americans succumbed to the disease during 1918–1919. Some historians today believe that even these numbers may represent underestimates by as much as 25 percent.

No effective treatment existed for the disease, other than quarantine to contain its spread. The flu attacked the United States in three waves through 1918–1919 and then left as suddenly as it had come. It had played a silent but devastating role in the war. In 1918, for example, 40 percent of the U.S. Navy fell ill; of U.S. Army deaths that year, 60 percent were the result of flu. The disease likely was chiefly responsible for bringing the Meuse-Argonne Offensive to a halt. Indeed, in the desperate final months of the conflict, Erich Ludendorff entertained the hope that flu would come to the rescue of his crumbling forces. But, of course, the disease knew no national allegiance, and it soon proved as deadly to the Germans as to the Allies. In later life, Ludendorff sometimes even blamed the failure of his five great 1918 offensives on manpower shortages caused by influenza.

From the Front

A certain number of the pandemic's survivors later contracted a form of Parkinson's disease popularly called "sleepy sickness." Characterized by extreme dullness and lethargy, in its worst form, "sleepy sickness" left its victims in a lifelong state of catatonia, apparently conscious, but unable to move or communicate in any way.

"Return to Normalcy"

Warren G. Harding took office in 1921, having promised America a "return to normalcy."

Just what did that mean?

The New Isolationism

To many Americans, "normalcy" meant calming the wartime madness and returning to the feeling that America was safely insulated and snugly isolated from the chaos of the rest of the world. As the war itself and the Red Scare (see Chapter 28, "The Tragedy of Versailles") that followed it proved, this feeling was an illusion. But, in the postwar years, many Americans—perhaps most—welcomed and embraced such comforting illusions.

How Ya Gonna Keep 'Em Down on the Farm?

Other Americans were not pleased with the status quo. Boys who would have followed in their fathers' footsteps as farmers or factory workers found that their experience of war had made them restless for something more meaningful and fulfilling in life. They had seen the cosmopolitan civilization of Europe at its most exciting as well as its most terrifying. In the space of a few months, they had grown—not only grown up, but, for many, grown beyond the confines of a working-class, a middle-class, or a rural American life.

For many young women, too, the war had been eye-opening and mind-expanding. With the men off at war, women left the confines of the house and housework to do war work, whether in a munitions plant or for such war-related relief agencies as the American Red Cross and the Salvation Army. Such experiences gave new impetus to a movement that had begun back in 1848 with a convention in Seneca Falls, New York. There, 240 women and men met to draw up a list of feminist grievances that included, paramountly, a petition for the right to vote.

The struggle for woman suffrage dragged on through the rest of the nineteenth century and into the early years of the twentieth, until President Woodrow Wilson approved the tersely worded Nineteenth Amendment, which was ratified by the states in August 1920. Women were now voters.

Woman suffrage arrived at the threshold of a decade in which women generally assumed a new identity in America. The cherished Victorian image of the innocent girl who married for love to become a chaste wife and mother dissolved into the "modern woman," a socially and sexually savvy female who was capable even of pursuing a career independent of husband and family. At her most extreme, the 1920s woman was a *flapper,* a sexually liberated female devoted to having a good time and beholden to no man.

Although women did not get the vote until 1920, African-Americans had had that right since 1870, which brought ratification of the Fifteenth Amendment, barring states from denying the vote to anyone on the basis of "race, color, or previous condition of servitude." Nevertheless, they, too, were in many respects disenfranchised within American society.

In the twentieth-century South, racial segregation was not only legal, but it was also supported by law. In the North, the law was silent on segregation, but prejudice and discrimination were no less real. During World War I, African-Americans served with distinction, albeit within segregated military units. In many U.S. Army units, African-American soldiers served in proximity to French *poilus* or even under the command of

From the Front

Many men assumed (and fretted) that women would tend to vote in a unified liberal bloc. They were wrong. Women voted for a variety of candidates from all over the political spectrum, but it was certainly the women's vote that helped put Warren G. Harding, product of a conservative "old boy network," into office.

Words of War

Flapper was the label for the "liberated" young woman of the 1920s whose interests were unabashedly worldly and whose inhibitions were few or none. The origin of the term is obscure but may refer to the wild flapping gestures associated with such 1920s dances as the Charleston.

French officers. In contrast to their white American counterparts, the French did not segregate or discriminate, and for some African-American soldiers, the overseas experience opened up a whole new world of possibility. They returned home no longer willing to accept second-class citizenship.

In many parts of postwar America, white attitudes toward blacks also began to change. Sophisticated white audiences flocked to the clubs and cabarets of New York's Harlem, a predominantly black neighborhood where such great jazz musicians as Louis Armstrong, Fletcher Henderson, and Duke Ellington played. They also found themselves attracted to the work of African-American artists and writers who were coming from all parts of the country to live in Harlem. A lively exchange between white intellectuals and black Harlem artists developed into what has been called the Harlem Renaissance.

Running parallel with these cultural developments was the social activism of such black political leaders as W.E.B. Du Bois, a principal founder of the National Association for the Advancement of Colored People (NAACP). Du Bois argued that blacks could not achieve social equality by merely emulating whites, but that they had to awaken black racial pride by discovering their own African cultural heritage. A host of African-American poets and novelists—most notably the poet Countee Cullen (1903–1946), novelist Rudolph Fisher (1897–1934), poet-essayist Langston Hughes (1902–1967), folklorist Zora Neale Hurston (1901–1960), poet James Weldon Johnson (1871–1938), and novelist Jean Toomer (1894–1967)—brought the African-American community an unprecedented degree of attention, interest, and respect.

Going Dry

As the rise of women and the growing equality of African-Americans played against the prevailing do-nothing conservatism of the Harding administration, so another prudishly conservative backlash counterpointed the perceived loosening of American morality in the Roaring Twenties. The Eighteenth Amendment was ratified in 1919, prohibiting the manufacture, transport, and sale of alcoholic beverages anywhere in the United States. It was called *Prohibition*—or the Volstead Act (which was the name of the legislation passed to enforce the amendment). Like woman suffrage, it had its origin in the nineteenth century.

By 1916, 21 states had voted themselves "dry." They, in turn, sent a "dry majority" to Congress. The lawmakers hammered out the amendment in 1917, and, over the veto of Woodrow Wilson, it was passed and sent on to the states for ratification.

Although politically liberal, President Wilson was as strait-laced a moralist as any, and he certainly

Words of War

Prohibition is the popular name for the law enacted by the Eighteenth Amendment to the Constitution forbidding the manufacture, transport, and sale of alcoholic beverages anywhere in the United States.

favored sobriety. But he believed that Prohibition would create a nation of lawbreakers—which is exactly what it did.

In 1919, state legislatures and Congress were dominated by rural lawmakers, whose constituents supported Prohibition. But the big-city neighborhoods always voted against such measures, and now urbanites began to brew their own beer and distill their own "bathtub gin."

Nor was all this production strictly for home consumption. Neighborhood *bootleggers* sold homebrew and booze to neighbors and even distributed the stuff through local ice cream parlors, grocery stores, pharmacies, and the like. As to the cop on the beat, well, he usually looked the other way—or, for a few dollars or a few bottles, could be induced to look the other way.

At first, bootlegging operated on a small scale, but soon it became a big business and formed the foundation of a new kind of American criminal activity: organized crime. Prohibition fueled crime on an unprecedented scale as a network of mobster gangs organized the illegal trade in liquor into an underworld enterprise of truly corporate proportions.

Words of War

A **bootlegger** was one who made, smuggled, or sold liquor during Prohibition. The term originated not in the 1920s, but in the nineteenth century, and came from the practice of hiding a whiskey flask in the upper part of one's boot.

The Jazz Age

Speakeasies—the eateries, clubs, and back-alley dives purveying bootleg liquor—sold more than booze. Also flowing freely was a new kind of popular music, called *jazz*. The American novelist F. Scott Fitzgerald even christened the decade of the 1920s the "Jazz Age."

New Music

After the war, jazz migrated north from the red-light district and French Quarter of New Orleans. Its ambassadors were such musicians as King Oliver, Jelly Roll Morton, and, paramountly, Louis Armstrong, the first great jazz soloist and one of the genre's greatest musicians. Jazz was rooted in African-American folk music, the music of the slaves, combined with the popular dance music of European immigrants. By the 1920s, the early practitioners of jazz were both black and white, but the prime movers of the music were African-American. The audience for the music, however, was mostly white.

Words of War

Jazz is a highly improvisational form of music primarily developed by African-Americans who combined European harmonic structures with African rhythmic complexities. These, in turn, were overlaid with European and white American dance and march rhythms, and with elements borrowed from the blues tradition. The word "jazz" is probably derived from a slang term for sexual intercourse.

The hot, expressive beat and tonalities of jazz came as an antidote to the cruel mechanical rhythms of war and of industries associated with war. At the same time, the longing, poignant emotionalism of jazz was in tune with the pain and despair that continually hovered around the postwar years—even when the Roaring Twenties roared their loudest.

Opting Out

While jazz was becoming a uniquely American postwar form of expression, many other American artists and writers, some of whom had fought overseas, were finding the Harding-era United States intellectually and morally oppressive. Many of the most exciting new American authors, people such as the poet e.e. cummings (whose fondness for lowercase type extended to the way he spelled his own name) and the fiction writers Sherwood Anderson, William Faulkner, Ernest Hemingway, and F. Scott Fitzgerald, gravitated to Paris after the war.

Many of the young American expatriates regularly gathered at the Paris home of yet another expatriate, Gertrude Stein (1874–1946), a rotund, homely woman with close-cropped hair and an ever-present mousey companion named Alice B. Toklas. With her brother, Leo, an art collector and dealer, Stein amassed a highly discriminating collection of modern art and developed enduring friendships with the likes of Pablo Picasso and Henri Matisse. Gertrude Stein also earned a reputation in her own right as the author of avant-garde prose.

The Lost Generation and a World Remade

In the epigraph to his novel *The Sun Also Rises,* Ernest Hemingway attributed to Gertrude Stein this remark: "You are all a lost generation." Although some have disputed the actual source of the quotation, all agree that the last two words of the sentence captured the mood of the postwar era, the period depicted in Hemingway's prose, the time of a generation that had come of age in the Great War, even as it had been physically, emotionally, and spiritually wounded by it.

The war had physically destroyed countless lives, but it had also scarred even those who lived through it without any physical wounds. From many, especially those with questioning minds and active imaginations, it stole faith itself. The old familiar beliefs, in God and country, in the essential rationality and goodness of humanity, and in the wisdom of one's elders, were blasted apart by a war fought for seemingly empty reasons to achieve questionable or even worthless goals.

In one respect, the result of the war was a generation cast adrift without a moral, intellectual, or spiritual compass. In another respect, however, this "lost generation" was a liberated generation, freed of the old beliefs, old ideas, and old ways that had culminated in a bloody catastrophe. World War I had shattered the world, and now it was up to the new generation to remake it. For all the despair and frenzy and cynicism of the postwar generation, there was also great creativity, idealism, and hope. And it was all aimed toward one end: not to make the same old mistakes again.

363

Tragically, World War I and the climate created by the Treaty of Versailles made it all too possible for the new generation to make *new*—and even more terrible—mistakes.

The Least You Need to Know

➤ The war spawned a worldwide influenza pandemic that was responsible for more deaths than the war itself.

➤ Following *its* triumphal role in Europe, the United States retreated into a policy of isolation from world affairs.

➤ The experience of war caused many Americans to rethink society and their place in it; ideas of morality and social justice changed, and women and African-Americans began to make major strides toward mainstream equality.

➤ The war produced an alienated "lost generation" of artists and writers, including a group of American intellectuals who chose to live in Europe, where they created a wealth of challenging new art and literature.

Who Was Who in World War I

Albert I (1875–1934)   King of Belgium celebrated by the Allies as the heroic defender of his small land in the face of German invasion.

Allenby, Edmund (1861–1936)   British field marshal who won signal victories in the Middle East against the Turks. His victory at Meggido (1918) is considered the most brilliant tactical achievement, by any side, of the war.

Asquith, Herbert (1852–1928)   British prime minister during the early years of World War I; after the failure of the Dardanelles Campaign, he was replaced by David Lloyd George.

Baker, Newton D. (1871–1937)   Secretary of War in the cabinet of Woodrow Wilson.

Beatty, David (1871–1936)   Excellent British admiral under Sir John R. Jellicoe; took a leading role in the Battle of Jutland (1916).

Below, Otto von (1857–1944)   German general who performed well on four fronts during the war and is best known for his vigorous drive against the Italians at Caporetto (1917).

Berchtold, Leopold von (1863–1942)   Austro-Hungarian foreign minister whose insistence on punishing Serbia after the assassination of Archduke Francis Ferdinand and his wife, Sophie, in 1914 most immediately triggered World War I.

Bethmann Hollweg, Theobald (1856–1921)   German chancellor through most of World War I; made peace overtures to Woodrow Wilson in 1917. He was compelled to resign after the failure of the last German offensive in 1918.

Brusilov, Alexei (1853–1926)   By far the best general in the Russian military; his offensive against Austro-Hungarian forces in 1916 nearly knocked that nation out of the war.

Bülow, Karl von (1846–1921)   German general usually blamed for the German defeat at the First Battle of the Marne (1914).

Cadorna, Luigi (1850–1928)   Italian general who led his forces in multiple offensives against the Austro-Hungarians along the Isonzo River. He was relieved of command in November 1917.

Castelnau, Edouard de (1851–1944)   French general who served Joseph Joffre as deputy chief of staff and vigorously supported Joffre's series of fruitless and costly offensives.

Churchill, Winston (1874–1965)   Best known as Britain's heroic and inspiring World War II prime minister. Churchill served as First Lord of the Admiralty in World War I and backed the disastrous assault on the Dardanelles.

Clemenceau, Georges (1841–1929)   French premier from November 1917. Clemenceau insisted on thoroughly humiliating and punishing Germany with the Treaty of Versailles.

Conrad von Hötzendorf, Franz (1852–1925)   Field marshal in overall command of Austro-Hungarian forces. Conrad, largely unsuccessful, was forced to turn over command to Paul von Hindenburg in 1916.

Drum, Hugh A. (1879–1951)   American general who served as the chief planner behind the American Expeditionary Force.

Enver Pasha (1881–1922)   "Young Turk" who became the chief military figure of Turkey in World War I. A failure as a strategist, Enver Pasha was largely responsible for the massacre of Turkish Armenians in 1916.

Falkenhayn, Erich von (1861–1922)   Chief of the German General Staff after the defeat at the First Battle of the Marne (1914). Falkenhayn was himself replaced after the costly failure of his campaign against Verdun in 1916.

Foch, Ferdinand (1851–1929)   Perhaps the most brilliantly aggressive general of World War I and certainly the most impressive of the French commanders. Foch became supreme Allied commander by the end of the war.

French, Sir John (1852–1925)   British field marshal who brought the British army to France and Flanders. After the failure of the Flanders offensives, he was forced to resign in December 1915.

George V (1865–1936)   King of Great Britain during World War I.

Haig, Sir Douglas (1861–1928)   British field marshal who replaced Sir John French at the end of 1915 and served through the end of the war as British commander-in-chief on the Western Front. He was associated with massive attacks costing huge numbers of British lives.

Hindenburg, Paul von (1847–1934)   As a commander assigned to the Eastern Front, he teamed with Erich Ludendorff to mastermind German victory there.

Hipper, Franz von (1863–1932)   German admiral who played a leading role in the Battle of Jutland, a tactical victory for the Germans, though a strategic win for the British.

Hoffmann, Max (1869–1927)   German architect of the great victories against the Russians at Tannenberg and the Masurian Lakes.

Jellicoe, Sir John R. (1859–1935)   British admiral in overall command of the Grand Fleet at the Battle of Jutland.

Joffre, Joseph ("Papa") (1852–1931)   As the first French commander-in-chief during the war, Joffre advocated a policy of "offensive to the uttermost," which proved a tragic failure. Despite early disasters, Joffre managed to keep the army together and fighting.

Kitchener, Horatio Herbert (1850–1916)   Britain's most celebrated commander at the start of the war. He served as secretary of state for war, but was killed in June 1916 when his ship struck a mine.

Kluck, Alexander von (1846–1934)   German general who led the right wing of the great offensive at the opening of the war. He is often (and too simplistically) blamed for varying from the Schlieffen Plan and thereby fatally compromising the offensive.

Lanrezac, Charles (1852–1925)   French general whose notoriously poor performance in the opening month of the war resulted in his removal from command.

Lansing, Robert (1864–1928)   U.S. secretary of state during World War I.

Lawrence, T.E. ("Lawrence of Arabia") (1888–1935)   Brilliant and controversial British leader of Arab guerilla forces fighting the Turks in the Persian Gulf. His monumental (but historically unreliable) memoir, *Seven Pillars of Wisdom*, contributed to his quasilegendary status after the war.

Lenin, Vladimir (1870–1924)   Architect of the Bolshevik Revolution of 1917. He agreed to a "separate peace" with Germany in March 1918 (Treaty of Brest-Litovsk), taking Russia out of the war.

Lettow-Vorbeck, Paul von (1870–1964)   Remarkable German commander who maintained brilliant guerilla operations in East Africa throughout the war and was the last German general to lay down arms.

Liggett, Hunter (1857–1935)   U.S. Army general who was the primary field commander during the difficult Argonne Forest operations.

Liman von Sanders, Otto (1855–1929)   German general who led Turkish forces as a field marshal of the Turkish Empire.

Lloyd George, David (1863–1945)   British minister of munitions from 1915 to December 1916, when he became prime minister. Often at odds with top British military commanders, he favored subordinating Sir Douglas Haig to Ferdinand Foch as supreme Allied commander.

Ludendorff, Erich (1865–1937)   Great but mercurial German tactician. With Paul von Hindenburg, he achieved victory on the Eastern Front and then effectively became generalissimo of German forces on the Western Front and virtual military dictator of Germany.

Mackensen, August von (1849–1945)   Highly effective German field commander on the Eastern Front.

Moltke, Helmuth von (1848–1916)   German chief of staff at the outbreak of the war. Moltke's deviations from the Schlieffen Plan, while at least partially justifiable, ensured the ultimate failure of the initial German offensive and thereby created the conditions that produced a long, stalemated war on the Western Front.

Nicholas II (1869–1918)   Last of the Russian czars; his assumption of personal command of the Russian military sealed its doom. Nicholas abdicated after the Russian Revolution of 1917 and, with his family, was executed by the Bolsheviks in 1918.

Nicholas, Grand Duke (1856–1929)   First overall commander of the Russian armies. After disasters at Tannenberg, Masurian Lakes, and Gorlice-Tarnow, he was relieved (in May 1915) by Czar Nicholas II, who assumed personal command of Russian forces.

Nivelle, Robert (1856–1924)   French general who replaced Joffre as commander-in-chief at the end of 1916 and mounted a spectacularly unsuccessful offensive (Nivelle Offensive), so disastrous that it provoked widespread mutiny throughout the French army.

Pershing, John J. ("Black Jack") (1860–1948)   Commander-in-chief of the American Expeditionary Force. Pershing stressed thorough training and an offensive strategy; he successfully prevented the AEF from being frittered away piecemeal by desperate French and British allies. He was a great logistician and an inspiring leader.

Pétain, Henri Philippe (1856–1951)   Rose from relative obscurity to share overall command of French forces with Ferdinand Foch. His defense of Verdun ("They shall not pass!") made him a national hero. Tragically, history remembers Pétain more for his role as head of the Nazi-collaborationist puppet Vichy government of World War II than as a hero of World War I.

Poincaré, Raymond (1860–1934)   President of France throughout World War I. Wielding significant power as a diplomat, he had almost no influence over the military and, toward the end of the war, yielded much of his authority to Premier Georges Clemenceau (who was France's chief negotiator at the Paris Peace Conference).

Potiorek, Oskar (1853–1933)   Austro-Hungarian general whose offensives against Serbia failed miserably, despite the great superiority of numbers he enjoyed.

Putnik, Radomir (1847–1917)   Extremely capable commander of Serbian forces who successfully repulsed initial Austro-Hungarian invasions but was defeated by overwhelmingly superior forces late in 1915. He succumbed to disease.

Rawlinson, Henry S. (1864–1925)   Highly capable British field commander under Douglas Haig who executed Haig's ill-conceived frontal assault along the Somme in July 1916.

Rennenkampf, Pavel K. (1854–1918)   Typically incompetent Russian general whose failure to coordinate his forces with those of Alexander Samsonov ensured the disastrous outcome of the Battle of Tannenberg. Rennenkampf suffered total defeat at the Battle of the Masurian Lakes. In 1918, he was asked by the Bolsheviks to assume command of the Red Army force in southern Russia. He refused and was summarily executed.

Richthofen, Manfred von ("Red Baron") (1892–1918)   German flier and most prolific ace of the war (with 80 confirmed kills). A legend among the Allies as well as the Central Powers, he was shot down in April 1918 and was buried by the British with full military honors.

Rupprecht, Crown Prince of Bavaria (1869–1951)   German field marshal who commanded the right wing of the army on the Western Front and was one of the toughest and most capable of German field commanders.

Samsonov, Alexander (1859–1914)   Disastrously incompetent Russian general who led his army to terrible defeat at the Battle of Tannenberg. During the chaotic retreat from this battle, Samsonov committed suicide.

Sarrail, Maurice (1856–1929)   French general with a quixotic socialist bent. He ineptly commanded the "Army of the Orient," a multinational force based at Salonika (Greece) and operating in the Balkans. Sarrail was removed from command in December 1917.

Spee, Maximilian von (1861–1914)   German admiral killed in an engagement with the British off Port Stanley, Falkland Islands.

Tirpitz, Alfred von (1849–1930)   Architect of Germany's prewar naval buildup and ardent advocate of unrestricted submarine warfare during the war.

Wilhelm II (1859–1941)   Germany's kaiser (emperor). During the war, he progressively yielded his authority to the military and, by 1917–1918, was essentially a puppet of Erich Ludendorff. Forced to abdicate on the day before the Armistice, he fled to Holland to avoid Allied prosecution as a war criminal.

Wilson, Woodrow (1856–1924)   U.S. president carried to a second term on the slogan "He kept us out of war." He struggled to maintain U.S. neutrality but was provoked to war by attacks on American shipping and by Germany's attempt to enlist Mexico as an ally against the United States. His "Fourteen Points" became the idealistic basis for the otherwise merely punitive Treaty of Versailles. He championed creation of the League of Nations, which was repudiated by the U.S. Senate. Exhausted by his vain effort to gain popular approval of the League in the United States, he suffered a massive stroke and served out the balance of his second term as an invalid.

Words of War

Allies   At the outbreak of World War I, Great Britain, France, and (until it dropped out of the war late in 1917) Russia. Japan played a minor Allied role; Italy joined in 1916, and the United States joined in April 1917.

amphibious assault   An attack in which ground forces are transported to the battlefield by ships and are deposited on shore by various landing craft. The land action of most amphibious assaults is supported by naval artillery bombardment from battleships or other warships.

annexation   The formal act of incorporating one political unit or nation into another.

ANZAC   Acronym for the Australian-New Zealand Army Corps; also used to refer to a member of that corps. More familiarly, ANZAC troops were called "diggers."

armed neutrality   The U.S. policy, initiated on February 26, 1917, of arming merchant vessels and taking other military steps—short of war itself—to protect American commerce.

armistice   A cessation of hostilities, or formalized truce, during which a definitive peace treaty is drafted, negotiated, and signed.

army   In the language of military organization, an army is the largest administrative and tactical unit into which a national army is organized.

artillery   Used as both singular and plural, artillery is the generic term for any large-caliber weapons, such as cannons, howitzers, mortars, and so on. Also the combat arm that uses such weapons.

automatic weapon   Any firearm that continuously fires as long as the trigger is squeezed and as long as it is supplied with ammunition. A machine gun is an automatic weapon.

Big Four, The   Principal Allied leaders at the Paris Peace Conference of 1919: Woodrow Wilson, president of the United States; Georges Clemenceau, premier of France; David Lloyd George, prime minister of Great Britain; and Vittorio Orlando, premier of Italy.

biplane   Aircraft with two sets of wings, one above the other in double-decker fashion, in contrast to a *monoplane,* which has only one set of wings.

Black Hand   Popular name for a secret society, founded in 1909, consisting of Serbian military officers and dedicated to the overthrow of Austro-Hungarian rule throughout the Balkans. The Black Hand sponsored the assassination of Archduke Francis Ferdinand in Sarajevo in 1914, thereby triggering World War I.

black powder   An easily ignitable explosive resembling gunpowder. It was widely used during the American Civil War but, for most purposes, had been replaced by high explosives during World War I.

blockade   The use of military forces, especially warships, to forcibly intercept goods and persons attempting to enter or depart from a particular place or an entire nation.

Boche   Familiar, derisive term for a German soldier or soldiers. Used especially by the French.

booby traps   Explosive devices triggered by some form of human contact and hidden in apparently innocuous places, such as houses.

bootlegger   One who made, smuggled, or sold liquor during Prohibition. The term originated not in the 1920s but in the nineteenth century, and came from the practice of hiding a whiskey flask in the upper part of one's boot.

bridgehead   A forward position seized and held by troops advancing into enemy territory as a foothold for farther advance.

cantonment   A group of temporary billets for troops.

capital ship   The largest and most powerful warship of any given era in naval history. The capital ship of World War I was the battleship.

carrier pigeon   A pigeon trained to carry messages in a small capsule fastened to the bird's foot.

Central Powers   In World War I, Germany, Austria-Hungary, Turkey, and, later, Bulgaria.

Chancellor   Appointed directly by the kaiser, the chancellor was, in effect, prime minister, the highest civilian official in the German government.

combat-loaded   An amphibious attack force is combat-loaded into ships—that is, loaded by unit and with all necessary equipment so that the force can be landed in good order, without having to take the time to assemble, and 100 percent ready to fight.

conscientious objector   An individual who declines compulsory military service on the grounds of religious, moral, or political belief.

conscription   The concept and process of inducting personnel into the armed forces on a compulsory basis.

convoy system   A method of grouping together supply, passenger, or merchant ships in formations that may be readily defended by warship escorts.

counterattack   An offensive response to an enemy attack. It is not merely a defense against attack.

counterbattery fire   An artillery assault directed specifically against the enemy's artillery, with the object of knocking it out.

counteroffensive   Aggressive action in response to an attack, as opposed to merely protective or defensive action.

crossing the T   Classic naval battle maneuver in which one maneuvers one's fleet so that it is perpendicular and broadside to the enemy. In this way, more guns can be trained on the enemy, who, in turn, cannot bring as many of his guns to bear.

demilitarized zone   A region declared neutral and in which no troops or armaments are permitted.

demobilization   The process by which a nation disbands a military force, typically after the end of a war.

depth charge   An explosive weapon launched or otherwise jettisoned from a surface ship and set to detonate at a given depth to rupture the hull of an enemy submarine.

dirigible   Word derived from the Latin *dirigere,* meaning "to direct" or "to steer"; it describes a steerable airship—that is, a *zeppelin.*

diversionary attack   An action intended to divert and distract the enemy, draining off his resources, while a principal attack or other action is launched elsewhere.

doctrine of war   A set of principles by which military forces guide their actions in support of particular objectives.

dogfight   Term generally used for air-to-air combat between fighter aircraft.

dollar-a-year men   Prominent U.S. citizens, typically industrialists and financiers, who volunteered their services to the war effort for the nominal salary of $1 a year.

double envelopment   Tactic executed by forces moving around both flanks of an enemy to attack those flanks or objectives to the rear of the enemy.

doughboy   The familiar name for American infantrymen in World War I. The origin of the term is obscure, but most authorities believe that it gained currency before World War I in the 1860s, when the large buttons on army uniforms were thought to resemble "doughboys," bread dough that has been rolled thin and deep-fried.

373

dreadnought   A revolutionary new style of battleship, bigger, faster, and more heavily armed than conventional battleships. The prototype of this class of vessel was HMS *Dreadnought,* launched in 1906. Through the end of World War I, the term *dreadnought* was used as a synonym for any modern battleship.

élan (or élan vital)   Term coined by the French philosopher Henri Bergson (1859–1941) to describe a "life force" he believed the French people possessed in abundance. The term was enthusiastically appropriated by French military planners.

emplacement   A prepared position for one or more weapons or other pieces of equipment to afford protection from hostile fire.

enfilading fire   Gun or artillery fire that rakes the enemy with gunfire in a lengthwise direction. This is also called "raking fire."

entente   An agreement between two or more nations for cooperative action. Somewhat less binding and more limited than a full-scale alliance.

ersatz   A German word, also borrowed into English, meaning "replacement" or "substitute"; it is a synonym for "artificial."

feints and demonstrations   Diversionary attacks by relatively small forces intended to decoy defenders away from the main attacking force.

field commander   Military officer at the front lines who actually executes the strategy and orders of top command, headquartered in the rear.

field of fire   The area that a weapon or group of weapons may cover effectively from a given position.

fire-step   Platform built into the forward wall of a trench from which soldiers can take aim and fire over the rim of the trench.

flapper   Label for the "liberated" young woman of the 1920s, whose interests were unabashedly worldly and whose inhibitions were few or none. The origin of the term is obscure but may refer to the wild flapping gestures associated with such 1920s dances as the Charleston.

flight   The basic tactical unit in the Army Air Service, consisting of at least four aircraft.

forage   For an army, to live off the land of the enemy, appropriating whatever food and supplies can be stolen.

Fourteen Points   The principal terms that President Wilson set forth in January 1918 as the basis for a satisfactory and enduring peace.

Freikorps   Collective name for German paramilitary groups, privately organized and without government sanction, formed by veterans after World War I chiefly to fight the incursion of communist forces in Germany.

friendly fire   Shells or other missiles that inadvertently fall on one's own position or troops.

frontier   For Americans, *frontier* connotes the borderland between settled country and the wilderness; in Europe, however, the word denotes the border and border region between nations.

garrison   A body of troops stationed in and assigned the defense of a fortress or fortified town.

Gatling gun   A predecessor of the machine gun, having a cluster of barrels that are fired in sequence as the cluster is crank-rotated; it was patented in 1862 by Richard Jordan Gatling (1818–1903).

Gendarmes   In France, members of the national police force; in Belgium, circa 1914, a national police force with specific paramilitary duties.

grand sherif   The chief magistrate of Mecca when that place was controlled by the Ottoman Turks.

ground attack   Use of aircraft against military personnel and other targets on the ground. When the ground attack is made in coordination with assault by ground troops, it is also called "close air support."

high-explosive (HE) rounds   Artillery shells employing powerful explosives that do their damage primarily by generating an intense blast wave rather than by creating shrapnel fragments.

howitzer   Any short cannon that delivers its shells in a high trajectory. The word is derived from an old German word for "catapult."

incendiary shell   An artillery shell loaded with highly flammable material, such as magnesium and phosphorous, intended to start and spread fire when detonated.

isolationism   National policy of refraining from involvement in political affairs beyond the nation's borders.

jazz   Highly improvisational form of music primarily developed by African-Americans who combined European harmonic structures with African rhythmic complexities. These are, in turn, overlaid with European and white American dance and march rhythms and with elements borrowed from the blues tradition. The word is probably derived from a slang term for sexual intercourse.

Jerry   Familiar, derisive term for a German soldier or soldiers. Used especially by the British.

jingoism   Extreme nationalism characterized by a chauvinist and belligerent foreign policy.

kaiser   The German equivalent of "emperor." Phonetically, it reflects the classical Latin pronunciation of *caesar*, the ancient Roman title for "emperor." The Russian word *czar* is another version of the Latin "caesar."

375

kepi   The traditional visored cloth cap worn by French soldiers since the mid nineteenth century. The caps worn by enlisted troops during the American Civil War were modeled on the French *"kepi."*

littoral plain   The flat region adjacent to the sea; the coastal region.

mine shafts   In a military context, tunnels ending in a "gallery" under an enemy position. Often, these galleries were packed with explosives, designed to detonate directly under the enemy.

minelayer   A ship either designed, modified, or simply used to lay explosive marine mines in patterns called "mine barrages."

minesweeper   Ship designed to locate and safely detonate explosive marine mines. Most World War I minesweepers were converted from fishing-type vessels, which worked two abreast, dragging a cable between them to snag the mooring lines of mines. The mooring line would be cut, and the mine would bob to the surface, where it could be safely detonated by gunfire.

mobilize   To put a nation on a war footing, calling up reservists to active service and putting regular forces on high alert. In nations with compulsory military service, conscription is also commenced.

monoplane   Aircraft with a single set of wings, either above or below the fuselage, in contrast to a *biplane,* which has two sets of wings, one above the other.

mutiny   Any rebellion against constituted authority. In the case of the French on the Western Front, mutiny was a kind of collective strike or work stoppage rather than a violent rebellion.

no man's land   One of the most enduring phrases produced by World War I; it originally described the contested territory between the trenches of the opposing armies.

open city   A city declared demilitarized during war and, by international law, that is therefore immune from attack.

over the top   The act of advancing out of a trench ("over the top" of the trench) to venture into *no man's land* for an attack on the enemy.

pandemic   An epidemic of global scope.

peripheral fronts   In World War I, all the colonial fronts, as well as the so-called Turkish Fronts (mainly the Dardanelles and Caucasus).

Pickelhaub   The spiked helmet that was the traditional German headgear, used on parade as well as in combat. The American army copied this style from the Prussians for its dress uniforms during the late nineteenth century.

pincers attack   Military tactic whereby an attacking force closes in on the enemy from two sides, so that the defending troops are "squeezed" as by a giant pincers.

plebiscite   A direct vote by a nation's entire electorate, which is invited to decide an issue with a vote of yes or no.

poilu   The World War I nickname bestowed on the French soldier; it translates, roughly, as "hairy one."

Prohibition   Popular name for the law enacted by the 18th Amendment to the Constitution forbidding the manufacture, transport, and sale of alcoholic beverages anywhere in the United States.

pusher configuration   Aircraft design in which the propeller is behind the engine and creates a thrust that pushes the airplane forward.

Q-ship   A warship disguised to look like a merchant vessel by hiding its guns and other weaponry. Its primary purpose was to lure submarines into ambush.

rear-guard action   Combat conducted primarily to protect a retreating main force, which is always vulnerable at its rear.

regulars   Members of a nation's permanent, standing army, maintained in peace as well as war. They do not include reservists or auxiliary troops, who are called on exclusively in emergencies or time of war.

Reichstag   The German parliament.

reparations   Compensation (usually monetary) required from a defeated nation as a condition of peace.

rolling barrage   In the context of a planned offensive, an artillery bombardment in which a "curtain" of artillery fire moves toward the enemy ahead of the advancing troops and at the same speed as those troops.

rout   The disorganized withdrawal of a military force from the line of battle; it contrasts with a retreat, which is an orderly—and, therefore, militarily effective—withdrawal.

salient   A battle line that projects into territory nominally held by the enemy.

scorched earth policy   The practice of deliberately destroying crops, food supplies, and other facilities to prevent an invading enemy from using them.

scuttle   To purposely sink a ship in a deliberate act of self-destruction, typically to prevent capture by the enemy.

separate peace   An *armistice* or treaty of peace made between warring nations regardless of other alliances in force. In 1918, Russia, though bound in alliance with France and Britain, concluded a "separate peace" with Germany.

shrapnel rounds   Artillery shells designed to detonate in the air, showering personnel with deadly fragments.

slackers   U.S. term for those who failed to volunteer for military service, who evaded the draft, who did not purchase Liberty Bonds or Liberty Stamps, or who otherwise shirked what was perceived as their wartime patriotic duty.

small-unit offense   The skills and tactics required to enable soldiers to fight as a team on the level, typically, of the company (in World War I, 256 men) and the platoon (128 men).

smoke screen   Heavy smoke purposely produced by ships (usually destroyers) to obscure the enemy's view of ship movements.

soviet   Any popularly elected legislative assembly. Soviets existed on local, regional, and national levels.

splendid isolation   Term that describes British foreign policy during the last third of the nineteenth century, a policy ended when England concluded the Triple Entente with France and Russia in 1907.

staff officer   Military officer attached to headquarters and typically acting as a liaison or link between top command and *field commanders*. Staff officers ensure that orders are executed and strategy is realized.

Stavka   The Russian supreme military headquarters during czarist days, including the period of World War I.

strafing   An attack on ground troops by machine guns fired from low-flying aircraft.

strategic bombardment   Aerial bombardment on a large scale, typically directed at civilian targets, especially those involved in the production of war-related materiel. Such a program of bombardment is "strategic" because it is intended as a direct means of shortening a war.

strategic victory   Term that describes attainment of long-term, overall objectives.

super dreadnought   Biggest battleship class of the war. The British *Queen Elizabeth*, for example, displaced 31,500 tons, had 13-inch belt armor, mounted eight 15-inch guns, and cruised at 24 knots, compared with the earlier *Dreadnought,* at 21,845 tons, with 11-inch armor, ten 12-inch guns, and a top speed of 21 knots.

tactical bombardment   Aerial bombardment of military targets at the front. Typically, tactical bombardment is on a relatively small or concentrated scale and is in direct support of ground operations.

tactical victory   Describes the attainment of short-term objectives in a given battle. It is possible to attain a short-term objective at the cost of a long-term objective, and thereby lose a campaign or an entire war.

Tommy   Familiar name for a British enlisted soldier.

torpedo   A self-propelled underwater projectile equipped with an explosive charge. It can be launched from submerged submarines as well as from surface vessels and even aircraft.

tractor configuration   Aircraft design in which the propeller is mounted in front of the engine, at the nose or on the leading edge of the wings. It creates thrust and lift by directly accelerating the air that passes over the plane's wings, in effect pulling (like a tractor) the craft forward.

triplane   Aircraft with three sets of wings, one above the other in triple-decker fashion. See also *biplane* and *monoplane.*

Triple Alliance   Military alliance among Germany, Austria, and Italy, concluded at the end of the 19th century. (Italy denounced the Triple Alliance during World War I.)

Triple Entente   Military alliance among France, Russia, and Great Britain, finalized in 1904, to counter the *Triple Alliance* among Germany, Austria, and Italy.

U-boat   Abbreviation of the German *Unterseeboot* (undersea boat); synonym for submarine.

unity of command   The concept of the Allied armies operating under the direction of a single final authority rather than wholly independently of one another.

unrestricted submarine warfare   The naval war policy instituted by Germany during much of World War I; it gave German U-boat captains a mandate to torpedo Allied merchant and passenger craft without issuing any prior warning.

war of attrition   War in which victory depends on wearing down the enemy rather than destroying him outright.

warm-water outlet, warm-water port   In northern countries subject to frozen winters, a *warm-water outlet* or *warm-water port* is one open year-round.

Young Turks   Mostly junior Turkish military officers, members of a military-political movement that overthrew the centuries-old rule of the sultans and sought to reform and modernize Turkish government and society.

zeppelin   Named for its inventor, Count Ferdinand von Zeppelin (1838–1917), the *zeppelin* was a hydrogen-filled airship constructed on a rigid frame and driven by propellers. Later, the zeppelin was called a *dirigible.*

zero hour   The precise time scheduled for a project to be launched; the phrase originated during World War I to describe the hour appointed for the commencement of a battle.

Further Reading

Axelrod, Alan. *Congressional Quarterly's American Treaties and Alliances.* Washington, D.C.: CQ Press, 2000.

——. *The Complete Idiot's Guide to American History.* Second Edition. New York: Alpha Books, 2000.

Axelrod, Alan, and Charles Phillips. *The Macmillan Dictionary of Military Biography.* New York: Macmillan, 1998.

Barbeau, Arthur E. *The Unknown Soldiers: African-American Troops in World War I.* 1974; reprint ed., New York: Da Capo, 1996.

Bean, C.E.W. *Anzac to Amiens: A Shorter History of the Australian Fighting Forces in the Western and Eastern Theatres of War 1914–1918.* Canberra: Australian War Memorial, 1946.

Bennett, Geoffrey. *The Battle of Jutland.* London: Batsford, 1964.

Burg, David F., and L. Edward Purcell. *Almanac of World War I.* Lexington, KY: University Press of Kentucky, 1998.

Churchill, Winston. *The World Crisis.* 5 vols. London: Butterworth, 1923–1931.

Clark, Alan. *Aces High: The War in the Air over the Western Front, 1914–1918.* New York: Ballantine, 1973.

Coffman, Edward M. *The War to End All Wars: The American Military Experience in World War I.* Madison, WI: University of Wisconsin Press, 1986.

Dupuy, R. Ernest, and Trevor N. Dupuy. *The Harper Encyclopedia of Military History: From 3500 B.C. to the Present.* Fourth Edition. New York: HarperCollins, 1993.

Dupuy, Trevor N. *The Military History of World War I.* New York Watts, 1967.

Farwell, Byron. *The Great War in Africa, 1914–1918*. New York: Norton, 1986.

Ferguson, Niall. *The Pity of War: Explaining World War I*. New York: Basic Books, 2000.

Fussell, Paul. *The Great War and Modern Memory*. New York: Oxford University Press, 1975.

Gardner, Brian. *German East Africa: The Story of the First World War in East Africa*. London: Cassell, 1963.

Gilbert, Martin. *The First World War: A Complete History*. New York: Henry Holt, 1994.

Gilford, Henry. *The Black Hand at Sarajevo*. Indianapolis, IN: Bobbs-Merrill, 1975.

Golberg, George. *The Peace to End Peace: The Paris Peace Conference of 1919*. New York: Harcourt, 1969.

Gray, Randal, and Christopher Argyl, eds. *Chronicle of the First World War*. 2 vols. New York: Facts on File, 1990, 1991.

Griffiths, William R. *The Great War*. Wayne, NJ: Avery, 1986.

Hoehling, Adolph A. *The Great War at Sea: A History of Naval Action, 1914–1918*. London: Baker, 1965.

Hough, Richard. *The Great War at Sea, 1914–1918*. Oxford: Oxford University Press, 1983.

James, Robert Rhodes. *Gallipoli*. London: Batsford, 1965.

Jameson, William. *The Most Formidable Thing: The Story of the Submarine from Its Earliest Days to the End of World War I*. London: Hart-Davis, 1965.

Jukes, Geoffrey. *Carpathian Disaster: Death of an Army*. London: Ballantine, 1973.

Keegan, John. *The First World War*. New York: Knopf, 1999.

Kennedy, David M. *Over Here: The First World War and American Society*. New York: Oxford University Press, 1982.

Kennett, Lee. *The First Air War, 1914–1918*. New York: Free Press, 1991.

Lawrence, T.E. *The Seven Pillars of Wisdom*. New York: Garden City, 1938.

Lewis, Jon E. *The Mammoth Book of War Diaries and Letters: Life on the Battlefield in the Words of the Ordinary Soldier, 1775–1991*. New York: Carroll & Graf, 1999.

Matloff, Maurice. *American Military History, Volume 2: 1902–1996*. Conshohocken, PA: Combine Books, 1996.

Messenger, Charles. *Trench Fighting, 1914–1918*. New York: Ballantine, 1972.

Rawls, Walton. *Wake Up, America!: World War I and the American Poster*. New York: Abbeville, 1988.

Shrader, Charles Reginald, ed. *Reference Guide to United States Military History 1865–1919*. New York: Facts on File, 1993.

Toland, John. *No Man's Land: 1918, the Last Year of the Great War*. New York: Doubleday, 1980.

Tuchman, Barbara W. *The Guns of August*. 1962; reprint ed., New York: Ballantine, 1994.

——. *The Zimmermann Telegram*. New York: Viking, 1958.

Tucker, Spencer C., ed. *The European Powers in the First World War: An Encyclopedia*. New York and London: Garland, 1996.

Venzon, Anne Cipriano, ed. *The United States in the First World War: An Encyclopedia*. New York and London: Garland, 1995.

Weigley, Russell F. *The American Way of War: A History of United States Military Strategy and Policy*. Bloomington, IN: Indiana University Press, 1977.

Winter, Denis. *Death's Men: Soldiers of the Great War*. New York: Penguin, 1993.

Zeman, Z.A.B. *A Diplomatic History of the First World War*. London: Weidenfeld & Nicholson, 1971.

Index

H

S

X-Y

Z